TRAINING INTERVENTIONS

Margaret Anne Reid, MA, CIPD, spent 15 years as a training officer in the clothing and engineering industries before moving into higher education. She directed the Postgraduate Diploma in Personnel Management at Leeds Polytechnic and was later appointed director of the MBA programme at the University of Leeds, where, having just retired from full-time academic employment, she now holds an honorary appointment. She is a past Vice President–Education of the Institute of Personnel Management. Having contributed to a number of publications, she currently edits two journals, *Personnel Review* and *Training and Management Development Methods.* She is a subject assessor for the Higher Education Funding Council.

Harry Barrington, BA, CIPD, formerly Company Training and Management Development Manager with Lever Brothers and Chairman of the UK Soap and Detergent Industry's Training Committee, is also a past Vice President of the Institute of Personnel Management and was the Institute's Chief Examiner for Employee Development between 1986 and 1991. He is perhaps best known as the originator of the 'continuous development' movement. An active Governor of Kingston College, whose governing body he chaired for several years during the 1980s, he is also the Treasurer of an associated educational trust and Chairman of the college's trading company. He has written and lectured extensively on all aspects of employee development.

The authors wish to express their thanks to John Kenney for his contributions to earlier editions of the work

The Institute of Personnel and Development is the leading publisher of books and reports for personnel and training professionals and students and for all those concerned with the effective management and development of people at work. For full details of all our titles please telephone the Publishing Department on 081 946 9100.

Training Interventions
managing employee development

Margaret Anne Reid
Harry Barrington

Foreword by Sir Geoffrey Holland

Fourth edition

Institute of Personnel and Development

For Maureen

First published 1986
Second Edition 1988
Third Edition 1992
Fourth Edition 1994

Typesetting by The Comp-Room, Aylesbury
and printed in Great Britain by
The Cromwell Press, Wiltshire.

British Library Cataloguing in Publication Data
A catalogue record for this book is available from the British Library

ISBN 0 85292 566 2

**INSTITUTE OF PERSONNEL
AND DEVELOPMENT**

IPD House, Camp Road, London SW19 4UX
Tel: 0181 946 9100   Fax: 0181 947 2570
Registered office as above. Registered Charity No. 1038333
A company limited by guarantee. Registered in England No. 2931892

Contents

SECTION B: MANAGING EMPLOYEE DEVELOPMENT

Foreword

by Sir Geoffrey Holland KCB
Vice Chancellor, University of Exeter
(formerly Permanent Secretary to the Department of Employment
and to the Department of Education)

As I look back over the past 10 years, and consider the developments in vocational education and training, I am impressed by the growing number of people and organisations committed to the creation of a world class workforce.

The reasons are simple. Technology can be transferred easily and cheaply throughout the world. The development of global businesses or global business partnerships means that decisions on investment, location and sourcing are now quite different from what they were even a short while ago. Throughout the world, demographic trends mean that there is no shortage of hands to do work, no shortage of young people, but critical shortages of more highly educated and more highly qualified people. And finally the rising expectations of customers and individuals mean that unless we match – and if possible exceed – the standards of quality set by the best in the marketplace, we shall simply drop out of contention.

One of the most significant developments recently has been the establishment, for the first time, of the national Education and Training Targets. They are not the CBI's targets. They are not the Government targets. They are not targets for the education service. They are targets for all of us. And we all have to work together to achieve them.

Of one thing I am clear: the targets are feasible and are capable of delivery. The Employment Department worked hard with the CBI and others to ensure that impossible objectives were not being set. But the targets will only be achieved if all of us work together consistently, purposefully and with commitment and energy to deliver them. And let us remember, as we do this, that the targets are the absolute minimum we need to achieve to be world class. The best in the world are constantly improving. They will not stand still and wait for us to catch up. They will move on and we must be up with them.

There are six key building blocks if we are to achieve the target and each and every one of them is, at least in outline, in place.

First, we have to ensure that all young people are educated and trained long, broad and to high standards. All the developments in the education service point in that direction as do developments in youth training, and projects such as Compacts and Education Business Partnerships.

Next, we must have employer commitment at every level: at national level; at sector level (the industry training organisations), at local level (the Training and Enterprise Councils in England and Wales and the Local Enterprise Companies in Scotland) and at the level of the individual organisation (the critically important new seal of approval as an Investor in People).

Third, we must have individuals who are motivated to take an interest in and some responsibility for their own personal development. It is encouraging that increasing numbers of employers are now agreeing with employees arrangements, including entitlements to time and money, to enable their workforce to do just this.

Fourth, we must have a modern, relevant, comprehensible qualification system. The National Council for Vocational Qualifications is well on course to deliver that framework.

Fifth, we must have high-quality information and advice available to all concerned: employers and individuals alike.

And, finally, we must have a research and development programme, at national, sector, local level – all three – which ensures that we continue to improve and keeps us at the frontier of developments in learning and learning technology.

Training Interventions shows us how much is on the move. We have a foundation and a framework capable of delivering world class standards. But we now need to secure performance and results from all parts of that framework.

Above all, we need to carry forward a revolution of higher expectations: by employers of what individual employees are capable of achieving and by individuals of where opportunities can lead and the rewards, both material and otherwise, that they can bring.

The potential rewards are great – for all of us. The alternative is not one we should remotely contemplate.

Preface to the Fourth Edition

The long-awaited amalgamation of the Institute of Personnel Management and the Institute of Training and Development to form the new Institute of Personnel and Development, the largest single professional organisation of its kind in Europe, has taken place since the Third Edition. The breadth of experience of its 70,000 members will provide an unprecedented wealth of knowledge and skill which augurs well for the enhancement of the training field.

At the same time, there is a gradually increasing recognition of the importance of the skills and knowledge of employees in the attainment of organisational competence and competitiveness. The role played by education and training in wealth creation is emphasised in the May 1994 White Paper 'Competitiveness: Helping Business to Win'. At this stage it is not possible to predict what influence the White Paper will have, but certainly the training scene remains a swiftly developing one. In fact, the various editions of *Training Interventions* and of its predecessor, *Manpower Training and Development*, provide a chronicle of the way in which training philosophies, strategies and methods have adapted to a rapidly changing environment. Changes sometimes follow a circular rather than a linear path, and those of us who have lived through developments since the early 1960s may be forgiven for occasionally experiencing sensations of *déjà vu*.

As in previous editions, we have found it necessary for several reasons to blend the old with the new. Rapidly developing technology and the organisational changes which accompany it have brought about the introduction of exciting new methods – some of which, such as electronic brainstorming and video-conferencing, are born of the technology itself. At the same time, however, some organisations and jobs have remained and are likely to remain in a more traditional mould, and time-honoured techniques such as job training analysis and task analysis are still highly appropriate. Unlike his or her predecessor in the early 1960s, the modern training officer enjoys a rich heritage of different approaches from which to choose. Some knowledge of the main historical events giving rise to these approaches is helpful in understanding the literature about them and to appreciate how and when they can best be used.

The need for employees to adapt to new systems at the workplace, sometimes without managers even fully realising it, has placed greater emphasis on learner-centred activity and continuous development. As in the Third Edition, we refer in Chapter 7 to a continuum with tutor-led interventions at one end and learner-centred activities at the other. We suggest that during the last eight years the pointer has moved further towards the learner-centred end of this continuum, and we prophesy that the trend will continue.

At the same time, however, we have a contrary emphasis on analytical methods, which presuppose the intervention of a trainer to undertake them. This trend has received an impetus from the accent on functional analysis, which is accepted as one way of meeting the criteria for National Vocational Qualifications.

Our central theme remains, as in previous editions, that an organisation is a learning environment: training is an intervention in an ongoing process. We believe that now, more than ever, those who manage employee development need to have regard to contextual factors when determining the way in which they assess training needs and objectives, plan strategies and choose methodologies. Although we offer details of approaches, systems, methods and techniques, the issue of how and when they should be used must rest with the professional practitioner: only the person on the spot can make these judgements. We have therefore endeavoured to raise questions, the consideration of which will, we hope, result in a deeper understanding of the basic issues and thus help to develop the necessary diagnostic and decision-making skills.

To this end, we have included examples and cases; we have also made suggestions for further reflection and discussion (both of which are important learning processes), and for further reading. Our cases are based on, but inevitably simplify, real life; the people in them have nevertheless been created as fictional characters, and do not correspond to anyone we know.

The structure of the book remains as in the Third Edition. It is in two sections. Section A, Employee Development Dimensions, sets the scene and incorporates a critical review of national issues as well as an examination of underlying philosophies and approaches to training and development. Section B is concerned with the practicalities of managing the employee development function in organisations.

We have always striven to keep a delicate balance between topicality and the danger of becoming outdated. The advantage of exemplifying principles and issues by reference to current developments has always appeared to justify the risk. The text is up to date as we go to press, but we must crave the reader's indulgence for failure to incorporate any changes after that time. We hope that readers in Scotland and Ireland will bear with us, in that their education systems have certain unique characteristics which it has not been possible adequately to address in this volume.

John Kenney has been unable to take part in preparing the new edition, but in retaining the title *Training Interventions* we wish to pay tribute to his pioneer work in earlier editions. We are grateful to Sir Geoffrey Holland for writing a Foreword to this book. We are also indebted to Ed Moorby, the late Ron Shepherd, Sue Wood, Jeff Gold, Raymond Gould, Mike Kelly and David Pierce for their helpful comments, advice and thoughtful criticisms of various draft chapters. We acknowledge our thanks to all authors and their publishers in allowing us to quote from their work. In particular, we thank Peter Honey and Alan Mumford for allowing us to reproduce parts of their work in Chapter 4, and Alan Mumford also for permission to reproduce the table in Figure 3.3; Len Holden and Yves Livian for allowing us to quote their work in connection with the Price Waterhouse Cranfield Project on European trends; Sue Wood for providing an example of her work in Chapter 12; Michael Pearn and R. Kandola for permission to reproduce the job-learning analysis question cards in Figure 9.3; David Sainsbury for permission to quote in Chapter 11 from his address to the TSB Forum; and to Prentice Hall for permission to reproduce the Kolb diagram. Thanks are due also to Safeway for their Basic Skills Training Card in Chapter 11, to the Department of Employment for several pieces of Crown Copyright material, and to the Skills and Enterprise Network for several other pieces of material.

Margaret Reid
Harry Barrington
July 1994

Introduction
WHAT IS EMPLOYEE DEVELOPMENT?

In this short Introduction, we offer some explanation of standard terms – education, training, learning – used by those who are involved in the management of employee development processes, and we emphasise the need to manage employee development in a situation-specific way. We also provide some initial evidence that managing employee development is becoming increasingly complex, purposeful and important within the world of work.

The Nature and Purpose of Employee Development

Training interventions are the means whereby employee development is designed and implemented. Its management is an art, and indeed a situation-specific art. Situations vary, in their suggestion of learning needs, opportunities, problems, objectives, options, preferences and priorities; hence, observation and decision skills are more useful to the employee developer than memory, and a creative impulse is needed alongside a respect for logical analysis and disciplined thinking. As in most other management fields, the professional's main asset is commitment – to a personal appreciation of the situation, and to the implications for action.

This may be the prime reason why employee development is not characterised by a set of terms with unique meanings, used consistently to explain the same things. In practice, the 'real life' meaning of terms often depends on the context within which they are used. For example, a group of training managers who are discussing 'management training' may be:

- assessing the strengths of a formal programme for others who are formally called 'management trainees'; or
- reviewing their own informal learning experiences among themselves; or

1

- criticising an external training course one of their number has attended; or even
- exploring what the nation might do to educate the next generation of managers.

This list is far from exhaustive; similar examples could be offered relating to any category of employee, and to most types of learning. We know, for example, of one organisation that uses the term 'training event' for six different types of planned learning activity, and we know of another organisation which uses the term 'development' with different meanings in at least five of its job descriptions.

This immediately leads us into problem areas. Text books traditionally suggest standard approaches and norms, implying that the reader might remember or copy them with confidence. But the student of employee development needs to build and respond to a 'moving dictionary'. The need can perhaps be appreciated in practical terms by looking at the following six examples:

1 Imagine you are a so-called Training Manager, who is en route to a local College of Further Education, to discuss with a lecturer a course which trainee employees are following and which is said to teach engineering practice (and which incidentally appears in the college prospectus under a heading 'vocational education'). Will it help your discussion if you stick rigidly to definitions of 'vocation' and 'education' that you have acquired in your past experience?

2 Now imagine you are a chairman of a company with a high turnover of management staff. You have a personnel manager reporting to you, but you believe that line management holds the prime responsibility for the performance of the workforce. You have taken to heart government and CBI pronouncements to the effect that 'the nation's human resources are the nation's prime resource', and you want education and training

activity to serve better the key aim of economic health, in order to provide a new, competitive cutting edge – especially at manager level. You have taken a position on the local Training and Enterprise Council, and are keen that that body should stimulate the creation of good quality management in the area, not least because you feel that you might not lose so many managers from your own company, and you might have replacements more easily available if and when they do leave. Within your own company, you have promoted a form of team development which has involved ongoing discussions, aimed both at welding departmental units together and at finding answers for real problems. Will your contribution in the TEC be about creating specific plans for individuals? Or will it take the group, or the firm, or the local community, or perhaps even the nation, as its unit? Will you call such plans 'training' plans, or 'educational' initiatives, or 'development programmes', or indeed something else?

3 You are a sixteen-year-old school leaver, who is just about to start a grant-aided 'youth training programme' approved by the local TEC, leading (you hope) to a job in a hairdressing salon. Will you hope the learning process will be like that you experienced at school? Will you feel confident of being able to use anything you learned at school? Will you view your YT grant as 'wages', or 'unemployment pay', or 'a reward for learning'? Will you expect your work experience and associated college classes to be neatly arranged in precise units and time periods, with others telling you how and when to do everything from wearing special clothing to dealing with difficult customers? Will you expect to get a

'qualification' as well as a job out of the programme?

4 You are a specialist in the production of 'open
learning', or self-study materials, creating TV programmes for the Open University, or computer-
based learning packages for mail order sale. You
are talking to a Training Manager, who plans a
course in French for sales representatives. You see
both education and training in a new and somewhat different light from that which assumes the
existence of teachers and trainers; you challenge
whether education and training should be of the
'autocratic' or 'telling people what to do' kind. You
are delighted that greater emphasis is now being
given to encouraging self-learning, i.e. individuals
are increasingly being asked and expected to
identify their own learning needs, and are increasingly being given more responsibility for planning
and managing their own learning. In this context,
how do you define the roles of the teacher and the
trainer? Will you perhaps expect the former to balance lecturing with questions, discussion and exercises? Will you want the latter to provide self-study
facilities as well as mount courses? And what will
you say if the latter says that this will mean much
time 'being diverted to removing structural or cultural barriers to learning'?

5 Now spare a thought for the people who may buy
self-study material: the sales representative who
wants to learn French, and is hoping for promotion;
the trainee accountant who is starting on the long
haul to becoming qualified; the housewife who
intends to return to work when her second child
reaches school age, and who is teaching herself
word processing with the aid of a new word
processor and a 'user guide'. Will they expect all

their future learning to be self-directed? Do they expect future employers to find ways to dovetail or merge learning and work?

6 Finally, imagine you are a young personnel manager who is beginning to treat change as normal in working life. In the past four years, you have experienced a change of ownership for your organisation, which has brought with it a range of new procedures; you have moved your head office; you have assimilated various changes in the law relating to personnel at work; your department has introduced computerised administrative systems; you have devised and introduced a new joint consultation scheme covering all levels of employee; and you have seen four major technical research projects produce four new products for sale. You are aware that each of these changes has demanded new learning on the part of existing staff, and that most of this learning has had to happen 'as part of work'. The rate of change has been such that separating out the training needs and planning formal courses has not been possible. How can you steer this organisation towards a 'continuous employee development' culture, with learning integrated with work?

These examples demonstrate the use of the term 'training interventions' in its widest sense, encompassing all ways in which learning might be helped to happen in the service of work goals – including any which aim at group (not just individual) learning, any which aim at developing self-study and self-development, and even any which aim at changing the work or the work environment to stimulate learning.

It is our intention to encourage and help the 'moving dictionary' process: our text aims continuously to expand its subject, and as it progresses the meaning of terms and concepts will become less 'standard', and more context-related. You will increasingly need to form your own conclusions. So, although we start by providing a few simple definitions and conclusions, we hope to stimulate a learning process which will eventually lead you to acquire a unique and personal view of what employee development means, and how it might be further developed.

Some Standard Definitions

The three most important concepts covered by employee development are *education, training* and *learning*. The last, learning, is critical and we will explore its meanings in a separate chapter (see Chapter 3). For the time being it should be noted that there is no universally accepted theory of learning. Until recently, most writers on the subject thought in terms of the acquisition (usually by some form of teaching process) of new knowledge, which is certainly one acceptable form of learning. But a learner may acquire new knowledge by memorising words which do not have meaning for that learner; learning may happen without understanding, or without sufficient understanding to allow the learning to be 'applied'. A person may learn to walk, swim, recognise objects, spot defects or develop any of a wide range of skills without consciously retaining the understanding of what is involved in practising it. At this stage, we suggest simply that *learning within the context of employee development must yield the ability to do something that was not previously within the learner's capability.* Precisely what the new ability is, and whether it has been acquired via a teaching process, and whether the 'learner' is a person or a team or a nation – these things are subordinate to a simple definition of learning as '*the process whereby a new capability is attained*'. They may of course become more critical as we move into other, more sophisticated definitions, which relate to specific aims and interventions, but for the present a simple definition will suffice.

Employee development is essentially about 'making learning happen' – any form of learning, although usually in the service of some work goal or goals. Learning can and does occur naturally as a by-product of everyday experience, but random learning is somewhat unpredictable, slow in performance, and may even be counterproductive (e.g. a random route to learning that an electric drill is a dangerous instrument may involve a nasty injury). Employee development usually involves ways of abandoning random learning routes in favour of more productive, planned routes.

'Education' and 'training' are ways of doing just that – abandoning random learning routes in favour of more productive, planned routes.

The (now defunct) Manpower Services Commission's 'Glossary of Training Terms' offered the following definitions in 1981:

> *Education* is defined as 'activities which aim at developing the knowledge, skills, moral values and understanding required in all aspects of life rather than a knowledge and skill relating to only a limited field of activity. The purpose of education is to provide the conditions essential to young people and adults to develop an understanding of the traditions and ideas influencing the society in which they live and to enable them to make a contribution to it. It involves the study of their own cultures and of the laws of nature, as well the acquisition of linguistic and other skills which are basic to learning, personal development, creativity and communication'.
>
> *Training* is 'a planned process to modify attitude, knowledge or skill behaviour through learning experience to achieve effective performance in an activity or range of activities. Its purpose, in the work situation, is to develop the abilities of the individual and to satisfy the current and future needs of the organisation'.

Both education and training are achieved by creating conditions in which the necessary attitudes, skill and knowledge can be effectively acquired by a learner who, as a result, becomes relatively confident of his or her abilities to apply them. It is important to understand that whilst confidence is not the only outcome of learning, and not the only generator of the will to develop further, it is central to the learner's ability to transfer what has been learned to novel situations – in a very real sense, it is the learner's confidence that allows the learning to be 'used'.

The underlying philosophy in these definitions is that education gives the general basis for living, and that training modifies and directs one's abilities towards a particular activity or activities. It can be seen that this philosophy assumes that the learner is an individual, and that plans are created by teachers or trainers to help, if not guarantee, learners' learning.

We can now offer a tentative early definition of employee development. It is part of personnel (or human resource) management, and involves the planning and management of people's learning – including ways to help them manage their own – with the aim of making the learning process more effective, increasingly efficient, properly directed and therefore useful. People's learning is typically classified as either education or training; education is 'for life', while training is for work. It all sounds logical, and fairly easy to remember.

We are, however, in danger of ignoring our early words of warning. Our definition remains based on generalised concepts. The reality is situation-specific. You might now like to revisit the examples given above, questioning whether our early definitions are 'contextually adequate'. For example, our first Training Manager visited a College of Further Education to discuss with a lecturer trainees' progress in engineering practice. This does not sound much like separating education and training, the former being 'for life', the latter 'for work'. The essential point is that employee development is a situation-specific art, and must be managed as such; a doctrinaire approach is likely to make communication difficult, and the biggest achievements rest with those who can observe, describe and promote change in ways which others find realistic.

An Increasingly Important and Complex Subject

Our six examples also illustrate how employee development has 'grown' – in importance, in complexity, and in purpose – during the past generation. They show that education and training are no longer in watertight compartments; that individual learning is no longer the only aim; that teaching is not the only way to ensure learning happens; that employee development concerns ALL employees, not just managers, and certainly not just personnel or training managers; that the employee development scene can be the nation, not just the firm or the college; and that the rate and pace of change have made employee development a fundamental part of work, not an add-on appendage to it.

We will explore these ideas further in Section A, where we will extend our understanding of:

- how the national and local scenes are evolving
- how attitudes and approaches to learning are evolving
- how employee development philosophies are evolving
- how employee development is becoming 'operational' at the workplace.

Throughout the remainder of the book, each chapter will include a summary of its main contents, under the chapter heading, and at the end of each chapter, a number of questions 'for further reflection and discussion' and a 'suggested reading' list. For now you might like to address this question:

> **'Given the ideas presented in this Introduction, is this book an educational or a training aid?'**

SECTION A

EMPLOYEE DEVELOPMENT DIMENSIONS

Chapter 1
NATIONAL TRAINING INTERVENTIONS

Training as an economic instrument – achievements and challenges – national initiatives 1964 to present day – a note on the Single European Market – which ways forward?

INTRODUCTION

From our viewpoint, the best answer to the question at the end of the Introduction is 'Both'. This book aims both to educate and to train: to offer generalised knowledge; to modify and expand the reader's attitudes and opinions and also to provide practical guidance. In this chapter, however, the emphasis will be on the former aim through the presentation of a summary of national initiatives – by government, quasi-governmental bodies, employer organisations, professional bodies, and others – all of which have been aimed at 'making training happen'. Much of the employee development activity that is now managed – and hence much of what we will outline in the second section of this book under the heading 'Managing Employee Development' – has been influenced by these initiatives; some of it has even been devised and introduced at national level.

'Why do you think we have chosen to cover "national" issues so early in this book?'

TRAINING AS AN ECONOMIC INSTRUMENT

During the past 30 years, education and training have increasingly commanded the attention of UK politicians, civil servants, professional

11

bodies, journalists, and many others who operate at national level. The increased importance of employee development matters is essentially linked to four major concerns:

1 The nation's declining economic performance.

a The balance of advantage in low-skilled labour intensive industry has shifted in favour of low cost labour markets, making 'third world' countries more competitive. The competitive edge for high cost labour now lies increasingly in the knowledge and skills of the workforce.

b In many of the UK's growth industries there is an imbalance between the skills and qualifications required by employers and those available in the nation's workforce.

c The aggregate investment in employee development made by employers is seen as inadequate in both quantity and quality (this is especially so in times of recession).

d Investment in vocational education and training – for ALL the workforce, not just 'elite' or management members – is seen as an essential ingredient of a competitive operation.

2 Unemployment – and employment – types and levels.

a Attempts by employers to restore productivity and profit levels by (in part) reducing manpower levels led during the eighties to high unemployment figures, particularly among young people. It was widely feared that a failure to find suitable work for these young people would produce major social divisions.

b At the same time, demographic trends showed a marked downturn in the number of young people leaving full-time education during the last fifteen years of the century, but a dramatic increase in the numbers of older women seeking paid work.

3 Rapid change – technological, social, and legal.

a New technology, new materials, new equipment, new processes, new procedures all demand the acquisition of new knowledge and skills by the nation's workforce, especially in the traditional craft fields, where sophisticated equipment typically replaces manual skills. New types of organisation structure have also evolved, requiring new styles of management: 'change' has become a way of life, with organisations allowing it to mould their cultures.

b New laws defining employee rights (e.g. equal opportunities) and employer responsibilities (e.g. health and safety), combined with demographic changes, are leading to new ways of organising people for work.

c The advent of the Single European Market whilst sharpening competition between member states has also added new constraints (e.g. anti-pollution measures). This has forced UK employers to address a new range of operational problems and opportunities, all of which involve potential learning on the part of employees.

4 The 'Training' Contribution.

a The role of personnel management has changed from one which was primarily to ensure the welfare of employees, and to manage the relationships between employees and employers, to one of managing human resources in the service of the organisation's commercial goals. This has increasingly been seen as serving at the same time the needs of the employee and the nation, through contributing to the prosperity of all.

b Learning achieved from early, full-time education has increasingly been accepted as inadequately serving vocational needs and also requiring periodic updates.

c New technology has brought with it new aids to learning. Self-study packages, often incorporating video and/or audio tapes, and sometimes making use of computers, allow learning to happen outside the traditional classroom. Satellite TV promises to further develop self-study methods.

Summing up all these statements, the UK is increasingly viewing education and training as potentially able to make a contribution to solving economic problems which are themselves growing more difficult to manage. This is the key reason why there has been a marked increase in government-led and other initiatives which promote employee development in many forms. These initiatives include the emergence of a national system of vocational qualifications (NVQs) overseen by a National Council for Vocational Qualifications (NCVQ), over 100 occupational standard-setting 'Lead Bodies', over 100 industry training organisations (ITOs – many of whom are also the lead bodies for their industries), a nation-wide network of Training and Enterprise Councils (TECs) and Local Enterprise Companies (LECs), plus government programmes of youth training (YT) and Training for Work (TFW) – previously Employment Training (ET). National training awards (NTAs) are

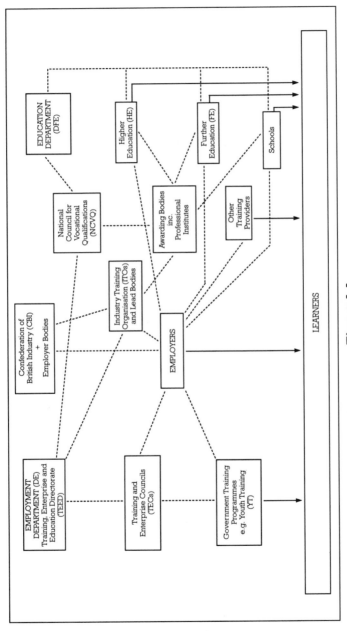

Figure 1.1
The National Training Network, Summer 1994

N.B. Dotted lines between boxes imply liaison links, but not necessarily command or responsibility relationships. As our main text explains, the system in Scotland involves some organisations with different titles.

now made annually. Progress against national training targets, which are defined largely in terms of numbers/percentages attaining NVQs (see page 29), is now regularly charted in government publications and reports from a newly-established National Advisory Council on Education and Training Targets (NACETT). In spring 1993, the *First Report on National Education and Training Targets* said 'these targets give us specific benchmarks against which to aim as we develop policy, set priorities and allocate resources . . . they will require a serious sustained programme of continuous improvement over the next decade'. A December 1993 strategy document entitled *Prosperity Through Skills: The National Development Agenda*, issued by the Employment Secretary, put the targets 'at the heart of the strategy'; an accompanying Department of Employment *Labour Market and Skills Trends 1994/5* report described them as 'what has to be achieved if Britain's workforce is to compete with their international rivals'.

Personnel and training managers are becoming proficient at recognising and remembering these new creations – usually by their abbreviated titles. The country's educational system is also now rapidly becoming involved. Figure 1.1 provides a much-abbreviated map of the evolving national network.

In the Introduction, we suggested that you might imagine yourself as each of several different people; one of these was a company chairman who had taken on a new societal role as chairman of a TEC. A multitude of similarly new roles has appeared, both outside and within the traditional industrial and educational settings, all of which involve promoting employee development: consider the civil servant, liaising with the local TEC on unemployment figures and skills shortages; the Further Education college lecturer, wondering what workplace examples to build into a lecture; the careers counsellor, advising a school leaver on a wide range of routes to a variety of qualifications; the administrator in the office of a professional institute, seeking to update membership rules to take account of best practice in the profession; or the editor of the Institute of Personnel and Development (IPD) journal, needing to keep members up to date; and so on.

ACHIEVEMENTS AND CHALLENGES

It is arguable that the upgrading of employee development activity via interventions at national, industry and local community levels is beginning to show results. The 1994/5 *Labour Market and Skill Trends* report mentioned above certainly records an improved *quantity* of training: 3 million employees (14.7 per cent of the employed workforce) were shown as receiving job-related training in the four weeks of a relevant 1993 survey, compared with 1.8 million (well below 10 per cent) in 1984. Over half (54 per cent) of all employees between 20 and 60 years old were said to have experienced job-related training during the previous three years, compared with about 33 per cent in a 1986/7 enquiry. Moreover, these advances were despite the 1991/3 years of economic recession, during which the volume of training, whilst reducing, held up reasonably well, especially within the larger firms (an Industrial Society survey in early 1992, when recessionary pressure was at its height, showed nearly 50 per cent of respondent employers predicting an increase in training expenditure). And although training away from the workplace (for those in organisations of more than 25 employees) dropped from 40 million to 26 million days between 1991 and 1993, the amount of time spent learning *at* the workplace has risen significantly, if employers' claims can be trusted (80 per cent of employers reported funding training in 1993). These results are important. Sustained economic health has almost certainly been thwarted in the past by undiagnosed mismatches between the 'competence profile' of the UK workforce and the changing needs of the workplace.

Moreover, whilst UK unemployment – and especially youth unemployment – increased during the 1991/3 recession, large numbers of young people (69 per cent) stayed on in full-time education, many moving into Further Education colleges to undertake vocational courses. In 1994, over 53 per cent of 16- and 17-year-olds are studying in FE colleges, many following 'General' national vocational qualifications (see pages 27–8, 382).

But there is little ground for complacency, especially if one looks beyond the generalised picture at the details. Among the less rewarding findings of the 1994/5 *Labour Market and Skill Trends* report are the following:

- planned training is still relatively rare in organisations with fewer than 25 employees (12 per cent)
- training is not equally available across all occupations: whilst professional staff report a one in four (27 per cent) likelihood, and managers one in six (16 per cent), operatives rate one in 16 (6 per cent), and engineering craftsmen one in nine (11 per cent)

- part-time and self-employed workers fare badly (11 per cent)
- training concentrates on young men (27 per cent), young women (21 per cent), managers (19 per cent), and those who already have qualifications (25 per cent); only 7 per cent of unqualified 50-year-olds below management identify with training plans.
- progress towards national training targets remains 'behind plan'
- Youth Training has declined in numbers under the influence of reduced government funding, and employers' unwillingness to recruit school-leavers
- at least 20 per cent of employers still do nothing to plan or provide training.

The last point perhaps understates the key issue. Even amongst those who do fund and plan training, there are many leading organisations (or, to be more precise, many opinion-moulders within those organisations) who still view learning to work, or to improve performance, as an alternative to work itself, and at best something that must be organised away from work. Such employers themselves have little-recognised but nonetheless critical learning needs, relating to their appreciation of the contribution that can be made by interventions aimed at promoting employee development, and (especially) at integrating learning with work.

Commercial, industrial and public sector organisations all operate in a dynamic environment. Market, technological, personnel, political and other changes have far-reaching effects on an organisation, and unless it is prepared and able to move with the times its efficiency is eroded and its opportunities for growth curtailed. But as Burns and Stalker pointed out as long ago as 1961, organisations often find it difficult to adjust to change. One of top management's key responsibilities is to develop their organisations to meet the challenges of the future. This responsibility is exercised by assessing the resources and opportunities available, defining objectives and efficiently managing the resources allocated to meet these goals. But if top management assume resources are 'static', ambitious goals are often seen to be beyond reach. A potential contribution of employee development within any organisation is to bring ambitious goals into attainable range. The potential contribution of national training initiatives is to create the environment within which the challenge – and the opportunity – are clear to all.

NATIONAL INITIATIVES: 1964 TO THE PRESENT DAY

The competence and commitment of the workforce largely determine the objectives that an organisation can set for itself and its success in achieving them. This fact of working life is not new; ever since the Second World War unstable labour markets have forced employers to pay particular attention to their personnel policies and practices. The rapid evolution of personnel management as a major business function is itself a direct result of employers' growing concern for the more effective use and development of their human resources (see Armstrong and Dawson, 1983). This concern has generated – especially in areas and times of full employment – the recognition that it makes good sense to have 'progressive' personnel policies. At one time such policies were assumed to need a 'welfare' orientation, covering rewards and conditions of employment; then, later, to focus on industrial relations and processes of negotiation; more recently, and especially since the 1960s, they have extended into employee development. Whether the Industrial Training Act of 1964 was the product or precursor of this recognition is a matter of varying opinion; but there is no doubt that the Act marked a turning point in the importance allocated to training matters at national level, and ushered in a very large number of initiatives – by government, by government agencies, and by other national bodies – all aimed, directly or indirectly, at making employee development more acceptable, more normal, more widespread and more effective.

Before we go on to describe some of these initiatives, here is another question:

> 'If you were responsible for promoting employee development throughout the UK, what types of initiative would you consider?'

The Industry-based Phase, or 'ITB Era'

The UK's first national initiative was a mixture of government prescription and industrial freedom. The 1964 Act forced most organisations to be 'within the scope' of one of the newly-formed Industry Training Boards (ITBs), and to pay levies determined by those ITBs. Each ITB was itself a tripartite body, representing employers, trade unions and educationalists; it was not a government department but a 'quango' (a 'quasi-autonomous non-governmental organisation') with a strong link to the Department of Employment but no responsibility to it. The main ITB instrument was a set of criteria which were devised by the ITB itself, and did not conform to any national pattern. If the employer met these criteria, the employer was allowed levy exemption or remission. The underlying aims were said to be:

* to ensure an 'adequate supply' of 'properly trained' employees at all levels
* to secure an 'improvement in the quality and efficiency of industrial training'
* to share the cost of training 'more evenly' between employers.

The last of these aims was never realistically attainable on a national scale, since ITBs were not established for all sectors, and administrative problems allowed small firms to remain out of scope.

Whilst hindsight may be an unfair aid, the strategic basis for the ITBs now appears somewhat naive. The ITBs appeared to some employers, and notably to those who saw training as an alternative to work, as a form of state interference, a new prescriptive tax collector, a bureaucratic diversion. ITBs' 'industry' base was not always respected and, despite their tripartite model, they appeared to clash with the prevailing wind of participation, which was usually promoted on a site basis (i.e. geographical units established their own participative systems and the pace of their development, without discussion at industry level). Whilst ITBs' main stock in trade – the 'standardised, systematic approach' – offered sound basic advice for employers without established training systems, it similarly clashed with an emerging practitioner view amongst the larger employers – the view that the key to improved performance lies in unique learning activities which are integrated with work and which often are not called 'training' at all. Those activities were often based on, and indeed complemented, the 'systematic approach'; ITBs were perhaps caught between the wish to publicise successful situation-specific (and sometimes confidential) case material, and their suspicion that it might frighten in-scope organisations who had not yet adopted 'the basics'.

Perhaps more important was the assumption that the key economic problem was one of supply: the ITBs tended to believe that skills shortages hindered competition and growth and made trainees poachable as soon as they became competent. Hence they preached *more* training by *all*. It is arguable that overmanning and earnings drift were more serious problems for industry during the sixties than the provision of skills, and that the main target for training should have been the updating and improved performance of the existing workforce. By the mid-seventies, technological innovation brought the need for *new* skills and *multi*-skilling; but centralised bodies lacking sophisticated intelligence systems were never able to judge the varying rate at which their member organisations were adopting the new technology.

Problems of administration and bureaucracy were also increasingly apparent, and ultimately became the focus of employers' criticism: levies grew; form-filling proliferated; complaints emphasised that money was being routed to administration and away from real training tasks. 'Fair' grants schemes were never possible, once the very small employer was exempted from scope; complaints became stronger when it became known that 'shop window' activity could sometimes minimise levy payments.

If employers had already respected and valued the training function, the ITBs might have developed into useful training managers. They did achieve some significant and valuable ends, some industries achieving more than others. For example, the Engineering Industry Training Board carried through a long-overdue revolution in craft apprenticeship norms and the Hotel and Catering Industry Training Board introduced discipline into training in an industry which hitherto had had none. The ITBs also did much to stimulate the training of trainers, and indirectly to influence the larger employers to place higher quality people in training jobs. ITB recommendations on such things as training policy statements, training needs identification, appraisal systems, the training of trainers, safety training manuals and training budgets provided new facilities for any employer or personnel manager who wanted such resources. Material in the second section of this book draws heavily for its detail on what was originally ITB material.

But there were not many supporters in evidence. And government's own response to employers' claims that they were 'having to pay too much for too much bureaucracy' distanced the ITBs further from those employers. A 1973 Employment and Training Act created a new national body, the Manpower Services Commission (the MSC), which controlled two agencies (the Employment Services Agency and the Training Services Agency) and was funded directly by the Treasury. A statutory limit was put on ITB levies, and all ITB administrative costs were henceforth paid nationally.

Whilst ITBs remained active until the eighties, and six even until the early nineties (with one, the Construction ITB, still extant, its industry continuing to believe in the approach), the 1973 Act effectively ended the industry-based approach, or at least dramatically reduced its thrust in favour of a more centralised strategy.

The 'Government as Manager'

It must be appreciated that the seventies were essentially years of reorganisation for UK industry: new technology and simple economic pressures were leading to new 'productivity deals' whereby overmanning was cut and improved profits were partly distributed to a smaller workforce. Recruitment was drastically cut, especially that of apprentices (craft apprenticeships quickly declined, despite ITB cries of alarm). High inflation towards the end of the seventies led to recession: the ranks of the unemployed grew, with large numbers of young people on the registers at government employment offices, and social security payments soared. In this politically-charged situation, the Manpower Services Commission (and of course the Treasury) came to see training primarily as an anti-unemployment tactic. The UK's first national youth training programmes were introduced, aimed at the young unemployed and delivered mainly in further education colleges or government skill centres. These programmes no longer exist, and hence they are not described here, but their introduction was a dramatic example of the growing feeling that vocational education and industrial training were both aspects of the same thing, and that new forms of education could be introduced via non-traditional routes.

A 1981 White Paper *A New Training Initiative: A Programme for Action* moved the national picture further forward. The objectives were expressed in the following way:

Objective One

To develop skill training including apprenticeship in such a way as to enable young people entering at different ages and with different educational attainments to obtain agreed standards of skill appropriate to the jobs available and to provide them with a basis for progress through further learning.

Objective Two

To move towards a position where all young people under the age of 18 have the opportunity either of continuing in full-time education or of entering a period of planned work experience combined with work-related training and education.

Objective Three

To open widespread opportunities for adults whether employed or returning to work, to acquire, increase or update their skills and knowledge during the course of their working lives.

These objectives show clearly the concern of government (or, perhaps more properly, their advisers the MSC) over employment and unemployment; but they also reflect concern over other, related issues. Skills training was henceforth to be 'appropriate to the jobs available'; entry to skills training was to be 'at different ages'; skilled people were, having regard to the changing technological scene, to expect 'progress through further learning'; youth training was to include *work-related* education and training; adult training was to cover all at work, including those 'returning to work' (not least a reference to the widespread return to work of married women). These factors were to be influenced by national programmes, and not merely left to be decided by market forces.

Less clearly, the 1981 White Paper reflected an enormous establishment concern that a whole generation of young people might, through wholesale unemployment, become alienated from the rest of the community – and might indeed become a permanent internal threat to existing democratic values. Government now saw anti-unemployment activity as imperative; yet the standard ITB philosophy, which preached the 'systematic' approach, improved work efficiency and numbers reduction, did nothing to promote it. Government now believed it was necessary to move without the ITBs, which could be dispensed with or bypassed. As a consequence in the early eighties:

- all but a handful of ITBs were abolished, to the delight of most employers, who happily agreed to replace them with non-statutory ITOs ('industry training organisations', who were expected to carry on the ITBs' work at much reduced cost)
- a new national 'Youth Training Scheme' (YTS) was launched – following frenzied discussions with employer organisations (notably the Confederation of British Industry) and specific large employers, who quickly saw the youth unemployment threat and promised active cooperation

- the MSC was disbanded and replaced by a new Training Agency (TA), which was organised as part of government's Department of Employment but was separate from its strictly 'employment' units. This was the agency whose 1990 report we noted earlier. The TA immediately took over the task of preparing strategic training initiatives, and the administration of national programmes.

Despite many and widespread administrative problems, YTS was a remarkably successful innovation. The scheme, administered via local area offices, yielded within three years an annual rate of over 300,000 traineeships. School-leavers who did not move into further or higher full-time education were promised, and received, the alternative of 'work related education and training' for periods of up to two years. Luckily the evolution of YTS coincided with the UK's economic upturn: well over half the YTS trainees found 'permanent' work before or when their traineeships ended.

YTS brought to the fore a number of important issues. The guarantee of a traineeship was for *all* school-leavers; a wide range of 'special needs' trainees existed for whom special programmes were desirable. Employers' long-stated complaints about school-leavers' inability to master the basic arts of reading and writing appeared even more frequently. Press coverage of accidents in the early days made safety training mandatory. And trainer training got more attention than ever. Perhaps most important was the spotlight YTS put on the 'qualifications' issue: it was generally agreed that low level vocational qualifications were too many in number and too academic in nature.

The initial success of YTS, unfortunately, did not reflect a new and widespread employers' attitude towards training in all its forms. The launch of an adult version – the Employment Training (ET) scheme (now Training For Work TFW) – fared much less well, and both were often pilloried by trade unions as opportunities for unscrupulous employers to obtain 'cheap labour'. Other TA products (for example, a 'Business Growth Through Training' scheme under which small employers could obtain financial aid for training activities linked with technical development) also lacked widespread support. It is not too cynical to say that many sponsored YTS because initially it was free – government met trainees' pay and scheme administration expenses – and as the boom of the mid-eighties rolled on, there was much publicity about a 'demographic time-bomb' in the form of a fall in the numbers of young people. But government was less than happy to continue

the level of funding when unemployment was falling, and each successive year brought an increase in what was to be provided by employers.
Predictably, employers complained and threatened to stop sponsoring
youth trainees. Once again, the problem of employers' lack of commitment to the 'alternative to work' was clear.

This problem led to the establishment of local 'employer-led' Training
and Enterprise Councils (TECs) and Local Enterprise Companies (LECs
– in Scotland). A 1988 White Paper *Employment for the 1990s*
announced the establishment of this network of local bodies, who were
given responsibility for tailoring national schemes (notably youth training) to suit local skill shortage requirements (and incidentally to help the
shift of funding onto employers). The old tripartite approach was
scrapped: TECs/LECs were to be managed by groups of local 'chief
executives', with training providers not allowed to join the main
boards. These TECs/LECs were also to be encouraged to promote
training serving specific local 'enterprise' initiatives. And to underline
the point, the Training Agency was abolished and the coordination of
the new bodies was placed in the hands of a new division within the
Department of Employment, called the 'Training, Education and
Enterprise Division' – henceforth known universally as 'TEED'.
Government was now keen to harness employer support behind both
its national programmes and its vocational education initiatives; linking them to enterprise ideals was seen as essential for that employer
support.

A 'National Training Awards' (NTA) scheme was launched towards
the end of the eighties, primarily as a vehicle for publicising examples
of excellence in training. This annual awards scheme quickly drew
over 1,000 entrants, ranging from small businesses with less than 20
employees to large multinationals; by the end of the decade, it was normal for some 150 organisations to be commended by the national panel
assessing the entries.

'Investors in People'

The need for employer support had been explicit in the 1988 White
Paper: in it, the key remit to TECs and LECs was 'to promote to
employers the necessity of their investing in the skills of the working
population'. The follow-up, after much discussion, was an 'Action
Programme' – or, to be more specific, an 'Investors in People' campaign, designed to stimulate employers' interest in what they called a

---

NATIONAL STANDARD FOR EFFECTIVE INVESTMENT IN PEOPLE

An Investor in People makes a public commitment from the top to develop all employees to achieve its business objectives.

- Every employer should have a written but flexible plan which sets out business goals and targets, considers how employees will contribute to achieving the plan and specifies how development needs in particular will be assessed and met.

- Management should develop and communicate to all employees a vision of where the organisation is going and the contribution employees will make to its success, involving employee representatives as appropriate.

An Investor in People regularly reviews the training and development needs of all employees.

- The resources for training and developing employees should be clearly identified in the business plan.

- Managers should be responsible for regularly agreeing training and development needs with each employee in the context of business objectives, setting targets and standards linked, where appropriate, to the achievement

of National Vocational Qualifications (or relevant units) and, in Scotland, Scottish Vocational Qualifications.

An Investor in People takes action to train and develop individuals on recruitment and throughout their employment.

- Action should focus on the training needs of all new recruits and continually developing and improving the skills of existing employees.

- All employees should be encouraged to contribute to identifying and meeting their own job-related development needs.

An Investor in People evaluates the investment in training and development to assess achievement and improve future effectiveness.

- The investment, the competence and commitment of employees, and the use made of skills learned should be reviewed at all levels against business goals and targets.

- The effectiveness of training and development should be reviewed at the top level and lead to renewed commitment and target setting.

Figure 1.2
Investors in People: The National Standard

Crown Copyright. Reproduced by arrangement with the Department of Employment.

'national standard for effective investment in people' (see Figure 1.2).

This national standard was claimed to be 'testing and credible'; firms were encouraged to meet the standard, and those subsequently doing so would be given public recognition. The job of deciding how to review and assess achievement against the standard was given to the TECs/LECs; the government made it clear that they expected mainstream national programmes such as YT and ET to be linked to the framework.

The 'employer-led' characteristic of TECs and LECs is critical. The strategy attempts to use people who are already recognised as successful businesspeople in their localities, and to influence the remainder through them. It is perhaps too early to say whether this strategy will work; but experience to date does not generate over-confidence. TEC and LEC leaders are finding the training world a difficult one to master; and government's reluctance to provide funds outrages many who are used to five-year (or longer) plans in their commercial life.

'Making Education Vocational'

In the mid-eighties, no less than four government departments (Education, Employment, Wales and Scotland) joined forces to announce a mammoth review and revision of national vocational qualifications. A 1986 White Paper, entitled *Working Together – Education and Training*, announced the setting-up of a National Council for Vocational Qualifications (NCVQ), whose remit was to evolve a system whereby 'competence-based' qualifications could be 'nationally approved' and given a new NVQ logo (separately SVQ in Scotland, where the supervising and approving body was the Scottish Vocational Education Council, or SCOTVEC. For the remainder of this book, our use of the letters NCVQ should be assumed to relate additionally and similarly to SCOTVEC).

The NCVQ's task was a large one. They had to design and adapt a new framework and a new national database of qualifications, which meant not only reviewing what existed but also ensuring comprehensive provision of new qualifications by the main awarding bodies. Arrangements for quality assurance and research had to be incorporated in the design. All occupational sectors must be covered: hence liaison with a long list of bodies was inevitable. Above all, they had to establish a strong image for NVQs/SVQs, especially among employers, professional bodies and the education sector.

The TA was simultaneously to galvanise the industry training organisations into adopting 'Lead Body' roles, drafting 'standards of competence', outlining what was required at the workplace. These standards of competence would form the bases of the new NVQs/SVQs. The justification for all this work was four-fold:

- qualifications must reflect real workplace needs if the associated learning was to be economically useful
- industries must 'own' (and develop) their own qualifications
- employers' views of what is needed at the workplace must dominate further education activity

- the advent of the Single European Market required a modern input to what would ultimately become common 'European' qualifications.

NVQs/SVQs would be arranged in a hierarchy of five bands or levels, numbered from 1 to 5, with professional or management level qualifications in the highest 'Level 5' – despite opposition from a number of professional bodies, and strongly expressed views that management competence could not be prescribed in abstract terms.

A number of future benefits for employers have been claimed, such as:

- easier recruitment and selection of competent employees
- improved training specification and design
- better standards of service and product to customers
- better strategic manpower planning
- increased cooperation between employers, training organisations and awarding bodies, based on a common understanding of statements of competence.

Summarised from a Training Agency videotape 'Standards for Action', 1990

We will look more closely in later chapters into the nature of NVQs/SVQs, and the ways in which workplace competence might be defined and assessed.

This was not the only centralised attempt to make education a more economic activity. Even more important was the creation of the National Curriculum for Schools. Hitherto, each school was its own master in determining the curriculum children would follow; in future, following a development period to be completed by 1995, all would have to implement a common curriculum which contained three 'Core' subjects (Science, Maths and English), plus seven 'Other Foundation' subjects. (We will explore this in more detail in Chapter 11.) Additionally, schools would be required to provide for 'important aspects' of education such as 'Economic and Industrial Understanding' and 'Careers Education and Guidance'. 'General' NVQs (GNVQs), designed to have wide transferability, were introduced in 1992; by 1995, these will be available in 14 occupational areas.

Further education-sphere initiatives have followed. Colleges of Further Education moved out of local authority control in April 1993, own their own assets and are managed by governing bodies with 'industrial' governors permanently in a majority; their funding is now

managed by a central funding agency, which has already introduced
incentives to increase FE student numbers and is firmly wedded to
national training targets (see Figure 1.3). In addition to the long-run-
ning Open University facility, which offers primarily degree-level
courses for those who wish to study from their home bases, an 'Open
College' now offers a range of technical courses on an 'open access'
(i.e. no entry qualifications) basis. Some three-quarters of all OC work
is aimed at NVQs/SVQs, with learning methods involving the use of
learning packages. 'General' NVQs/SVQs and new vocational diplomas
are also now available for those who stay in full-time education but take
studies biased towards industrial activity. Higher education institutions,
prompted by government pressure, money, and an 'Enterprise in Higher
Education' (EHE) initiative, are developing vocational learning within
degree courses. A system of 'Youth Credits' was introduced in 1991 in
11 TEC/LEC areas, and extended to a further nine areas in 1993, covering about 33,000 school-leavers; these young people receive vouchers
which must be spent on approved vocational courses, which in practice
means NVQs/SVQs. Government funding is steadily being geared to the
achievement of targets which are expressed in terms of NVQs; all YT
trainees, for example, must attain 'Level 2' NVQs, or funding is reduced.
Fees for NVQ/SVQ courses are now reduced by 'deduction of standard
rate income tax' – the first time any tax incentive has applied to training.

A separate but related initiative came from the 'Management Charter
Group' (MCG), comprising a network of employers who put their
names to a new initiative (MCI) and a new charter, both designed to
stimulate management education and training. The original idea
appeared in a report on management training from a team led by
Professor Charles Handy (the 'Handy' report): the team had compared
management development practices in the US, Japan, Europe and the
UK; they concluded that a UK 'relaunch campaign' was required. The
early work of the MCG concentrated on reviewing and redefining management competences and producing the equivalent of a Lead Body's
prescription for management qualifications, which NCVQ readily
adopted as the basis for NVQs in management subjects.

Another, and far more widely acknowledged, sign that employers
supported the overall strategy came from the Confederation of British
Industry, who welcomed and further developed it by launching a
'World Class Targets' campaign in summer 1991. The initiative, which
was quickly supported and shared by other bodies, including the
Employment Department and the Trades Union Congress, set out dates

NATIONAL TRAINING TARGETS

For Young People

* **By 1997** at least 80 per cent of young people should gain NVQ/SVQ level II (equivalent to 4 GCSEs at grades A-C) in their foundation education or training.

* **A right** to structured training, work experience or education leading to NVQ/SVQ level III for all young people who can benefit.

* **By the year 2000** at least half the 16 to 19 age group to gain NVQ/SVQ level III or equivalent, as a basis for further progression.

* **All** education and training provision should be structured and designed to develop self-reliance, flexibility and broad competence as well as specific skills.

For Employees

* **By 1996** all employees should take part in training or developmental activities as the norm.

* **By 1996** at least half of the employed workforce should be aiming for qualifications or units towards them within the NVQ/SVQ framework.

* **By 2000** 50 per cent of the employed workforce should be qualified to at least NVQ/SVQ level III or equivalent.

* **By 1996** at least half of the medium and larger organisations should qualify as 'Investors in People' assessed by the Training and Enterprise Councils or Local Enterprise Companies.

Figure 1.3
The UK's National Training Targets

Crown Copyright. Reproduced from *Skills and Enterprise Executive*, October 1991, by arrangement with the Department of Employment.

by which targets, mostly expressed in terms of NVQs/SVQs or their academic equivalents (see Figure 1.3) should be attained.

These targets are ambitious, to say the least, and we have already noted that progress towards them is 'behind plan'. The annual increase in young people attaining NVQ Level 2 has not matched the aimed-for 5 per cent; and by July 1994, only 1,000 employers had achieved the 'Investors in People' standard. But the former will benefit from the national launch in late 1994 of a 'modern apprenticeships' initiative which is to be promoted by TECs/LECs (who are increasingly arranging joint action with local Chambers of Commerce), and aims annually to create over 40,000 apprenticeships (with 150,000 in the system at any one time); and over 6,500 organisations are said (mid-1994) to be committed to becoming 'Investors in People'.

These developments have dramatically altered the national VET (vocational education and training) scene. The emphasis in YT (now Training For Work TFW) is no longer on anti-unemployment activity, but on qualifications. Training needs are now assumed by government, by TEC/LECs and by the major UK employer body to be determined in line with what industry lead bodies say constitutes workplace competence as built into the new NVQs. These 'workplace competence' national vocational qualifications are seen as offering employers a new incentive to train, employees a new degree of job mobility, and the nation a new educational structure to match the formalised qualifications of continental countries. So, remembering what we explored in the Introduction, perhaps the UK is beginning to bring together its education ('learning for life') and its training ('learning for particular work skills') activities.

It is also arguable that at last the UK government views these activities as affecting much more than unemployment or literacy statistics: a White Paper entitled 'Competitiveness: Helping Business to Win', which was introduced in May 1994 by the Secretary of State for Trade and Industry (flanked by the Prime Minister and no fewer than seven Cabinet ministers), spelled out within a broad economic context the importance of NVQs, youth credits, TECs, national training targets, and so on – and it went on to promise new-style vocational courses for 14-year-olds, new general diplomas for those staying in full-time education after age 16 ('to show employers that the holders have mastered the basics'), and a £300 million increase in Treasury funding. We will return to this subject in Chapter 11, which we entitle 'Towards 2000 – Preparing Tomorrow's Workforce'; for the moment it is sufficient to note that training interventions at national level have grown significantly in both scale and ambition since the first Industrial Training Act of 1964.

Attitude – and Organisation – Development

However, the nation has not yet become passionate about, nor heavily committed to, training interventions; there is a long way to go before training becomes generally accepted as an economic instrument. A paper presented by one of the present authors to an autumn 1991 seminar mounted by the former Institute of Personnel Management said in its opening sentence 'The United Kingdom has never had a strategy which appropriately addresses the need to improve the economic performance of its workforce'. That paper went on to stress that the basic problem lay in UK society's attitudes, and especially those of the nation's managers. We have already seen how the government and the CBI are working towards this end; but three other initiatives, taking different forms and using different catalysts, should also be mentioned.

1 The 'Continuous Development' movement

In the early part of the eighties, the Institute of Personnel Management (now the Institute of Personnel and Development – IPD) announced the inception of an 'ABCD' campaign. 'ABCD' stood for 'A Boost for

Continuous Development'; a 'CD Code' followed shortly (it is now available in a twice-revised form as a 'CD Statement'; we reproduce it as Appendix 7). The essence of continuous development philosophy was the integration of learning with work and the promotion of self development; the Code called on employers to promote learning *in* the workplace, endlessly raising standards and not waiting for others to say what they should be. CD means creating learning objectives as part of commercial plans, devoting time to review activities, providing self-study materials and so on. CD ideas were for personnel management what 'Total Quality Management' – another eighties development – was for production and commercial management: an attitude-based approach to managing change, in an era of boundless change, by making it work for you, and without using someone else's model of what was desirable. CD ideas have been taken up by a number of professional bodies (and are incorporated into the Management Charter Group's charter), and a 'continuing professional development' (CPD) movement is now gaining impetus.

We will explore the theoretical basis for CD in our chapter on 'learning and training' (Chapter 3); we also include a chapter explaining CD in greater detail as the last in this book. CD ideals stress learner motivation, and insist that learning is at its strongest when it is unique to the learner's objective; hence CD advocates tend to view standardised programmes as second best, or 'lowest common denominator', alternatives. CD also claims to be relevant to all levels of learner: the individual employee, the team, the department, the site, the company, the industry, the nation.

2 The 'Learning Organisation' movement

Whilst the IPM were developing their CD philosophy, other researchers/writers were increasingly searching for ways to define the same thing in organisational terms. Work in the mid-eighties by Pedler, Burgoyne and Boydell in what was known as the 'learning *company* project' led to the detailing of a wide variety of factors which are related to a learning culture but have not traditionally been seen as 'mainstream employee development' – such factors as organisation structure, worker participation, and management style. A team of researchers from Warwick University reported at roughly the same time on specific organisations which seemed to be 'practising organisational learning' (see Pettigrew *et al.* 1988). Interest has since been growing in this field, which aims at establishing a set of conditions which might be regarded as necessary for employee development; work has also been progressing in the USA. The term 'learning company' is now tending to be replaced by the less restrictive term 'learning organisation', with both public and private sectors under review.

The concept of the 'learning organisation' is still developing; definitions vary from the simplistic 'a lot of people learning' (see Jones and Hendry 1992, pp 3–4) to the Pedler et al report's (1988) 'an organisation which facilitates the learning of all its members and continuously transforms itself'. There is clearly a significant overlap between what is here being addressed and the CD movement; indeed, their aims could be said to be identical. The main difference between CD concepts and the 'learning organisation' models is mainly one of emphasis. CD advocates believe that, given the existence of an attitude wholly supportive of continuous learning, appropriate organisations will follow (serving both operational and learning ends). Hence they accept *any* organisational culture and *any* management style: the CD attitude is expected to continuously adjust the culture. The 'learning organisation' approach, on the other hand, tends to assume that an appropriate organisation is needed to ensure that the positive attitude towards learning can survive; hence it tends to suggest social and structural interventions which should ensure that learning takes place. This issue of the relationship between employee attitudes and organisational design is an important one, to which we will return later (see Chapter 4: on 'the learner and the organisation'); for the moment we would simply suggest that each will in the ideal complement the other.

3 The 'Learning Pays' movement
In April 1991 the Royal Society of Arts (RSA) mounted a series of regional consultations on the subject of post-compulsory education, under the 'Learning Pays' label. The RSA's interim report champions the ideal of a 'learning society', suggests a number of impediments to learning in current UK society, and offers possible solutions. Its strongest recurring theme concerns attitudes and aspirations; its provisional findings relate mainly to methods in schools and colleges (i.e. for post-16 education and training), but they emphasise the importance of helping people to 'learn how to learn' without dependence upon teachers. (As such, they probably owe much to the evolution of 'open', 'distance' and 'flexible' learning methods pioneered by the Open University and publicised by more recent satellite or cable TV companies; learning at one's own pace and in one's time

are growing in attraction). They include a plea for industrial cultures to change to raise the status of employee development, including self development, within them. The report suggests a three-phase model of 'Foundation' (up to age 16, concerned with establishing habits of learning, and covered by the National Curriculum), 'Formation' (16 to 18, concerned with workplace learning, and covered by NVQs/SVQs to Level 3), and 'Continuation' (beyond 18, concerned with self-development, and covered by higher NVQ/SVQ Levels). Other phases ('Transformation – learning how to change; and 'Transfiguration' – learning to cope with change) have since been added during a consultation process which has lead to the definition of activities which might be needed for each of these phases.

The RSA model, with its emphasis on educational influences, supports both CD and the 'learning organisation' approach *sequentially*. The Foundation stage is said to develop attitudes, and 'learning to learn'. The Formation stage emphasises learning about 'workplace readiness'. The Continuation stage allows the organisation to make increasing demands on the learner, who in turn is encouraged to be more innovative. We must wait and see the extent to which these ideas grow; some critics see them as full of insight, others as an elaborate piece of contrived architecture.

It seems probable that the three initiatives will tend to merge over the next few years: their conceptual bases and strategic aims are close enough to ensure that each draws from the others. Their importance lies primarily in their common sources: an increasing belief among both educationalists and training practitioners that improved economic performance cannot be *imposed* by national edict or plan, and emerging evidence that developments in both workplace attitudes and organisational design are essential. This is not to say that the supporters of these movements reject ideas of value accruing from the various other initiatives we have described; the aim is less to abandon traditional methods than to achieve a new balance – or perhaps, more properly, a new set of balances – between:

- learner dependence and learner independence
- formal and informal learning methods
- standard programmes and unique, self directed plans
- learning and work as separate processes and learning and work as an integrated whole.

A NOTE ON THE SINGLE EUROPEAN MARKET

We cannot leave national perspectives without mention of the European Union. So far, our only reference in this history to its influence has been in relation to the NVQ system. UK industry has during the seventies and eighties shown little interest in vocational education and training systems or norms across the Channel, and the idea of a common system has drawn little enthusiasm. But the European Commission's own Social Action Programme looks forward to a different future; indeed, the Community's stated aim of implementing a charter of basic human rights includes clear vocational training objectives, which Commission documents report as being 'at the forefront of the Commission's priorities'. EU initiatives include:

- an instrument on access to vocational training – for every worker, throughout working life
- rationalisation and coordination of training within 'a common vocational policy'
- comparability of vocational qualifications – including extension of work to cover levels above that of 'skilled worker'
- specific action programmes.

The UK government has opposed the EU Social Charter (which is basically a declaration of fundamental rights for all workers within the community, and has been adopted by the other member states), but without referring to that part which gives employees training rights. The UK is nevertheless signed up to the Social *Chapter*, which is contained within the treaty of political union, and which is effectively the way in which the Social Charter can be transformed into legislation. But the Social Chapter is modified by a 'subsidiarity clause', under which the EU, if it wishes to improve workers' rights by its own directives, must prove that national governments cannot achieve the same ends for themselves. Hence the room for continued debate.

The scope of the Social Charter is wide: apart from such things as freedom of movement and the right to receive training throughout one's working life, it covers, for example, rights to information and consultation – including information on planned technological changes and the restructuring of operations. Most importantly, it requires a number of health and safety standards to be met (including arrangements for firefighting, first aid and evacuation, with possible later extensions to include safety induction whenever an employee moves into a new job or area). The necessary legislation on health and safety is expected before the end of 1992, and in this particular area it seems probable that the UK will implement any directive without any challenge.

There is also the important issue of vocational qualifications – an obvious target for harmonisation in the interests of mobility and equal opportunities. Principles for a common vocational training policy were established as long ago as 1963 (at which time such a policy seemed to be limited to establishing common qualifications); these principles have been declared 'still valid' as recently as 1991. At national and trans-national levels, the debate on 'integration or diversity' (or a new, acceptable, mix of both) is already being promoted by the Commission, and will continue throughout the nineties. A European social policy document dated February 1992 promised this, and reported that work which compared existing vocational qualifications at 'qualified worker' level was nearly complete. A directive is expected to be agreed by the end of 1994; this should establish mutual recognition of qualifications in some 200 occupations and professions, covering technical qualifications involving up to three years' training and approved (in the case of the UK) at NVQ/SVQ Levels 3 or 4. The ongoing debate should also lead eventually to a set of guidelines being promulgated, with measures to stimulate trans-national cooperation. It seems unlikely that the UK will need to invoke the 'subsidiarity' clause and argument to retain its qualifications system.

Employees' rights to training (as for example in France, where the law requires employers – subject to some defined limits – to grant leave of absence for vocational training) are a more controversial issue. If such rights are confirmed throughout the Single Market, the impact upon UK employers is likely to be considerable. An EU 'Directive' (i.e. a piece of legislation which all member states must build into their own national laws) was for years expected on 'access to vocational training'; instead, a (less binding) 'Recommendation' appeared in 1993. This document states unequivocally that 'all Member States should ensure that every worker in the EU has access without discrimination to vocational training through their working life'; to that end, it then suggests that each Member State should:

- encourage organisations to 'make continual training and development a priority, and establish training plans'
- provide specific incentives (e.g. financial) to encourage smaller organisations to invest in training

- provide specific retraining incentives for organisations which are 'restructuring'
- develop local and regional networks to 'encourage and assist . . . training which reflects local need'
- ensure that workers know about their organisations' training policies
- promote skills assessment and training needs assessment 'at work or in other centres'
- encourage worker consultation when training plans and programmes are developed
- encourage 'competence-based training which leads to recognised and transferable qualifications'
- promote open and distance learning
- 'pay particular attention to those who have received little training in the past, are unemployed or disabled, to women – and particularly to women returners'.

The European Commission has already launched and funded a variety of cross-border 'action programmes' aimed at specific training goals – for example, 'Erasmus' (furthering the exchange of students in higher education), 'Lingua' (promoting foreign language training), 'Petra' (encouraging vocational training for young people), and 'Comett' (fostering cooperation between education and industry without regard to state frontiers on new technology). Some of these programmes end in 1994; but a major new programme ('Leonardo') is due to be launched in January 1995, coordinating and expanding such activities. 'Leonardo' is one of the outcomes of a long-awaited and intensely debated EU White Paper entitled *Growth, Competitiveness, Employment: the Challenges and Ways Forward into the 21st Century*, which was issued in December 1993. The White Paper focuses on unemployment as the main feature of Europe's economic and social crisis, and includes among its proposals:

- the promotion of life-long vocational training
- labour market flexibility through retraining

These twin goals could be said to represent in a mere dozen words the priorities to which all training interventions at the level of each EU nation might be linked.

WHICH WAY(S) FORWARD?

Although all these developments during the past 25 years can be seen as sequential and complementary, and certainly as adding up to a considerable surge in employee development activity at national level, they are diverse in their emphases. One can detect at the same time:

- centralism AND devolution
- conformism AND development of local initiative
- national programmes AND tailor made plans
- prescribed qualifications AND self development
- permanent institutions AND temporary campaigns
- teacher-led AND learner-led approaches
- the separation of learning from work AND its integration with work.

Recently, government's strategy has been to steer activity towards the standardised programme and the national qualification, whilst limiting its own financial contribution and pressing employers to increase theirs. At the same time there have been strenuous efforts to make state education more vocational. But the key problem – that of the commitment of the nation's managers – remains as yet unresolved.

The Institute of Personnel Management issued early in 1992 its own 'agenda' for further national initiatives; an 'executive summary' heading their paper acknowledged that 'much has been achieved', then stressed the following points:

- people development must be recognised as top priority
- higher goals must be set for youth education and training
- adults must be helped to cope with changes
- a more forward-looking continuous development approach must be applied to the development of 'people-skills'
- a new 'investment' approach is needed to sharing the costs of training
- a more coherent method is needed for setting and maintaining standards of education, training and attainment
- an evolutionary approach to change must be generated, with full consultation to ensure continuity and commitment.

Adapted from 'Towards a National Training and Development Strategy' IPM, 1992

A 'Positive Policy' paper was attached as an appendix to this (now IPD) document: the paper is reproduced in this book as Appendix 1.

National training interventions during and throughout the nineties will need to be made with all these challenges in mind.

Now we can return to the question we posed at the start of this chapter:

'Why do you think we introduced a chapter on "national" issues so early in this book?'

Like most propositions in the field of Employee Development, there are several reasons for this particular strategy.

1 No Personnel and/or Training manager can avoid being interested in developments of this magnitude, even if some mix a measure of trepidation along with their interest. They themselves need to form views on what they must discuss with their day to day contacts.

A day in the life of Samantha Bloggs, Personnel Manager for Random Articles Limited, may include any of the following: conversations on the shop floor with first level management, who may have conflicting views on workplace competence as described at industry level, and equally conflicting views on the desirability of workplace assessment; a telephone call from the managing director, who does not understand papers sent to him by the local TEC director and a trip to the local further education college, when information about new qualification courses is shared. It will help Sam considerably if she understands 'how things came to be this way'; this knowledge can be used to help explain the present, and also to anticipate further developments. Sam must help any contacts – on both sides of her company's boundary – to work out what must be done, what might be done, what should not be done, what cannot be done, within the contexts of the new national and local developments AND her organisation's operational needs. Observing these things, judging them, deciding what should be done, and then persuading others – this is what boundary management is for Sam, and how people like Sam try to influence the boundary itself.

2 Observation and understanding of national moves can help the manager to understand her/his own role inside the home organisation.

Jack James, a Production Manager in Random Articles, can remember when he first made this connection. The occasion was a branch meeting of his professional institute. The theme of the meeting was 'The Management of Change', and proceedings livened up when members who worked in the public sector challeged others from the private sector, the latter having asserted that 'the only stimulus for change is competition'. Jack learned several truths, in fact: that change happens at national as well as organisation level; that governments and boards of directors equally try to make change work for them; that strategies to make change happen do not always work in the same direction, either within a level or between levels; that political decisions are needed from all managers at all levels and that the most effective stimulus for change is management itself.

Jack has since realised that some employee development decisions in Random Articles are similar in content to those being taken at national level. How can we get learning to happen: do carrots or sticks work best? Should we build up resources in case they are needed, or wait until we are sure, then run crash programmes? Should managers be treated differently from others? Should standards be laid down at the centre, or indeed from the top, or should everyone be urged to continuously develop, setting new standards as soon as old ones are achieved? Should responsibility for training be carried by all, or given to one or more special units, or should we have a mixture of the two?

Right now, Jack and Sam are pondering several specific issues which reflect national developments:

- Should we be creating internal TECs of our own?
- Should we mount a new review of our management training practices?
- Should we move into YT, which we have so far ignored?
- Should we make new recruits study for NVQs?
- Should we search for ways whereby we can use distance learning instead of formal courses?
- How can our appraisal practices better stimulate improved performance, as CD philosophy preaches?

These issues have all been raised by Sam. It is not difficult to see how she has been influenced by national developments – and so perhaps not difficult to understand her interest in the national scene.

3 Learning from life is sometimes superior to learning from theory – and case material based on the nation is often easier to understand than case material based on another organisation. There are several approaches to learning; the most usual involves coming to terms with abstract concepts, and then understanding their application by studying case examples which show the concepts in applied form. But it is possible to explore from the other direction, studying case material and deducing the issues and concepts.

Jack has made a habit of this. He finds text books too logical, too structured, too contrived; his ideal learning ground is biography. He has read Harvey-Jones, MacGregor, Iaocca, DeLorean and so on, but would not recognise such names as Schein, Argyris and Kolb. Sam finds she cannot easily discuss her specific Random Articles development issues with him if she talks theoretically, but sharing an understanding of national case material is relatively easy. Again, it is not difficult to see why Sam is interested in the national scene.

And, perhaps, not difficult to see why we chose this as our first main chapter (although there is in fact a further reason, which we will be covering in the next chapter). The examples of Sam's and Jack's 'specific issues' will also provide a sample answer to the question we posed half way through the chapter.

FOR FURTHER REFLECTION AND DISCUSSION

1 **If you were Sam or Jack, how might your attitudes towards education and training have changed in the last few years?**

2 **What would you yourself like or expect to see in a statement on 'national policy in the field of education and training'?**

3 To what extent do you see changes in training and education at national level during the past generation demanding changes in the management of employee development at the workplace?

SUGGESTED READING

There are no standard texts covering the material in this chapter. Appendices 1, 2 and 3 provide an opportunity to review some of the key national issues and specific initiatives, many of which are referred to by their respective abbreviations.

A 1987 MSC/NEDO 'Action Pack' entitled 'People: the Key to Success', comprising a videotape and supporting literature, comprehensively presents the case for 'training as an economic instrument' without referring to specific national initiatives.

Keeping up to date with new developments is not easy; the problem can best be met by continuing reference to journals, especially:

- The Employment Department's *Labour Market Quarterly Report* and annual *Labour Market and Skill Trends*
- The Institute of Personnel and Development's *Personnel Management, IPM Plus,* and *European Update.*
- The Employment Department's *Insight* and *Competence and Assessment*
- The National Council of Industry Training Organisation's *The NCITO Independent*
- Longman's weekly journals *Education* and *College Management Today.*

Training and development in the other EU member states is dealt with comprehensively in one volume of the former Institute of Personnel Management's 'European Management Guides' series: *Training and Development* (IPM, 1992).

For organisations and practitioners, the Employment Department's Skills and Enterprise Unit at Moorfoot, Sheffield, S1 4PQ operates a 'Network' membership scheme. Depending on the level chosen, members regularly receive briefing and updating material covering most aspects of the national training scene.

Chapter 2
ATTITUDES TOWARD EDUCATION AND TRAINING

Education, training and work – changes in attitudes – philosophies of training

INTRODUCTION

If you have not already done so, you might like now to look at Appendix 1, a 'positive policy statement', created a few years ago (and revised in 1990) by the former Institute of Personnel Management's National Committee for Training and Development: The words 'education' and 'training' both loom large in this document. This perhaps reinforces the view in our last chapter that perhaps the nation is beginning to bring together its education ('learning for life') and its training ('learning for particular work skills') activities. But we must still remember what we said earlier, when defining the two terms: the training reality is ALWAYS SITUATION-SPECIFIC. And don't forget that not all national developments are working in the same direction.

The last chapter contained much to suggest that the success or otherwise of national training interventions is heavily dependent upon society's attitudes towards learning – and especially the attitudes of those at the workplace. The same is true of training interventions within any given organisation. This chapter explores assumptions which have generally been held about education and training within the work context, and the extent to which attitudes have changed in recent years; it then outlines a number of training philosophies, and suggests some generalised implications for all who feel responsible for 'making learning happen'.

Is your attitude towards education and training based on:
- your own past learning experiences?
- support for one or more national initiatives?
- support for one or more clear-cut philosophies of learning?
- workplace responsibilities?
- your hopes for the future?

EDUCATION, TRAINING AND WORK

A number of writers, including Stringfellow (1968), Tannehill (1970), and Handy (1989) have discussed the nature of education and training within a work context, and have drawn attention to problems which arise from assumptions which people make when they use these two terms. The word 'education', for example, is at times used narrowly to mean the formal process of studying a subject syllabus, with the traditional assumption that this entails attendance at an educational insitutuion, conforming to a plan drafted by someone who is a teacher. Such assumptions can be expected to work against the growth of self-study or distance learning methods. Or 'education' might be used in a very much broader sense, as in 'life itself is the best educator', with the idea that developing one's values, opinions, and personality is achieved independently of institutionalised education. Such an assumption will tend to work against attendance at formalised courses, and will promote on-the-job training.

Distinguishing between the purposes and methods of education and those of training is not always possible, as the two overlap. However, as we shall see later, our assumptions can make differences between them which are of more than academic and semantic interest. Indeed, the assumptions that employees, especially managers, make – about what each aims to achieve, and by what means – can lead to costly mistakes. For example, when the UK converted to decimal currency in the seventies, some companies ran expensive formal teaching sessions before 'D day' for their accounts clerks and canteen till operators; others, who recognised the 'education' that was happening naturally to all via official TV and press information services, and who believed that learning would be quick without any formal input, managed their operations with little more disruption than short briefing sessions.

A more complex, classic example of incorrect assumptions lies in the widespread practice of giving graduate management trainees – who are recruited as top managers of the future – nothing more than a 'Cook's Tour' of their companies during their early (often twelve to eighteen months) training period. One assumption here is that these graduates are already superior learners, with 'fast track' ambitions, but need *knowledge* – knowledge of how the company operates. Another assumption is that they will rapidly show their superior management qualities wherever they go. Yet another is that training for general management (i.e. corporate) responsibilities is best left until they, years later, move into general management jobs. The strategy is a sequential one, with education dominating in the early days and training taking over a long time later. In practice, this strategy has often failed, for several reasons. Firstly, academic success is not necessarily a guarantor of management development; the latter demands more than knowledge of operations, and notably a set of political skills which existing staff recognise and respect. Since academic programmes offer little opportunity for such skills to be developed or displayed, 'fast track' promotion is often delayed. Here the planners' assumptions have obscured a fair definition of the trainees' training needs. Secondly, trainees' work experience is usually below management level, at a time when they have strong ambitions to test their ability to take responsibility. Here the planners' assumptions ignore the raw material: it is not surprising that trainee turnover often proves high.

Thirdly, corporate vision is rarely possible from a few months in production, a few months in accounts, a few months in selling and so on: the tendency is to acquire departmental loyalties (and disloyalties) which make the later transition to general management a more challenging task. Here the assumption that later training will easily build on earlier education is faulty: there is an educational element in preparing corporate managers which would be better covered first, allowing it to influence the ongoing experience. It can be seen that graduate trainees' programmes are both difficult to plan and need a sophisticated blend of both education and training, regardless of one's definitions of those two words. The overlap between the two effectively requires a concept of employee development that is not wedded too strongly to a simple definition of either.

Further examples of attitudes which ignore the education-training overlap with unfortunate results can be seen in managers' attitudes to formal off-the-job course attendances. Some managers assume that a two-week course is sufficient to turn a clerk into an office supervisor, or a research chemist into a leader of a research team. Others assume that, however charismatic the trainers, a course cannot reproduce the real-life language and culture of the workplace, and hence anything learned will be impossible to transfer. Both treat the course as an isolated learning experience; neither see the potential value in generating pre- and post-course learning (e.g. discussions, special assignments) at the workplace, to help the learner to bridge the divide between reality and concepts.

Bearing these examples in mind, and remembering also that both education and training are concerned with promoting and guiding learning and assisting in the achievement of goals, which gives the trained person the confidence to apply learning, we can now consider how education and training *differ* and *yet* can *complement* each other.

Education or Training?

As our examples demonstrate, education and training differ in the following ways:

1 In the degree to which their objectives can be specified in behavioural terms
2 In the time normally taken to realise learning objectives
3 In their methods and content of learning
4 In the context within which learning materials are used.

1 Objectives

To most observers, a characteristic feature of a training objective is that it can be expressed in behavioural terms. Many trainers specify 'learning objectives' as part of their training plans; those objectives detail the work behaviour required of the learner at the end of the training, i.e. the criterion behaviour. In contrast, educational objectives have traditionally been less specific, because, as Otto and Glaser argued (1970) 'they are too complex or . . . the behaviours that result in successful accomplishments in many instances are not known'. These objectives have usually been couched in more general and even abstract terms; indeed, it has been argued that this gives the learner a broader and stronger opportunity, allowing her to interpret and apply a basic understanding to specific situations without constraints imposed by teachers or planners. Educational objectives have tended to stimulate personal development, and in the past could reasonably be viewed as 'person' rather than 'job' oriented – even in vocational education. This is still largely true of primary and secondary educational activity, and of undergraduate education in the universities. But the work of the National Council for Vocational Qualifications, and more particularly that of the Lead Bodies who have set standards as the basis for NVQs/SVQs (see Chapter 1, page 26), has changed matters in relation to further education, so that – as we shall see in Chapter 5 – these new vocational qualifications are based on 'what can be done at the workplace', not 'what can be demonstrated in the examination room'. They are not concerned with personal strengths or weaknesses, except in so far as these allow or prevent competence in a particular job.

It is not surprising that the NCVQ development has raised much debate among professional educators and trainers. Critical professional educators complain that the approach is limiting, backward-looking, unduly constraining on teachers, and bureaucratic; critical professional trainers complain that its national base cannot prescribe what competence is on a single work site, and in accepting workplace assessment it can only promote 'national' standards on a 'lowest common denominator' basis. It nevertheless remains a significant attempt to bring education and training together, and constitutes the prime focus for much future discussion between employers and training providers.

2 Time

Whilst examples might be quoted to disprove the point, it remains generally true that training plans are shorter than educational plans. For example, a young person entering an office may complete a course in word processing in a matter of months, but it has taken the same person over ten years to develop a mastery of the language that allows the training to be undertaken.

3 Methods and Content

Some ways of learning appear more appropriate to education than to training, and it is useful to refer to Tannehill's (1970) distinction between mechanistic and organic learning. Mechanistic learning is achieved as a result of stimuli and responses, reinforced by practice; many industrial training programmes are designed with the assumption that mechanistic learning is involved. Initial training of apprentice fitters or plumbers, for example, will typically involve teaching how to handle and use tools in a relatively standardised way. Organic learning, on the other hand, involves a change in the individual rather than in what can be done. For example, a move from a production job into a personnel job may require a new understanding of what the day's work can involve – a new set of concepts – and is much less amenable to external direction, since the outcome is much less easy to predict. Hence a change of this kind might involve following the professional body's education scheme alongside planned work experience.

There is also usually a difference in the learning content of training and of educational programmes. As we have seen, training aims to provide the learner with the knowledge, skills and attitudes necessary to carry out specific work tasks. It is essentially 'practical'. Much of its content will, in the ideal, be derived from within the organisation itself. In contrast, educational programmes contain theoretical and conceptual material aimed at stimulating the learner's critical and analytical faculties. Detail is usually included to illustrate principles or relationships, rather than to be copied slavishly. It is probably for this reason that we hear frequently about 'management education' and 'professional education' but normally about 'craft training' and 'operator training'. The regular use of the term 'sales training' is probably a reflection of the fact that it has traditionally been based on the teaching of sales techniques and not on a body of principles or concepts.

4 Context

Baron (1981) makes the point that the distinction between education and training is at times a function of the context within which either is used. He quotes as an example the study of the principles of company law, which can be a part of an education programme in legal studies for law degree students, but equally a part of a training course for managers. Another example lies in the title we have chosen for this book: we have chosen to include the word 'training' and ignore the word 'education' (despite its relevance), because the former is much more usually associated with the management of employee development at the workplace. These examples perhaps serve to confirm that most learning experiences mix educational and training processes, yet these processes will often be described only in terms of their 'majority' usage or purpose. Some education almost invariably exists in training, and vice versa: the common factor is learning.

Or, perhaps, 'development' – and, within our work context,

'employee development'. This term was not used in the title of the earlier editions of the book; we have now incorporated it because, as we shall explain shortly, it has become a generally used term to denote 'learning at work'. The former Institute of Personnel Management divided its professional studies syllabus into three essential areas – and 'Employee Development' is the one which covers all those elements relating to the management of learning at work. From now on we will increasingly use 'development' and 'training' rather than 'education' or 'education and training' to describe our area of interest. But we hope the reader will not forget that *both* education and training are parts of any employee development process.

CHANGES IN ATTITUDES TO TRAINING AND DEVELOPMENT

Prior to the introduction of the Industrial Training Act of 1964, as noted above, successive governments and most employers (and hence most managers) had a *laissez-faire* attitude towards the development of their employees, expecting that:

- employee development should be primarily educational in nature
- education should happen away from work, and in a person's own time.

Whilst some organisations provided sophisticated training plans and programmes for some of their employees, most saw no advantage in spending money to this end. Why should they? With the exception of the long-established apprenticeship arrangements in industries such as engineering and printing, employers appeared to have little need to train. Much of the work they wanted from their weekly-paid employees was of an unskilled, routine nature, capable of being learned quickly by watching and imitating other, established, workers. An employee who did not manage to do the job satisfactorily after a short period of 'sitting by Nellie' could be asked to leave, and replaced by one who might. There were not many who did need to be replaced; most learned as expected, and met traditional standards of competence. Such an attitude was understandable, at least in economic terms, when there was a plentiful supply of labour in the marketplace capable of doing the work employers required.

However, during the period of relatively full employment from the

1950s to the early 1970s, employers' and managers' attitudes to workers began to change. Replacements were not always as good as those who had been 'dropped'; staff shortages inevitably produced higher unit costs, through overtime arrangements; overseas competition challenged the continued relevance of traditional work specifications; and trade union pressure for improved worker benefits called for better opportunities for established workers. The larger employers were already investing in management and supervisory training, and seemed to be moving ahead commercially at the expense of their competitors; they did not resist the advent of the ITBs in 1964/5, and indeed they supplied part-time members of some ITBs' committees.

Wellens (1968) was one of the early writers to see the change emerging (he was the editor of a training journal, who had for years urged attitude changes). He argued optimistically that changes in management's attitudes to training were predictable, and that they depended primarily upon the state of technology in society. He considered that the increasing complexity of business and industry in the UK had reached a stage when only by pursuing a policy of training could employers ensure that their staffs' skills kept pace with technological progress. Training, he argued, would soon claim 'a place in the mainstream of management'.

The EEC commissioners put this message even more clearly in their 1971 *Preliminary Guidelines for a Community Social Policy Programme*:

> 'Progress is itself gradually raising the general level of skills; the faster rate of progress is tending to blur the nature of these skills by the swift and radical change in machinery, materials, methods of work and organisation. Knowledge, know-how, techniques and acquired attitudes are quickly left behind and re-adaptation, which was recently the exception, is becoming the rule. As a result, occupational skills can no longer be defined by reference to the job and the nature of the occupation involved. They are now seen as the permanent ability to adapt to the technical pattern of work.'

We have seen in the last chapter how the ITBs generally failed to change attitudes to training among the smaller and medium-sized UK companies. It was their larger competitors, perhaps because of their wider horizons and more established forward planning routines – but also because they understood better the challenges within their markets – that made the running. The oil crisis in the early 1970s, the increasing impact of new technologies affecting product design and manufacturing, the new methods of communication, the decline in international competitiveness, and not least the discussions that took place on the inability of ITBs to affect 'the bottom line' were all major factors influencing the larger companies to train. Their first action was to appoint people of calibre to personnel and training posts; these people slowly began to produce and preach the conceptual lead that the function needed. These were the people who filled the ITBs' committees, and who significantly influenced (and sometimes compiled) the ITBs' recommendations; it was these people who were the main advocates of the 'systematic approach' that we have mentioned as the major ITB product, and which is still considered the essential base for training activity by many personnel and training managers (we will outline much of this base in Section B). In 1977, in another somewhat ambitious and perhaps political statement, the Training Services Agency was able to report:

> 'The whole environment in which training and the trainer has to operate has changed rapidly and in all probability will continue to change, e.g. through the increasing stimulus and direction from the Training Services Agency and the MSC; increasing external demands through legislation; availability of investment monies; inflation; competition in the market; and, increasingly important, unemployment and the changing values and expectations of the workforce, especially among young people.'

> *'An Approach to the Training of Staff with Trainer Roles'*

Within their own large organisations, the training practitioners pioneered much new work. They drafted training policy statements (for their top managements to sign and distribute); they wrote employee handbooks and mounted induction sessions (to ensure new recruits received basic information about such things as conditions of employment and safety rules); they produced apprenticeship and other trainee programmes, often dictating movement between jobs through time; they arranged attendance at day release classes, in support of selected qualifications; they developed appraisal systems (to yield data for themselves on training needs, which offered a first stage in the process of creating training plans); they drew up budgets; and, most of all, they arranged formal courses – on a wide range of topics, from safety to leadership, and from interviewing skills to debt control. It is important to realise that except in a very small number of cases, the early growth and sophistication of training came essentially from these practitioners, not (as in other new functions such as marketing or computing) from top management. Top management discussions on training were infrequent, unless they happened without warning as part of discussions on broader personnel or industrial relations issues. The function was developed 'from below'. This may be the essential reason why during the seventies little training was aimed at long term corporate needs, and management generally failed to appreciate that in a changing world the organisation must be viewed as a learning system and managed as such.

Whilst this evidence at the end of the eighties suggested that the training function was beginning to come of age, we believe it would be wrong to suggest, even now, that training has achieved in all, or even most, organisations a 'mainstream place'. We must repeat the realistic view that perception of the increasingly important role of training and development in modern society is not shared by all employers or even most managers. We have seen in Chapter 1 that industry as a whole is not yet firmly committed to national vocational qualifications, and cannot yet be said to 'invest in people'. The norm must still be described in negative rather than positive terms; regardless of size, and despite the substantial attention now paid to employee development in many different types of organisations, it is still our belief that the main descriptors of training in British industry *taken as a whole* remain as follows:

- it is only rarely integrated with mainstream operations
- it still has a low operational priority
- it does not normally appear amongst strategic plans
- it is a peripheral activity for most line management
- it usually functions via *ad hoc*, unrelated events
- it is not normally mentioned as part of new capital projects, nor product launches, nor reorganisation plans, nor notices of new administrative methods
- it is viewed not as investment but as expense
- few managers aspire to a superior understanding of learning processes
- management takes the view that, whilst properly organised training costs money, unplanned training, which relies on informal assistance from fellow employees, is inexpensive.

PHILOSOPHIES OF TRAINING

The above list of negatives might have included one which read 'trainers do not appear to hold any clear-cut philosophy of training'. But this would be open to dispute: the vast majority of personnel and training staff do appear to believe that:

- the organisation is a learning system
- employee development is essentially that part of the organisation's planning activities which aim to make learning happen
- training interventions can serve at the same time the individual and the organisation (unlike the 'conflict' base for some employee relations activities).

Within these generally held principles, there are a number of 'philosophies of training' which underlie and inform attitudes in the field of employee development. If they are rarely written into work documents, they are often implicit in the decisions that are taken, and the activities that result.

A complex range of influences accounts for the values, ideals, opinions and preferences that affect decisions relating to training in a work organisation. Among the more important of these are:

- the political ideologies of governments, employers and employees
- the expectations of people with regard to access to training opportunities
- the degree to which a learning opportunity carries with it an obligation on the learner to the provider
- the traditions and power of established groups (including, for example, professional bodies and trade unions) to regulate entry and to confer status
- the variety of relationships between existing occupations in the workforce
- the relative stability or otherwise of occupations
- the stock of 'competent' workers compared with expected future work needs
- the scale of unemployment in the catchment area.

As we shall see in the following paragraphs, different philosophies of training reflect the range and mix of responses to such questions as:

- who is considered responsible for funding training (the employer, the employee, or both?)
- whether the training to be planned will be narrowly focused or broadly based and transferable (e.g. single skilled or multi-skilled, specific job related, or general management related?)
- the impact of new technology (e.g. how revolutionary, how much, how fast?)
- the responsibility for creating the learning plan (e.g. government, lead body, external consultant, local college, line manager, training officer, learner?)
- the nature of the expense (e.g. long term investment, essential expense, unavoidable cost to be minimised?)
- the priority accorded to certain groups (e.g. young, unemployed, women, disabled, 'fast track' trainees, selected department's staff?).

Thus a philosophy of training has its foundations in the cultural, economic, social and other values and experiences of the individual, organisation or nation. Yet the purpose of training is to promote change, and often to disturb these values, or to offer new experiences which outdate those that have been valued. It is this potential conflict which underlies many of the more intractable issues facing training and development at all levels in society.

Elitism

This philosophy of training can take many forms, and has its roots in long established patterns of provision which are seen to have served a country or organisation well over a substantial period of time (for this reason it is sometimes referred to as 'Traditionalism'). For example, in a country where traditional craft skills reflect the degree of technological advance and where the great majority of the workforce engage in semi-skilled or unskilled work, the tradition may well be that training is necessary and 'reserved' for high status work (i.e. the craft and technician jobs) but unnecessary for the rest of the working population. Similar examples might restrict training to 'members of the family', or to 'managers over a certain grade', or might link success in well established but apparently unrelated fields (e.g. higher education, regardless of the studies undertaken) with the training priority.

Such a philosophy of training was dominant in the UK throughout the industrial revolution, and has persisted in some organisations despite changing social norms and changing technologies.

Voluntarism

A *laissez-faire* philosophy of training assumes that requirements for skilled and professional staff will be produced as a result of initiatives taken by individuals and/or by their managers, as and when they seem appropriate – that is, that the working conditions do not need to contain an injunction to learn or train, and the continuing work system does not need to provide for its regular or periodic planning. This philosophy places much of the onus for initiating and paying for training on the individual as, for example, in the standard 'evening classes' route towards professional qualifications for some workers in the UK pre-war. A more modern example can be seen in the UK subsidiary of a major US computer manufacturer, who send new technical videotapes monthly across the Atlantic ocean, but who do no more than inform their UK technologists of what is being sent; learning via the use of the tapes is left to the discretion of those technologists. A more easily recognisable UK example is in the public library – and in modern 'learning resource centres', where facilities are available on an unplanned basis.

One important outcome of this philosophy of training is that the skills and knowledge acquired may not be 'recognised', since they are unique to the individual and are not catalogued anywhere (a fact that may be considered favourable by an employer who does not want to lose scarce resources).

Centralism and Authoritarianism

These are not strictly training philosophies, but as complementary management philosophies they inevitably make an impact upon training wherever they co-exist. They assume that learners will not or cannot take their own decisions on learning; those decisions must be taken as a result of a bureaucratic process and imposed by 'someone in authority'. This was the philosophy underlying the introduction of ITBs and ITB levies and, whilst they have now disappeared, within individual organisations it remains the most predominant influence on training. Typically, training interventions are drafted and imposed from a central personnel or training unit, acting with the assumed authority of top management: most training programmes and plans follow a more or less systematic identification of needs by someone other than the learner, plans to meet those needs are prepared by specialists acting in conjunction with line management, and those plans are implemented again without regard to the views of the learner, who moves through the ensuing learning experience with the assumption that it will prove beneficial.

This is the philosophical basis for the 'systematic approach' (see page 19). Whilst that 'systematic approach' may be modified to include a planning role for the learner, it is unusual for this to happen in relation to large groups of learners below management level. This fact is not necessarily to be criticised: it is no more than a reflection of the existence of elitism, centralism and authoritarianism in most work cultures today. But such cultures might themselves be criticised in rarely providing for learner motivation – which as we will see later is an important element in any training plan. We will explain the 'systematic approach' in more detail in Section B; see also Harrison (1988).

Conformism and Non-Conformism

Once again, these two alternative philosophies cannot properly be called philosophies of training *per se*, but their impact on training activity is critical. In a society which is predominantly conformist, learners tend to wait to be told how and what to learn, expecting or at least hoping for a centralist lead. The non-conformist alternative develops 'from the fringe'; innovation is encouraged.

The belief that voluntarism is an inadequate and inappropriate approach to satisfying a nation's training requirements has led some to argue that the state has a duty to provide a centralist training culture, and to stimulate conformism by such methods as financial pressures and even statutory requirements. We have seen in the last chapter how this view has influenced some of the UK's key developments during the past 25 years – firstly via a statutory ITB operation, then via the introduction of national training programmes, and most recently via the introduction of the 'national vocational qualifications' (NVQ/SVQ) system, under which standards are set at national level and then transformed into qualifications, with government funding being restricted to training aimed at these qualifications.

It is something of a paradox that the Conservative government of the eighties, which preached a philosophy of open market competition and self sufficiency should have moved towards a centralist training philosophy. The reasons, and the attitudes which back them, are political rather than doctrinaire. NVQs/SVQs are the UK government's answer to several problems. Firstly, the vocational qualifications scene has for too long been confused and confusing: employers and potential students have found it difficult to understand what exists, and again what any given qualification 'means'. The range of options has been particularly great at the lower levels, i.e. those serving young people in their periods of early employment. The lack of an easily understood route to a widely accepted qualification has led to students sometimes addressing levels which were too difficult for them, producing failures and a high drop-out rate. Secondly, qualifications have often been biased towards academic rather than practical ability, with written examinations which test knowledge but not necessarily its application. These problems made the UK system look inadequate compared to the simpler, more structured yet more occupation-based qualifications in cross-channel countries such as Germany – at a time when the impending Single European Market heralded pressure towards a common system. But perhaps the greatest influences were the twin perils of skills shortages and unemployment – and government's need to reduce both, by making skills 'more portable'.

We have allowed our discussion of training philosophies to divert us into an explanation of why centralism is currently strong within the UK. And we will explain more of the new conceptual and procedural NVQ/SVQ approach in later chapters. But we should stress that these training interventions are not totally authoritarian and prescriptive – certainly not as prescriptive as was the ITB levy. To date, the effect on the individual employer of NVQs/SVQs is simply that a choice must be made. Adopting the externally produced standards may be an attractive choice, since it fills a gap for those who do not analyse their own needs, offers a ready-made blueprint instead of time-consuming analysis of one's own, and is likely to be supported by the employee, whose learning is portable. But it may be at the risk of failing to match one's current targets, which may be more closely defined or aimed at moving above the national standard. Management may choose to adopt the new system for some employees (e.g. fitters, drivers) but not for others (e.g. sales representatives, managers). One of the most intriguing aspects of the next few years will be to see the extent to which employers, and indeed employees, opt in to the new arrangements and adjust their own internal training systems to them.

The degree to which choices are open inside any given organisation is of course a reflection of the existing work culture. Hence training interventions may vary in their basic assumptions, even within an organisation: safety training may be prescribed and imposed, whilst attendance at further education classes may be voluntary; production departments might be expected to accept externally written manuals, whilst marketing departments might be encouraged to build their own; sales representatives might be taught techniques, whilst personnel managers might engage in open-ended discussions and training for joint consultation representatives might (logically) require prior agreement within joint consultation committees. Nonetheless, in planning training interventions, the training specialist who makes uninformed assumptions about conformism and non-conformism is engaging in high-risk management.

Humanism

Humanism makes human interests paramount – by implication, paramount to those of the organisation. This philosophy gives the learner rights – to decide what most serves the learner's interests, and how. An example exists in France, where the law requires employers to provide facilities for education (subject to certain maximum obligations) at the request of the employee. In practice, many current work cultures in the UK have developed to the point where *specific individuals* can and do influence decisions on their training – in terms of its content, its methods and its timing. It has also become increasingly normal for course leaders to gather information on course members' own wishes and aims at the start of courses, with attempts to adjust course programmes following. And courses which are aimed at helping learners to understand group dynamics often start without an agenda; the content is the product of members' own processes, which are themselves studied (with the aid of a process consultant) as they evolve.

Continuous Development (CD)

This is the latest philosophy of training to gain attention in the UK. Put briefly, it assumes that learning should be endless for all, and throughout life. In this it mirrors the earlier continental philosophy of *education permanente*. But it is more closely directed to the world of work, maintaining that the frequency and pace of change in the modern world demand:

- that organisations are structured and managed in such a way as to help the learning to happen
- that employees, especially managers, maintain an attitude of mind which believes in learning, promotes the integration of learning with work, and seeks to learn about learning itself.

It is the emphasis on this latter attitude of mind which justifies the use of the term 'continuous': while development itself is not expected to be continuous, the attitude – in the ideal – is.

CD has evolved largely from the work of consultants from the Tavistock Institute (e.g. Rice, Emery, Trist) and the US Sloan School of Management (e.g. Schein), who concentrated on the mix of social and technical elements in industrial organisation, and concluded that 'efficient' groups acknowledge that continuous learning is needed to manage both their work tasks and their internal process (i.e. the ever-changing relationships between people, goals, technology). The (former) Institute of Personnel Management's *Statement on Continuous Development* (see Appendix 7) reflects this new and radical philosophy, which shares the responsibility for identifying and proposing training with all members of an organisation and, by extension, with society as a whole. The final chapter in this book is given to this subject, with the sub-title 'The Ultimate Intervention'.

At the close of the last chapter we gave you two case-studies and asked you to think about how the attitudes to training of the two people in each case, Sam and Jack, might have changed over the past few years. At the start of this chapter, we asked you to consider what most affected your OWN attitude to training and education. We now offer some more mini-case material, giving examples of evolving attitudes; you might like to 'criticise' these attitudes – that is, to account for them and to judge whether they are likely to be respected by the people with whom they work.

Mary Maddocks is a Personnel Manager in a large, five-star hotel. She has watched the development of national standards with satisfaction. She has to cope with much movement of employees: she has learned to accept an annual staff turnover figure of between 85 per cent and 100 per cent, notably amongst those working as room and catering staff, where people leave and join every week of the year. She has liked the 'Caterbase' programme and material devised by the now-defunct industry training organisation (the Hotel and Catering Industry Training Board), which breaks work down into neat 'bricks' and is established as the basis for NVQs issued by the City and Guilds of London Institute (the C & G). She has a standing arrangement with the local catering college, which allows students to gain work experience at the hotel during their full time studies leading to different C & G qualifications (also approved as NVQs) and which provides her with a steady flow of potential young recruits – who continue to study on a part-time basis after joining. Much of the discussion – with and between employees and supervisors – on the issues of what they can and cannot do, whether they need to improve, what their current training needs might be, and what they themselves want to do, draws on the 'Caterbase' material. As Mary has often said, the HCITB documents take away the need for her to have unique training specifications, and even help her to create or update job descriptions. Liaison with the tutors at the college is easy: they both speak the same language. Mary cannot understand why all industries do not operate the same sort of system.

John French, however, has less interest in any form of national system. He works as Education and Training Manager in a soap-making factory, and has consistently urged the industry's training organisation, on whose national committee he sits, not to create such a system. He is not used to high staff turnover rates; indeed, throughout the past decade his establishment numbers below management level have been steadily falling as new plant has been installed and productivity improved. His new plant differs from what his competitors use and in general the industry's soapmaking processes vary widely between factories. Equipment tends to differ in age, source and method; raw materials and packaging vary in type and quantity, and the degree to which operations are labour intensive ranges from nil (full automation) to 100 per cent (hand mixing, hand finishing, hand wrapping, etc). John's prime aim regarding training is not the new but the established worker, whose range of competences must be continuously widened, and whose 'standards' cannot properly be equated with any national norm (John actually thinks the 'desired standard' is always 'one notch above what has just been achieved'). Like Mary, John has worked with local college staff, but in his case they have produced tailor-made courses which he (and those who attended) would quite like recognised at national level, but which cannot carry an NVQ logo and which would not directly serve other employers. John thinks NVQs tend to undermine the more important workplace efficiency goals.

Peter Critchley is a YT trainee in a boat-building firm. He hopes to be offered proper employment by the firm when his two-year programme ends. He enjoys his work in the boatyard, where the older workers have accepted him easily, and although he still has to spend most of his time fetching and carrying (not least the tea tray), he likes the boat-building atmosphere. His weekly day at college, where he is studying the early stages of marine engineering, is less pleasant: it reminds him of school, which he never enjoyed. He wishes he could be allowed to drop these studies but his traineeship demands them, and his supervisor simply orders him to 'get on with them and stop complaining'. The older workers make jokes about 'back to school', but they never question the supervisor's orders.

Unknown to Mary or John or Peter (who in any case do not know each other), Samantha Bloggs (Chapter 1) is 'not sure about all these national developments'. She has great difficulty in keeping up to date with all the changes that have been reported, and has reached the position where she doubts whether anything will last for long. She is seriously considering whether to press for a specialist training officer to be added to the department's complement. On the subject of NVQs she is somewhat ambivalent: making national qualifications less academic and more work-related sounds 'a good thing', and will surely be applauded by line management; but the latter do not yet know that through time they may be called upon to introduce assessment of competence at the workplace, and might have to become much better at it (and much less biased when carrying it out). She wonders whether management will accept the idea of having NVQs at their own management level – that is, some sort of qualification which implies that they are competent (and, by implication, that they are NOT competent if they do not possess it). All she can be sure about is that the world of employee development is becoming ever more complex and demanding.

FOR FURTHER REFLECTION AND DISCUSSION

1 Has your attitude to education and training changed as a result of reading this chapter?

2 What do you think is required within an organisation to ensure that training can properly be said to occupy a 'mainstream place'?

3 To what extent do you think the philosophies outlined in this chapter are mutually exclusive?

4 What attitudes to education and training would you expect to exist in
 (a) a university administration office?
 (b) a fire brigade?
 (c) a trade union?
 (d) a professional football team?

SUGGESTED READING

ARGYRIS C. and SCHON D. *Organisational Learning: A Theory of Action Perspective*. Addison Wesley, New York, 1978. This is still the most thought-provoking book in this area, but it is not 'light reading'.

SCHEIN E. H. *Organisational Psychology*. Prentice Hall, New Jersey, 1970. This offers substantial material on the links between attitudes and organisational patterns – but it is less than illuminating in its brief treatment of training activities.

HANDY C. *Understanding Organisations*. Penguin, London, 1985. This contains much on concepts and their application, and has its own 'Guide to Further Study'; *The Age of Unreason* by the same author (Hutchinson, London, 1989) offers stimulating ideas on how attitudes to education and training might change in the years ahead.

Chapter 3
LEARNING AND TRAINING

What do we understand by learning? – reinforcement theories – cybernetic and information theories – cognitive theories and problem solving – experiential learning theories – learning to learn and self development – mental processes – other horizons.

INTRODUCTION

Learning theory merits a detailed study in its own right, and a comprehensive overview would be beyond the scope of this book. For this we would refer the reader to a psychology text such as one of those given in the Suggested Reading at the end of this chapter. Our aim is to whet your appetite to pursue more specialised texts by demonstrating some of the ways in which learning theory can be related to training processes and to some of the training methods and techniques which will be found in Appendix 6.

Six main groups or sets of learning theory will be outlined:

- *reinforcement theories*
- *cybernetic and information theories*
- *cognitive theories and problem solving*
- *experiential learning theories*
- *learning to learn and self development*
- *mental processes.*

The chapter concludes with two examples of the ways in which trainers are endeavouring to build upon the findings of researchers.

Think of three recent occasions when you think you learned something.

Does a consideration of what happened help you to define learning?

How did your learning take place?

Was it the same kind of learning in each case?

WHAT DO WE UNDERSTAND BY LEARNING?

It might help to consider the following examples:

1 Mary is a trainee in the sales department. Her first boss never seemed to notice when she attracted new business, and so she concentrated on looking after her 'regulars'. She now has a new boss, who makes a point of congratulating her immediately she gains a new customer, and if a large order ensues she is straightway given a bonus. Mary has now set herself a monthly target of new customers and has brought considerable business to her company.

2 A child picking wild flowers innocently grasps a nettle and stings his fingers and cries. After having made the same mistake two or three times he recognises the nettle and avoids it.

3 The experienced car driver has learned to recognise the condition of the road surface and potential hazards and monitors her speed accordingly.

4 Whilst sitting in his bath, the Greek scientist Archimedes suddenly shouted out 'Eureka!' (I have found it), when he had a flash of inspiration which enabled him to formulate his famous principle concerning the displacement of water.

These examples have at least one common factor: they all involve a change in behaviour. How did your own examples compare? Did they support the definition given by Bass and Vaughan (1966) that learning is 'a relatively permanent change in behaviour that occurs as a result of practice or experience'? We may be fully aware of what we have learned from the experience; on the other hand, until our attention is drawn to it in some way, we may be oblivious to the fact that we have modified our actions.

This definition also distinguishes two different aspects: 'practice,' which tends to be related to events which are deliberately planned, and 'experience', which may have been intentionally arranged (such as a short secondment to another organisation/department), or may have occurred spontaneously in the natural course of events. People cannot be brought together in an organisation to achieve any kind of common purpose without this 'spontaneous' learning taking place. As a result they will change their behaviour in various ways. At the simplest level, they learn each others' names, technical terms and the location of equipment; and at a more sophisticated level, they learn about the behaviour of their colleagues, supervisors and management and thus develop attitudes which can have complex effects on their behaviour. This in turn will confirm or alter the manager's attitude towards the subordinate. The process is interactive, both learning about each other and modifying their behaviour accordingly. People learn by imitating others (modelling), by perceiving and interpreting what happens in the organisation and by the cumulative experience of trial and error. In this sense, therefore, as King (1964) stressed, learning is an inevitable organisational activity. Later in this chapter, we shall show that many of the learning opportunities presented by the organisation pass by untapped because they are unrecognised, and we shall suggest that the ability to identify them is the 'take off runway' for the process of 'learning to learn'.

This book derives its title from the fact that in managing employee development, we are continually attempting to decide whether some kind of deliberate training intervention is required into the natural learning process. If we decide that this is the case, the next question is what specific form the intervention might take. Prior to examining the range of possibilities (see Chapters 5, 8 and 10, and Appendix 6) we first consider some of the ways in which the intervention might reflect the assumptions made by the trainer about how people learn. These assumptions may be well informed, on the basis of careful study and deliberation, or they may be implicit, the trainer or learner relying solely on intuition, or purely anecdotal sources. Anyone responsible for training should have a working knowledge of the processes which are involved before committing an organisation to considerable expenditure.

This brings us to the second and third of our questions above, as to how to define learning and how it takes place. Even the few examples we quoted demonstrate that there is a variety of different kinds of learning. The range of human abilities is extremely wide, from psychomotor skills, such as operating a keyboard or styling a client's hair, to the negotiating skills of an industrial relations expert, the symbolic skills of a computer programmer, or the decision making skills of a financier. The training officer searching for one set of simple rules which adequately encompasses such varied activity is going to be disappointed. Researchers have concentrated on different aspects of this complex process and have been able to demonstrate certain principles, but no one theory is in itself complete and none can claim to cover all eventualities. We have selected four main types of theory for discussion.

REINFORCEMENT THEORIES

On a television programme a volunteer was told to watch the numbers moving round on a counter on the wall. He was promised £20 every time the counter moved to a new number. He was not told what caused the counter to move, but it actually did so every time he blinked his eyes. The camera showed a rapidly increasing rate of blinking as the counter moved around. After a few minutes he was asked if he could state what caused the counter to turn, or if he could suggest how his behaviour had changed since the beginning of the programme. He replied that he did not know.

A very basic concept in learning is that of 'conditioning' or 'shaping' behaviour, the main exponent being Skinner (1965), who tested his theory by carrying out numerous experiments, the most famous of which concerned pigeons. By means of rewarding his experimental subjects with corn every time they made an appropriate movement, he was able to teach them many things even including how to play 'ping pong' with each other. Although behaviour in animal experiments cannot be considered an infallible and accurate reflection of complicated and sophisticated human conduct, it has been claimed that conditioning is an essential ingredient in many types of learning. In fact, the first of our examples about Mary and her new customers may be seen to incorporate this type of learning. Praise or reinforcement from her new boss engenders confidence, which acts as a strong motivator for her to continue and extend the desired behaviour.

Another instance is provided by techniques of programmed learning and its current, more sophisticated development into computer-assisted learning. The assumption is that receiving a 'reward' (which for humans is not corn, but might be being told that they have answered correctly, or 'done well') gives positive reinforcement to that response, and so motivates them to continue and extend their learning.

Conditioning applied to social systems

Skinner (1976) extended the application of his theory from experimenter and subject (trainer and trainee) to the whole area of the structure of social systems. In his novel, *Walden Two*, he developed the concept of an entire society based on the use of positive reinforcement. He conceived systems which were designed to reward behaviour functional to the society. In other words, the citizens were not controlled by law but by the way in which the environment was designed. Other writers, e.g. Nord (1969), have attempted to apply Skinner's ideas to management through positive reinforcement, embracing items such as job design, compensation and rewards, organisational design and change. For instance, Nord suggests that annual merit interviews and salary increments are very inefficient development techniques, as the rewards are so delayed that they have little feedback value.

This brings us back once more to the title of this book. Training is an intervention into an on-going learning process; the culture, philosophy, policies and procedures of the organisation form a very powerful learning environment, which must be taken into consideration. We shall discuss the influence of organisation culture on approaches to training later in this book (see Chapters 5, 7 and 10). On a note of caution, however, Skinnerian theory goes only a limited way towards assisting understanding of the process by which human beings acquire a whole range of knowledge and skills. His concept of 'social engineering' by the provision of positive reinforcement is now regarded as too simplistic, but it constitutes an important reminder of the need to consider the organisation's culture and to provide feedback or knowledge of results, without which planned learning is unlikely to be effective.

Punishment

Now consider example 2 of the child and the nettle. In this case a particular action was *suppressed*, not promoted. Some researchers, e.g. Estes (1970) have investigated the effect of punishment in suppressing an inappropriate response. His experiments (which mainly involved giving mild electric shocks to rats) demonstrated the principle that punishment may temporarily suppress a response, but will not *extinguish* it. After having been 'punished' for pressing a bar, the rats made fewer trials, but later after the punishment was withdrawn, they resumed their original behaviour patterns.

Whilst positive feedback can bring about a relatively permanent learning outcome, negative feedback or harsh criticism may be effective only as long as some threat appears imminent. What then are the implications for safety training, where it might be said that the trainee is being taught to avoid possible punishment (in the form of accident or injury)? The nettle stung the child every time it was touched and would always do so even if further trial attempts were made. Accidents have been described as chains of events when a number of different conditions all coincide at one fatal moment. Because these events do not normally all happen together, the threat does not continuously appear imminent; it may be possible to ignore certain safety features for a considerable time without necessarily meeting with an accident, and therefore on occasions malpractices go 'unpunished'. If safety equipment is irksome to wear, and a worker has managed to do without it and no accident has occurred, the habit of neglect will be reinforced as thoughts of danger recede. An illustration is provided by car seat belts, which, until legislation was introduced, large sections of the population refused to wear for the sake of their own safety (largely because the habit of ignoring them had been reinforced – it was easier and no accident had 'happened to them'). It was not until the threat of prosecution became constantly imminent that the correct usage began to approach 100 per cent!

This is one of the major reasons why safety training is often ineffective, and you might like to think of ways in which the imminence or possibility of danger can be *constantly* emphasised. For instance, in some countries there is a practice of leaving a wrecked car at the side of a road which features particularly dangerous hairpin bends. We will return to the question of making safety training more efficient later in the chapter.

Learned helplessness

During a severe recession an enthusiastic worker loses his job and applies for over one hundred jobs in a year without any success. He finally abandons the attempt and sinks into depression. Six months later, the economy recovers, but he is too depressed, and so convinced that he cannot get a job, that he does not even try and remains permanently unemployed.

A development of reinforcement theory which has significance for those concerned with trainees who are suffering from depression, perhaps as a result of a long spell of unemployment, is that of Seligman (1975). He concluded from his experiments that just as subjects can learn to carry out certain behaviours for some kind of reward, they can also learn that certain situations are 'uncontrollable', i.e. that no behaviour they can display will produce any satisfactory result. Just as we learn by positive reinforcement, when we are exposed to uncontrollable events, we can learn that responding is futile. This learning undermines motivation to respond and persists even when events actually become controllable.

Seligman argues that when we are faced with trauma, fear is reduced if we learn that we can take some action to control it, but that if we learn that the trauma is uncontrollable, fear gives way to depression.

He relates his findings to chronic depression, and to the situation of the long-term unemployed and racial minorities. The theory may have a message for trainers of people who are disadvantaged or handicapped in some way or are long term unemployed. They may not display much motivation to learn and initially may not perform effectively. If, in addition, they are constantly being told that their work is poor, the conditions will be reinforced. A very considerable 'unlearning' process has to take place before they will make any attempt to behave in a positive manner.

CYBERNETIC AND INFORMATION THEORIES

A trainee sewing machinist finds that he is unable to concentrate on controlling the foot treadle and at the same time guide the material correctly through the machine. After special exercises in machine control and demonstrations and supervised practice in handling the material, he gradually becomes proficient and is able to increase the speed and quality of his performance.

These theories concentrate on how information is received and monitored. Stammers and Patrick (1975) and Duncan and Kelly (1983) liken the way in which feedback can control human performance to the manner in which a thermostat controls a heating system. The temperature is monitored and regulated because information fed back from the thermostat determines the level of power input to the system. See Figure 3.1 which is based on Stammers and Patrick's model.

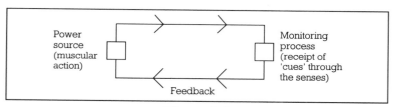

Figure 3.1
The monitoring and regulating process

This monitoring is a constant process in all activities. For example, someone who is profoundly deaf may develop an unusual speaking voice because he cannot hear it and must monitor it in some other way, possibly by the feel of muscles in the mouth and throat. The motorist in our example 3 was receiving 'stimuli' from the environment, by which she monitored and regulated her performance, or in other words, her input to the system. She received these stimuli through the senses – touch, sight, hearing, kinaesthesis (the sense of muscular effort or the 'feel' that one's limbs are in the correct position) and balance. For instance, the machinist above might interpret the sound of the machine, the pressure required by his foot to operate at the correct speed and the appearance of the work in the machine. Similarly, a cook or a wine taster might be relying on her sense of smell to monitor performance.

In a training situation, the most usual form of feedback is provided by comments from an instructor, but sometimes it can be given by simulators, which act as artificial 'thermostats' and help the trainee monitor his performance.

An important part of skills analysis (see Chapter 9) is to determine by which 'cues' or 'stimuli' an experienced worker is being guided and by which of the senses they are being received. Probably the best known example is to be found in the job of a typist. Observation of a skilled performer reveals heavy reliance on kinaesthesis, or the 'feel' and positioning of the fingers on the keyboard. Left to his own devices, it is likely that a beginner would rely upon sight, looking intensely at the keyboard and using what has been described as the 'hunt and peck' method. Anyone who has taught himself to type in this way finds it difficult to learn to touch type because he has to unlearn all his bad habits. A skills analysis, which includes not only a record of exactly what is done but also the details of exactly what 'cues' or stimuli are being used to monitor performance and trigger action, can provide the basis for an efficient training programme for many psychomotor jobs. The training time can be shortened by providing practice in recognising and reacting to the stimuli used by those with experience, rather than allowing the learner to work unsupervised and thereby reinforcing less efficient habits, such as the 'hunt and peck' method.

Since recognising stimuli is central to learning, a training officer should understand the process of perception. For instance, training for inspection tasks is largely a matter of organising the perception to highlight certain stimuli or details and ignore others. (For more detailed study, see Thomas (1962) and Wright and Taylor (1970)). During the learning process the 'selectivity' of stimuli becomes increasingly automatic, and the experienced worker ceases to think consciously about it (in other words 'sheds the perceptual load'). Think of a learner car driver, who initially has to concentrate hard on braking, accelerating and changing gear; after sufficient practice these operations become second nature and are carried out almost without thought. Similarly, when learning to ski, the beginner has to concentrate hard on cues which assist his balance, the correct position of the body in relation to the skis, how to traverse, how to turn or stop. After a number of painful experiences, he may look wistfully at the experienced performer, who seems to carry out all these operations naturally and apparently without thought, although possibly observing other matters such as the texture of the snow, or the position of other skiers on the piste. In other words, certain of the experienced skier's actions have been 'pre-programmed'.

Seymour (1968) advocates training programmes where the tasks are subdivided into small parts so that the learner can concentrate on one item at a time (part analysis). Each part then becomes programmed more quickly, the training period is shortened and fewer errors are made. For instance, the beginner can attend dry ski school and, wearing shorter skis which are easier to manage, can learn such skills as correct body position or how to carry out a 'kick turn'. On reaching the ski slopes, some pre-programming will already have taken place, a little of the perceptual load can be 'shed', and some of the discomfort taken out of learning. (See also Plateaux of Learning, page 95). The principle has often been similarly applied in craft apprentice and operative training programmes, especially those based in special training workshops.

You should now be in a better position to answer the question posed earlier in this chapter:

How can safety training be made more efficient?

Far more effective than the threat of punishment to persuade people to avoid accidents is the positive aspect of ensuring that from the beginning the trainee will always perform in a safe manner (compare the example of the use of car seat belts above). Cultivation of safe working methods and habits must therefore be the prime concern, and will help to ensure that even when the perceptual load is 'shed', the *safe* way has become automatic.

Kay (1983) gives a useful explanation of accidents as enforced changes from programmed to unprogrammed activity. For example, someone walking along a pavement is carrying out an activity which has been programmed since childhood; she therefore does not need to think consciously about it. If, however, her foot slips on a banana skin, the programmed activity will not suffice and she has to concentrate rapidly on new style evasive action. Injury may result if she cannot think out and effect this action in time. Someone trained in the art of falling could probably manage this because her mind is pre-programmed to do so, but the rest of us would most likely fail!

An important part of safety training, therefore, is to pre-programme trainees for possible hazardous situations (e.g. training vehicle drivers on a skid pan) so that they can more rapidly recognise and interpret the stimuli they receive in the monitoring process (e.g. the first feel of the vehicle's wheels sliding); because an appropriate response pattern has been pre-programmed, the trainees have a much improved chance of avoiding an accident. This theory has a further implication for safety: because learners have to concentrate on many items at once and cannot shed the perceptual load, they have less ability to anticipate potential hazards, and are thus more prone to accidents. Trainers need to pay special attention to this fact, particularly when dealing with young employees and students and school children on work experience, where not only is the trainee attempting to cope with cues and signals from the job itself but also has to become acclimatised to a whole new work environment, as opposed to the familiar background of school or college.

COGNITIVE THEORIES AND PROBLEM SOLVING

Craft trainees are confronted with a model of a live electrical wiring system. By operating levers and watching the results, they can work out the principles of electricity for themselves and apply them to their work.

In direct contrast to reinforcement theories, which are concerned with the establishment of particular behaviour patterns, cognitive theories draw attention to behaviour which we might ordinarily describe as 'insight'. They reflect the way in which we learn to recognise and define problems or experiment to find solutions, whether by trial and error, by deductive reasoning, by seeking information and help, or by a combination of all three. We see the situation as a whole and begin to organise it. Eventually we conceptualise or 'internalise' the solution and methodology, so that we are able to extend their use and adapt them to future situations. Sometimes the solution comes by sudden insight, as in the case of Archimedes in example 4 above.

These theories are not new. In 1925, Kohler was experimenting with an ape which was required to solve the problem of retrieving a banana placed beyond its reach outside the cage. It first tried to grasp it by frantically stretching its arms through the bars but gave up after several unsuccessful attempts. After retreating to the back of the cage for some time, the ape returned to the bars, reached for a stick which was lying outside, and managed to poke the banana and pull it nearer the cage. The experiment was then repeated but this time the banana was further away and the ape had to use a short stick to pull in a longer stick before being able to reach the desired food (see Kohler 1973). This experiment demonstrates the close relationship between cognitive theories and the training technique called discovery learning. In this technique the trainee is given tasks which require him to search for and select stimuli or 'clues' on how to proceed. The aim is to provide a means of unassisted learning and appropriate experience to develop insights into key relationships. The success of this method obviously depends upon the effectiveness of the task design.

The craft trainees in our example learn with the aid of a practical working model, but the technique is very versatile. For instance, depending upon the method of presentation, a case study, a project or assigned task can provide discovery learning. This training technique has the advantage of assisting transfer of learning to the job, because, as the learner has found an answer for himself, it becomes internalised. However, this method requires careful structuring of the situation to the learner's needs, as long periods spent in vain pursuit of a solution which is well beyond his current capability, can prove an extremely frustrating and demotivating experience. In these circumstances, anger and irritation are likely to be turned upon the trainer. As we have seen from reinforcement theory, however, finding the solution acts as a well-earned reward to reinforce the learning. Obviously it is usually quicker to tell the learner than to let him find out for himself, and therefore discovery learning sessions tend to be time consuming, although by providing better learning transfer they are likely to be more effective in the long term.

EXPERIENTIAL LEARNING

A personnel manager conducts a disciplinary interview, and when writing up the results for her records discovers that she does not really know enough about the offender's side of the story. Upon reflection, she realises that she did not give him the opportunity to explain, most of her questions having required a 'yes' or 'no' answer. She then decides that in principle when she needs to obtain information in an interview, she will ask at least some questions which are open ended to encourage the interviewee to talk. She tries out this idea at the next interview and discovers that it works; she therefore resolves to do this on all future occasions.

We can see that there are really four stages here: the experience; observation and reflection; theorising and conceptualisation; testing and experimentation. To be effective, the learner correspondingly needs four different but complementary kinds of abilities. This is how Kolb (1974) conceived the learning process which he illustrated in the model in Figure 3.2 below.

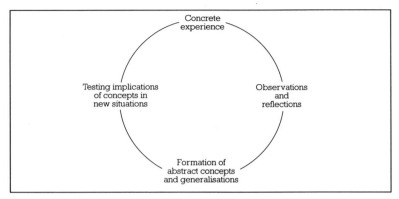

Figure 3.2
The Kolb learning cycle

Source: David A. Kolb, 'On Management and the Learning Process', in *Organizational Psychology: A book of readings*, ed. Kolb, Rubin and McIntyre, 2nd edition, 1974, page 28. Reprinted by permission of Prentice Hall, Englewood Cliffs,.New Jersey.

Kolb suggests that this ideal is difficult to achieve and argues that in fact the required abilities might even be in conflict. He claims that:

'as a result of our hereditary equipment, our particular life experience, and the demands of our present environment, most people develop learning styles that emphasise some learning abilities over others'.

In other words, most people are better at, and prefer, some of the four stages rather than others. For instance a mathematician might give preference to abstract conceptualisation and active experimentation, whilst a manager may have greater concern for concrete experience and the active application of ideas.

Building on Kolb's theoretical base, Honey and Mumford (1992 and 1986) defined four major categories of learning styles: activist; reflector; theorist; pragmatist. These correspond with the four stages in the Kolb Cycle, viz. concrete experience; observations and reflections; formation of abstract concepts and generalisations; testing implications of concepts in new situations. Honey and Mumford have kindly given us permission to reproduce in full their descriptions of people strong in each of their four styles:

Activists

Involve themselves fully and without bias in new experiences. They enjoy the here and now and are happy to be dominated by immediate experiences. They are open-minded, not sceptical, and this tends to make them enthusiastic about anything new. Their philosophy is 'I'll try anything once'. They tend to act first and consider the consequences afterwards. Their days are filled with activity. They tackle problems by brainstorming. As soon as the excitement from one activity has died down they are busy looking for the next. They tend to thrive on the challenge of new experiences but are bored with implementation and longer term consolidation. They are gregarious people constantly involving themselves with others but, in doing so, they seek to centre all activities around themselves.

Reflectors

Like to stand back to ponder experiences and observe them from many different perspectives. They collect data, both first hand and from others, and prefer to think about it thoroughly before coming to any conclusion. The thorough collection and analysis of data about experiences and events is what counts so they tend to postpone reaching definitive conclusions for as long as possible. Their philosophy is to be cautious. They are thoughtful people who like to consider all possible angles and implications before making a move. They prefer to take a back seat in meetings and discussions. They enjoy observing other people in action. They listen to others and get the drift of the discussion before making their own points. They tend to adopt a low profile and have a slightly distant, tolerant unruffled air about them. When they act it is part of a wider picture which includes the past as well as the present and others' observations as well as their own.

Theorists

Adapt and integrate observations into complex, but logically sound theories. They think problems through in a vertical, step by step logical way. They assimilate disparate facts into coherent theories. They tend to be perfectionists who won't rest easy until things are tidy and fit into a rational scheme. They like to analyse and synthesise. They are keen on basic assumptions, principles, theories, models and systems thinking. Their philosophy prizes rationality and logic. 'If it's logical it's good.' Questions they frequently ask are: 'Does it make sense?' 'How does this fit in with that?' 'What are the basic assumptions?' They tend to be detached, analytical and dedicated to rational objectivity rather than anything subjective or ambiguous. Their approach to problems is consistently logical. This is their 'mental set' and they rigidly reject anything that doesn't fit with it. They prefer to maximise certainty and feel uncomfortable with subjective judgements, lateral thinking and anything flippant.

Pragmatists
Are keen on trying out ideas, theories and techniques to see if they work in practice. They positively search out new ideas and take the first opportunity to experiment with applications. They are the sort of people who return from management courses brimming with new ideas that they want to try out in practice. They like to get on with things and act quickly and confidently on ideas that attract them. They tend to be impatient with ruminating and open-ended discussions. They are essentially practical, down to earth people who like making practical decisions and solving problems. They respond to problems and opportunities 'as a challenge'. Their philosophy is: 'There is always a better way' and 'If it *works* it's good.'

The concept of learning styles is an important development because it helps to throw light on how people learn from experience. It indicates firstly that a variety of training methods might be planned in sequence. In the example of the interview situation above, immediate experience requires a practical interview session (either 'for real' as part of the learner's daily work, or as a simulated exercise in a classroom situation) whilst observing and reflecting might take place by individual thought, or by discussion with a coach or mentor, or observer and tutor in the case of the classroom exercise. Generalising and theorising might involve the learner in comparing her findings with relevant literature and formulating and re-examining her own principles and guidelines on, for example, the use of specific techniques and strategies. The next stage would be testing out these perceptions in a new situation and so back to experience. This example demonstrates the need for all four stages. However, when planning specific learning programmes or selecting participants for external courses, it is wise to allow for the fact that some people learn better by one style than another and some may reject certain styles altogether; hence programmes will ideally be planned with a knowledge of learners' own preferences, and diagnostic activity will be built into the early stages of (flexible) plans.

It is also important for the trainer to realise that she has a natural learning/teaching style, and that in choosing appropriate techniques she should consider the trainees' preferred or desired learning style as well as her own, insofar as it is practical to do so.

A rich menu is on offer to those who can take advantage of all four learning styles. For instance, consider in how many ways we can learn a sport such as tennis or golf. Your list is likely to include methods such as practising, experimenting, coaching, reading, watching others, watching oneself on video cassette, talking to other people, thinking about one's game, and of course, playing. Each of these methods involves one, or more, of the four learning styles, and taken collectively, they encompass the whole of the experiential learning cycle. The successful professional will ideally take advantage of them all.

Similarly, many learning opportunities are available to managers. Mumford (1989) points out that learning opportunities do not have to be manufactured; they already exist in the real environment. Many of them pass unnoticed and unused, and managers need help in learning to recognise and take advantage of them. Figure 3.3 lists examples of situations which may provide these opportunities within organisations and

---

Situations within the organisation

Meetings	Modelling
Task – familiar	Problem solving
– unfamiliar	Observing
Task force	Questioning
Customer visit	Reading
Visit to plant/office	Negotiating
Managing a change	Mentoring
Social occasions	Public speaking
Foreign travel	Reviewing/auditing
Acquisitions/mergers	Clarifying responsibilities
Closing something down	Walking the floor
	Visioning
Situations outside your organisation	Strategic planning
	Problem diagnosis
Charity	Decision making
Domestic life	Selling
Industry committee	
Professional meetings	**People**
Sports club	
	Boss
Processes	Mentor
	Network contacts
Coaching	Peers
Counselling	Consultants
Listening	Subordinates

The opportunities identified here are not necessarily separate. You may, for example, think of something first in terms of something happening at a meeting – or you may think of the way in which one of your colleagues achieved success at a meeting.

Figure 3.3
Learning Opportunities

Source: *Management Development: Strategies for Action* (IPM, 1989). Reproduced by kind permission of Alan Mumford.

in private life. The right hand column lists the *processes* by which managers can learn, and again it will be seen that taken together they embrace all four learning styles. Managers who rely on only one learning style are restricting themselves unnecessarily to just one course on the menu.

Considerable developmental work on learning styles has already taken place and there is now a wide range of literature. For example, Richardson and Bennett (1984) have examined the structural and cultural barriers to behaviour at each of the stages in the experiential learning cycle. They suggest that one can think of the organisation itself as having a preferred learning style, which influences those within it. You might compare this concept with the discussion of the different approaches to training in Chapter 5. Although further research and validation of this work is still necessary, it is important for the trainer to realise that her own natural training style may be at variance with the culture of her organisation and with that of the learners.

Furthermore, a traditional difficulty of group training activities is the effect of the composition or 'chemistry' of the group and the influence it can have upon individual learning. Although the concept of learning styles does not produce instant answers to this problem, it nevertheless contributes an explanation, and may help to promote useful discussion and understanding within the group. During the course of their research, Honey and Mumford (1986 and 1992) developed a Learning Styles Questionnaire based on self description and established norms for different types of manager such as those engaged in research and development, production or finance. Such a questionnaire is a useful measuring instrument for the trainer and could ultimately yield data relating to the influence of different learning styles on group activity, thereby constituting a valuable guide in, for instance, determining an optimum composition of learning groups. For the individual it provides a tool for self diagnosis as a guide to building on strengths (best learning styles) and overcoming weaknesses (least favoured learning styles), leading to the use of a richer variety of methods. Honey and Mumford (1986) give advice on making the best use of your learning strengths and how to improve and practise each of the four styles.

LEARNING TO LEARN AND SELF DEVELOPMENT

In 1979, we wrote: 'Our cyclical economy and the speed of technical change suggest that "learning to learn" is the central training problem of our time' (Kenney, Donnelly and Reid 1979), and we suggested the need for further research in this area. Attention has been gradually focused away from mechanistic formulation of objectives and the conditions which surround learning, to the activities of the learner, and the means of equipping him with strategies and a range of styles which are appropriate not only for present learning but which will transfer to future situations and enable learning from experience to take place. The emphasis has moved from activities largely controlled by the trainer, to the learning process, and where possible to self-directed and self-managed learning using opportunities provided by new technology such as computer-assisted programmes.

In 1981, a report, 'How do I Learn?', was produced for the Further Education Unit (FEU), by a team from the then Industrial Training Research Unit (ITRU); the team had been asked to look into what the FEU called 'doing' learning (as opposed to 'memory' and 'understanding' learning). The team made two important points:

- learning is something one does for oneself
- the most effective ways of learning involve conscious mental activities such as checking, self testing and questioning.

These points emphasise the fact that whatever the activities of a trainer, it is the learner who is really in the driving seat.

Much training theory assumes that learning objectives represent a static work state, in which case, competence depends largely upon memory and the acquisition of basic skills which will last a lifetime. Knowing 'what' and 'how' and 'when' is a matter of remembering what the manual (or text book) says; and/or what worked last time. However, memory proves unrewarding if the content, or indeed the context, of work is constantly changing. For example, if manual book-keeping changes to computerised bookkeeping, the individual's memory of mental arithmetic will not suffice: the computer now performs this task. Confidence in the relevance of one's knowledge base diminishes and must be replaced by some new knowledge (e.g. how to make the computer perform calculations), plus keyboard skills. The whole process is illustrated in Figure 3.4.

It will be seen that there are both positive and negative factors affecting attitudes: initial confidence and sense of achievement in attaining competence, which in terms of reinforcement theory act as a motivator to further learning, followed by apprehension and fear of

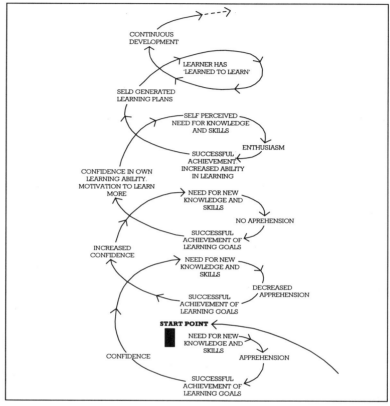

Figure 3.4
The Continuous Development Spiral

change which would demotivate. In ideal circumstances, the desire to learn might be regarded as self generating, the sense of achievement from successful learning giving rise to confidence in one's ability *as a learner* and reinforcing the desire for further learning. The learner remains competent and 'learns to learn', eventually creating new 'improved performance' objectives and managing the learning process required to realise those objectives. This is the essence of self development.

Furthermore, learning is like opening a door in a corridor which gives a view into a room beyond; the room has other doors which had not previously been in view; on opening these doors further doors appear. Curiosity is a strong motivator (see page 93) and the natural learning process is really a continuous progression of self testing and questioning. There are, however, a number of barriers to learning, for example fear of failure, inability or unwillingness to expend the time and effort. In a rapidly changing environment it is not sufficient to acquire the standard knowledge and skills, the process has to be constant; the successful organisation will be one where attention is paid to minimising the demotivating factors by creating a supportive climate and by developing employees' confidence in their ability to tackle and overcome barriers to learning; in other words a 'learning organisation' which fosters and encourages the natural self-generating learning process. This is a critical aim. Learners who have grown to believe that they are competent *as learners* take the lead in managing change and develop themselves in the process. Writers such as Hayes, Anderson and Fonda (1984) have stressed that interest in continuous development is one of the main features which distinguishes workforces in countries such as Japan and the USA from those in the UK, where the training emphasis tends to be placed more upon short term considerations. The concept of continuous development is discussed more fully in Chapter 12.

MENTAL PROCESSES

We start with a consideration of memory, and the dual memory theory which has important implications for trainers. It is possible, however, that exciting discoveries about learning may lie in extending our knowledge of cerebral processes and a fruitful avenue of exploration has been the study of the effect of brain damage on cerebral functions. In more recent times, new technology, particularly the use of sophisticated scanners, has facilitated more comprehensive investigations into the functioning of various areas of the brain. We give an outline of the activities of the right and left hemispheres of the brain, followed by examples of the ways in which educationalists and trainers claim to have built upon research findings.

Memory
Think of the last time you looked up a telephone number in the directory. Unless you wrote it down you may well have forgotten the number whilst you looked up the code. If the number was engaged and your

telephone did not have a memory facility, you would probably have had to look it up again to redial. If you want to remember a friend's number, you have to keep repeating it. This is explained by the *dual memory theory* which distinguishes between short-term and long-term memory and postulates that rehearsal is necessary, if we wish to transfer material from short-term to long-term memory. The average number of discrete items that the human mind can comfortably take in at one time is seven. We can remember much more if we combine small items into larger 'bits'. For instance, it is only possible to remember about seven random letters of the alphabet, but if we combine them into meaningful words or sentences we can remember many more. The implication for the trainer is that meaning assists memory. It is very difficult and time-consuming to remember something we do not understand.

The two factors of long-term and short-term memory have serious implications for the lecturing technique. Any matters which listeners cannot recall shortly after a lecture are unlikely to have entered long-term memory and will therefore not be retained. Two other phenomena are worth noting: *sharpening* and *levelling*. When material is recalled later, certain items are remembered for their peculiarity or particular interest (although they may not necessarily be the most important items of content). The jokes or amusing stories in a lecture or training film may be remembered long after the serious content has been forgotten. Other items are glossed over and a 'levelling' process takes place. The material is remembered in very general terms, the only detail being that which has become 'sharpened'. From a trainer's point of view it is crucial to make sure that it is the important items which are 'sharpened' in the listeners' minds. One way of assisting this to happen is to plan the presentation logically – making sure that every point is clear and likely to be understood and to summarise succinctly at the end. Other methods of assisting memory are mental imagery (see the example of learning electrical coding in Chapter 10), appealing to more than one sense (for example, using an overhead projector involves sight as well as hearing and helps to 'sharpen' the main points), and finally, overlearning (see page 102). A good account of the process of memory can be found in Atkinson and Atkinson (1985).

The right and left hemispheres of the brain

Researchers have found that the two hemispheres of the brain have very different ways of processing information. The connecting network which sends messages from one side of the brain to the other is called the 'corpus collosum'. When this is unimpaired the two hemispheres are effectively integrated, but studies of patients in whom the 'corpus collosum' has been severed, have shown that the two hemispheres function separately without communication with each other. For instance, such patients are unable to match an object held unseen in the right hand with one they cannot see held in the left hand. By studying these patients, researchers have been able to demonstrate that each side of the brain appears to have its own specialisations. Experimental work indicates that the left hemisphere is analytical; logical; associated with spoken language skills, number and scientific skills and reasoning, whilst the right hemisphere is related to art; three dimensional forms; music awareness; imagination; creativity; insight and holistic perception. The right side also has a visual learning capability. There are still many questions to be answered concerning these complementary abilities and the way in which the two hemispheres are co-ordinated. It must be emphasised that neither has a complete monopoly of its particular cognitive style, the specialisms of the two hemispheres now being regarded as a matter of degree rather than as an absolute. Studies have shown that individuals vary greatly in the ways in which the hemispheres are habitually activated, and such factors as sex, age, handedness, education and special training appear to have an effect. For a brief but informative account, see Gregory (1987).

New technology has enabled more extensive and accurate research in scanning the brain and measuring its electrical activity whilst the subject is exposed to different kinds of stimuli, such as a conversation, a piece of music or synchronised words and music. Researchers claim that by this means they have obtained scans which show the particular areas of the brain which are activated by these different stimuli (see Rose, 1991).

Johnson and Indvik (1991) consider the implications of these findings in relation to the job of a manager, and suggest that the integration and synthesis of both the analytical left- *and* the intuitive right-brain activity are critical. For instance, too heavy reliance on the analytical left can result in loss of intuitive powers on the right side of the brain. They indicate that left-brain oriented managers pursue rational and logical reasoning and work in a highly structured way, but may quosh imaginative ideas generated by more intuitive right-brain oriented colleagues. It is suggested that where policy issues are complex, right hemisphere and integrative skills are needed more than purely left hemisphere skills, because the complete data on which to base a totally calculated and logical decision is not always available. In addition, advances in computer technology will diminish the need for managers possessing left hemisphere analytical skills, whilst the demand for those with creativity, imagination and the ability to take a holistic perspective will increase.

What, then, are the implications for employee development? First, it would seem important that employees are aware of the functioning of the two hemispheres, and of their own particular dominant skills, as well as of the effect they might have on colleagues and subordinates. Johnson and Indvik suggest that this knowledge might be used in career management, to ensure that people are placed in jobs appropriate to their particular mental strengths. Secondly, they indicate that the advantage possessed by 'great minds', lies in the inclination to use both hemispheres effectively and they suggest exercises to enhance brain interaction.

Thirdly, from a training perspective, it would seem sensible to attempt to involve both hemispheres in any structured learning activities. For instance, learning which relies upon logical interpretation appeals to the left hemisphere, and can be effectively reinforced by the use of visual aids, imagery, or sensory stimuli which relate to the right side of the brain.

From work with patients who have suffered brain damage, researchers have discovered that certain mental functions appear to be associated with particular areas of the brain. These discoveries have led to theories that types of mental processes may be discrete activities, and to the hypothesis that ability (whether learned or innate) in one activity does not necessarily transfer to another activity. These theories obviously have important implications for learning transfer.

The Theory of Multiple Intelligences

Gardner (1987), suggests that intellect is modular and postulates seven different intelligences, namely: linguistic intelligence; logical mathematical intelligence; musical intelligence; spatial intelligence; bodily kinaesthetic intelligence; interpersonal intelligence; intrapersonal intelligence. (He defines the latter as 'an effective working model of oneself and the ability to use that model effectively in the light of desires, needs, wishes, fears and skills'.) Whilst traditional psychology propounds 'horizontal' theories of learning, which cut across all kinds of content, Gardner proposes 'vertical' theories, i.e. that principles of learning, perception, memory etc. can vary according to the seven different types of intelligence. He hypothesises that each type has its own set of learning principles. In other words, 'the mind is organised in terms of content', and it makes a difference whether we are dealing with language, music, space, other people, or ourselves. Quoting the example of memory, he suggests that the way in which someone remembers a dance step taught some months ago is different from the way in which the same person remembers a group of people who came to a dinner party the previous year.

He claims that each intelligence has its own 'developmental trajectory' and suggests that 'capacities like logical thinking develop in a very different way from capacities such as personal intelligence'. Moreover, development and training in one intelligence is unlikely to affect another: 'Our minds and our brains are composed of different modules, and it is difficult to get transfer from one module to another.'

You might like to think about the implications of Gardner's propositions for some of the traditional theories outlined earlier in this chapter. To what kind of 'intelligence' do you think traditional theories might apply? In a number of chapters of this book you will read about transferable core skills, and national standards of competence; you might like to consider what Gardner's theories might be telling us in relation to these concepts.

OTHER HORIZONS

Trainers and educationalists have endeavoured to devise techniques based on the interpretation and application of research findings such as those described above. Within the context of this book, it is not possible to describe any of these in detail, but we conclude the chapter with a brief outline of two examples.

Accelerated Learning

The exponents of Accelerated Learning have devised methods for which they claim spectacular results. These are described in detail by Rose (1991), who suggests that the average human uses only four per cent of his or her potential brain power, maintaining that we have a cultural legacy of self-imposed limitation, produced in part by the way in which we are taught to learn at school. Rose claims that most schools relegate right brain activities to two or three hours a week, the main emphasis being on the left brain functions required by verbal and deductive subject matter. Furthermore, as a society we tend to value logical and analytical thinking more highly than artistic or intuitive ability, and in the main we do not reward independence of thought or creativity. Thus we starve the right hemisphere of development and *systematically damage* the brain. Accelerated Learning methods stimulate the whole brain, not just one hemisphere, and emphasise the role played by emotional content in learning because it effects a higher state of arousal, thereby making the learning more likely to be retained. If the whole brain is to be used there is a need for imagery as well as logical thought, and (as we exemplify in Chapter 10) visual association assists memory.

A novel feature of Accelerated Learning is the use of music as part of the learning event, as it is claimed to stimulate right brain functioning. In particular, it is suggested that the Baroque composers produced exactly the right frequency and sound to harmonise with the rhythm of the brain, thereby inducing a state of relaxed alertness and calm conducive to learning.

It is also maintained that in every learning activity there is a focused and central component, but also an area of peripheral activity, in which the brain subconsciously processes more than the learner realises (peripheral, subconscious and paraconscious often being used interchangeably). Peripheral learning contributes strongly to what is retained, and therefore Accelerated Learning builds in techniques which appeal to the subconscious. These include visual presentations which take into account peripheral vision; the use of posters and cards arranged around the room; materials directed to visual, auditory and, where possible, kinaesthetic channels; games and role playing which distract the attention and allow information to be subconsciously assimilated.

It is not possible here to give more than this brief summary of the underlying concept of Accelerated Learning, but a much fuller account will be found in Rose (1991).

Neuro Linguistic Programming (NLP)

NLP was developed from research in the USA in the early 1970s, by John Grinder, a professor of linguistics, and John Bandler, a mathematician. They selected three communicators (all of whom were therapists renowned for their excellence) and studied them at work with their clients. The purpose of the research was to identify the precise behaviours which contributed to this excellence, and to produce a framework or model of excellence in one-to-one communication, which could be used by others. By combining the skills of linguistic analysis and mathematical notation, they were able to organise their data into a set of hypothetical 'rules' which could be used by other therapists, who thereby improved their performance (see Bandler and Grinder 1976).

Since this original work, practitioners have applied the use of NLP to education, training and development. Whilst the original work related to self management and one-to-one communication, later work by Dilts and Grinder extended the scope to leadership and management of groups and organisations. The exponents of NLP draw attention to the fact that each person's concept of reality is actually his or her subjective interpretation, as the mind is a filtering mechanism. The interpretations made by each individual are influenced by their experiences and attitudes relating to other people and the world around. From birth onwards, individuals learn to programme their reactions and develop strategies, which are then likely to become automatic or unconscious; these strategies are of two kinds, those involving language, and those relating to body movements and physical reactions. From their studies of the strategies used by 'excellent performers', the researchers developed a framework which can be used to help an individual identify his or her own strategies and those of others. Having been made consciously aware of his or her own strategies, the individual can begin to have choice and control, by adjusting what would previously have been 'automatic' responses and behaviour.

NLP embraces many different techniques and approaches, which cannot all be described here. Some of them relate to self management, an example being 'outcome thinking' – thinking of the positive outcome required in a particular situation, and rehearsing it by imagining it through as many senses (sight, sound, feeling etc.) as possible. The next stage is to identify the personal resources (e.g. confidence) needed to bring about that outcome, and to summon those resources using stimulus/response techniques which require the individual to think of a time when he possessed the particular resource, to relive how it felt and to recall how he reached that state, in order to help himself recreate it. The final stage is to rehearse the use of that resource in the new situation in order to bring about a positive outcome. Other skills are concerned with the micro-skills of communication, to enable the individual to become aware of how he is progressing towards the desired outcome, and to help him acquire the flexibility to adapt as necessary. For fuller accounts see Johnson (1991) and Kamp (1991).

It must now be obvious that no one theory explains the complex processes of learning in all situations. This chapter was intended to provide a background to help you to choose and devise training strategies which will be discussed in more detail in Chapter 10. In the meantime, the discussion of the value of curiosity and the barriers to learning leads to a consideration of contextual factors, which are the subject of Chapter 4.

FOR FURTHER REFLECTION AND DISCUSSION

1 'Health and safety training never ends'. Why should this be so? What arrangements would you recommend to ensure that on a regular basis workplace behaviour does not contribute to sickness and/or lost time accidents?

2 Study the 'Quick guide to training methods and techniques' to be found in Appendix 6 of this book, and see if you can identify the different learning styles to which they might appeal. Select any subject matter (or skill), with which you are familiar, and identify training methods which could be used:

(a) appealing to only one learning style.
(b) involving all four learning styles.

Compare method (a) with method (b) in terms of potential interest/enjoyment and effectiveness, when related to different groups of learners.

3 A child is backward at reading. Is the suspicion that he cannot learn likely to be extended to learning and training in general? What can be done to help him?

4 To what extent do you think it is desirable for learners to know about theories of learning? What would you recommend to enable adult learners in your organisation to develop their own learning plans?

SUGGESTED READING

ATKINSON R. L., ATKINSON R. C. *et al. Introduction to psychology*, 10th edition, Harcourt, Brace Jovanovich, New York, 1985. A good general introduction.

DOBSON C. B. and HARDY M. Weidenfeld and Nicolson, London, 1990. Chapter 3, 'Learning and conditioning', Chapter 4 'Remembering and forgetting'.

GREGORY R. L. (ed.) *The Oxford companion to the mind.* Oxford University Press, Oxford, 1987 (pages 740-47, on split brain and the mind).

HONEY P. and MUMFORD A. *Manual of learning styles.* Third edition, Honey, Maidenhead, 1992.

PATRICK J. *Training: Research and Practice.* Academic Press, London, 1992. Covers many aspects, and relates them in a practical way.

STAMMERS R. and PATRICK J. *Psychology of training.* Methuen, London, 1975. (Essential Psychology Series, Heriot P. General Editor).

Chapter 4
THE LEARNER AND THE ORGANISATION

The learner – the organisation as a learning environment.

INTRODUCTION

As we have explained in the preface, and indeed stress throughout this book, the learner does not exist in a vacuum, but in an environment which influences the behaviour and learning of its inhabitants, and which is in turn influenced and shaped by them. This interaction is reflected in the two sections of this chapter; the first section deals with contextual factors with an emphasis on how they affect the individual, whilst the second section develops the theme introduced on page 81, the organisation as a learning environment, which both influences, and can be influenced by, learning/training events.

THE LEARNER

The aspects we have chosen to highlight are as follows:

- motivation
- knowledge of results (or feedback)
- attitude formation and change
- the age factor
- learning transfer.

Motivation

A large manufacturing company wished to provide the best possible training for school leavers enrolled as trainee machinists. Accordingly, an off-the-job induction programme was provided for them during the first week of their employment. It was held in a classroom away from the noise of production and consisted of films, discussion and talks by various managers in the company. The trainees appeared to have little interest in the programme and from the difficulties they experienced later, it was obvious that they had not absorbed the information which was given to them and the results of a 'quiz' to test their knowledge of the company left much to be desired. Occasionally trainees handed in their notice at the end of the first week, saying that they were bored.

As part of the programme evaluation, they were asked to write a short description of their feelings the night before they started work. They produced comments such as:

'I was frightened; I wondered whether I would be able to do what they asked me.'
'I wanted to get to a machine and have a go.'
'I wondered what my supervisor would be like.'

Because of these comments, the programme was reorganised and trainees were taken straight to the training department workshop, introduced to their supervisors, who showed them their machines (already labelled with their names). They then learned how to operate them in a completely safe manner, and were allowed to try them out on a specially designed exercise. At a later stage, the films, discussions and talks provided a welcome break at appropriate times from skills training sessions; for instance a session explaining a pay slip was given in the afternoon before the first pay day. Trainees were also given a checklist of items to find out for themselves.

Under the new scheme trainees reached target performance much quicker and the results of the knowledge 'quiz' were greatly improved.

Motivation is a complex concept and it is most important to recognise that, as this example shows, people are multi-motivated and that they can be motivated towards or against specific behaviours.

Otto and Glaser (1970) suggest a useful classification of motivation factors based on the kind of rewards which are involved in learning:

• achievement motivation, for which the reward is success

- anxiety, for which the reward is the avoidance of failure
- approval motivation, for which the reward is approval in its many forms
- curiosity, for which the reward is to explore the environment and be exposed to novel stimuli
- acquisitiveness, for which the reward is something tangible, such as money or material benefits.

None of these classification groups should be regarded as excluding the other, for instance both achievement and anxiety motivation are possible in the same person at the same time. The trainees in our case study were motivated by both curiosity and anxiety. All the factors are influenced by the immediate experience of the learner, and as motivation is a personal matter, the case for careful discussion of individual programmes is obvious. Frequently, however, a variety of people are undertaking the same programme and it is necessary to bear all the general motivation factors in mind. For instance, achievement motivation requires that learning should be a successful experience. This has implications for the size of the learning 'steps' in relation to the target population; for timing; for the provision of ample knowledge of results or feedback to trainee and trainer, and assistance in case of difficulty. If the training is lengthy and possibly daunting, the setting of intermediate targets can be a useful means of effecting a sense of achievement, as can the introduction of a competitive element for younger trainees, although older learners tend to react unfavourably to that type of atmosphere. Approval is also concerned with knowledge of results, and psychological theory suggests that it is more effective to approve, and so reinforce correct actions, than to punish and ridicule incorrect ones (see page 67).

It is likely, however, that there is an optimum level of motivation. Learners who are too eager can suffer from excessive anxiety, which may inhibit learning. This can apply particularly to older workers, who may be anxious for financial reasons, for prestige, or because of domestic problems; a good trainer should be prepared for this and allay any fears. As in the case above, it is useful to help the trainee to face the cause of the anxiety and thus overcome it. If this does not happen, the learner either wastes time worrying about failure or practises very hard. This is beneficial if he is practising an effective method, but if not, he may be reinforcing errors which may be difficult to eradicate. It is not always true that 'practice makes perfect'.

An office supervisor took delivery of a new piece of technical equipment which he wanted all staff to learn to use. He left it covered up in the office and claimed that within two weeks every member of staff had found out what it was and how to use it!

Curiosity can be a very powerful motivator, as experience with small children will show; for this reason, discovery methods (see pages 72ff) are often very effective. They have been applied in machine handling, with colouring and numerical cues being used to minimise the safety risk. Curiosity is one of the trainer's most powerful allies and should be nurtured by building on the learners' interests whenever practicable rather than destroying them by a rigorous insistence on logicality. Our induction course case study illustrates the importance of considering motivational factors such as curiosity and anxiety when timing learning events so that as far as possible they occur at the most appropriate point for the learner.

There can be difficulties in establishing a direct link between the acquisitive instinct and successful completion of training. The relationship is probably at its most obvious in the field of operator training for pieceworkers, where a resultant increase in output will be reflected in a higher overall wage. In management development, however, the outcome is likely to be less clear, as exemplified by a survey of managers who had attended courses. The results demonstrated that not one of them thought that attending the course would lead to a pay rise (Marks Group 1985, see also Chapter 10 page 280). The relationship is more likely to be indirect, in that if the training leads to better performance, an increase of salary or promotion may result, but as many factors contribute to improved managerial achievement, it can be extremely difficult to attribute cause and effect.

Knowledge of results

Knowledge of results
This is a form of reinforcement, without which it is difficult for learning to be retained and applied. It has important implications for the way learning situations are structured. Imagine trying to learn to play the piano without being able to hear the sound you are making, or being given any feedback about it. Your performance would be unlikely to improve and you would soon tire of the attempt. The more prompt and

specific the reinforcement, the more effective it is likely to be; in the case of learning the piano, it is more effective to hear a wrong note at the time of hitting the key, than three weeks later. In the case of development where results are longer term (such as certain managerial skills) it is useful to set criteria for adequate performance to act as subgoals to final achievement. There are also obvious relationships with continuous assessment of progress, behavioural objectives, target setting or goals in managerial jobs.

Extrinsic knowledge of results

Is provided artificially, for example, by comment from the manager, trainer or fellow trainees, or by information derived from a simulator such as a monitoring screen in simulated pilot training.

Intrinsic knowledge of results

Relates to the monitoring and guidance the learner is able to gain from cues within the job itself. Unless the learner can internalise knowledge of results, i.e. convert it from extrinsic to intrinsic, and know himself whether he is performing well or badly, the effects may not last after removal of the extrinsic provision, and may not transfer to the working situation. Success depends upon drawing attention to the intrinsic cues so that the trainee recognises them. For example, a learner driver may initially look at the speedometer to decide when to change gear, but with trainer help and experience will learn to know instantly, from the feel and sound of the engine.

Learning curves

These depict the rate at which learning takes place, thus providing knowledge of results to trainer and trainee. Progress is plotted on a graph, with the vertical axis representing a measure of achievement, such as output per hour, and the horizontal axis denoting the time period or number of attempts made (see Figure 4.1).

The curvature can be described by the way the gains vary from trial to trial – in the case of sensorimotor skill the curves are most often of decreasing gains (the change in performance from the current trial to the next is frequently less than the change that took place on the previous trial): this is one reason why the learning of a skill is often discouraging. Sometimes it is practicable for trainees to plot their own learning curves and seeing their own progress can act as a motivator.

Fleishman and Hempel (1955) have suggested that as the attainment

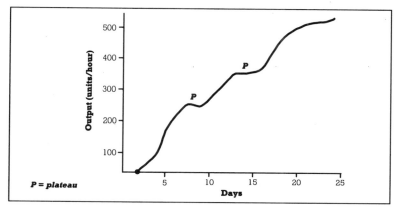

Figure 4.1
A Learning Curve

of skill level in a task increases, the importance of certain ability dimensions can vary. For instance, having gained more competence in the task, the learner's further progress may be affected by his reaction time and rate of movement, while other abilities, such as spatial relations, may have a decreasing influence on performance improvement. The learning curve may therefore not be measuring the acquisition of one skill, but of different skills which are called in to use as the learning progresses. This may be one cause of a plateau of learning.

Plateaux of learning
These are periods of no improvement. They can sometimes be explained by a shift from a lower order of learning to a higher order (e.g. from letter habit in typing to word habit i.e. learning to type familiar words as a single unit rather than concentrating on one letter at a time.) A plateau is often followed by a rapid burst of progress. The trainer should attempt to discover the causes of plateaux, particularly those which occur regularly, in order to assist the trainees to overcome them. For instance, there may be certain stages when trainees become demotivated, indicating an alteration should be made to the training programme. They may need to concentrate more on one aspect, perhaps in the example above in learning to type particular combinations of letters where errors are most frequently made, or as Fleishman and Hempel maintain, they may have reached a stage when they are dependent on a different type of ability which has not yet been adequately

developed. The exponents of part analysis (see page 70) claim that by learning one small part of a job at a time and combining the parts gradually, learning plateaux may be minimised or avoided. (For a discussion of the use of learning curves, see James 1984.)

Attitude formation and change

Attitudinal aspects of training are extremely important as they predispose learners to action. The relationship between attitudes and action is, however, by no means a simple one: in outline, we would state that attitudes are formed through our relationships with other people and are notoriously difficult to change. The concept of cognitive dissonance (Festinger, 1957) provides an explanation based on the premise that we normally like our attitudes to be in harmony with each other. Admiring a superior who actively supports an organisational practice of which I strongly disapprove, I am left in an uncomfortable and dissonant state of internal inconsistency, in that someone whom I admire is supporting something I dislike. The problem can be resolved by modifying my attitude about my superior, or about the organisational practice, or by a decision that the practice is not very important anyway. Whatever the outcome, I shall have altered my attitude in some way. In a training situation, cognitive dissonance can occur in role playing where, while acting to a brief, I may be required to give a convincing argument from a standpoint other than my own (such as that of a subordinate). If this is done in public, I am left with an uncomfortable state of dissonance and may begin to move slightly nearer my subordinate's viewpoint. In other circumstances, however, it may cause me to reject new learning as unimportant, possibly even subconsciously, because it is inconsistent with my other firmly held attitudes. A useful discussion of this phenomenon in relation to management development is given by Mumford (1980).

Group discussion has been found to be one of the effective ways of attempting to modify attitudes. Examples may be found in Study Groups, and other forms of social skills and leadership training.

Another method of attitude change is by providing new information. For instance, attitudes towards certain medicinal drugs can change radically upon learning of research which indicates harmful consequences. This fact is particularly important in training as preparation for organisational change. If little or no information is given on important issues, people may develop attitudes to the change which may harden and be difficult to alter. When a particular attitude has been adopted, the natural tendency is to seek confirmation which reinforces it, unless there is extremely strong evidence to the contrary. For a fuller discussion of attitudes see Hewstone (1990).

The age factor

The climate and the approach to teaching in schools is usually different from that in industry, and school leavers can experience considerable difficulty in adjusting to a different kind of learning situation. Trainers must take this into account when designing programmes if young people's natural enthusiasm is to be channelled in the right direction. Young trainees usually react favourably to intergroup competition and appreciate variety in their programmes. They prefer to keep within their original training groups, membership of which gives them confidence. Leaving school and looking for work is a big and worrying step for many young people and self-destructive behaviour, such as over-confidence or shyness, often results from a feeling of insecurity. A patient and supportive trainer can do a great deal to help; this is particularly true with those taking part in Youth Training, who may be discouraged if they see little hope of obtaining a permanent job. A perceived and desired outcome is an essential motivator, and YT schemes include skills which are likely to transfer to a variety of jobs, as well as social and life skills. An important feature is that learners are consulted about their programmes, and are thus participating in training which is seen by them as interesting and relevant.

Gradually, as we become older, the reproduction of new cells to replace those which die, slows down and those which continue to reproduce start yielding a higher proportion of unhealthy offspring. The result is that speed of performance can decline. For example, as they grow older the majority of people will perform less well on a timed test. Welford (1962) found that the process of ageing impairs the central decision processes. This affects the time taken to reorganise information, monitor movements and deal with a number of matters at one time. Short term memory deteriorates, resulting in time increase and errors in complex cognitive tasks. On tasks involving number matrices, Welford's older subjects were unable to cope with a large amount of information arranged according to different criteria. This involved not only short term memory but the reorganisation of behaviour to shift from one aspect of the task to another. This appears to emphasise the potential value to the older worker of certain types of modern computer software such as spreadsheets. Certain tests, such as those of vocabulary and comprehension, demonstrated an improvement with age, but reasoning and numerical sections of intelligence tests showed a decline for older people and therefore, although they were able to score as well as (or possibly even better than) in their youth, the marks were obtained in different ways.

It is generally agreed that a number of factors are likely to affect achievement in later years and that age is by no means the sole determinant. The first of these is the original level of intelligence. Vernon (1960) gives evidence that the rate of decline is slowest among those whose original score was high. There is therefore an accentuation of individual differences.

The second factor is stimulation and use of intellectual ability. A number of studies suggest a slow decline among those who make the greatest use of their intellectual ability and a more rapid decline in intelligence amongst those who do not. It is also possible that stimulation may have physical consequences for the brain. Evidence from animal studies shows that the weight of cerebral cortex is affected by stimulation from the environment (Bromley, 1990). Evidence was found by Vogt (1951) of slower deterioration in brain cells of those whose level of intellectual activity had been high. A third factor is education and training. Welford (1962) suggests that the manipulative, occupational, mental and social skills acquired through experience help to offset a decline in abilities as a result of the ageing process. Other important factors are state of health and motivation.

For information on designing training programmes for older people entering the labour market see Plett and Lester (1991).

Our knowledge of the ageing process is imperfect, but there are a number of important implications for the trainer. Demographic trends indicate the availability of fewer young people in the work force and an increasing dependence upon the services of older people. There may have been a time when people in their fifties and over were deemed to be unsuitable for job change and retraining. Organisations of the future are unlikely to be able to take this view. In fact already one supermarket has opened a store staffed entirely by people over fifty (see page 311).

Secondly, if people are at their most receptive to learning in youth, and in later years draw upon their attainments, it is essential that the young are given every opportunity to learn. Thirdly, if those with lower cognitive ability are likely to show greater deterioration than those with above average potential, it is extremely important that a broadly-based training is given to young people, so that through vertical transfer (see below) they may find it easier to learn a variety of skills when they are older. The National Curriculum exemplifies this philosophy. These arguments also provide a strong case for Youth Training schemes and supply a justification for the prevention, albeit at a high cost in financial terms, of a young unemployed workforce.

Learning Transfer

Having learned to drive a particular model of car, we expect to be able to drive different models; whilst some of the controls may be alien to us, we can adjust ourselves to them without having to repeat the entire learning process. This is because of *positive learning transfer*, which is said to occur when learning that has already taken place on one task assists later learning on another. Positive transfer can be either vertical or lateral. We shall discuss each type in turn.

Vertical transfer

Occurs when one subject area acts as a basis for another. For example, a basic knowledge of mathematics can transfer vertically to make it easier to learn statistics. The justification for starting many training schemes with a basic foundation course, before allowing the learner to accept specific modules, is that as well as providing an overview, the content will transfer vertically in a number of different ways. This is also the rationale of providing a broader general education in schools. In a rapidly changing environment, pupils can make better use of vertical transfer to assist in the acquisition of a wider range of knowledge and skills later in life.

Lateral transfer

Occurs when the same type of stimulus requires the same response. Training simulators are devices for teaching a skill which will transfer, usually laterally, to the real task. For example, a trainee pilot can practise in a 'safe' situation provided by a computer-controlled flight simulator which imitates the effect of using different controls. Care is required, however, in the provision of simulators, as the extent of transfer obtained by their use is complex (see Annett 1974).

On- and off-the-job training

Off-the-job training relies upon lateral transfer to the working situation and was recommended, and in some cases demanded, by many of the Training Boards, in preference to what was then a 'sitting with Nellie' approach. It can have many obvious advantages including: the provision of conditions conducive to learning away from the noisy rush of the workplace; properly trained instructors; planned training methods; a carefully prepared programme at a pace governed by the trainees' needs; the creation of safe and inexpensive situations in which to try out and practise newly acquired skills and techniques; use of a greater variety of training techniques (e.g. discovery learning, case studies, films, closed circuit television) and the opportunity to emphasise all four stages of the Kolb learning cycle, particularly observation and conceptualisation.

On the negative side, learning undertaken in a specialised environment may hinder the learner's ability to cope with the actual situation. For example, case studies are useful in the consideration of a variety of possible courses of action, and of principles and concepts, but they can be criticised on the grounds that in the 'real' world we frequently have to decide on one best course of action and undertake personal responsibility for the results. What is learned during a leisurely contemplation of alternatives, may not transfer to a stress situation. Furthermore, if the on-the-job climate is not supportive of what has been learned in the training situation, it is unlikely to be transferred.

Whilst it is generally agreed that off-the-job training can often be beneficial, it is necessary to introduce factors from the 'real' world, (e.g. workplace jargon), and on-the-job experience, when it becomes appropriate. There has, for instance, been a progressive increase in the number of 'organisational placement periods' as an essential part of educational courses, and a significant increase in the on-the-job element of teacher training. The NCVQ insistence that training shall be carried out and tested to workplace standards emphasises the importance of obtaining learning transfer.

The concept of 'core competences' which underlies the philosophy of Youth Training and NVQs relies heavily on the concept of learning transfer, the rationale being that training geared to national standards will stand the trainee in good stead for a variety of jobs. It has been argued, however (Duncan and Kelly, 1983), that the components which give rise to transfer may be very precise and it is suggested that insufficient research has been carried out to substantiate the claim that competences achieved in one organisation will necessarily transfer to similar sounding competences in a different industry or line of business.

Hayes *et al.* (1983) use the concept 'Skill Ownership' defined as 'the ability to redeploy learned skills and knowledge in new and unfamiliar circumstances'; they suggest the addition of a new dimension to the acquisition of knowledge and skills, which involves the trainee in taking the conscious step of learning how to 'find out what he needs to know and be able to do'. In this way the potential for transfer to new situations can be built into the original learning situation.

Negative transfer

Sometimes, however, old learning or past experience can hinder performance on a new task, that is when the same stimulus requires a different response. For instance, having learned to drive on one side of the road can make it difficult to drive on the other side when touring abroad. Literature suggests that although negative transfer can interfere, it quickly gives way to positive transfer and may actually result in more flexible performance in the long term (see Duncan and Kelly, 1983).

In matters relating to safety, as in our driving example above, or where dangerous or expensive material may be involved, early learning may be vital and it is necessary to overcome negative effects immediately. Duncan and Kelly (1983) indicate that the more similar the responses required in the two tasks, the greater is the likelihood of negative transfer: it increases with response similarity until the point is reached where the required responses are identical and transfer becomes positive. There is no guaranteed method of overcoming the problem; one precaution is to check the learner's previous experience of similar tasks and carefully point out the differences and possible consequences of negative transfer. It is worth noting that it is most likely to occur when the learner's attention is distracted, for example, by situational factors or new elements of the task, such as approaching a roundabout when driving abroad as in the example above.

Factors which assist transfer

Transfer of knowledge and skills to new situations is essential for continuing development and the attainment of flexibility. It is a complex area and there is no one set of infallible rules but the following points may be helpful:

Understanding of general principles: transfer occurs through the understanding of general principles and concepts rather than by concentration on one narrow application. It can be facilitated by discovery learning. It is necessary both to understand the general principle and to be able to apply it under different conditions. For example, a knowledge of employment law is less likely to transfer to the working situation if the learner has had no practice in applying it to the actual procedures in an organisation. Examples of training methods which might assist this process are discovery learning, case studies and histories, structured exercises, assignments and projects. Group discussions and any means of associating and integrating new learning with existing knowledge also help. You might also like to consider the relationship of learning transfer with the reflection and conceptualisation stages of the Kolb learning cycle described above.

Overlearning (i.e. practising beyond the level of minimum competence): in situations where confusion could be caused by the acquisition of several similar skills, minimum negative transfer will occur if the learner obtains a really good grasp of the first step before proceeding to the others. Systematic rehearsal and mental practice assist in the maintenance of skills already acquired.

Association factors: the transfer of learning will be assisted if the trainee can associate and integrate new learning with other learning which has already taken place. Any structured exercises which help to achieve this aim are therefore useful.

THE ORGANISATION AS A LEARNING ENVIRONMENT

If we accept the link between experience and learning in Bass and Vaughan's (1966) definition of learning (quoted at the beginning of the last chapter) and consider Nord's (1969) application of Skinnerian theory of reinforcement to organisations, we find a number of important implications for the training officer.

A continuous learning process

The first implication is that the training officer is really intervening in a continuous learning process, and therefore requires diagnostic and analytical skills of a far higher order than is commonly realised. People learn by example and reinforcement and the influence of a superior upon his subordinate is very powerful. It is particularly strong when the superior holds the key to what may be termed the rewards and punishments of the organisation. Successful training requires active management support – ideally it should start at the top and filter down through the organisation, each superior being involved in the training of his subordinate. McGregor (1960) maintains that:

> 'every encounter between a superior and subordinate involves learning of some kind for the subordinate (and should for the superior too). The attitudes, habits and expectations of the subordinate will be reinforced or modified to some degree as a result of every encounter with the boss . . . Day by day experience is so much more powerful that it tends to overshadow what the individual may learn in other settings.'

Range of training interventions

Secondly, formal training encompasses much more than the provision of courses and off-the-job training: it includes *any* activity which provides organisational experience relevant to training objectives. Such activities range from short periods of work in different organisations, jobs or roles, to problem solving discussion groups, projects and giving advice. Removing barriers to learning constitutes an important intervention and can include the provision of open learning facilities to counter practical difficulties such as shift work and geographical location, as well as attempting to overcome attitudinal constraints. A highly skilled training officer can extend his role by helping the whole organisation to learn more effectively from its experience, for example, by reviewing the group processes and conducting a meeting.

Influence of organisation climate

Thirdly, off-the-job training requires reinforcement at the workplace: the attitude of the superior and the climate of the organisation are both powerful influences in determining whether training is likely to be transferred to the working situation. For instance, it is difficult for a manager to put into practice what he has just learned about the adoption of a participative and democratic style if the organisation structure and atmosphere is autocratic. During courses for supervisors, a common cry is 'It's our managers you ought to have here'. However, in reality, it is not always possible to start at the top, as we shall discuss later.

Unexpected repercussions

The fourth implication is that training may be likened to a game of skittles where aiming at one target may have repercussions in a variety of other areas. The 'skittle effect' suggests that it may be impossible to train one group of people effectively without changing the behaviour of another group. For example, the early ITBs, for a variety of reasons, put their first efforts into operative or craft training but soon found that in order to gain the benefits from the trained operators it was necessary to start training the supervisors. Apparent inefficiencies on the part of one section of employees may in reality be caused by poorly maintained equipment or defective materials, indicating training needs for a totally different section of the workforce. Training of one group of people can sometimes act as a catalyst in triggering change in other parts of the organisation and may have unexpected consequences: in one instance, a complete redefinition and reappraisal of the organisation structure resulted from an in-house training course for managers.

Development of attitudes to training

Everyone in the organisation, not least management, is learning something about training and formulating attitudes towards it. Favourable management attitudes are particularly important in influencing political decisions about training. The advantages of planned training have to be 'sold' and clearly demonstrated; this may be no easy task and because organisations are all different there is no one recipe for success. The credibility of the training officer is an important factor and may come originally from his personality, but can ultimately only be maintained by successful training results. The starting point is crucial and it needs little imagination to see why the recommendation that training should start at the top is not always practicable. It is a question of weighing up the situation and deciding whether to start where success seems to be the most likely, or to begin, in an idealistic and politically sensitive manner, at the top.

Necessity for commitment

The sixth implication is expressed by McGregor (1960) who suggests that:

> 'knowledge cannot be pumped into human beings the way grease is forced into a machine. The individual may learn; he is not

taught. Programmes do not produce managers; we cannot produce managers as we do products – we can only grow them.'

Skill and knowledge are required in the design of training programmes to meet specific needs, but the most difficult task is often that of gaining enthusiasm and whole-hearted co-operation because people will normally only learn if they want to do so. It is all too easy to pay lip service to training. We could extend McGregor's horticultural analogy a little further and suggest that a gardener will succeed in cultivating a delicate plant if he starts by allowing it to grow in appropriate conditions and encourages and feeds it to help it bloom. We must never lose sight of the fact that commitment comes from involvement and if we involve people we must attempt to use their suggestions, even if they do not necessarily accord with neat and tidy models of systematic training. It is necessary for a training officer to be fully conversant with planned methods but the skill of adapting them to specific situations is paramount.

Organisation development

The final implication is that people learn from the organisation and that, as Greiner (1972) maintains, 'their behaviour tends to be determined primarily by previous events and experience, not by what lies ahead'.

He extends this analogy to the organisation itself and suggests that a company can become:

'frozen in its present state of evolution, or ultimately in failure, regardless of market opportunities . . . [because of] . . . the inability of management to understand its organisation development problems. [For example] Key executives of a retail chain store hold on to an organisation structure long after it has served its purpose, because their power is derived from this structure. The company eventually goes into bankruptcy.'

Learning processes are involved in organisation development and if we recognise that training can include group activities which might trigger organisational change, then the link between training and organisational development is clear. A sophisticated assessment of training needs would therefore include not only details of the future development of individuals but also a framework for discussion of the future potential of the organisation and the changes in climate and structure which would be necessary to achieve it. The simplest example of this is to be found in the small established company which is owner managed. It often appears that such an organisation has no training needs: all employees know their jobs as the company has been running the same way for years. If, as a result of his own training, the owner manager sees the potential of his company in a different light and installs new methods, then the company may require not only new skills but a new organisation structure. Training and organisation development needs can therefore arise at the second level when a fresh assessment may be required. The whole operation must be seen as a dynamic process, not as a once and for all event.

Some of the ideas in this chapter may seem very conceptual, and it may need some thought to turn them into practicalities. You should be able to draw upon the concepts and ideas and examples and apply them to the design of situation-specific training/learning programmes and opportunities and to be able to relate them to the concept of the 'learning organisation'. Considering the questions below should help you to operationalise what you have learned.

FOR FURTHER REFLECTION AND DISCUSSION

1 What do you consider to be the main reasons why a person is, or is not, motivated to learn? What action would you recommend within your own organisation to ensure a higher commitment to learning? This question can be considered in general terms, or in relation to a specific example.

2 What arrangements can you suggest to assist the transfer of learning from a formal off-the-job course into a work situation? What do you recommend to make this transfer process more effective?

3 Suggest ways in which line managers can give positive feedback to assist the learning of their subordinates.

> 4 What do you understand by 'barriers to learning'?
> Using the headings, 'Personal' and 'Organisational'
> list any barriers you encounter in your own
> learning. Is there anything you can do about
> them? Do you need to add any further headings?
> What 'barriers to learning' do you think might
> apply to a new entrant to your organisation?
> Could anything be done about them?

SUGGESTED READING

PLETT P. and LESTER B. T. *Training for older people.* ILO, Vincent House, Vincent Square, London SW1P 2NB, 1991.

BROMLEY D. B. *Behavioural gerontology. Central issues in the psychology of ageing.* Wiley, Chichester, 1990.

ATKINSON R. L. and ATKINSON R. C. *Introduction to psychology.* (10th edition), Harcourt Brace Jovanovich, New York, 1985.

DOBSON C. B. and HARDY M. *Understanding psychology.* Weidenfeld and Nicolson, London, 1990. Chapter 13, 'Attitude Change'.

HEWSTONE *et al.* (eds.). *Introduction to social psychology.* Blackwell, Oxford, 1990. (For discussion of attitudes.)

PATRICK J. *Training: research and practice.* Academic Press, London, 1992. Useful all round text. With reference to the content of this chapter, see learning transfer, retention of skill and knowledge of results.

Chapter 5
APPROACHES TO TRAINING INTERVENTIONS

Organisations' learning systems – generalised approaches – planned training interventions – costs and benefits of training interventions

INTRODUCTION

This is the last chapter in this first section of the book. We hope that by now you have come to appreciate that:

- *employee development is an art*
- *the art of employee development is itself developing rapidly, with training interventions increasingly being made at all levels – the nation, the employing organisation, the training provider, and the learner*
- *managing employee development is about 'making learning happen', which involves all forms of education and training for all employee levels*
- *to manage effectively, one must have both contextual and conceptual understanding*
- *contextual understanding relates to the scene within which learning happens, including the history, culture, aims and assumptions of both the surrounding organisation (up to and including the nation, if relevant) and the learner*
- *conceptual understanding relates to learning processes themselves, and associated factors (e.g. motivation) which help or hinder those processes.*

This chapter aims to move one more step towards making these things 'operational': that is, to suggest approaches to using one's contextual and conceptual understanding to decide first on the organisation's learning environment, and then on specific training interventions.

108

Here are a few questions to which you might like to draft answers. The material in the chapter should help you to confirm, refine or revise your answers as you progress.

---

1 Should training benefit people, or organisations, or both?

2 Should training be planned for individuals, or larger groups?

3 Should decisions on how to learn be left to the learners?

4 How important are learning objectives?

5 Should the nation spend more on training?

ORGANISATIONS' LEARNING SYSTEMS

Managing employee development in the real world invariably requires more than a good philosophy of learning and/or a set of learning principles. The essentials of day-to-day management are purpose and choice; decisions must be taken on such matters as who will learn, what the learning objectives should be, how the plans will be drafted and implemented, the duration of the learning and so on. These subjects will be addressed in some detail in the second section of our book; for the time being, it will help to summarise some of the most frequently observed (even if often unplanned and misunderstood) approaches which influence the minds of those responsible for taking the decisions. The fact that there are many such approaches suggests that no one approach is likely to satisfy all organisations' needs.

The Learner or the Organisation?

Shrivastava (1983) studied organisations' learning systems and found a number of different approaches corresponding to differing mixes of two variables. The first variable was what he called the 'Individual-Organisation Dimension': learning activity is seen as being for the good of either the individual or the organisation (or – in the case of a mix of the two – reflecting an emphasis towards one of them).

Individual _____ Organisational
Learning   Learning

'Individual' learning was seen as accepting personal development as
the only planned aim; 'organisational' was seen as fitting individual
learning into a coordinated pattern which would also serve the organisation's work needs. Examples of each are not difficult to find; imagine
first a company where the only planned training involves the sending
of individual employees on external courses, and compare this with
one where departmental training plans are created as part of annual
operating plans.

> A Merseyside company used to issue to local schools a booklet
> entitled 'Career for Life', in which the claim was made that all
> employees would be trained 'to the fullest extent of their capabil-
> ities'. Newcomers were given release facilities to follow further
> education courses of their own choosing. The approach changed
> following increased competition for labour in the area when
> 'overtrained' staff sought and easily found better opportunities
> elsewhere.

Systematic or *Ad Hoc*?
Shrivastava's second dimension related to how learning is expected to
happen: it is either allowed to evolve in its direction and time, or it is
'designed' via a master plan or a set of procedures which ensure that it
takes certain forms (or, once again, there is a bias towards one of these
two alternatives).

Evolutionary _____ Planned
Learning   Learning

Shrivastava described the former as 'lacking any conscious effort to
contrive the learning mechanisms that emerge in any organisation', and
the latter as 'formally introducing these mechanisms to serve stated
learning and/or information needs identified [we might add usually] by
managers'. Here again the distinction is easy to appreciate: compare an
organisation with a policy of placing people in jobs for, say, fixed

twelve-month periods, but without any formal training inputs, with another which automatically arranges attendance at an external business school course for each person newly promoted to junior management grade. (It is of interest to note that Shrivastava saw Japanese industry as offering many examples of the evolutionary approach – group cohesiveness, participation and team spirit being the cultural bases which he suggested provide the stimulus for learning.)

Until relatively recently, craft apprentices in a Midlands engineering firm 'served their time' by accompanying established craftsmen, the latter deciding what the apprentice could be given to do. The same firm now uses formal training plans which itemise what must be learned against a calendar plan, with trained instructors providing instruction and overseeing progress. Learning times have been cut dramatically.

Shrivastava defined six 'types' of organisational learning system, and placed them into the matrix he had created using these two parameters. And although his research used data from the USA, it seems that these variables also reflect common differences between UK organisations' learning systems.

It also seems reasonable to suggest that in recent years organisations with substantial training activities have been adjusting their learning systems in two ways:

1 They have been increasing the planning, and decreasing the evolutionary, emphasis
2 They have put organisational learning in front of individual development, whilst trying to achieve both.

Other Variables

Many practising training professionals see the two parameters mentioned above as incomplete descriptors of what characterises any given organisation's approach to learning, and hence its learning system. They suggest a large number of equally important variables as follows:

1 The learners themselves

Some training systems are specifically geared (in terms of both resources and methods) to graduate management trainees, or technical specialists, or people with disabilities (e.g. the Royal National Institute for the Blind's centres).

2 Training methods

During the sixties, many large companies bought or built residential training centres, which became the focal centre of their (formal) learning activities. More recently, self-study has become a new focus for some.

3 The size of the learning unit

Some organisations define needs in terms of individuals; others group people in departmental units, or occupational groupings (e.g. managers, drivers). The larger the organisation, the more likely it is that group activities will at least have a place in the system.

4 Training resources

Many organisations feel they cannot afford their own training resources, preferring to use local providers (e.g. further education colleges).

5 Lead times

Plans can be 'long term general' or 'short term specific'. The former are most usually seen in organisations which are internally stable; but even such organisations may abandon long lead times in periods of recession.

6 Status and power

The status and power of those pressing for the learning to take place.

7 Operational purposes

Whether mainstream operational priorities are served or not.

A long-established food manufacturing company maintained a strategy of recruiting school leavers and graduates for many years, 'growing its own future management', and promoting from within to fill all management vacancies. When local competition for labour increased with the arrival in the area of three new major employers, top management were forced to review their strategy, as traditional recruitment sources dried up. Top management concluded that they wished to continue with the system as it was, believing it had produced key operational strengths. Training staff were asked to maintain the learning system; recruitment staff were asked to improve their links with schools, colleges and universities.

This last case example makes clear that the learning system is as much a matter of operational decision-making as other mainstream systems, e.g. those relating to production or accounting. But decisions on its make-up are rarely taken as consciously as is suggested by the example. This is partly because not many top managements make explicit their training priorities and norms, which therefore continue to exist not as 'standards' but as relatively vague perceptions, the general impression being that training approaches are not really the basis for decisions but their product. It may also be because the influences mentioned above – all of which might be important to top management – actually impact on each other, any traditional ranking order being difficult to sustain. For example, a group learning approach is threatened if specific learners come to oppose it; group training may be impossible in-house if a company moves its offices and the necessary physical resources do not exist in the new buildings; external resources may not be covered by a small budget; and money may be unavailable unless the idea came from the chairman. A long list of similarly overlapping issues might be offered. Even if such problems do not exist, past norms are unlikely to be sustained if they are not explicit and their justification is in doubt; hence many organisations' learning systems are best described as 'flexible'. Hence also decisions on specific training interventions are quite likely to depart from tradition, or from what is generally believed to be the 'standard approach', especially in times of change. An *ad hoc* culture can emerge, or at least one which allows specific interventions to depart from norms. As Pettigrew and his Warwick team (1988) discovered when researching specific training interventions, organisations' approaches to training can dramatically change when competition is fierce and results are deteriorating.

It nevertheless remains true that professional trainers, and all management working in organisations which aspire to professional employee development practices, should try to understand, to be able to describe, and to take decisions with conscious reference to, the basic assumptions in the learning systems for which they are responsible.

In a London office, much discontent was fostered by a sequence of what were seen by clerical and administrative staff as 'unfair' decisions on further education facilities. Some workers were given paid release to attend classes which they, the workers, had chosen; others were refused similar requests. Some refunds of travelling expenses and book expenses were authorised; other, similar, requests were turned down. Most employees' complaints implied that they wanted equal treatment. The Training Manager believed in equality, but any idea of establishing rights on a collective basis had always been strongly challenged by top management as 'uncommercial', and the Training Manager had himself insisted in the past that he must be consulted before release was granted to any employee. He talked with various line managers, and with several day release students; virtually all wanted a tighter set of rules. The Training Manager drafted new 'rules' governing these release decisions; these rules were quickly approved by the board. In future, support would only be given for classes which were appropriate to the work that staff were undertaking or expected to undertake in the near future; approval required both the line manager and the Training Manager's signatures on a newly designed form. Support would follow prescribed rules concerning paid time away from work, payment of fees, refund of travel and book expenses, with payment coming out of the Training Manager's budget.

In this example, the Training Manager reviewed and re-established his norms as follows: first, learning must be in both the company's *and* the employee's interests as expressed in work arrangements; second, decisions on facilities would be individual, not group; third, the power to decide would rest jointly with the line superior and the Training Manager; and fourth, resources would be provided from a central budget which the Training Manager would control. Other variables (e.g. the nature of the learners, lead times) were not considered important enough to influence the new system, which once agreed was imposed on and quickly accepted by all. Discontent disappeared overnight. The 'singles versus groups' issue was treated as an important one, and resolved in favour of an individualised system; but it was subordinated to the issue of company need, and again made subject to the twin issues of management control and available resources.

The essential points are that:

- each specific training intervention is an 'operational' and a political one, not to be dominated by philosophy or theory, although both may have influenced it
- whilst specific training interventions may depart from past norms, their appreciation is a powerful aid to discussions between line management, personnel or training management, and learners.

GENERALISED APPROACHES

Any attempt to understand the basic assumptions in a given learning system can be helped by comparing it with one or more 'generalised' approaches, examples of which are often to be found.

The 'Sitting by Nellie', or 'Learning by Exposure', Approach

XYZ Limited is a manufacturing organisation, the managing director of which believes 'we cannot afford to train'. The firm recruits 'ready-made' workers, paying them higher wages than local competitors. Learning happens solely 'on the job', with supervisors and established workers giving new recruits whatever information they (the supervisors and established workers) think is needed, and with the recruits picking up routines and standards as they go along.

This is not, strictly speaking, an approach to employee development; it is an 'anti-approach'. But, since learning still happens, it can be considered a management option; and it is of course widely preferred, albeit perhaps by default. In so far as it can be said to positively reflect any of the variables we set out earlier, it assumes individual learning, and no resources (but the hidden costs of poor or slow learning might involve a high level of hidden resource).

In this situation, the learner is assumed to be able to gather knowledge and to use it without any help other than that randomly offered by colleagues. There are no obvious incentives to learn or disincentives not to do so. The trainers are not themselves trained, nor are they prepared in any way for their roles.

The last two sentences suggest ways in which this approach might become less haphazard and more useful. First, experiential learning can be improved *if learner motivation is increased*. In the case above, this may involve no more than offering the incentive of 'removal of probationary status once competence is demonstrated'. A different example might relate to the introduction of explicit learning objectives against which the learner can measure progress. Second, *Nellie can be trained to train*. This is both likely to change the way Nellie works and talks, making it easier to appreciate and copy what Nellie does, and to introduce into the system an 'authority' to which the learner can direct questions without feeling embarrassed. We know of one company which selected and trained nearly three hundred 'operative trainers' within a factory complement of over 2,000. These part-time 'trainers' compiled manuals, briefed newcomers and provided tutorial help (they also reported progress regularly to a central training officer), although they never actually provided formal initial instruction – the system assumed that job placements and replacements were all that needed to be planned. But such interventions are already beginning to move into different approach categories.

The 'Educational' Approach

A local authority has a policy of recruiting wherever possible young people direct from school. All employees below the age of 25 are encouraged, and in some cases REQUIRED (as a condition of employment) to study for appropriate qualifications, paid leave being given to attend day-release classes, and other costs such as essential books being refunded. Promotability is linked to success in examinations. Staff who are promoted into supervisory and higher posts are similarly encouraged (regardless of age) to study for further professional and management qualifications. Training activity within the council is sporadic and largely unplanned.

This approach essentially serves individual needs, although the learning content of most formal education programmes has in the past been prepared externally with large groups in mind. Since educational syllabuses are typically substantial, leading to recognised qualifications, the approach is characterised by 'long term' planned activity which involves attendance at formal classes, and/or home study.

For many small organisations, local educational resources are the only training resources believed to be available, and they have traditionally been inexpensive – except perhaps in terms of time lost from the workplace. The approach generally guarantees teaching staff who are experienced in teaching (and now increasingly in flexible learning) methods, and of course it offers assessment against nationally accepted norms. Off-the-job vocational education, as we have seen, is a requirement of YT programmes; it is also the basis of most professional bodies' current schemes of study leading to membership.

Government's establishment of the National Council for Vocational Qualifications (NCVQ – see Chapter 1), to which we will return under a 'Competences' approach heading below, represents an attempt in part to revitalise the educational approach, rationalising the many national qualifications that exist, but at the same time linking them more closely to the reality of the workplace. The national training targets support this goal, as will the range of 'modern apprenticeships' when they are launched in 1995. Youth Credits may similarly be tied to NVQs/SVQs. Further education funding is also likely to provide increasingly colleges with financial incentives to offer the necessary NVQ/SVQ courses.

NCVQ developments nevertheless only offer a limited application of the 'educational' approach. Training is at its most 'work specific' when it is organised as part of the work itself. Educational courses which cater for learners from diverse origins cannot be specific in the use of workplace language. Whilst qualifications might be recognised nationally, no general assessment system can guarantee standards which apply in any one organisation. FE colleges also struggle to keep up to date in vocational terms; it is no use teaching mechanics if the firm is developing robotics, no use giving practice on electric typewriters when the firm has bought the latest wordprocessors and a range of modern software. Moreover, almost by definition, established employees in a changing world need *post*-qualification courses. It is this need that is most likely to lead to the 'educational approach' being developed. Educational institutions at all levels are now offering tailor made course facilities, and are building new consortia-type arrangements with employers to plan new activities. Professional bodies are beginning to offer multi-media packs and tutorial services (sometimes using college staff) which can be the basis of a self-directed educational approach, a modular structure allowing the learner to vary both the content and the pace of study. The educational approach will become more sophisticated and more in *vogue* in the next decade.

The 'Problem-centred' Approach

> An advertising agency includes in its organisation a part-time
> 'trouble-shooting' team comprising five senior managers, who
> attend the monthly board meetings as observers and meet imme-
> diately thereafter to determine corporate plans stemming from
> any specific problems identified by the board. Since agency per-
> formance levels are often criticised, it is usual for plans to
> include training interventions. The company does not employ its
> own training manager or training department or training budget,
> and *ad hoc* plans have usually taken the form of formal in-house
> 'teach-in' events, arranged and led by external consultants.

Predominantly short-term and *ad hoc* in nature, this approach is dominated by operational problems, which can determine learning needs for
either the individual or the group.

The essence of this pragmatic, and perhaps 'temperamental',
approach is the use of special monies for special operational needs – in
this case with top management deciding what those needs are. The
approach is often highly acceptable throughout the organisation: it is
seen to serve real work problems, it produces quick action and is usually
believed to produce cost-effective results.

However, the success of the approach depends on high level identification skills, and not merely the redefinition of an operational
problem as a lack of expert knowledge in the named sphere. True
diagnosis may be a lengthy process when no one carries the continuing responsibility for assessing learning needs; failure to diagnose
the training need adequately may lead to a misuse of resources
and/or new operational problems. A useful example comes from a
City office where the output from the audio-typing pool was criticised, the diagnosed need being little more than 'put those typists
straight'. In the predictable course which was hastily mounted, the
external trainers became quickly convinced, and agreed with the typists, that the operational faults lay essentially with line managers,
who lacked the skills to use the pool effectively. Those managers
never became the subject of a training plan; a number of the typists
went to work elsewhere.

The 'Action Learning' Approach

John Smith is currently half way through a six month attachment to a large computer software establishment; under normal circumstances he is a Shift Manager at a power station. He has been asked to look into the system which governs distribution of software packages to a variety of types of outlet; the company is concerned at delays in delivery which have been reported from too many clients. John has gathered data from many sources, and has set up several *ad hoc* 'action sets', incorporating selected line managers from the host firm and a transport manager from a mail order house; collectively they have agreed on a number of measures which should eradicate the existing problems.

'Action learning' is basically the study of real-life problems, and their resolution within a real-life environment. Its justification as an approach to (mainly management) training is twofold: it offers a challenge, which in turn provides all-important motivation, and it demands the transformation of problems into opportunities. 'Action learning' has been used in a variety of forms; the approach was pioneered by Revans (see Revans 1980 and 1983), who arranged for managers to be seconded to firms and placed in existing work teams or part-time working parties (e.g. value analysis teams), and added a mentor (i.e. advisor) whose role was to help the group devise appropriate work processes. Hence the learning extends to matters of organisation, leadership, and teamskills: a 'task culture' must be set up and maintained, and the experience of achieving this whilst addressing a real-life problem can create powerful feelings of achievement and confidence.

The 'Systems' Approach
Since there is no one single 'systems' approach to training (indeed, Goldstein (1980) noted that there are almost as many different 'systems' approaches to training as there are authors on the subject!), we will omit an example. Basically, systems thinking is thinking about relationships between parts of a system, about their appropriateness, and especially about *feedback*, which acts as a judging mechanism and feeds new operational decisions. (For a comprehensive treatment of the systems approach to learning, see Argyris and Schon, 1978).

A systems approach to training views the organisation as a complex set of sub-systems, and expects changes in one sub-system to yield potential needs in another. It is therefore 'organisational' – but it can produce individual or group plans aimed at long- or short-term objectives. For example, if an organisation seeks to reduce its workforce dramatically by offering large-scale early retirement options, *prima facie* there will be (a) some 'early retirement' training needs – assisting employees to understand the options being offered; (b) a change in work requirements, and some learning needs, for those who remain; and (c) a shift in the age patterns of the workforce, which may justify long term adjustments to recruitment patterns, and hence eventual changes in past training patterns.

A systems approach may equally address the training system *per se*: assessing the impact of training policy; challenging the quality of data which comes from appraisal; suggesting new ways of evaluating actual training activities; comparing the effectiveness of different training methods; identifying whether learning transfers easily between off-the-job training events and the workplace; redefining trainer roles – and so on *ad infinitum*. It can immediately be seen, however, that this approach cannot normally replace others: it will seek to refine and improve those others by continually reviewing them.

The 'Analytical' Approach

A sales force of some 200 representatives employs a Sales Training Department, managed by a Sales Training Manager. Initial training takes the form of a three-week skills course in a residential centre. The STM has created, and has had circulated to management, a training policy statement which includes a commitment to a detailed sales training manual. That manual, which forms the basis of the initial training course and later refresher courses, lists procedures to be followed by salespersons, and explains in great detail the techniques that they will be expected to use. The manual is reviewed and updated by the STM himself (using specialist job analysts) every two years; changes lead to imposed refresher courses in the residential centre.

In some organisations, the analytical approach is a static one, lacking the updating operation in our example. The approach has traditionally been associated with a careful and specialist assessment of organisational training needs, followed by detailed analyses of knowledge, skills and attitudes required for each job. Job Descriptions and Job Specifications are typically created and/or drawn on for this information. Where programmes are created for new, as yet unrecruited, staff, the norm is to assume no knowledge, no skills, and no relevant attitudes: a Training specification is then drawn up, which is essentially a work-specific version of the sort of learning profile that the 'educational' approach designs. Where employees' performance can be measured against the analysis, a so-called 'Learning Gap' is said to exist, and a more specific plan can be drawn up.

We will cover analytical methods in much greater detail in the second section of this book (see also Pearn and Kandola, 1988). For the present, it should be appreciated that the approach usually relies on job characteristics standing the test of time – the analysis is rarely completed quickly, and is a costly investment. It requires the application of logic on the part of someone other than the learner – usually a teacher or a work study specialist. It is particularly applicable in situations where the overall task requires that a number of people work consistently in accordance with laid down rules – although, as our example shows, it does not necessarily assume close supervision of workers. The local fire brigade operates with such rules, and might make huge errors if it were not trained to observe them; similarly a group of packaging machine operators might justify the analytical approach, as their work is dominated by high-speed moving machinery, and undisciplined behaviour might lead to accidents.

The analytical approach was the first to be preached by the ITBs when they appeared in the sixties. The ITBs assumed that logic and order could improve training practices, and made this the first brick in their 'systematic training' wall of recommendations. It was ironic that industry was at that time simultaneously moving beyond work study into more dynamic approaches. But, as we shall see next, the approach has persisted and been further sophisticated.

The 'Competences' Approach

A small bus company has paid a fee to engage in the Vehicle Engineering Competence Assessment scheme developed by its industry training organisation, Bus and Coach Training Limited. The fee entitles the company to receive literature explaining the scheme, the forms on which its administration is based, plus the training of several of its own supervisory staff as trainers and assessors. The central aid is a manual which sets out in substantial detail the elements of vehicle fitter jobs in the bus and coach industry; the manual has been approved by the National Council for Vocational Qualifications. The job elements are collected under a number of generic headings; a requirement of the scheme is that each fitter (the scheme extends to all ages, not merely apprentices) should be trained to master all the essentials of the actual site job, which MUST include some elements from each generic heading. When the learner believes s/he is 'competent', s/he completes a 'claim form'; an assessor then visits the workplace and tests the learner, using real life materials and processes. Minimum standards must be attained on all tests, and each generic heading must be covered. Satisfactory results allow the award of NVQs.

Analytical work on 'occupational families' during the sixties and seventies, which was aimed at establishing a national set of competencies (NB not quite the equivalent of the more modern 'competences') and a framework of 'transferable skills' led to the Training Agency adopting this as their preferred approach for the establishment of standards for the new NVQs/SVQs; over 150 Lead Bodies and occupational groups have since produced competence manuals which are now accepted as the definitive national standards in their respective industries.

Our example above shows how the competences approach can serve the needs of the nation, the industry, the employer and the learner. It does this by prescribing the outcomes, not the learning method (the approach has been termed the 'outcomes' approach); how the learner becomes competent is left to the learner and/or the trainer to determine. Standards are described in terms of:

- 'Elements of Competence', which each describe 'what can be done' – that is, 'an action, behaviour or outcome which a person should be able to demonstrate'
- 'Performance Criteria', which are 'statements by which an assessor judges the evidence that an individual can perform the activity . . . to a level acceptable in employment'.

All quotations from the MSC's 'Development of Assessable Standards for National Certification' Guidance Note Number 3: 'The Definition of Competences and Performance Criteria', 1988.

A set of performance criteria may also be backed by one or more 'Range Statements': these outline the range of applications in practice which are considered 'good practice' (i.e. the normally acceptable uses of the given competence).

These standards are 'national': they are defined by Lead Bodies approved by government to represent each industry or occupational group (the latter in cases where work crosses industry boundaries – e.g. clerical work). An example of an occupational standard, covering an element within the Training and Development role, can be seen in the next chapter as Figure 6.3 on page 151.

The detailed work of compiling standards requires that four aspects of job competence are covered:

- the technical activities to be performed
- contingency management – dealing with things that go wrong, and with 'the unexpected'
- task management – allocating time, setting priorities, etc.
- handling the environment – ensuring safety, interacting with colleagues, etc.

From the point of view of the employer, the approach brings together the educational and analytical approaches already described above (we will explore this in more detail in Chapter 9), but without requiring the individual employer to undertake the time-consuming analytical work. It has the added appeal of offering qualifications which are more vocational and less academic than their predecessors. Support from government, industry Lead Bodies and TECs/LECs means that it is certain to develop further during the nineties. What is less certain is whether it will serve improved performance goals, or indeed whether it will provide the competences that are actually needed at any given workplace.

Critics have challenged the lack of interest in learning processes, stressing how an outcome can be affected by the learning route. For example, a maintenance fitter who has learned 'breakdown procedure' as a sequential procedure will operate differently from one who has acquired diagnostic skills. This suggests that at least in some cases the learning method and the actual job need to be matched. It also confirms that workplace assessment is critical – but which is the 'right' workplace? One job may require a type and level of competence that is not appropriate for another job, nor indeed for the industry as a whole, which in turn means that through time employers may view

NVQs/SVQs as something other than 'national'. Moreover, it is unlikely that workplace supervisors will assess impartially; regardless of any central training they receive, they are political animals in a highly political environment. External assessors can be assumed to be less biased, but they incur additional expense, and their assessments may ignore the specific needs of the workplace. Since much of the training actually takes place in a college setting, simulation of the workplace within the college will almost certainly become widely acceptable. (There are additional problems for college tutors, such as the tendency for Lead Bodies to ignore links between theory and practice, which have traditionally promoted understanding alongside memory.)

GNVQs – the *generalised* qualifications available to young people still in secondary or further education – have come in for some of the strongest criticism. Competence here is described in terms of 'core skills', emphasising communication, the application of number and information technology. The first piece of major academic research into GNVQs, mounted by a team from Manchester University's Centre for Education and Research, concluded that GNVQs' performance criteria fail to distinguish the essential from the desirable among hundreds of elements, and equally fail to offer valid assessment arrangements.

Such problems and challenges may eventually undermine the value of the 'competences' approach, although it is now firmly established as the means whereby UK employees will become 'qualified' in the eyes of employers in all EC countries.

The 'Training Process' or 'Procedural' Approach

A local authority has recently appointed a Training Manager to work within its personnel department. The Training Manager's job requires first and foremost the creation of training plans for all the authority's departments; the new manager has already set about the task of systematising the identification of training needs, and has established relations with heads of department to allow draft plans to be discussed and, hopefully, agreed. A central training budget has been allocated to the personnel department; all major training expenses except salaries will be charged to it. The Training Manager is committed to producing in the future an annual training review document, which will summarise training achievements during the past year and suggest improvements to the training system.

This approach owes its origins to Fayol's ('plan-organise-do-review') process theory of management, plus the ITBs' strong advocacy of it through their recommendations and levy-grant mechanisms (it was for a time synonymous with the ITBs' widely-preached 'systematic training' ideal). In its early form, the training process was assumed to be based on the simple, four-stage process of (a) identifying training needs; (b) designing training plans; (c) implementing the plans; and (d) evaluating the results. But whilst the simplicity of this model made it attractive, its reputation suffered as trainers gained experience and came to appreciate the complexities that arise both within and between each stage in the cycle, and hence demand a more sophisticated model, and one which accepts the political dimension. But despite this, the 'training process' approach has grown stronger, especially in organisations which have a personnel department but no full-time training management, and it now offers and mirrors what many firms have come to regard as 'basic system requirements' – accepting that training interventions will be a regular phenomenon throughout an organisation's life, with people explicitly responsible for seeing that appropriate procedures exist and are followed. Typically, those procedures are seen as including:

- the promulgation of training policy
- the inclusion of training responsibilities in job descriptions
- the regular, periodic definition of training needs
- the creation of training plans
- the provision of training resources
- the implementation of training plans
- the assessment of results.

Our example above does not cover all these elements, but we will say more about them before this chapter is finished.

Although this is the most 'accepted' approach to training interventions in the UK, some experienced trainers still see it as flawed. As with many management activities, the definition of a relatively simple set of procedures in a simple sequential model (such as we present as Figure 5.1) is unlikely to describe best practice, they say. For example, evaluation is covered in the model as a discrete post-learning procedure, the final stage in the process; yet it is actually managed by many trainers as a natural part of each of the other parts, and hence conditions ALL decisions as they are taken. Determining needs is likewise

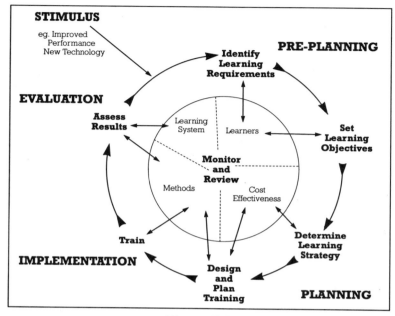

Figure 5.1
The Training Process

said to be not a discrete set of procedures, being affected by such matters as planning options, yesterday's experiences and management opinions. These critics argue further that the 'annual training plan' tends to prejudice and delay key training priorities which subsequently appear at unexpected times. Hence they see the approach as once again serving a static state which is never realised.

Other Approaches

We have chosen those approaches which are most visible in present-day UK organisations, omitting several which readers may individually believe are more important, useful or interesting – for example, the 'political' approach (spotlighting and serving primarily the wishes of opinion moulders), the 'organisation development' approach (applying behavioural science techniques to organisation change), and the 'welfare' approach (using training as a reward for individuals to improve personal prospects). We have also left the 'Continuous Development' approach, and the very important complementary 'self development' approach (see Mumford, 1980), together with their supporting 'socio-technical' and 'open systems' theoretical bases, to be covered in full in the last chapter of the book.

It remains true that approaches to learning systems are not mutually exclusive, and that organisations invariably develop their own learning systems without a particular model in view. As we have said above, the value of appreciating generalised models lies in being able to understand and compare one's own reality, and hence in alerting oneself to possible future directions. The management of employee development remains a situation-specific art which demands the endless reappraisal of priorities, preferences, and purposes in the service of new goals. Planning training interventions is never likely to be satisfied by rigid adherence to a single approach.

PLANNED TRAINING INTERVENTIONS

Whatever the underlying learning system, a training intervention is a conscious attempt to make learning happen in order to achieve improved performance. It may be aimed at any level – the nation, the organisation, the site, the department, the team, the individual. It may be made at any of these levels. It may be made by a body or a person responsible for promoting the learning of others, or again by one or more learners working in their own interest. A training intervention will usually aim to improve the performance of both the learner and the organisation; indeed, some training professionals argue that the invariable need to choose between alternative ends for limited resources rules out goals which only serve one of these ends.

Despite criticisms of the 'training process' approach, it offers the most useful basis for describing a standard guide to the planning of training interventions.

It can be seen that there are several requirements:

- **a stimulus** which produces one or more provisional learning goals. The stimulus, which might be appreciated in the form of a problem or an opportunity, might typically spring from an external development (e.g. new legislation), or an internal work change (e.g. the purchase of a new machine), or a new awareness of an available training resource (e.g. an advertised course), or simply a desire for improved performance
- **a pre-planning stage** during which the learning requirements are

identified (NB some interventions may stop here, if they deduce a need simply to change the learning environment but no actual training need – for example, procedures may need to be rewritten), learner characteristics reviewed, detailed learning objectives set, and cost effectiveness judged

- **a planning stage** involving decisions on the learning strategy, the design of learning methods, and the creation of specific calendar plans;
- **an implementation phase** when the training takes place
- **a monitoring and review process** which overlaps the various stages, and in which progress is watched, adjustments being made where needed to such things as objectives, resources, learning methods, and time span
- **a post-learning evaluation stage** when the overall effectiveness of the activity – including the ongoing review system itself – is appraised.

An Illustration of a Planned Training Intervention

The following simplified example describes in practical detail the stages set out above. In this case the chosen strategy option for the initial training of newly recruited employees is that of an internal course. The example also illustrates the roles played by line managers and the training specialist.

Stimulus

The Works Manager of a successful electronics manufacturing business has been pleased to see his company's sales results rising, and the marketing estimates justifying larger output targets. He plans to meet the increasing demand by introducing shift-work, with new employees being recruited to undertake several specialised jobs. There are no job descriptions currently written for these jobs, and no established training programmes available externally or internally. The Works Manager is certain that the new recruits will not be competent to carry out their new specialised duties without training; he contacts the Training Officer, and opens discussions on how this need might be met.

Pre-planning

The Training Officer agrees that the skills cannot be 'bought in', and hence must be 'created' – unless the work methods and machines can be altered for use by unskilled labour, which might make a small reorientation programme for existing workers possible at much reduced cost. The Works Manager rules this out: it would call for much MORE workplace cost, and would need a longer lead time than is available – he is not prepared to accept a loss of orders due to failure to meet delivery dates, and he feels the company should be able to provide the necessary training resources. After discussion with her personnel manager superior, the Training Officer contacts the Works Manager to say that she is ready to work on the training intervention, but her budgets will not allow large-scale external consultant-trainer fees; it seems therefore that the development will need to be managed entirely in-house. They agree the overall objective (newly designed in-house training to follow company induction arrangements and to be completed four weeks from the day of recruitment).

The Works Manager sets up a meeting between his own Departmental Manager, two of his Shift Supervisors, the Trade Union Representative, and the Training Officer; it is agreed at the meeting that the Training Officer should, with the assistance of the others, mount a training analysis of the work, producing training specifications which detail fairly precisely what the new recruits must be able to do, the acceptable 'tolerance limits', key parts of the work where errors would be costly, duties which the trainees are likely to find difficult to master, and (not least) some special safety requirements. The analysis is completed quickly by the Training Officer – quickly enough to communicate to the Recruitment Officer that each new worker must be entirely free of eyesight problems, and must be capable of reading simple gauge instruments entirely without errors. The analysis clarifies the performance standards to which the recruits must be trained.

The Training Officer then compares the trainees' anticipated present levels of competence with those required by the training specification. She emerges with a list of learning objectives, and sets up another meeting of the departmental group, where – after several hours of hard discussion – the final documents and revised learning objectives are determined.

Planning
It is clear to the Training Officer that much of the learning involves new knowledge, and must be taught; arrangements must

follow for practice, either in a specially reserved workplace setting or via a simulation. She decides a formal course is necessary, and drafts a programme, taking advice from the Departmental Manager and one of the supervisors (who becomes her main instructor) on the learning sequence. Her draft timetable includes periods of practice at the workplace, when two experienced workers (detailed by the Departmental Manager) also act as instructors and monitors of progress. She easily 'sells' the programme to the Works Manager.

Implementation and Monitoring
The recruits join, and attend the course. The early lecture sessions flow well – in the training officer's view – and a high level of commitment seems to be emerging. The practice sessions are less uniformly successful: some trainees appear to have mastered the work, whilst others vary in their handling of specific aspects, and one suffers a minor accident when overlooking a safety rule. Special new arrangements are made for these 'slow' learners: one-to-one coaching is provided by the experienced workers, and the training officer intervenes without warning to check awareness of key points. These measures work well. All but two of the recruits are installed in shifts inside the four-week deadline; the others follow two days later.

Evaluation
'Post-mortem' discussions are mounted by the Training Officer, with the whole working party attending, three weeks later, and (with the Works Manager present) after a further three weeks. The Training Officer carries to the meeting copies of questionnaires completed by the trainees at the end of their course; they have rated it highly, but make individual criticisms of several sessions. Discussion centres on the transfer of learning to the workplace proper: the shift supervisors are highly satisfied that the specified standard has been attained. The Works Manager speaks even more highly, saying that ex-works targets have been met and no client complaints received – at least, none that point to sub-standard worker performance. He alerts the others to a probable further increase in demand, and a probable further recruitment need covering both skilled and unskilled jobs; it is agreed that the team will meet again as soon as these needs are

made definite, and that they will bear in mind several ideas for improving the detail of the specialist training.

In this illustration of a planned training intervention, the Training Officer leads the way in proposing and drafting a course programme, external facilities being unaffordable and in any case unknown. It is probably true that in many real-life situations, a much less time-consuming process might be adopted which takes advantage of known external resources. But the simple intervention is often the least effective; the example above, with all its simplifications, shows how many issues might need to be managed to ensure success. We would furthermore stress that in most pre-planning situations, the training options are many and varied, and decisions on the preferred option should not be taken lightly. The more comprehensive the approach to the training intervention, the more likely it is that the learning objectives will prove reliable and will be realised.

THE COSTS AND BENEFITS OF TRAINING INTERVENTIONS

Our 'Planned Training Interventions' model contains an element headed 'cost effectiveness'. This is perhaps the key element for the majority of employers, even if it is generally accepted as the most difficult to monitor and manage. Since training is only rarely a condition of employment, and the lack of training is rarely likely to lead to illegal acts, training interventions are not often seen to be 'imperative', or justifiable regardless of cost. They must therefore be justified; and in a commercial context, this means *financially* justified.

Investments of all kinds, including training, contain an element of uncertainty. In all except a few non-profit-making and charitable associations, prudent management demands that before an investment decision is taken, a convincing case can be made showing that the expected return is greater than the expected cost, and that the expected return will probably be forthcoming.

In order for British Airways to justify the training of Concorde pilots which was expected to cost £100,000 per pilot, it was estimated as desirable to spread the training cost over a seven-year period, which in turn made it necessary to plan for at least seven and a half years of post-training service before retirement, and in turn demanded an upper trainee age limit of 47.5 years.

Alternative strategies (i.e. those not involving training, such as recruiting people who are already competent – clearly not possible in the Concorde case) must also be shown to be less appropriate as part of the convincing case.

But what is a 'convincing case'? Some training managers argue that however strong the need and however unchallenged the proposal as the only or best solution, a degree of pure faith must accompany management's commitment. They cite comparisons with research and advertising expenditures; both are held to be essential for ongoing competitiveness, yet in neither case can proposals for specific expenditures be supported by guarantees of success. An element of trust is needed, coupled with a strong commitment to ensure that the investment will be 'made to work'.

Whilst recognising the validity of such arguments, we suggest that they must not be allowed to obscure the need for professional managers to develop their ability to manage the financial aspects of their roles. Far too few personnel and training managers can yet talk confidently with accountants about the benefits and costs of training – *prima facie* evidence for a training intervention in its own right. And even those who argue that employee development is based on faith do not claim that *specific* training interventions must be taken *primarily* on trust; they usually prepare a case, collecting up to date evidence to support answers to three basic questions:

1 What benefits can the organisation obtain?
2 What costs are involved?
3 What is the net result?

What Benefits Can Be Expected?
It is probably true that in organisations with a long tradition of training, the following benefits tend to be accepted by at least a majority of management:

- training helps recruits to learn their jobs more quickly
- established staff need training to keep up to date in a changing world, and at times to improve their performance

- trained and retrained staff are unlikely to make as many errors as untrained staff, and can eliminate the costs of correcting errors
- training can help to minimise labour turnover in times when labour is scarce and 'poaching' rife
- an organisation with a reputation for good training attracts recruits
- regular training in safe working practices reduces accidents, which are costly in both financial and morale terms
- training can significantly stimulate the creation of a versatile workforce, that is, one in which workers can efficiently carry any of several jobs, and hence provide a flexible resource.

But these are essentially 'general' benefits. The case for a specific intervention will usually itself need to be more specific in its estimate of the returns to the organisation. It is of some importance to remember that in most organisations top management are not strong promoters of training: knowing little about the function, and preoccupied with decisions affecting products or processes, they tend to wait for those below them in their hierarchies to suggest what must be done. Lacking this top management lead, the case for a training intervention must be justified in operational terms. Here are two examples of successful operational interventions – both from sources close to one another, the marketing and technical departments of a fast moving consumer goods company – to illustrate the types of issue that can be expected to attract top management interest:

Technicians who controlled the flow of raw materials into a spray drying plant spent many working hours watching a set of gauges, and adjusting the input of different materials in response to the information supplied by the gauges about the 'moisture content' (i.e. the volume of water in the mixture). Typically, the technicians reduced that moisture content by adding chemicals whenever the gauge showed a certain level. If that level was never reached, the mixture was allowed to continue unimpeded. Experience had shown that setting a high input of chemicals at the start of a batch meant that few further adjustments would be necessary. The Technical Training Officer, working with a Development Technologist, deduced that a considerable saving in the cost of chemicals would be possible if the technicians could be trained to start up with lower levels of chemical input, and to control the various flows by making more frequent adjustments within a set tolerance band. The Technical Director was persuaded. The training, with the Development Technologist as teacher, took two days: the resultant annual saving in chemicals cost was over £250,000.

Several brand managers, responsible for heavily-promoted brands, operated a six-month-lead-time system for the planning of specific promotions (e.g. competitions, joint merchandising schemes, free on-packs, etc.). Instructions to advertising agencies were given at the start of the six-month period; draft artwork for leaflets, packs, etc. was supplied by the agencies some three months later. The original specifications were often changed at this stage – and again even later, in many cases – with more ambitious print requirements being requested. The agencies simply 'double billed' (i.e. they properly charged for work against both specifications), and of course they charged heavily for the more sophisticated and 'more urgent' work. The Training Manager heard of the problem from the Print Buyer, whose budget carried these costs, and who had frequently tried without success to explain to the brand managers how they were escalating costs by asking for complex printing work (he estimated an undue cost of over £200,000). The Marketing Director agreed that all brand managers should be given a tailor made course in print methods, costing for some 22 people a total of £6,000. The apparent saving in print buying during the following half-year was £178,000, with nearly all 'mid-term' alterations to specifications being easy to satisfy.

The first example was one where the future benefit was not clear, but the cost (two days' time x three people, plus the technologist) was minimal. It illustrates the lessons that 'a low or uncertain return usually determines a low-budget training intervention', and 'a high potential return justifies substantial training expense'.

Estimates of benefits must be as realistic and situation-specific as possible. But they are not necessarily only to be found in the precise area where the training is mounted: as the second example shows, training within one department can yield savings in another. Similarly, reducing the running or maintenance costs of a company fleet may be effected by training sales representatives or top managers; a costly external market research task might be reduced to a small expense by being given as a project to a team of laboratory chemists after an initial period of training.

What Costs are Involved?

The list of benefits may convince top management that investment in training merits serious consideration, even after taking into account the practical difficulties associated with the training – for example, having staff unavailable for other duties whilst learning proceeds. But it is unlikely finally to convince *in cost-benefit* terms until the advantages are considered in relation to the resources needed to achieve them.

For more comprehensive coverage of cost-benefit analysis of training, see Talbot and Ellis (1969), and Chapters 11 and 12 in Pepper (1984).

One approach to training costs is that adopted by economists who argue that the actual cost is not the financial expenditure directly related to the plan, but the opportunity costs involved. Garbutt (1969) argues:

> The opportunity which a firm foregoes may be a better measure of its cost than its accountancy procedure. In other words, we may spend £100 on training, but if in doing so we lose the opportunity to make £200 the opportunity cost of training is £200.

However, as Garbutt continues:

> Measures of opportunity cost are hard to establish and even harder to agree between conflicting interests.

The opportunity cost approach is therefore not usually a practical one to adopt in trying to establish the cost of a training investment, except perhaps where the level of investment is very high, or very low, and the training need bordering on the 'imperative'.

The more usual alternative approach is to consider the various costs that an organisation will be forced to incur as a direct result of the required learning happening through (unplanned) experience – the 'learning costs' – and then to determine how these can be minimised or even replaced by new earnings through expenditure on training – the 'training costs'. Talbot and Ellis (1969) have shown how learning costs are unavoidable; training costs are a means to control these learning costs and to improve upon their yield, in terms of the quality and speed of learning.

A new brand was introduced by the company we reported on above when considering 'benefits'. The company's sales force called on grocery outlets, mainly supermarkets; the new brand was designed to be sold into these stores, but first it was felt desirable to mount a limited test market over a period of four months in hardware shops, of which the reps had little experience. The Personnel Manager advised against this plan, believing the impact on the reps would be considerable – in terms of varied journeys, disruption to normal sales, and morale (hardware shops were considered 'low status' outlets). His alternative solution was to invite several reps who had retired early during the past four months to return to complete the test market work – first attending a two-week course on the hardware trade and the new product. The Personnel Manager estimated the relative saving as 'enormous'. His advice was accepted; the course generated a high level of enthusiasm among the returning reps; and the test marketing was concluded satisfactorily, with all targets being reached in less than two months' selling.

The following are examples of Learning Costs:

- payments to employees when learning on the job
- the costs of materials wasted, sales lost or incorrect decisions made by employees who are less than competent
- supervision/management costs in dealing with 'incompetence' problems
- costs of reduced output/sales caused by the deleterious effect on an established team of having members who are less than competent
- costs attributable to accidents caused by lack of know-how
- costs resulting from employees leaving – either because they find the work too difficult, or resent the lack of planned learning, or feel they have no prospects.

'*Training Costs*' are defined as those deliberately incurred to facilitate learning and with the intention of reducing learning costs. Some such costs might be aimed not at planned training *per se* but at the learning *system*; for example, a training intervention might involve investing in appraisal procedures in order to get better data on learning needs, and by clarifying learning objectives the data might be expected to generate some learning of its own volition. But most training costs are more directly related to planned training itself. They may conveniently be described as being of two kinds: *fixed* costs, which are not expected to change with the amount of training that takes place (e.g. salaries of permanent training staff); and *variable* costs, which must vary directly with the training (e.g. materials used, or college fees paid).

The following are examples of Training Costs:

'People' Costs:
- wages, salaries of trainers and instructors
- managers'/supervisors' salaries while training/ coaching
- fees to external training providers
- fees to external assessors
- travel and subsistence of trainees and trainers.

'Equipment' Costs:
- training equipment and aids
- depreciation on training buildings and equipment.

'Admin' Costs:
- wages/salaries of admin backup staff
- telephones and postages
- office consumables
- systems and procedures (e.g. post-training questionnaires)
- hire of rooms.

'Materials' Costs:
- films and tapes
- distance learning packages
- materials used in practice sessions
- protective clothing
- books and journals.

Large-scale initial costs relating to buildings or major items of training equipment (e.g. a simulator) will normally be 'capitalised' – that is, they represent a transfer of liquid funds into 'fixed assets', the costs of which are spread over a long term via the annual 'depreciation' item. Additionally, the upkeep of a training centre (i.e. a purpose-maintained building) will incur all the normal costs usually associated with buildings e.g. community charges, insurance, cleaning, heating, lighting, decorating and general maintenance. Personnel and training departments will also usually be required to carry a proportion of the organisation's overheads.

Ideally, the relationship between learning costs and training costs should be such that both are minimised, since any expense is only justified if it reduces the costs of unplanned learning. However, since the degree of certainty attaching to any estimates must vary, and must reduce when the rate of change itself varies, decisions are invariably made on incomplete information. This in turn demands that the organisation sets an upper limit in advance, i.e. a 'budget' on what can be spent in a given period (usually a year). Some organisations adopt a 'zero-base' budgetting system – that is, each budget must be built up from a clean sheet, with each entry being justified in its own right as a realistic estimate of a necessary expense (alternatives which use previous actual costs as 'norms', and simply adjust those norms on the basis of what can be afforded, are notoriously poor predictors or controllers of costs). A budget will usually be detailed under a number of headings (such as those listed above, but essentially conforming to the accounting conventions of the organisation). The training budget acts as a major constraint on decisions to promote training interventions; but in the ideal it will also offer some scope for realising new opportunities, whilst regularising 'standard' (i.e. traditional) training activities which have been justified in the past. Some organisations mount annual reviews to reappraise the relationship between learning and training costs with regard to these standard activities, prior to fixing the next year's budgets.

Like all other management procedures, budgeting can be abused. In the days of the ITBs, training managers were known to persuade other managers to move funds into their training budgets to convince ITB visitors that the training investment was high. A more persistent abuse involves unnecessary end-of-year spending against, but within, a given budget in order to raise the chances of the level being retained for the next year – which in turn allows a new proposal to be accompanied by the claim that 'we have the money budgetted'. Such practices can be expected ultimately to reduce rather than increase the credibility with which top management (and their advisers, the accountants) view the training function.

In practical terms, a useful starting point to find out what training costs an organisation incurs is to examine its training budget, and the actual expenses that have accrued under the various category headings. But not all organisations budget for training in one, single account – and for good reasons. If line management are expected to carry a prime role in delivering training, they need to own and manage their own training budgets; a central budget, under the control of a training man-ager, is likely to be used mainly for corporate ends, with line managers rarely suggesting how and on what it should be used. The answer is usually to have *both* central and departmental training budgets; but the way the latter are detailed may vary (e.g. wages costs may not be sepa-rately allocated to training for short training periods), and any attempt to build a comprehensive picture of what has been spent may itself prove a costly and unreliable process.

Linking Benefits and Costs

It will by now be amply apparent that a proper cost-benefit analysis, whereby *all* results of the training intervention are systematically quan-tified and compared with *all* the training costs, is rarely possible or economic. The management of training remains a situation-specific art. 'Best practice' in determining training interventions is achieved not by attempting any single rigorous and ultimately imperfect method, but by those responsible for training efficiently mastering four ongoing, situa-tion-specific, needs:

- awareness of mainstream operational goals and priorities
- awareness of how, why and at what cost resources are currently deployed
- up to date intelligence on what is being achieved (and not achieved)
- accessibility of information on potential resources.

Mastery of these four needs allows a competent response to requests from top management to provide justification for any intervention, and indeed to take the initiative in suggesting interventions.

FOR FURTHER REFLECTION AND DISCUSSION

1 What would you expect to be the 'preferred approach' to learning by the staff at your local public library?

2 What do you think will be the long-term effect to the UK of government's introduction of competence-based qualifications?

3 What measures would you recommend to an organisation whose top management expect to authorise frequent training interventions, and who want to monitor progress on each?

4 To what extent can cost-benefit analysis be used to justify training interventions?

SUGGESTED READING

MOORBY E. *How To Suceed in Employee Development.* McGraw-Hill, Maidenhead, 1991. Offers a practitioner's approach and adds the political dimension.

Department of Employment. *Development of Assessable Standards for National Certification,* 1991. This comprises a series of papers by people at the centre of the 'Competences' initiative, and provides a thorough description of the 'Standards Development' process. NCVQ and SCOTVEC publish literature on all aspects of NVQs/SVQs. The Department of Employment's quarterly journal, *Competence and Assessment,* supplemented by special issues, offers authoritative views on all aspects of the 'competences' approach.

PEPPER A. D. *Managing the Training and Development Function.* Gower, Aldershot, 1984. This publication does justice to cost-benefit issues in the employee development field.

SECTION B

MANAGING EMPLOYEE DEVELOPMENT

Chapter 6
THE TRAINING FUNCTION IN ORGANISATIONS

The training function – management's responsibility for training – creating an appropriate structure – the training of personnel and training staff.

INTRODUCTION

The first part of this book presented the background (economic, historical, and philosophical) to employee development. This is the context within which employee development should be understood. We must now approach issues of managing the function.

Most of what follows throughout Section B will concern the level of the operating organisation. We should perhaps remind you that managing is an art, and a situation-specific art, serving and at the same time being constrained by the environment in which it is carried out.

This chapter sets out to outline what the 'training function' comprises, and the key conditions necessary if it is to secure and maintain a relatively stable place in the organisation – including the main roles which must be defined, their constraining boundaries, and a range of structural alternatives.

Think of any organisation with which you are familiar – perhaps your local bank, or the local supermarket, or an airport, or a leisure centre. What do you immediately think of as 'the things that must be managed' within the training function? Now assume for a moment that you are responsible for managing these things. Who would you expect to be working for and with? What do you think would be your main

---

> daily worries? What do you see as the probable main
> constraints which would affect what you did and
> how you did it? How would you map your ideal
> organisation chart to cover these things?

THE TRAINING FUNCTION

The word 'function' comes from the Latin verb 'to perform or to act',
and a useful definition of the training function (based on that contained
in the former Manpower Services Commission's *Glossary of Training
Terms*, 1981) is:

> 'the purposes, structure and specialised activity of training and its
> relationships with other activities within a working organisation'.

You should appreciate that the training function is a relatively recent
addition to UK organisation structures compared, for example, with
production, accounting or sales. Donnelly (1984), in his review of the
evolution of training as a specialist function, drew attention to the fact
that, prior to the 1960s, training activities were very restricted and dif-
fused within organisations. Not surprisingly, therefore, there was an
almost complete absence of any objective analysis into the job
demands of the training officer, and (in the minds of top management)
the nature of company training activities rarely justified the status of a
'business function'.

We are then dealing with what is a relatively recent feature of organisational life, and moreover one which, often from a zero base, enjoyed
a spectacular but ephemeral growth.

Although a number of large companies (e.g. Ford, Lever, Cadbury,
Pilkington) had training units in operation before the Second World
War, training departments first appeared in quantity during the late
sixties – in the form of off-site course centres, or wings of existing
personnel departments, and occasionally as mere one-person administrative units. There was no general pattern of organisation, nor was a
standard pattern preached by the 1964 Act or the industrial training
boards, which were the main stimulus for the development. In later
years, when the legislative support was withdrawn, many of these

training departments failed to consolidate their position. As might be anticipated, there were great variations in the ways in which training functions evolved, in their perceived purposes and achievements, and in the extent to which they were accepted and valued within their organisations. At one end of the spectrum, the function had no real impact but existed as a token presence to satisfy minimal internal needs, and perhaps also to justify an ITB grant. At the other extreme, training units were developed which enjoyed a high status and influence and came to be embedded in the mainstream activities of the organisation.

Bearing in mind the very limited 'stock' of training expertise that was available, the low calibre staff frequently appointed to the training positions and the limited training they were given, the expectations which organisations had of their training departments at that time were often unrealistically high. A warning note about the range of activities of training officers was sounded by Rodger, Morgan and Guest (1971). In their study, carried out in the mid-sixties, they sought to clarify the function of the training officer and the limits of the function, and they commented that:

'Training is a means of making better use of human resources in the organisation by developing people to meet the requirements of the job to be done . . . Any attempts to extend the expertise of training officers into broader human resource specialist roles is to change the trainer into . . . a more exotic role that would be beyond the aspiration of all but a minority of training officers.'

A Study of the Work of Industrial Training Officers, 1971

This quotation should not be taken to mean that training *per se* has no part in organisation change and the creation of a flexible workforce. On the contrary, it is a primary vehicle for these developments. But their achievement demands the exercise of a high order of training expertise, and this was in short supply at that time.

The economic recessions of the 1970s and 1980s provided the *coup de grâce* for many weak training departments, especially those in small organisations, typically resulting in the cessation of planned training activities in the host organisation. In more robust organisations, some training departments lost their independent functional status, and the responsibility for the activities which survived cost-cutting was dispersed to other functions. Thus in many small and medium-sized organisations the training function which had enjoyed a departmental state in its own right regressed to its pre-1964 state.

But the seed had germinated: some organisations, and particularly those with buoyant personnel departments, had increasingly appointed good quality human resources to their employee development positions. They found during the eighties that employee relations problems were less in evidence: hence employee development could wrest more resource time from the personnel professional. The economic recovery of the eighties, coupled with the success of government's Youth Training scheme, further renewed many organisations' involvement with employee development, and although the recession of the late eighties and early nineties hit companies hard, the tendency to abandon the training function has not been so evident; indeed, by 1990 some commentators were coming to describe employee development as the 'leading personnel function'.

Rodger, Morgan and Guest (*op. cit.*) noted a wide variety of activities in response to variables such as:

- the status and importance of the training function as expressed by top management's interest and support
- the extent to which there is a need and demand for training within the organisation
- the natural development of training in the firm
- the managerial calibre of those held responsible for training.

Similar data emerges from studies twenty years later. We shall see later how strategic, political and organisational constraints influence, if not mould, the training function: but it is still possible to suggest three main conditions which must be satisfied if the function is to secure a relatively stable place in the organisation. These three conditions are as follows:

1 The management team should accept responsibility for training
2 The training function should be appropriately structured within the organisation – with roles that are perceived as relevant to such aspects as boundary management, organisational culture, operational strategy, management style, and the organisation's geography
3 Specialist training staff should be seen as professionals – trained, with clearly defined roles.

These prerequisites for success are discussed in the remainder of this chapter.

MANAGEMENT'S RESPONSIBILITY FOR TRAINING

Although, as we shall see, there are different types of managerial responsibility for training, all managers, without exception, ought to accept personal responsibility for the training and development of their own staff. This involves taking an active interest in their careers, providing opportunities to improve and extend their abilities, especially by using day-to-day work tasks, and, above all, by encouraging them to continue learning (Singer, 1979). An organisation should ensure that each of its managers accepts the importance of this particular role when contributing to the corporate training effort and that their success in exercising this responsibility will have a bearing on their own career prospects. Unlike other training responsibilities, this cannot be delegated.

These assertions of good practice, however, are not universally accepted by managers. 'More urgent tasks have to be given priority' and 'general pressure of work' are the usual reasons given by managers for not being involved in employee development. While not discounting these reasons, it is true to say that a critical aspect of the management process is concerned with identifying and dealing with priority tasks, and for many managers training is simply not perceived to be a priority. We have drawn four conclusions from numerous discussions we have had with senior, middle and junior managers attending management development programmes:

- a significant obstacle to progress in exercising this responsibility is that, for many, the task is perceived as being difficult – and is hence avoided
- it is unusual (perhaps for the same reason) for managers to be assessed rigorously on this aspect of their work (in appraising managers and determining their own training needs, much more emphasis should be placed on expertise – or the lack of it – in this sphere)
- many training activities demand a heavy and sustained allocation of a manager's time
- it seems that many managers have adverse feelings about learning which stem from their early experience of formal education – feelings which are both uncomfortable and unpleasant, and which they

hoped to leave behind them when they entered adulthood. Such feelings act as powerful anti-development influences, and ensure that trainer training for managers is itself a complex and lengthy process.

The nature of the responsibility for training, and how it is exercised, varies with the level of management. Top management have four main responsibilities as follows:

- they bear the main responsibility for creating and sustaining a positive attitude to employee development in all its forms
- they determine the organisation's employee development policies, and the level of resources to be allocated in support of them
- their personal involvement in training decisions, and in formal training events, and their own self development practices, offer an example to ambitious subordinates
- their training interventions (not least via critical comments on what they observe) provide a quality control service for the training function.

Middle and junior managers are responsible for implementing the organisation's training policy within their own spheres of influence. They must themselves communicate information linked with work plans, for example, new work schedules or new output targets. They must ensure workplace competence despite such hazards as raw material variances, machine breakdowns, variable hours of work, sudden workforce sickness, and frequently changing specifications – all of which require a flexible workforce, with trained deputies available at short notice. They must honour conditions of employment, for example, those allowing leave of absence to attend external courses; but above all, they must encourage subordinates' learning on a continuous basis, to ensure that all these other operational learning processes can flow smoothly. As with their own top management superiors, their own training decisions, their involvement in discussions, their self development, and their training interventions give to their own subordinates an ongoing justification for learning.

CREATING AN APPROPRIATE STRUCTURE

Defining Roles
Following the 1986 White Paper *Working Together: Education and*

Training (see page 26), a Lead Body was set up to define occupational standards for training and development occupations. These standards were published in draft form early in 1991; after a period of consultation, the final 'National Standards for Training and Development' document emerged one year later.

The basic approach used is one of 'functional analysis': as with all standards aimed at approval for NVQ/SVQ use, a model of the function is broken down into elements, these being described in terms of what people in the relevant roles are expected to be able to do at the workplace. Each element is backed by performance criteria and range statements; the whole constitutes a 'national standard'.

The T & D Lead Body first defined the key purpose of training and development in a single sentence as:

'To develop human potential to assist organisations and individuals to achieve their objectives'.

To break this down into elements of competence, a variant of the 'Training Process' approach was used (see Chapter 5, and especially Figure 5.1, pageₒ 126), which is called the 'Systematic Training Cycle' (Figure 6.1):

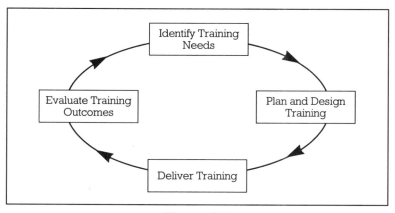

Figure 6.1
The Systematic Training Cycle

Crown Copyright; reproduced by arrangement with the Employment Department from the Training and Development Lead Body's *National Standards for Training and Development*, 1992

From this model, the Lead Body constructed:

- five main functional 'areas of competence'
- twelve sub-divisions of these areas
- further sub-divisions of these twelve sub-areas into 44 'Units of Competence'
- 132 'Elements of Competence', each carrying up to eight 'Performance Criteria' and a number of 'Range Statements'.

The main areas of competence, and their sub-divisions, are reproduced here as Figure 6.2; an example of a standard follows as Figure 6.3; a complete list of 'Elements of Competence' can be found as Appendix 4.

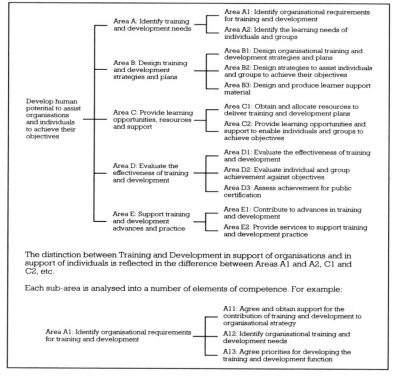

Figure 6.2
T & D National Standards: Areas of Competence

Crown Copyright; reproduced by arrangement with the Department of Employment from the Training and Development Lead Body's *National Standards for Training and Development*, 1992

Performance Criteria

a coherent and accurate proposals are presented which specify realistically how learning needs will be met

b agreed organisational priority needs are described accurately

c relevant standards of performance to be achieved as outcomes of the strategy are described accurately and coherently

d individuals and groups for whom strategies are required are identified accurately and clearly

e proposals clearly define appropriate design parameters

f negotiations and agreements are conducted and concluded in a manner which preserves goodwill and trust

g specifications are accurately recorded and summarised, stored securely and made available to those who require them

Range Statements

1. Descriptions of priority needs/proposals:
   - oral
   - written

2. Types of specification:
   - formal
   - informal

3. Presentation and negotiation methods:
   - oral, including group presentations
   - written

Performance Evidence Required

	Performance Evidence Required	Assessment Guidance	Observation of activity	Examination of Product
1.	Proposals presented and agreements made on specification of learning needs (pc a, b, c, d, e, f)	Proposals presented against two different organisational priority needs. Proposals and descriptions presented orally and in written form.	1	1
2.	Specifications recorded and summarised (pc g, b, c, d, f)	Specifications recorded and summarised against two different organisational priority needs. Both types of specification covered. Summaries presented orally and in written form.	1	1

Notes: On completion of evidence collection (performance and supplementary) there is evidence, overall, that oral presentation/negotiation to a group has been included.

Supplementary Evidence Required

Knowledge of methods to:
Specify learning to meet needs
Set outcomes in terms of standards of performance
Identify individuals/groups with learning needs
Define parameters for designing training and development strategies

Knowledge of data/information about:
Learning needs to be addressed
Types of learning needs
Agreed organisational priorities
Types of parameters to designing training and development
Categories of individuals and groups with learning needs
Ways of summarising and recording specifications of requirements

Role of Supplementary Evidence

Range:
If performance evidence produced (as above) does not, of itself, provide full coverage of the range statements, further evidence to supplement that which is available will be necessary

Knowledge (methods to ... and data/information ...)
Knowledge underpins performance. If performance evidence produced (as above) does not, of itself, provide sufficient evidence of the underpinning knowledge, further evidence to supplement that which is available will be necessary

Figure 6.3
T & D National Standards: An Example of a Unit of Competence, or 'Standard'

Crown Copyright; reproduced by arrangement with the Department of Employment from the Training and Development Lead Body's *National Standards for Training and Development*, 1992

As can be seen, Performance Criteria employ terms such as 'relevant', 'appropriate' and 'adequate', and so may need to be further defined within the context of a specific work operation. Range Statements suggest a possible range of applications for the element. The definitive 'National Standards' document also lists against each element the types of performance evidence that are required for proving competence; 'supplementary' evidence (knowledge) is also listed, and assessment guidance is added.

There is no doubt that the Lead Body's work represents the most detailed and most comprehensive description of the training function ever completed. It offers an exhaustive description of employee development roles, and in adding performance criteria it clearly aims at establishing common national standards. Herein lie problems: workplace standards are likely to vary from industry or national standards, and the definition of performance criteria has only been possible by using terms such as 'relevant' or 'adequate', which allow variable workplace meanings. Critics have also pointed to the inadequacy of range statements, which sometimes seem alien to the realities of many workplaces.

The Training and Development Lead Body's standards suffer from their very size and complexity: while attempting to cover all aspects of the function, they still cannot offer a specific blueprint for each individual training job, and the process of adapting their 'standard' to fit any given job description demands sustained hard work. A more fundamental criticism is that the bureaucratic assumptions in the standard do not stand four-square with all cultures (perhaps no single approach could). Important among these assumptions is the insistence that knowledge and understanding are not part of the competence, but simply 'underpin' it; a strong practitioner view to the contrary has led to the inclusion of long lists of knowledge items in each element as 'supplementary evidence required', but these lists are unlikely to satisfy the critics, who see the knowledge need as extending beyond the elements into general management – and as forming a job-specific role in its own right. (The Employment Department issued in December 1993 a special broadsheet on 'the place of knowledge and understanding in NVQs/SVQs'; whilst continuing to assert that neither is part of competence *per se*, the broadsheet acknowledged that in some instances performance may be heavily dependent upon a person's knowledge, and evidence of knowledge and understanding may be crucial to making a decision about a person's competence.) The same critics also argue that the standards can have no meaning to a learner without a conceptual framework, which they say must have a foundation in broader-based knowledge than that supporting any given element of competence. There are moreover other critics who feel management level qualifications should be outside NVQ/SVQ scope altogether, as management competence itself incorporates the endless redefinition by managers of their own performance criteria.

But despite these criticisms, it remains reasonable to stress that the Training and Development Lead Body's national standard document offers an invaluable aid to anyone who wants a sophisticated, detailed checklist of 'what the training function comprises'. It must be the first port of call for any organisation wanting to clarify training roles.

There are nevertheless other views, other emphases, and other approaches to the definition of training roles. Studies during the late seventies by Pettigrew and his team at the University of Warwick (Pettigrew, Jones and Reason, 1981) confirm the view that there is no one common set of roles that is carried out by all, or even most, people with responsibility for training (they also suggest that the function is most active in large firms when those firms' operational goals are under threat). These studies provide interesting data about training and development roles and the factors influencing their effectiveness. The Pettigrew team reviewed a sample of training managers, training officers and training advisors in companies of varying size in the UK chemical industry. Using semi-structured interviews, they collected data on: the relational aspects of the trainers' jobs; the activities which they performed or felt they ought to be performing; the degree of satisfaction they achieved and the ways in which they influenced decisions. The research underlined the importance of congruence between these variables: the roles of the people, the cultures of the organisations in which they worked, and the types of people concerned.

Pettigrew and his colleagues identified several types, or perspectives, of training officer roles and associated behaviour, stressing that these perspectives, or role interpretations, should not be considered as watertight categories but as 'broad descriptions', and that no judgemental assumptions should be made that one role type is 'better' or 'worse' than another. (See Pettigrew, Jones and Reason, 1981).

The 'Provider'
Has a generally accepted though limited role in offering training expertise geared towards the maintenance and development of the organisational performance – but not with organisation change. The 'Provider'

works within the current culture in a manner which is congruent with its expectations, i.e. operates in the standard ways expected by contacts and colleagues of a training officer in that organisation.

The 'Training Manager'
Concentrates personal effort on the management and performance of subordinate training staff, and on the development of the training function. The 'Training Manager' tends to describe the role primarily as one of management rather than training, and is likely to be involved with policy development and co-ordination issues.

The 'Change Agent'
is the classical organisation development consultant (the antithesis of the 'Provider' role). As the title suggests, the 'Change Agent' is concerned with the definition of organisational problems and with helping others to resolve problems through changing the culture. The role is very difficult and demanding, and its legitimacy is uncertain.

The 'Passive Provider'
Role is similar to that of the 'Provider' (i.e. it is concerned with maintaining, not changing, the activities of the organisation) but it is characterised by a low level of influence – which the researchers attribute to personal difficulties in managing the role. The 'Passive Provider' takes few decisions, waits for others to make demands or requests, is low in self-esteem, and is not politically skilled in securing support. In some cases, the role becomes one of simple administration due to the inability of the job holder in articulating what distinctive services can be offered.

A fifth identified role type was that of the 'Role in Transition', where the job holder has some characteristics of the 'Provider' role, coupled with others of the 'Training Manager' or 'Change Agent'.

Pettigrew's team identified two key issues from their research. First, successful training activities depend (as in many other management level jobs) upon the training officer's personal effectiveness, which itself is a function of the degree of 'fit' or 'congruence' between the organisation culture, the personality and style of the job holder, and the role assumed. A training officer therefore needs to recognise that there may be a choice of roles that can be played, and to select the most appropriate one (for her/him in the particular working context), and then to be able to meet others' expectations of what the role involves.

Second, questions of influence and survival 'result from the way the trainer, on an ongoing basis, manages the boundary between his or her activity and the rest of the organisation'.

These researchers examined the essential but largely ignored theme of role relationships in training through the concepts of power resources, legitimacy, and boundary management ('the system of exchanges a function, activity, or role, has with its environment'). This part of their study was concerned with five major requirements, how the training officer:

- acquires resources and disposes of inputs
- exercises influence
- builds relationships and activates an image
- protects territorial integrity
- coordinates activities with other roles and units of the organisation.

Pettigrew and his co-authors considered the training officer's 'power bases' and 'cultural identification' (expertise at using aspects of the organisation's culture) to be central to the effective functioning of the job. They developed the theme of power resources available, e.g. political access, cultural identification, credibility, and access to information, and argued that successful boundary management and cultural identification are much more important than technical competence. Assuming this argument is accepted, these things would seem to need to be grafted on to the standards published nearly a decade later by the Training and Development Lead Body by further sophistication of specific performance criteria set out in those standards.

While the main contribution of the work of Pettigrew, Jones and Reason is that it offers a much needed theoretical framework for the analysis and understanding of training officer roles in the context of power and relationships, it is necessary to appreciate that the sample was relatively small and that the study relates to the perceptions of training officers only. Nonetheless, the research provides an important basis for further conceptual analysis of the place of the training function within the work organisation.

Mapping the Boundaries

All functions must be managed within a set of prevailing constraints, which effectively map and define their 'boundaries'.

The more easily defined constraints are external. The law, for example, imposes requirements and barriers in employment matters (e.g. in the health and safety field); in some European countries employment law extends to training matters, giving some employees rights and regulating employers' responses to employee requests for training facilities. Similarly, involvement in UK government-sponsored national training schemes makes demands on any employer who participates. At a less regulatory level, a decision to use external training resources imposes constraints (e.g. courses mounted by a local Further Education college must conform to the college's three-term timetable).

But the main constraints are likely to be less obvious 'internal' demands, imposed by the organisation itself, affecting *intrinsically* the type and depth of training interventions, and the way the function is organised. Managing the function in a way that accepts and supports these constraints is critical to making the training function 'operational' in the eyes of management generally. There are four key internal constraints: policy, strategy, resource, and culture (the latter including management style).

Policy
During the period of the ITBs, it was normal for them to 'recommend' a written policy statement on training; that statement would appear in careers handbooks, in recruitment and induction material, in management manuals, and on notice boards. It might contain explicit commitments – for example, to provide paid release facilities for certain categories of staff, or to grant pay increases to all attaining a specific qualification, or even to 'train all employees to the limit of their abilities'. It might specify certain training schemes – for example, apprenticeship and management traineeship schemes. And it might stress the importance of certain processes – for example, induction, appraisal, or safety.

Whilst some organisations may have allowed their written statements of training policy to gather dust since the demise of the ITBs, others have built upon them. The interim period has of course seen the emergence of newly important policy messages – on, for example, equal opportunities, disabled persons, and health and safety, all of which have implications for the training function. ANY policy statements will act as a constraint on management: managers must work within them if they are properly to represent their organisation in their decision making. Training policy statements typically contain a statement of principles, and perhaps aims, which must be followed, plus a set of procedures and regulations which guide decisions. But even if there is no written policy statement, the training function will in practice be conditioned by whatever top management, or the main opinion moulders in the organisation, are perceived as expecting under these headings (see also pages 211ff).

Strategy
Similarly – and much more frequently – operational strategy is likely to constrain many decisions on employee development (unless, as in the continuous development ideal, learning is itself explicitly given priority in the strategic plan). Strategy is essentially about purpose and choice: priorities emerge which should be reflected in management decisions. For example, if XYZ Limited's strategy makes Brand A superior to all other brands, it is likely that training investment should be weighted to that end (in other words, the organisation's learning strategy should reflect its operational priorities). We will explore later in this book how an organisation might set up its own learning strategy.

Resource
It is fairly obvious that large organisations, with substantial central service units, have more resources available than their smaller colleagues. The latter may not even have anyone explicitly responsible for developing the systems that stimulate training interventions. But 'internal' resources may perhaps be extended to include resources easily available – for example, a nearby Further Education college or a group training scheme run by a consortium of local employers. Such resources will both facilitate and constrain: they may offer training means, but within an approach which is not preferred.

Culture, including Management Style
Organisational culture is not easily defined (see Williams, Dobson and Walters, 1989 – who cite one text which itself cites 164 definitions of the term). It is essentially a collective term, bringing together the ideas, beliefs, attitudes and values that exist within the organisation, the form of which few employees are likely to appreciate. It is perhaps most easily 'seen' in the way management manage: the prevailing management style reflects the culture. And as with all other management functions, decisions on employee development will be influenced by the prevailing management style, especially that of the chief opinion moulders in the organisation. It follows that the influence may be either 'for' or 'against' training activity, and that where it is 'for' it may be selective in its favours. This is

the prime reason why so many textbooks on personnel and training management stress the importance of top management giving a lead: they recognise that the absence of such a lead imposes an effective straightjacket on less powerful staff who seek any new development.

Personnel and training managers typically accept responsibility for describing their organisation's culture and management style. The description needs to be unique; few if any organisations mirror simple stereotypes, and a given culture is likely to comprise a series of subcultures, not all of which are consistent with each other. Nevertheless, five main culture types prevail, and their implications for training interventions are clear (see Handy (1985) for a summary treatment of the first four):

1 The Power-based (P1) culture

The P1 organisation is recognised by the efforts of its opinion-moulders to exercise power over subordinates, colleagues and contacts of all kinds. (See Schein (1970) for a useful summary of Etzioni's (1961) substantial treatment.) Whilst the alignment of power does not necessarily conform to the formal organisation chart, decisions are usually taken by individuals, not groups, and training is essentially something that is 'imposed on others'. Training plans are likely to reflect attempts by those in power to improve the performance of those who are not.

2 The People-based (P2) culture

P2 means 'process first': consensus is prized, and group decisions are encouraged. Training activities will often reflect individual requests (e.g. for attendance at external events), and projects, attachments and even job movements will be arranged to give employees the opportunity to develop themselves.

3 The Role-based (R) culture

The R organisation is bureaucratic: it operates largely on the basis of 'rules' i.e. norms which are written down and seen as being collectively owned. Training systems may be similarly defined by written documents, and 'standard' programmes and courses are likely to be followed by all in specific categories or groups.

4 The Task-based (T) culture

T organisations put task before process, and concentrate their activity on whatever happen to be current work goals. Training needs are therefore similarly defined, and training plans reflect the latest work-based appraisal data or newly defined competences. T cultures also typically put much human effort into organising and managing group or team activity in the service of the common task; hence training plans will often be determined and described on a group basis.

5 *The Quality-based (Q) culture*

Recent years have seen a dramatic increase in interest in a philosophy which sets quality before everything else. The so-called 'Total Quality Management' approach demands that all employees understand a common language concerning quality, and commit themselves to conforming to detailed standards. (See Collard (1989) for a comprehensive discussion of the TQM approach.) In such a culture, structured 'quality education courses' are a norm (a fifteen-step education process is not unusual), and each department houses quality improvement teams which, often with the aid of a consultant, devise new techniques; group learning events are mounted to train in new techniques, and to confront employees with discrepancies between their beliefs and their behaviour. Training is not itself likely to be stressed as a function: all types and levels of employee are expected to learn 'to the required standard'. Training staff are nevertheless firmly integrated into the system.

Much more might be written here concerning the impact of culture on employee development. Many professional trainers argue that the cultural constraint is also the opportunity: those carrying responsibility for the training function can, if they are themselves capable enough, propose training interventions aimed at changing the constraint itself. We will say something about training as a cultural change agent when we come to address the continuous development culture (which you will notice we do not offer as one of the main cultural types already in existence) in Chapter 12; for the time being, however, it would be wise merely to record that as with other management functions, any given training function will have developed, and will probably further develop, in line with the assumptions governing the organisation's operational activities in general.

Arranging the Structure

The need to structure the training function 'appropriately' within the organisation is easy to prescribe and difficult to describe. There is no one correct way of 'positioning' the training department within organisations which vary in such respects as employee numbers, employee types, geographical sites, organisation charts, historical tradition, management style.

In a very large number of small organisations, and a minute proportion of large organisations, the employee development function is not itself detailed at all. Responsibility is held to rest with line supervision and management, and corporate decisions are taken by the owner, managing director, or whoever else is the senior executive. In organisations which number more than 100 but less than 250 employees, it is often the case that a personnel function (or department, or unit) exists, and the personnel function is taken to subsume that of employee development; in many such organisations, the personnel manager is unlikely to be served by substantial resources, and he or she will not be able to spend a large proportion of working hours on employee development matters; typically, the department will arrange for external training activity (e.g. vocational courses at local colleges) to be patronised. Some small companies meet their needs and obtain much valued resources by joining group training schemes or consortia, which plan and manage training for specific categories of staff, or use an external training consultant/advisor on a permanent contract.

But the vast majority of middle-sized to large organisations, both public and private, do now formally describe and place the function in their charts. Role designations vary considerably, as can be seen from the following list of existing titles (which is by no means exhaustive):

- Human Resources Director
- Human Resources Controller
- Human Resource Development Manager
- Human Resource Development Officer
- Personnel Director
- Personnel Controller
- Personnel Development Manager
- Personnel Operations Manager
- Group Training Director
- Group Training Manager
- Group Training Officer
- Group Employee Development Manager
- Company Training Manager
- Company Training and Development Manager
- Training Manager

- General Training Manager
- General Training Officer
- Training Officer
- Training Adviser
- Employee Development Manager
- Employee Development Officer
- Employee Development Adviser
- Mangement Development Manager
- Management Development Officer
- Sales Training Manager
- Sales Training Officer
- Technical Training Manager
- Apprentice Training Officer
- Instructor

Some of these positions – notably those in the second half of the list – are sometimes observable as 'part-time' posts in specific organisations, or perhaps held in conjunction with other positions (e.g. the Company Secretary may also handle the Management Development role; a Regional Sales Manager may also be the Sales Training Manager). The essential need for an 'appropriate structure' is not met simply by choosing titles for those carrying responsibilities. The function must attempt to 'fit' all those strategic, political and cultural items already discussed; above all, it must be integrated with the overall personnel management function, and, equally importantly, with other operating functions. Here are a few examples of this sort of integration:

Example A is a smallish company which operates on only one site, apart from a small field sales force, and it does not itself run training events of any kind, except for a short induction course for new starters. Training needs have always been satisfied by sending young entrants on part-time courses at the local college of Further Education, or (in the case of supervisors and managers) to selected short external courses run by various providers. The employee development function is not itself to be seen in the formal organisation chart: it is in fact carried by the Personnel Department.

Induction courses are run about once every two months by either of the two Personnel Officers, who draw on others (e.g. the Safety Officer) to handle individual sessions. The Admin Supervisor keeps information on external courses, makes all bookings, and arranges for the fees to be paid. She also records course attendances on personal files. The Admin Supervisor also issues blank appraisal report forms (covering only management grades); reports incorporate salary recommendations, but not training needs. Line management and supervision determine who attends what courses, and when.

This is an authoritarian, tight-knit organisation, run by management who believe in helping young people to acquire formal qualifications, but have no current belief in the need to plan learning on a continuing basis, and do not aspire to any sophisticated employee development plans.

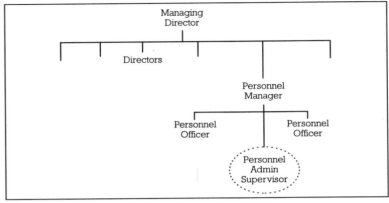

Figure 6.4
Organisation Chart – Example A

Example B is somewhat larger than A in numbers of employees, although it also operates from a single site; and it does have a Training Department. That department is responsible directly to the Chairman, who is an enthusiastic supporter of youth and management training but believes the company should manage these matters internally, to ensure learning is geared to the actual workplace. The Training Department is in reality a Training Centre: it comprises a youth training workshop (covering engineering and secretarial skills) and a residential building in which management courses are run. Induction courses are also held in the Training Centre.

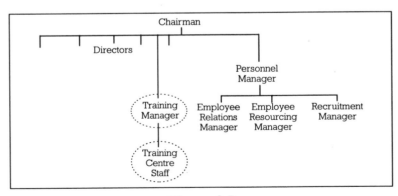

Figure 6.5
Organisation Chart – Example B

Recruitment, appraisal and other personnel procedures are managed from within the sister Personnel Department. In recent years, the Chairman has insisted that his Training Manager develops (mainly by purchasing appropriate hardware and software) a range of self-study facilities, with the result that the Training Centre is now called a 'learning resources centre': employees can apply to attend and have access to audio-visual and computer-based programmes. Access is guaranteed outside normal working hours; during working hours, the decision to allow the use of these facilities is shared between the Training Manager and the line manager.

Example C is a small provincial building society, which has 35 branch offices all within about 40 miles of the company's head office. The company is diversifying into a wide range of new customer services; these developments are led by a Marketing Department, staffed by so-called Development Managers. Branch offices are closed to the public until 11 a.m. each Tuesday: this time is 'operational training time', and is used both to train in new procedures and to discuss problems with office staff. Branch Office Managers lead the Tuesday morning training sessions, but their formal content is agreed in advance with the relevant Development Manager, who often attends and indeed sometimes operates as an instructor.

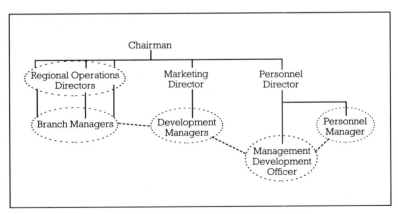

Figure 6.6
Organisation Chart – Example C

The Personnel Director, the Company Personnel Manager, and a Management Development Officer all operate from Head Office; they handle all other employee development activities, including central induction, further education regulations, liaison with outside training providers, attendance at management courses and conferences, management trainee programmes, and 'one-off' programmes created for managers before or on promotion. Line Directors have a major role to play in the management development system, maintaining succession plans and mounting periodic interviews with all who are on promotion lists.

Example D is an 800-strong County Surveyor's Department within a 3,700-strong County Council. The department has been run on a geographical and 'public service' basis, but has had to restructure in order both to meet new budget constraints and to become more openly accountable. The County Surveyor and his immediate subordinates have agreed a new structure for the department as follows:

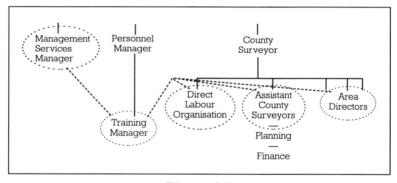

Figure 6.7
Organisation Chart – Example D

In this arrangement, the 'DLO' ('Direct Labour Organisation') manages the maintenance and works staff, and produces tenders for jobs in competition with outside contractors – a new approach which did not immediately engage employee support. The County Surveyor's team has therefore promoted a major training programme aimed at changing the departmental culture; in conjunction with the authority's central Management Services

Department, management seminars have been held using specially prepared computerised simulations (business games) which demand consideration of issues of business strategy, plus open discussions on topics such as 'The New Philosophy' and 'Customer Awareness'. The leaders at these seminars are the County Surveyor and his team; some administrative arrangements are handled by the central Personnel Manager's Department, but seminar resources are all supplied by officers from Management Services, who are well versed in the computerised games. The Personnel Manager is himself somewhat concerned at the speed with which a strong sense of identity is being developed, and work is often being completed against external contracts; his concern is not for the efficiency of this unit, but for the jealousy emerging in other authority departments.

Example E is a supermarket chain, with many branches and an annual intake of around 350 retail management trainees, whose recruitment is a major annual operation, and whose later development has justified the emergence of a large central training unit. This unit reports to a member of the board known as the Management Development Director; to him a number of managers are responsible, including a Career Development Controller, and several Training Officers.

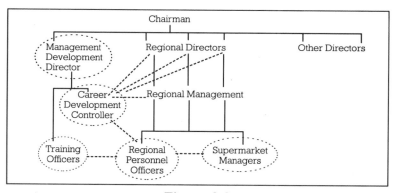

Figure 6.8
Organisation Chart – Example E

Apart from engaging in the annual recruitment 'milkround', and running specific management courses and conferences, the main role of the Management Development Department has been to manage the management training system and its outputs. This involves endless discussions – with trainees, and with regional and district personnel office staff – about the objectives and methods in individual programmes. The department has detailed some forty 'areas of competence' (e.g. stock control, running wines and spirits, opening new stores) which must be mastered by a trainee before an initial management appointment; specific plans are worked out for each individual, the vast mass of actual learning being completed in real-life shop circumstances. The final say on what is included in a personal plan rests with the central Career Development Controller; but in practice, decisions are invariably jointly taken, with regional personnel officers handling the liaison with supermarket management (who themselves take on the day-to-day training and instructor roles).

Example F is a large company, with several thousand employees (including several hundred managers), and operations involving a Head Office, two manufacturing sites and a regionally organised national Sales Force. The company has a long history of training – applied to all departments and all levels of employee. Full-time Training Managers exist in each functional department (Technical Department has one in each factory). Company and departmental training plans are created every six months.

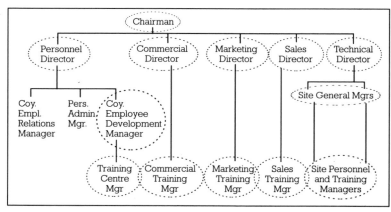

Figure 6.9
Organisation Chart – Example F

In this company, a matrix arrangement ensures that responsibilities are often shared, but one person will always carry PRIME responsibility for training within each site or department, or for training applied to a specific category, or for a given training task. The nature of the matrix can be appreciated from this extract:

Responsibility	Chairman	Pers'l Director	Other Dir's	Site Gen. Mgr.	Coy. Empl. Dev. Mgr.	Training Centre Mgr.	Functional Training Mgrs.	Site P&T Mgrs.
E D Policy	★	●	★					
Corporate Trg. Needs/Priorities	★	★	●	★	†			
E D Systems		★	★	★	●		†	
E D Budgets		★			†	★	★	★
Mgt Development	†	•	★	★	★			
Mgt Trainee Programmes		★	★		●		†	★
Departmental Training Needs + Plans			●	†	★		†	★
Individual Training Needs + Plans							†	●
Formal Course Management					★	●	★	
Liaison with Outside Training Providers						†	†	†
etc.								
etc.								

Key: ★ = Some responsibility   † = Major responsibility   ● = Prime responsibility

Figure 6.10
Matrix Organisation – Example F

Example G is perhaps more than a little futuristic in character. It reflects the currently developing concept of the 'virtual organisation' – a term borrowed from computer terminology, where it is defined as 'not physically existing as such, but made by software to appear to do so'. This is not easy to translate into an organisational model, but might typically describe an operational set-up which is project-based, with new projects appearing frequently and project teams endlessly re-forming to tackle them. Each change brings with it new roles, new relationships, and (most importantly) new and unique information needs. These information needs are satisfied by access to external databases – which, programmed properly and married with simulation methods, provide new knowledge *and* suggest how it might be used, *and even* offer a forward view of what the results of adopting the information will be (hence 'not existing, but made by software to appear to do so'). In our example, project teams are formed and re-formed by the project leaders, who also operate as team members but carry the prime responsibility for resolving detailed day-to-day problems in the ongoing management of each project; team members access the databases using their own computers and telephones. Project work moves forward as members, operating in 'chains' or networks, feed their personal findings to colleagues via unique processes which are regularly reviewed at team meetings. Training interventions are frequent and commonplace, but the word 'training' is rarely used, as the learning system is effectively integrated with the project work (see the 'Open System' model in Figure 12.3, and 'Key CD concepts', pages 358–62). Everyone nevertheless has a 'training function', and a contribution to make to the corporate learning system, even if in most cases they are serving temporary ends. Two key roles exist, however – that of the IT specialist/s who maintain and develop the information system, and that of the process consultant/s, whose job is to understand *and help project leaders and team members to understand* their own process reality. There is no 'training officer' *per se*; personnel officers handle induction training as part of the induction process, and provide the process review expertise.

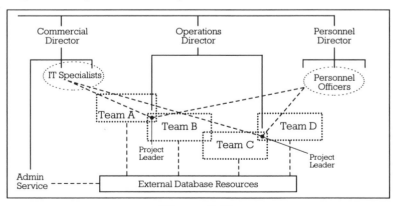

Figure 6.11
Virtual Organisation – Example G

It can be seen that advanced information technology is likely to promote flatter and more flexible organisations. It also tends to merge learning with work, and to make the individual the master of his or her unique learning process. An article in the *Independent on Sunday* (6 March 1994), discussing recent work by the well-known commentator Tom Peters, drew a picture of an environment in which 'independent contractors such as freelance journalists, software programmers and gardeners, wake up knowing that before sunset they must (i) prove themselves again with their clients, and (ii) learn a new wrinkle to improve their odds of survival'. The article then went on to suggest that everyone in salaried employment might need to achieve this same attitude. The key point is that the training function effectively becomes a learning function, and it is organised as part of work processes, not as an extra.

These seven examples underline the wide variety of possible ways of organising employee development activity in organisations. There is no one model that can be suggested as appropriate for any given size of unit, category of work or type of worker: each organisation must develop its own, aiming to 'fit' employee development into its operational activities in line with its policy, its purpose, its environmental constraints and opportunities and the imagination of its personnel and training staff. As we shall see in future Chapters, the nature of this 'fit' is an important determinant in the selection of the most appropriate training approach and methodology.

THE TRAINING OF PERSONNEL AND TRAINING STAFF

From the above discussion of the many roles that training staff undertake, and their dependence upon their own organisational environment, it follows that the knowledge, skills and attitudes required for effective trainer performance will vary from individual to individual, and indeed will be subject to change in response to the dynamism of the workplace. Despite the 'definitive' list of competences set out by the Training and Development Lead Body, there is no one set of abilities needed by all trainers. We shall explore various ways whereby a specific person's training needs can be identified and an appropriate training programme constructed. The Lead Body's list may well prove a useful reference document during this task, but it must be complemented by information on the precise roles to be carried out in the organisational setting, and the abilities which those roles demand.

We have already noted that the Lead Body excludes knowledge from its competences list: knowledge is held to *underpin* but not to constitute competence. There are nevertheless some 'common areas of know-how', as recognised by the 1978 Manpower Services Commission report entitled *Training of Trainers*, which are fundamental to trainer jobs, and these must clearly be satisfied in any new appointment. These common areas of know-how are:

- the organisation, its business and its employees
- the training function and its specialist roles
- learning and the design of learning
- national education and training systems and resources (including any key EU requirements and trends)
- people in organisations.

The first of these can only be satisfied by a training programme which is specific to the employing organisation (this alone justifies the claim that *all* newly-recruited training staff, however experienced, require an initial training programme). Organisations must judge for themselves whether other areas must be covered by in-house activities. For many years, employers accepted satisfactory completion of either the Institute of Personnel Management's final professional examinations or possession of the Institute of Training and Development's diploma as adequate evidence of basic know-how in these areas; external recruitment advertisements typically demanded one or either of these. The picture is now perhaps less clear, as these two institutes merged in mid-1994 to form the Institute of Personnel and Development (IPD – which, with over 70,000 members, is now Europe's largest body of personnel and development professionals). At the time of writing (also mid-1994), the impact upon ex-IPM and ex-IPD professional qualifications is still to be clarified: it is certain that corporate membership already approved by either former Institute justifies corporate membership of the new one, but possession of the ITD diploma alone is unlikely to give future exemption from all IPD professional examinations. IPD have announced that it will be at least July 1995 before the task of defining, maintaining and developing the new professional membership requirements will have been finalised. The relevant part of the ex-IPM syllabus, and that for the ex-ITD diploma, are summarised in Figure 6.12.

IPM	**ITD**
• National Policy and Practice	• The Management of Training
• Learning Philosophy	
• The Role of T&D within the Organisation	• Individual and Group Learning
	• Management Development
• The Training and Development Process	• Training for Change
• Specific Approaches and Issues	• The Organisation and its Environment
	• Management and the Management of Resources

Figure 6.12
Former IPM and ITD Syllabuses

We have seen earlier (pages 149–51) that the Training and Development Lead Body's national standards have a different conceptual base. That Lead Body have announced that their standards apply to NVQs/SVQs which are at Levels 3 and 4: that is, below the normal professional qualifications level. It has also been announced that NVQs and SVQs in Training and Development will be offered by:

• the Business and Technology Education Council (BTEC)
• the City and Guilds of London Institute (CGLI)
• Pitmans Examinations Institute
• the Royal Society of Arts Examinations Board
• the Scottish Vocational and Education Council.

The former ITD were also included in this list before their merger with IPM; that merger has surely established the new IPD as the predominant body capable of planning future qualifications in this sphere, but as yet

(July 1994) there has been no announcement of an impending IPD diploma to succeed the ITD qualification. It should perhaps be stressed that IPM, and indeed the new IPD, have rigorously defined the employee development function as being *within* the personnel (or human resource) management function, and whilst allowing a degree of specialisation in preparations for their final examinations, have insisted on the 'fundamental requirement' of studying the sister functions of employee relations and employee resourcing – demanding in particular an understanding of the working links between these functions and employee development. The IPD can also be expected to continue IPM's insistence on practical assignments, and a major work-based management report (which can be tailored to fit the learner's workplace needs, and involves employer collaboration) within the mainstream qualifying process.

Yet another major influence exists – the *Personnel* Standards Lead Body (PSLB), who sit alongside their older TSLB sister but whose work inevitably overlaps, since they have with what seems good reason included as one of their five defined areas of personnel management an area labelled 'Development'. In common with other Lead Bodies' standards, those from the PSLB incorporate units and elements of competence, performance criteria and range statements (see pages 122–3, 150–2 and 248–9); but unlike some, they also include 'underpinning knowledge and understanding', 'evidence requirements' and 'personal qualities', the latter expressed as behaviours.

In July 1994 the PSLB standards were launched in a 'consultative third draft' form; at that time the 'Development' area was subdivided into seven competence units and a total of 27 competence elements. It is worth noting that functional and occupational surveys conducted by the PSLB during 1993, and covering some 1,000 personnel practitioners, showed 'Development' area competences as all of high importance for organisational success, but likewise *not* (to date) performed well; the PSLB thus decreed these as 'priorities for competence development'.

The work of the PSLB may be considered conceptually superior to that of the TDLB, in that it has stressed a strategic approach, addressed *both* specialist *and* generalist personnel management, acknowledged line management's personnel and training roles, extended into both management units (some of which have been copied from the Management Charter Group's lists), and even incorporates professional and ethical competences, the latter including a continuous development aspect. Future personnel and training professionals are clearly to be expected to understand all their organisation's other functions (e.g. finance), and are expected to stand up for continuously reviewed professional principles and ethical goals.

The PSLB and the TDLB are due to come together (along with the Lead Body for Trade Union staff) within a single Occupational Standards Council during the autumn of 1994. Whether thereafter we will see an attempt to standardise where overlaps exist, or perhaps to rationalise differences, seems unlikely, at least in the near future. At the time of the July 1994 launch, only one unit of competence – 'Introduce Improvements to Training and Development within an Organisation' – had been copied verbatim by the PSLB from TSLB standards. The PSLB did, however, promise that NVQs/SVQs would be developed by early 1995 at all of Levels 3, 4 and 5; these were described respectively as 'basic', 'professional' and 'seasoned professional'. At each of these levels a draft structure set out a *core*, plus several *compulsory* competence units, and some further *options* from which the student may choose. The structure could be further modified dependent upon whether a generalist or specialist qualification is sought. The PSLB has stressed its intention to promote flexibility to the point where qualification routes do not have to be completed in total, thus serving line management's and established professionals' specific needs without a 'sausage-machine' imperative. This is in total a complex and ambitious aim, and it remains to be seen whether tomorrow's personnel professionals will value the amount of sophistication involved. Whether the draft PSLB qualifications structure will be adopted, and/or how TDLB and PSLB standards themselves might be adapted by bodies offering qualifications, and in particular by IPD, is far from clear; presumably IPD is currently addressing this very task. IPD has however properly stressed that the attainment of professional IPD membership means more than the attainment of a qualification.

It seems certain that a definitive description of what constitutes an 'employee development professional' remains some way off, if indeed it can ever be achieved; perhaps a single, common stereotype will never emerge, whilst a range of alternative qualifications, only some of which treat employee development as an integral part of personnel management, will satisfy the variable requirements that the UK generally accepts. If this proves to be the case, the appearance of a standardised qualification throughout Europe (see pages 35 and 308) can be expected to be delayed for quite some time.

Whatever the future for qualifications, the work of both the TDLB and the PSLB offers extensive reference material for use in the establishment of specific training plans and programmes for personnel and training staff, and again for line management in their employee development roles. TDLB majors in implementation areas such as identifying needs and creating specific training plans; PSLB majors in strategy, organisation and system improvement, plus (as part of general management competences) team building and working relationships. A mention should also be made of two other Lead Bodies – those for Open Learning Staff and for Advice guidance and Counselling – both of which have similarly created detailed standards in their own fields.

Before their merger, both IPM and ITD had their own codes of professional practice (also now under review). Both contained 'rules' relating to personal behaviour, relationships with employers and employees, and responsibilities to others. IPM went further than ITD in describing members' 'primary' responsibility to be to their employer; ITD exceeded IPM in detailing specific responsibilities (e.g. 'establish realistic plans to meet stated learning objectives'). Both codes stressed the importance of commitment to improved performance. The ex-ITD Code is reproduced as Appendix 5.

You might now review your own learning from this chapter by working on the following short tasks:

1 Imagine you are the first Training Manager appointed by a newly-formed company, which operates from a single site and includes a small manufacturing unit and an adjoining suite of offices. You work in the Personnel Department, reporting to the Personnel Manager. Fill in for yourself the details concerning numbers of staff, type of operation, top management, etc.

(a) List the main work areas for which you expect to be responsible.

(b) List the people with whom you expect to be regularly in contact.

(c) Draw a chart/map describing your place in the organisation.

2 Now imagine you are in the same job five years later – by which time the company has expanded to control two sites plus a small sales force. People are being recruited regularly, and formal courses are being run on site (again, fill in any further details for yourself). You now have three subordinates working for you in what is called the 'Training Department'.

(a) List your main responsibilities.

(b) List the main work areas for which each of your subordinates is responsible.

(c) Draw a chart/map describing the position of the Training Department within the company, and its internal organisation.

FOR FURTHER REFLECTION AND DISCUSSION

1 You are a personnel manager in an organisation which has just appointed a new training officer, who will report to you. You have not previously worked with the newcomer. You feel strongly – on both 'cost' and 'results' grounds – that training is first and foremost a line management responsibility, and that training should be primarily aimed at improving workplace performance. What would you include in your brief to your new subordinate, and why?

2 Do you agree that if and when personnel or training managers publicly criticise line management for their lack of interest in training, it damages the image of the personnel and training functions?

3 What are the main factors influencing the way in which the training function is (a) described, and (b) organised?

4 What are the advantages and disadvantages of an organisational arrangement that places the employee development function outside the personnel department?

5 How should small businesses, whose top management believe they cannot afford full-time or part-time trainers, organise to ensure that training happens?

6 Take any organisation with which you are familiar. How would you expect the training function in this organisation to be influenced by the upgrading of communication and information systems to the point where it operates as a 'virtual organisation'?

SUGGESTED READING

Texts which specialise in the organisation of the training function are rare.

HARRISON R. *Training and Development.* Institute of Personnel Management, London, 1988. Offers a stimulating mixture of guidance, case material and 'activities'.

CHILD J. *Organization: A Guide to Problems and Practice.* Harper and Row, London, 1982. This is a comprehensive outline of the many choices that must be made when attempting to organise ANY function.

MOORBY E. *How to Succeed in Training and Development.* McGraw Hill, Maidenhead, 1991. Opens with an illuminating chapter entitled 'A Week in the Life of a Training Manager'.

As our text explains, the TRAINING AND DEVELOPMENT LEAD BODY's *National Standard for Training and Development* is the most detailed description of Training roles yet produced.

Chapter 7
ASSESSING ORGANISATIONAL TRAINING NEEDS

The levels of organisation needs – types of organisational reviews – before starting the review – reasons for an organisational review – carrying out an organisation-wide review.

INTRODUCTION

'Recent research in France has revealed that a prominent French banking organisation achieved rather negative results after a large investment in an extensive training programme, primarily because of the failure to analyse the training needs within the organisation. There was thus an inability to relate the training investment to the overall HR and business strategy. The authors suggest that this is much more representative of the way organisations operate than their management teams would care to admit.'

Holden and Livian (1992)

This quotation comes from an account of an international survey carried out as part of the Price Waterhouse Cranfield Project, which showed a high percentage of organisations claiming to analyse their training needs systematically. The highest percentage was 85 per cent in France, followed by 80 per cent in the UK, whilst the lowest was Germany at 55 per cent. This appears impressive until the authors point out that the respondents to the survey included many 'good practice' organisations, of which it can be seen that nearly a quarter in the UK and nearly a half in Germany, did not do a systematic analysis. As you read this chapter, you might try to decide why you think this is. The favoured method of assessment varied from country to country, France, Italy and the Netherlands preferring 'analysis of business plans', Sweden and the UK considering staff appraisal to be the most important, whilst Switzerland, Denmark and Spain opted for 'Line Management Requests'. (Holden and Livian, 1992 op. cit.)

If an organisation is to achieve its goals it must have sufficient numbers of people with the appropriate skills. The training function's strategic contribution to corporate objectives is to help to provide this vital expertise. In this chapter we explain how training needs analysis at a corporate or organisational level is a critical step in the process. We show that training needs exist at different levels within organisations and we consider a variety of approaches to identifying organisational needs. We give examples of the reasons why top management decide to investigate training needs at a corporate level and illustrate the stages in carrying out an organisation-wide needs review.

Such a review was the first requirement stipulated by the ITBs for the payment of training grant. This was usually carried out by the training officer, or a consultant, or a member of management responsible for the function. The rationale was that in order to prioritise the training effort towards the strategic objectives of the business, it was necessary to undertake a careful analysis of all that was required. This is still sound logic, but there is another side to the coin: an organisation-wide exercise can be expensive and may require much time and energy to produce a vast amount of paperwork before any much needed training is started.

You might also be wondering how such a review relates to some of the concepts and developments already outlined in this book; for example, the 'self-generating nature of the spiral of continuous development', illustrated in Chapter 3, and the concept of a 'learning organisation'. You might also ask how a training needs review focused on broadly (or even narrowly) defined objectives of the business fits into a 'learner centred' environment. It is obvious that there is no one best method of assessing needs; on the contrary there is a variety of approaches, each of which can be adapted to suit particular contexts.

Imagine a continuum, featuring at one end the strictly analytical and controlled, such as the 'global' review outlined on page 180 below, whilst at the other extreme will be found processes based on the philosophy that people are capable (or can learn to be capable) of defining their own training needs either individually, or more usually, in groups. In between come a variety of measures, or combinations of measures, which might contain elements of either extreme. The analytical movement flourished under the early training boards and is receiving new impetus from developments such as NCVQ and competence based approaches. Action learning reigns at the other end of the continuum, along with project groups and quality circles, the exact position of which might vary according to their terms of reference.

Before discussing these approaches it will be helpful to define the parameters of this chapter, by distinguishing the different levels of training needs.

THE LEVELS OF ORGANISATION NEEDS

A retailing company suffered bad publicity due to press and TV coverage of unfortunate incidents in some of its branches. In a number of cases the company's employees were alleged to have had a very poor attitude towards customers' requests for after-sales service. The Chairman called for an urgent investigation. The subsequent report accepted the criticisms but showed that in almost every case the employees were competent in selling, but, because of work pressure in the branches and management emphasis on high sales targets, there had been insufficient attention paid to the importance of after-sales service. The report stipulated that this weakness must, as a matter of priority, be addressed both by management directives and training, and the Training Officer was instructed to take immediate action. She worked with line management in reviewing, and amending, as necessary, the job specifications of both managers and staff, and then provided training for those employees who were assessed to require it.

This case illustrates that training needs, as Boydell (1983) has suggested, can exist at three levels:

At the organisational level
There was a general weakness in the way the organisation had perceived its priorities and the prescribed remedy would require modification of the organisation culture.

At the job or occupational level
There was recognition that certain groups of employees needed to improve performance; most, if not all, jobs had to be redefined in terms of competences required to meet new standards.

At the individual employee level
The present abilities (skills, knowledge and attitudes) of each member

of staff concerned had to be assessed against the higher standards now needed to carry out their work satisfactorily, and any shortfall remedied through training.

It is the first of these levels with which we are immediately concerned; the second and third levels will be the subject of Chapter 9.

The needs at these levels can sometimes conflict; for instance, a school leaver requires training to stand him in good stead for future promotion or job seeking elsewhere, (hence the justification for programmes such as YT), but the short-term organisation need may be very narrow and specific. If there are insufficient promotion prospects or opportunities for wider experience, the long-term development of the employee may be sacrificed to the specific requirements of business objectives. Although management may be aware of the need for new experience and fresh challenges, it is not always possible to provide them at the right moment, particularly in times of recession, when budgets are reduced; the enthusiastic may thus become frustrated. However, the current trend towards flatter organisation structures (where the tiers of the hierarchy are reduced and more staff require a broader base of skills, reward often being based on output and value added contribution rather than rank), should encourage learning contracts and help towards providing wider experience, as may the use of project teams. NVQ programmes, both external and in-company, offer a framework for career progression, providing recognised and 'portable' qualifications for the individual, and possibly at the same time meeting organisation needs.

TYPES OF ORGANISATIONAL REVIEWS

The 'Global' Review

This was the type originally specified as a condition of grant by the early training boards. The review started with an examination of the organisation's short-term and long-term objectives, the purpose being to ensure that the training effort was correctly targeted to the strategic needs of the business. In its extreme form it was a very time-consuming exercise; the training officer, in a mechanistic way, would analyse every job category in the organisation, from the least skilled to the managing director and produce job specifications. Each employee was then to be assessed against the appropriate specification and training provided when a shortfall was identified. In many cases, the result was the production of a mass of paperwork, which in some cases was mainly used for the purposes of trying to reclaim grant from the appropriate ITB. The current NCVQ approach (see Chapters 2, 5, 9 and 11) requires a specification of competences and standards which could obviously provide a similar basis for training needs review.

These criticisms should not be taken to mean that a global approach is never an appropriate strategy, although it is difficult to imagine circumstances in which the extremely mechanistic approach we have just described would be justified. It can, however, also be used differentially, that is, applied in a very detailed way in some departments where there may be a specific justification, but not in others.

Performance Management Approach

A well known contract catering group announced recently that they have taken a major step from old-style 'systematic' training to a new 'performance management' approach. They 'cascaded' the whole philosophy of training throughout the organisation, bringing the improvement of standards down to 'unit level'. Managers were required to draw up job descriptions for every member of staff, specifying standards against which performance was to be reviewed. Line managers accepted that training was an integral part of their management role and they were expected to possess or acquire the necessary skills. They then had to put together a systematic training programme for new staff, which provided a framework which could be related to NVQs.

This analytical approach consists of identifying specific and recognisable standards of work for all staff against which their performance can be assessed and their training needs established. It is attractive in that it is firmly related to outcomes, and provides a potential basis for performance related pay. It can easily be imagined that such schemes may involve much detail and computerised systems can be a great advantage. As the above example demonstrates, the standards can pertain to NVQ competences, and as the incidence of organisation-based NVQ programmes with their emphasis on workplace assessment increases, this may become a very common approach. It is useful in that, if used as in the example above, responsibility can be 'cascaded' down the hierarchy of line management and training becomes an integral part of the managerial responsibility. The process of 'cascading' responsibility is also compatible with the concept of Total Quality Management, which can then be linked with the continuous development of staff. The role of the training officer then becomes one of process consultant providing expert skills and advice.

For further information and in-depth cases studies of performance management see Neale (1991).

Critical Incident or 'Priority Problem' Analysis

In this model, the objective is not to produce a comprehensive list of every possible training need, but to identify and prioritise the main problems of the organisation which appear to have a training solution. An important point to note about the case of the retail company, is that it was not just the sales staff who required training to higher quality standards, but managers also, in that they needed an awareness of the concept of Total Quality Management and the ability to design appropriate procedures. This is an example of the 'skittle' effect described on page 104, where in order to achieve the desired effect, it may be necessary to include other targets before tackling the one which appears to be the most obvious. Priority or problem areas therefore require careful examination to determine where the problem really lies, and whether the solution also necessitates training for levels of staff who did not at first appear to be involved. This approach is nevertheless extremely important, as the main message for training officers must be *to determine which areas are vital to the strategic objectives, or possibly even the survival, of the organisation, and concentrate the main effort upon them.*

Critical incident analysis is a strategy which is likely to be suitable for small to medium-sized enterprises (SMEs), particularly at an early stage in their development. A study by Warwick University's Centre for Corporate Strategy and Change (1991), suggests that in an SME, particularly in its early stages, when markets are evolving, goods or services are being refined and the customer base broadened, training needs unfold rapidly and an *ad hoc* approach is required in order to maintain current viability. Flexibility and adaptability are more important than systematic across-the-board analyses of training needs based on job descriptions and specifications. After five to seven years, however, when the organisation has become more complex, and the numbers of staff have increased, new problems can arise, indicating the need for a different approach. For instance, people have not had time to develop their skills and keep up to date, or they have continued to learn on the job as the complexity has increased and there are difficulties in training new inexperienced staff to replace them. The findings suggest that 'there may be a natural life cycle of training, which matches the intake and progression of employees', the precise nature of the cycle differing from firm to firm. One wonders whether this could have had any influence on the international rankings of most important methods of assessment in the Price Waterhouse Cranfield Survey, mentioned above.

The report also emphasises the important role of the entrepreneur; this is reminiscent of the experience of the ITBs, which found that in the first instance, chief executives of SMEs often declared that they had no training needs; it was not until the entrepreneur was persuaded to undertake training himself that the need for more efficient methods of operating was recognized and training needs for other people began to unfold.

Learner Centred Analysis

We have implied that these types of analysis require the intervention of a training officer or consultant. Now imagine that you are a member of an organisation-based action learning set with important company goals to achieve (see Chapter 5) where, although, if circumstances demand it, your 'set adviser' might, albeit reluctantly, act at an appropriate time as a catalyst, an important part of your 'set's' functioning is to work out for yourselves how to determine what training and development you need in order to achieve your objectives, and to take steps (possibly assisted by the 'set adviser') to acquire it. Your learning in the 'set' is essentially targeted directly at organisation needs, because it is encapsulated in the action itself. At the same time it is highly developmental and an embodiment of 'learning to learn', thus bringing together the needs of the organisation and those of the individual. The whole process is an important part of your learning experience, and unless an intervening training officer approached her task in a highly participative and democratic manner, the culture and norms gradually developed by your 'set' might cause you to resent the 'external' person probing into your training needs.

Similarly, in a 'task' culture (see Handy, 1985), where knowledge and skill requirements might vary from one project group to another, the first, most important *group task* might be to determine its own learning needs in order to complete the project. Quality Circles are likely to display the same characteristic. Although she might be called upon for assistance, the uninvited intervention of a training officer might well be regarded as an interference. The approach to identifying training needs and the manner in which the task is carried out, will therefore be influenced by the organisation culture. A mechanistic form of global analysis is likely to be most suitable for a 'role' culture, where the content of jobs can be specified in detail, and is likely to remain constant for long enough to make all the necessary analytical work worthwhile. Current trends, particularly those relating to NVQs, are analytical; but is there a contradiction here? The pace of change is accelerating, and in such a climate, will top managers not tend to assign the key problems of the company to project teams, whose responsibility it will be to determine their own needs, and possibly those of others whose jobs impinge upon the task in hand? Perhaps the question we should be asking is 'how can we develop people to develop themselves?' Training needs are never static, they *unfold* as situations develop, even more so in a changing environment. Whilst it is logical and necessary to produce an overall assessment as a basis for a company training plan targeted at organisational objectives and for boardroom justification of the budget, such a document rarely offers more than a snapshot in time.

BEFORE STARTING THE REVIEW

Now imagine you are the senior training officer of a large national building society, which has decided to instigate a formal training review, to be carried out every three years; you have been asked to draft proposals for its content and process and to create an appropriate statement for discussion at a future top management meeting. What would your first considerations be? How would you set about your task? Would it be different from that of Joe Brown, who was at the same time undertaking a training review in the small sweet factory in which he was employed?

Congratulations if your first query concerned the purpose of the review! This would determine whether it would require an audit, and possibly an evaluation, of existing training, or an investigation into current and/or future training needs. It would also help to establish whether the review should be total or partial, as well as who might attend the top management meeting and the items on the agenda on which decisions need to be taken. Every review should relate to the strategic objectives of the organisation, but these are likely to be much wider than the all-important one of achieving profit targets. Most organisations have objectives relating to public image (the public are usually customers!) and to compliance with the law (on matters such as health and safety and equal opportunities). Adapting to national and international developments, such as EU regulations, or coping with government economic policy may well be reasons for companies to consider their training needs. A partial review may relate to one of these, or a variety of other, objectives. In an industrial relations audit, the questions which would arise and the composition of the meeting would probably be different from that convened to discuss a training needs review for Total Quality Management. This very obvious example emphasises the fact that the first step must be to make sure of your objectives as it is all too easy to waste time in irrelevant discussion and information gathering.

REASONS FOR AN ORGANISATIONAL REVIEW

Despite the apparent contradictions between analytical, problem-centred and learner-centred approaches, there are circumstances, such as those outlined below, when a review might be necessary in *any* organisation, regardless of its culture.

Establishment of a training department

An organisation which has appointed a training officer for the first time will be aware of some of its training requirements; it rarely possesses all the information necessary to formulate an appropriate training policy and plan of action. In these circumstances the new training officer might expect to carry out an audit to assess the strengths and weaknesses of the present policies and activities and to see how training can be more effective. Whether the review would be organisation-wide, or confined to certain departments, would depend upon the seniority of the training officer as well as other factors, such as immediate pressing problems pointed out to her by management. As we shall see later, in carrying out the review, the new training officer would discuss a range of issues with line and other staff managers, which would provide an opportunity to explain and clarify her roles and responsibilities. Similar comments can apply when a new training officer is appointed to an existing department.

Corporate planning and longer term training needs

Organisations monitor trends in the demand for their goods or services and attempt to forecast possible threats and opportunities which would affect their survival or growth. These forecasts should take account of critical factors such as economic conditions, government policies, including possible legislation, financial constraints, anticipated market changes, competitors' activities, technological developments, investment programmes, new products or services planned, and personnel issues. A useful technique is that of SWOT analysis, which involves identifying organisation strengths and weaknesses (internal factors), and opportunities and threats (external factors).

Data from these sources is used to construct possible future operating scenarios which top management evaluate in deciding the organisation's future policies and strategies. Human Resource Planning should play an important part in these processes.

Human resources specialists should help to develop the scenarios and offer advice to top management when the strategies are being formulated and later translate the staffing implications of the agreed strategies into operational plans. The organisation's anticipated manpower profile, expressed in numbers by occupational category and competences required, is then compared with the existing workforce, and after making adjustments for retirement and other anticipated staff losses, surpluses and shortages of staff are identified and succession plans are drawn up. This is the first step in developing a comprehensive human resource plan for the organisation, which by co-ordinating recruitment and training, retraining, career development and other personnel responsibilities, will help to ensure that appropriately trained and experienced staff are available when required. For a detailed discussion of human resource planning, see Bramham (1988), and also Bennison and Carson (1984).

The preparation of a training budget and plan

The organisation's training requirements. may be reviewed annually in order to prepare a budget and training plans for the following year. These result in a statement of intent which shows how the training department, in co-operation with others, proposes to meet the specific training objectives required by the company's manpower plan. The draft will specify what has to be achieved, how it will be done, whom it will affect, what benefits will accrue to whom, and what financial expenditure will be required. Whilst this seems an obvious requirement, the findings of a survey conducted in the UK for the Department of Employment (1991) across all industries except agriculture, forestry and fishing, revealed that only half of the respondents had formal written business and training plans and training budgets, whilst 38 per cent said they had a formal written manpower plan. By 1993 the position was slightly improved with larger establishments being the most likely to have training plans and budgets. See Figure 7.1.

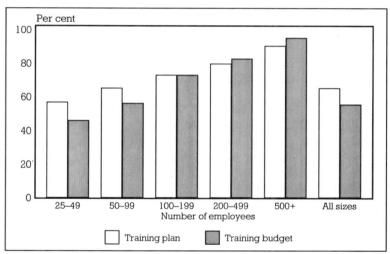

Figure 7.1
Establishments with training plans and budgets

Source: 'Skill Needs in Britain 1993'. Reproduced with the permission of the Department of Employment. (In Labour Market Quarterly Report Nov. 1992. Crown Copyright.)

These findings are illuminating when considered alongside the criteria for the *Investors in People* standards, launched in the Autumn of 1991, and administered by the TECs (see Figure 1.2, page 25).

A major change in an organisation's activities

Training plays a major organisational role in preparing people to be more ready to accept change and, when necessary, in equipping the staff concerned with the expertise they need to do the new work expected of them.

> Imagine you are employed by an airline which has just decided to buy a new type of aircraft, and consider the range of training which will be required. New skills and knowledge will be needed by some of the pilots, navigators, maintenance engineers, marketing and sales staff and, in varying degrees, by other employees. The successful introduction of the new aircraft will depend in part upon all the staff concerned being trained to undertake the new tasks required of them. The training implications must be identified if the changeover problems are to be minimized, and the benefits gained at the earliest possible stage. Policies, priorities, costs and schedules of training must be determined and co-ordinated at an organisational level and, eventually, detailed training programmes prepared. In tackling this type of problem there are advantages in adopting a systems perspective of training, as described in Chapter 5, i.e. the airline is viewed as a total system and as a series of sub-systems which interact with each other. Working with and using data obtained from planning and senior line management, the training officer examines in turn the list of activities which will be undertaken by each function, how each function will interact with other parts of the airline (the boundaries of the sub-systems) and with the external environment. It is then possible to clarify the specific and general training which will be needed, and prepare a schedule of priorities, sequences of training programmes, costings, etc.

Profound changes or discontinuities which affect the whole of an organisation present formidable challenges to the training function as in the case of the privatisation of a nationalised industry. For instance, one of the new water boards carried out a major review of operations following privatisation. This resulted in an extensive 'upskilling' programme involving the BTEC national certificate in water and water-waste operations, for the incumbents of about 700 new operations controller posts. A lower order, but still powerful challenge is presented by a major change in the way part of an organisation operates, for example, when a decentralized computer-based management information system is introduced. This type of change can be deceptive in that it may ultimately result in a new style of management, requiring totally different abilities. Many companies are turning to the 'flat organisation', which needs staff with a broader base of skills, thus eliminating the need for many specialisms; traditional boundaries and practices change. A survey by Coulson-Thomas and Coe (1991) for the BIM, indicated a wide recognition of training needs in this type of organisation, 95 per cent of respondents indicating that 'managers need to be equipped with new skills'. Many of Coulson-Thomas and Coe's recommendations focus on developing these skills. They suggest that the restructuring should begin with a skills audit, and that financial resources should be allocated to pay for its recommendations. They contend that in this type of organisation particular attention should be paid to team building skills; development activity should be linked to the achievement of change; people should be encouraged to identify their own qualities and strengths and relate them to the organisation's objectives; employees should take responsibility for their own learning; the focus should be on learning rather than teaching; flexibility is required to cater for the needs of individuals.

Requests from management

The responses to the Price Waterhouse Cranfield Project (Holden and Livian, 1992), showed that in some countries line management requests were considered a very important method of defining training needs. This might indicate the lack of a more systematic approach, but on the other hand, training needs can arise suddenly, particularly in small organisations, and may not occur at the time of regular audits. Such requests may have political significance in encouraging line managers to accept responsibility for defining training needs, and in demonstrating that the training department can play a useful role in helping to achieve organisational objectives.

Incorrectly identified training needs

It is necessary to approach an assessment objectively and with an open mind, without being unduly influenced by the assumptions which management and others may make about the cause of a problem and how it should be solved. On occasions it will be found that a difficulty is in fact not a training problem, although it has been presented as such. For example the training officer in a civil engineering company was asked to prepare a training programme for supervisors in the sub-contracting department. On investigation he found that the supervisors' apparently inadequate performance was caused by the irregular flow of work into the company and therefore into the department. The problem was an organisational one and could not be solved by supervisory training.

Partial training needs

A training officer's help may be sought in tackling such problems as removing bottlenecks in a production department, the assumption being that the shop floor workers concerned have not been trained to do their jobs correctly. While this could be the case, an investigation might show that inadequate operator training is only partly responsible for the poor quality of the work or slow working: the major causes may be poor supervision or machine maintenance, discontent over pay, or recruitment of unsuitable employees. The training officer has to distinguish between those problems which are wholly or partly due to ineffective training, and are therefore likely to have training solutions, and those which result from non-training factors, for which other answers must be found.

'Displaced' Training Needs

Problems are sometimes not initially referred to the training department because they are attributed to other causes, and are not recognised by management as training needs. Consider the following example:

An investigation into the backlog of work in the Accounts Department of a rapidly expanding company showed that the root of the trouble was not, as the Chief Accountant had claimed, a shortage of staff, but a deterioration in the calibre of accounts clerks which the company had employed. Previously the recruitment position in the area had been favourable and new employees had not needed formal training. When the labour market was tighter, less able staff were recruited and still no attempt was made to train them. The newcomers were eventually able to learn how to do the work (without training) but this took time and in the process they made many more mistakes than their predecessors.

A good training officer will endeavour to keep herself well in touch with the mainstream of activity, so that she will be aware of such problems and prepared to offer assistance when the timing seems appropriate.

Training audits
An audit of existing staff's competence in a particular facet of their work is another example of an organisation-wide training-needs analysis. Such an analysis may be undertaken for a variety of reasons, such as an industrial relations audit (Jennings and Undy, 1984) or a discrimination audit, or an audit of needs relating to membership of the EU. For a substantial treatment of the 'triggers' of training audits, including case examples, see Pepper (1984).

Total Quality Management
The decision to attain Total Quality Management and/or the attempt to reach British Standard 5750, requires a careful audit of training needs throughout the organisation. Every facet of work must be performed to the highest standard, and quality targets must be defined and met. This requires not only initial training, to make staff aware of the targets, and to assist them to attain the necessary competence, but also continuous monitoring to ensure that standards are not allowed to slip, and are kept up to date, taking into account the implications of any organisational changes. Procedures for continuing professional updating and 'upskilling' are also required.

Ensuring that statutory requirements are met
Organisations, their executives and employees are variously affected by both new and long-standing statutory obligations. Ignorance of the law is no defence for failure to comply with it. Nor are an organisation's legal obligations necessarily met by a once and for all training intervention. The training function has a continuing role to play in helping to ensure improved compliance with legislation and this can be achieved by the maintenance of a checklist of statutory responsibilities,

to use in reviewing training needs for a department or for the organisation as a whole. Such a list would include the following areas: health and safety; industrial relations; race relations and sex discrimination.

Health and safety

The Health and Safety at Work Act, 1974, specifies that it is the duty of every employer to provide:

> 'such information, instruction, training and supervision as necessary to ensure, as far as reasonably practicable, the health and safety at work of his employees'.

Part 1 Section 2

Subsequent sections of the Act are concerned with a written statement of policy on health and safety and the 'arrangements' (which presumably include training) for its implementation, together with the appointment in 'prescribed cases' of safety representatives and safety committees. The philosophy of the Act is clearly supportive of employee participation and consultation and this has training implications. It will also be necessary for employers to be aware of any complementary legislation adopted by the UK in connection with membership of the EC.

It must be emphasised that Part 1 Section 2 of this Act (quoted above) mentions the provision of supervision. It is generally recognised that safety training must be an integral part of a company's training schemes, and must be included in programmes for supervisors and managers as well as in induction courses and in operator training. School leavers and 'work experience' assignees are particularly at risk and require special attention. The problems associated with YT trainees are relevant here.

Industrial relations

The inept handling of what appear to be relatively minor problems by supervisors and managers unaware of the law can lead to major industrial relations issues. Furthermore, if a case is brought against an organisation at an industrial tribunal, it is extremely damaging if senior managers cannot support the actions of their subordinates. In cases of unfair dismissal because of incompetence, one of the first questions which arises at a tribunal concerns the amount and quality of the training and counselling provided and whether sufficient warnings were given. In addition to a knowledge of the relevant law, skill in devising the procedures necessary to comply with it, and training in company policies and practices, as well as in union agreements, are necessities.

The Employment Protection (Consolidation) Act, 1978 places the employer under a legal responsibility to allow trade union officers time off with pay during working hours to take part in industrial relations training relevant to their duties.

Race relations

Training will not solve problems of race relations or equal opportunities but it has a contribution to make. Awareness of the special needs of particular groups of workers is likely to be achieved most effectively when included as an integral part of the organisation's training plans for managers, supervisors and other employees. There are obvious needs relating to job-centred training. The Race Relations Act, 1976, encourages positive action (it is not a legal requirement) to promote entry of racial groups into new areas of work by stipulating that the employer or trade union can provide training facilities, exclusively for members of a particular racial group, to fit them for work in which they are under-represented. For examples of positive action in this field see Prashar (1983). Another important aspect is induction to the organisation and to the trade union, including knowledge of all relevant procedures. This training can help to prevent the painful consequences that may otherwise arise from later misunderstandings. Language teaching may be necessary and there is evidence that such programmes must be supported by the indigenous English-speaking population and related to shop floor practices. Race relations audits have shown that ethnic minorities tend to be under-represented in more senior posts and point to the necessity for improved opportunities and training for career development.

Advice on problems, ranging from provision of language training to courses for managers and shop stewards, can be obtained from the Commission for Racial Equality.

Sex discrimination

Organisations have a legal responsibility to comply with the requirements of the Sex Discrimination Act, 1975. As in the case of the race relations legislation, an organisation should ensure that its managers and supervisors understand their obligations in this field and, where necessary, they should ensure that appropriate training is provided for their subordinates. Appropriate management development including advice, and where appropriate, mentoring should be available to assist women to progress up the career ladder. As the number of school leavers declines, women employees are going to constitute an increasing proportion of the workforce and special measures may be required to ensure that they are adequately represented in the upper levels of management. Special training arrangements during career breaks, as well as for those returning to work after a number of years' absence, are likely to become more commonplace (see Chapter 11).

CARRYING OUT AN ORGANISATION-WIDE REVIEW

Although an organisation-wide review can be time-consuming and expensive, it is nevertheless worth considering in closer detail how it might be carried out, as a model or 'standard guide' which can be adapted for many purposes and used differentially. Although sections of the review may be delegated and responsibility for identifying training 'cascaded' throughout the organisation, and collective discussion will often take place, one person normally takes overall responsibility for the review, and for the purposes of this example, we are assuming that the 'reviewer' is the training officer.

The usual reason for an organisation-wide review is to provide objective data about the training investments required, in the short and longer term, to meet corporate goals. It provides top management with professional advice on human resource development and enables them to decide the nature and extent of the role of training in the achievement of corporate objectives. Top management's decisions determine the operational training policies and plans for the organisation.

The organisation's corporate policies and plans set the context within which the review takes place. It comprises:

- the identification, at all levels in the organisation, of the certain and probable needs for training
- a critical review of this data
- the submission of a report which sets out the priority training and development issues and recommends action plans, supported by cost estimates.

Figure 7.2 shows the sequence of steps which might be followed in reviewing training needs at the level of the organisation.

Step 1
Preparation for the review

Step 2
Collection of data and initial interpretation
Identification of problems with 'non-training' solutions

Step 3
Detailed interpretation of data
Identification of 'key areas'
Development of recommendations

Step 4
Preparation for implementing the recommendations

Figure 7.2
Steps in identifying organisational training needs

Step 1: preparation for the review

The importance of preparation as a key to the success of a training-needs investigation cannot be overstressed. This involves obtaining a clear brief, specifying the precise objectives of the exercise. The brief should cover the scope, objectives, and the time horizon of the review, the degree to which it is confidential, the authority which the reviewer is given for access to relevant information, when the results are required and the person to whom the final report is to be sent. In deciding what essential investment in training must be made, the reviewer must constantly bear in mind the organisation's goals.

When the objectives of the review have been clarified, the next step is to ensure that all employees who are likely to contribute to it are informed. This is necessary for three reasons. First, the training officer relies on the co-operation of senior managers and others to help her to carry out the review. It is, therefore, important that the purpose of the investigation, and how and when she proposes to carry it out, are fully discussed in advance with the appropriate staff. For example, it should be made clear that the review is *not* part of an organisation and methods or work study exercise. This initial activity has an important part to play in the formation of attitudes and will help determine the acceptability of any resultant training activities.

Second, the investigations may involve asking searching questions, which may cause adverse reactions from some employees who might adopt a less than co-operative attitude if, as can easily happen, they misconstrued the training officer's intentions. This is particularly likely if the organisation climate is unsettled. A review taking place soon after a company has been taken over, or when a number of people have been made redundant, or during an industrial dispute, may well run into difficulties which are not of the training officer's own making. Even if the organisational climate is favourable, she should nonetheless explain the purpose of the review to the staff concerned and obtain their co-operation. The review should be regarded as an opportunity to nurture positive attitudes to training, but training needs are often weak spots in an organisation and those concerned tend to be sensitive when questioned about them, especially if they regard the investigation as an implied criticism.

A third reason for advising those involved of the impending review is that, given advance notice, they can collect the information which will be required, for example, by up-dating organisation charts or job specifications, where available, and by preparing labour turnover statistics. This can save everyone a great deal of time, and is particularly important where line managers are taking responsibility for drawing up job descriptions and standard specifications for their subordinates.

Finally, the most appropriate starting point must be determined. This will depend upon many variables, such as urgency of action in particular areas, staff availability, the purpose of the investigation, the personal choice of the assessor, and the degree to which line management is prepared to co-operate.

An organisation chart showing the relationships of different departments and the formal lines of responsibility is a useful document for the training officer, but it is important to remember that these charts often show much less information than may be needed. To be of value, they must be up-to-date and indicate the real areas of responsibility and lines of communication, not just those of the formal organisation. If, as is often the case, no chart exists, the training officer may have to draw up new-style 'maps' as she progresses with her review. The data shown on such 'maps' must be continually cross-checked against the perceptions of other managers. Organisational mapping is an important skill within this context, and must be practised as a standard technique;

the nature of a given map must reflect management's view on future operational priorities.

Step 2: collection of data and its initial interpretation

Although, in theory, information has first to be collected before it is interpreted, in practice it is artificial to separate these two processes, as they tend to take place simultaneously. The training officer interprets the facts and opinions that she gathers about the organisation as she records them, at times seeking more detail and at others deciding more information is not required. Later (Step 3) she evaluates the data more critically in relation to the broader picture which has emerged.

In the process of collecting information for the review, the training officer will also receive comments on current and former training policies and interventions. Whether this feedback is agreeable to her or not, the perceptions which her clients have of the training department's services must be taken into consideration when helping to formulate the organisation's training plan. The amount of support which line managers are prepared to give to the training function will certainly influence top management's decision as to the resources which will be made available for her department. Organisations are always faced with the problem of competing claims for limited resources. The training function requires as much support as possible and the best way of achieving this is to argue a case which has wide support within the organisation. The case must be based on acknowledged training priorities, the rationale for these priorities must be explicitly expressed, and alternative strategies, for example, job redesign or the recruitment of ready-trained employees, shown to be less cost-effective than training interventions.

Methods of collecting information

Depending on the focus of the investigation, information might be obtained by:

- reference to strategic planning documents relating to marketing, production, staffing, etc
- analysing minutes of management meetings
- selecting data from operational records such as personnel statistics, job descriptions, accident records, training reports and staff appraisal

forms. Accounting records can often also be very revealing. For example, costs/returns of waste board or metal can yield dramatic evidence on precision in manufacturing, which in turn may reflect on operator competence

- formal and informal interviewing, especially with people in charge of key departments. Senior managers often have major operational aims which are not to be found in the published forward plans
- questionnaire surveys
- discussions with the training committee, which can provide information on training requirements and the priority areas. (Do you recollect that in Chapter 1, Jack and Sam were pondering whether they should be creating internal TECs of their own? These would indeed be invaluable in the situation we are discussing, and as they would be of very senior level, might in fact steer the whole process of the review)
- direct observation of work.

The training officer often has to ferret out information, since it is not necessarily available in the form in which she needs it. For example, job specifications prepared for recruitment purposes are useful but at best only a starting point for any training analysis (see Chapter 9).

Sources of information

There is no one correct sequence to follow in collecting relevant data; a potentially successful plan will reflect top management's current views on operational priorities. The following are likely to be the main information sources: external influences, top management, personnel department, other service departments, departmental managers, and their staff and trade unions. But each organisation has its own key sources and idiosyncrasies: for example, XYZ Ltd. may have recently developed its Joint Consultative Company Council as a major forum for discussion on efficiency, in which case Company Council minutes and an interview with alternating chairmen might be front runners.

External influences

No review should be undertaken without reference to the context in which the organisation operates, as its training needs are directly influenced by the external environment. Economic factors such as interest rates, stock exchange movements, or general recession all have an impact on organisational activity, as well as international events, politics, markets, raw material prices and exchange rates. Competitive activity may suggest and even force, new or more technical development activity, changes in product presentation, etc. The demand for its goods or services provides the *raison d'être* for the organisation's existence and any changes in demand can have a considerable impact on the training function. The reduction or discontinuation of apprentice recruitment in a recession can have a major effect on a training department, whilst a policy of non-replacement when staff leave eliminates the need for induction and initial job training. Conversely, an increase in demand for the organisation's goods or services can lead to an expansion of training activities, particularly if the organisation has a policy of retraining its staff when jobs become redundant.

Top management
The training officer should begin the investigation by discussing with each of the directors or senior executives, their objectives and the human resource problems likely to emerge in meeting them. However, an organisation's objectives are not always clearly defined nor will they necessarily be fully disclosed to the training officer. If senior management do not supply strategic information about the company's present and future operations, ideally making available strategic forward plans, the validity of the review will be in doubt. If the training officer is not considered a suitable custodian of this type of classified information, the review should be carried out by someone else. Without this information, there is no objective means of assessing the significance of the data collected, no certain basis for determining priorities and other training recommendations, and therefore no satisfactory ways of measuring the standards and effectiveness of existing and future training.

Furthermore, if the organisation's goals have not been clarified it is possible that the company's structure is inappropriate and that operating problems may occur because managers are unknowingly working to different ends. This can give rise to situations where training is apparently being applied successfully to remedy a problem: in reality it is only a palliative which treats the symptoms of a problem, whilst its cause, for example, an out-dated policy, remains unaltered.

The training officer must therefore obtain from top management indications of any anticipated variations in the business such as technical, product or market changes, future capital expenditure, and any predicted adjustments in the labour force. These variations have training implications if they result in a demand for new expertise, or an increased requirement from existing staff categories (e.g. multi-skilling). The training officer records these changes in detail and notes when they will be implemented, their scope and estimated effect. At this stage she will also be able to list a wide variety of *questions*, answers to which will be sought in the later stages of the review. Armed with this information, she will be able to assess the relevant factors when discussing training needs with managers of departments affected by these changes.

Personnel department
A personnel department can supply valuable information, including job descriptions, job specifications, job evaluation documents, recruitment plans, the industrial relations climate, bonus payment and assessment systems and promotion policy. In addition, it can provide employee statistics of three main kinds: labour turnover, length of service of leavers, age distribution, all by department and section. These statistics are of great importance in an organisation-wide review and are illustrated in Figures 7.3 and 7.4. Obviously a good computerised record system is invaluable in its capacity to provide analyses in many forms.

Local availability of skilled labour is also essential information. The personnel department may have its own list of 'improved performance' priorities (e.g. timekeeping, lost time, accidents) or procedural changes (e.g. new appraisal systems, new flexi-time arrangements), or external threats (e.g. competition for labour in the locality). Industrial relations officers can usually be relied upon to communicate shop floor attitudes regarding any known innovations or problems.

Labour turnover: Labour turnover statistics are of significance to the investigation because where there is a high turnover of new staff there is also likely to be a substantial need for induction and job training for recruits. An investigation of the reasons for high turnover of labour may reveal that it is caused by inadequate training or by non-training problems. The organisation may need to solve some of the latter, such as low wages or inadequate supervision. If it fails to do so, a disproportionately heavy expenditure on training is the penalty.

Organisations sometimes find that the cause of a high labour turnover lies outside their control. For instance, the demand for technicians skilled in a rapidly developing technology is likely to exceed the supply, and in spite of attractive salaries and work conditions, these staff may leave within a year. Faced with this situation, the training officer might recommend the introduction of training having decided that the costs of providing it would be outweighed by the benefits. Staff turnover may not be significantly reduced by training new employees but it would help to ensure that they would be more productive sooner. If the average length of service of the programmers was a year and, without formal training, they took three months to be fully productive, they would give, on average, only nine months' productive work before they left. If, with a planned training approach learning times were reduced to about a month, even though the new staff still left after approximately a year, then at least for eleven of these months they would be pulling their weight.

It should be noted that staff turnover as an index of labour instability is only valid if related to small, homogenous groups of employees. When dealing with large numbers of staff, marked variations in labour turnover tend to be 'evened out' and their significance lost. Analyses by job category or department category can often be illuminating. Caution is necessary in deciding what constitutes a 'high' or 'low' figure. Comparisons should be made only with the same type of industry and areas which have similar recruitment problems. For a helpful guide to the use of quantitative methods by managers, see Cuming (1984).

Length of service of leavers: An unstable workforce can be expected if staff are not trained correctly and find the work too difficult to learn unaided. The 'length of service of leavers' should be checked to determine whether, as in Figure 7.3, many staff have left within a short period of joining. Even if this pattern emerges from the figures, it cannot be assumed that inadequate training is necessarily to blame, as non-training reasons, such as poor selection, or tight bonus may be the cause.

As with labour turnover figures, the training officer should initially regard leavers' length of service data as general indicators for further investigation. Finding out why employees leave is not easy; sometimes the departure is multi-causal, or they are often reluctant to give the real reason and this kind of data can be misleading unless interpreted by experienced staff.

Job	Length of service					
	Up to 3 months	4 to 8 months	9 to 23 months	2 to 5 years	Over 5 years	Total
Sales assistants	48	25	9	6	4	92
Section supervisors	—	3	2	2	1	8
Departmental heads	—	—	—	1	1	2
Buyers	—	1	—	2	4	7

Figure 7.3
'Length of service of leavers' data (taken over a one year period)

Job	Age range						
	Under 25	26–30	31–40	41–50	51–60	61–65	Total
Office supervisors	1	2	2	5	7	8	25
Senior clerks	—	3	3	2	1	—	9
Word processor operators	6	6	3	—	—	—	15
Typists	15	7	4	7	8	6	47
Clerks	32	26	20	17	18	15	128

Figure 7.4
Data showing 'Age distribution' by job category

Age distribution: The purpose of an age distribution analysis, in this context, is twofold: to discover how many employees in a department or staff category fall within certain age groupings, and to interpret the training implications of any imbalances in the age structure.

A department may have a very young labour force, in which case both inexperience and staff mobility are likely to create considerable demands on training resources. Conversely, a department may be staffed largely by older employees, perhaps with a number of its key personnel approaching retirement. For instance, in Figure 7.4, eight out of 25 office supervisors are over 60, and a total of fifteen are over 50, a situation which could give rise to problems in the not too distant future, unless succession plans are being prepared. An ageing workforce is not revealed by labour turnover statistics; on the contrary, a low staff turnover might appear to suggest that little training is required. Both turnover and age distribution statistics should be considered.

Ideally, the labour force will match the local labour market profile in terms of age, sex and type (e.g. ethnic minorities); few do so. The extent to which an organisation is 'top heavy' (i.e. biased towards older workers), or young male dominated, or 'at a management standstill' (i.e. managed by unpromotable middle aged people) can strongly influence the later stages of the review.

Other service departments

In medium and large companies there are usually other specialists from whom information can be obtained. For example, planning, maintenance, accounts, management services, quality control, and research and development departments all have data about the company's activities which can be of direct value to the review.

Planning departments accumulate much data on problems – especially regarding manufacturing and distribution, but also in the area of 'lead times', which are often a direct reflection of decision making abilities and speed of transforming decisions into action.

Maintenance departments have information about machine utilisation and efficiency.

The accounts department may be able to provide such details as: training expenditure in the company, with a breakdown by department, and the system of recording training costs (see Chapter 5). A review of company training, expressed in financial terms, provides a valuable measure of the scale on which training is taking place. However, the level of expenditure must be carefully interpreted. For example, a department's high training costs may be due to inefficient training or fully justified by high demand, while low expenditure might indicate inadequate training or little requirement for it; or it might reflect an economical training methodology, such as the use of self learning packs.

Records in the 'Management Services' department can be an important source of information for certain types of job. Work procedures, job specifications and grades, training times, work standards, all provide a clear picture of the structure and work of a department. Moreover, since these specialists are concerned with analysing existing work as well as implementing new systems, they can often suggest where training requirements already exist in the organisation, and where in the future, training is likely to be needed.

Similar help can be given by the quality control and research and development departments. The former can provide quality standards for particular work and indicate where employees have difficulty in achieving these standards. Research and development staff will know of anticipated technological changes and when they are likely to be introduced in the company. They may also be able to predict some of the human resource implications of the proposed changes, such as the grades of employee that will be required in the future and the feasibility of retraining existing staff for new jobs, e.g. operators to undertake more highly skilled work associated with the introduction of higher technology.

The costs of unplanned training are often hidden but are usually well worth investigating, both to help 'sell' an improved scheme and to use as a yardstick in later evaluation. These costs can be expressed in inadequate equipment utilisation, damage to equipment, high scrap levels, time taken by supervisors or others in instruction, lack of recruits and, as already mentioned, in staff turnover and length of training time.

Department managers and their staff
The training officer is by this stage well prepared to start the major part of the investigation: discussions with line management. Using the information already collected about the organisation's current operations and its objectives, she discusses the following questions with each departmental manager:

1 Problems of the department: many of these may be later ruled out as not having a training solution, but the knowledge gained from discussion can be very helpful in determining training priorities.

2 Present training arrangements in the department:

- Who is responsible for training?
- What training has the nominee had to do this job?
- How much is training costing the department?
- What is the scope of the present training?

- What plans are there for training new and existing staff?
- Do these cover job and career training?
- Are these arrangments regarded as satisfactory?

3 *Quality of present training:*

- Have training programmes been based on identified needs?
- Have training standards been established, and if so, on what basis?
- How are trainees assessed?
- What records of training are kept and why?
- Are training resources adequate, and what is the basis for their allocation?

4 *Departmental management's attitude to training:*

- Is the manager well-informed about the training in his department?
- Is he aware of the organisation's training policies?
- Does he regard the policies as satisfactory?
- Has he developed his own departmental policy? For example, is it his practice to train staff to be able to do more than one job?
- Can senior management, or the training department, give him any further assistance?
- Are there any training problems which are particular to the department?

5 *Future training requirements:*

- What are the likely future developments affecting the department?
- What future training needs have been recognised in the department?
- What plans have been evolved to meet them?
- Which requirements should have priority?
- What departmental and other resources will be required to meet these needs?

The training officer then interviews the junior managers and supervisors concerned with day-to-day training who are therefore well-qualified to discuss the quality of existing arrangements and recommend improvements. The close involvement of junior managers and supervisors is vital. Their perception of training needs is often insightful and they are one of the organisation's most important training resources. These discussions also give the training officer an opportunity to assess the managers' actual and potential performance as trainers.

Other employees who can help are staff currently under training or who have recently completed their training. The consumer's point of view is often very illuminating.

Finally the trade union's attitude to, and policies on, training matters are important factors which must be considered both during and after the review process.

Having collected data under these headings, the training officer should have a comprehensive record for each department's present arrangements, its anticipated training needs and priorities and the resources required to meet them. At this stage, it is often possible to identify those problem areas which are unlikely to have a training solution, and such information can be discarded.

Step 3: detailed interpretation of data: determination of 'key' areas and development of recommendations

At this stage the information which has been collected is reviewed and the results analysed. At times, there will be gaps and discrepancies in the data necessitating a return to particular information sources. Some of the problems which have emerged will be identified as requiring solutions other than training, and can be discarded from the review. An attempt is then made to weigh the relative importance of the identified training needs, initially on a departmental basis and subsequently for the organisation as a whole, bearing long- and short-term objectives constantly in mind.

Ranking training priorities is difficult and requires careful judgement and it is helpful to refer to criteria such as the terms of the original brief, existing training policies and strategies, the availability of resources which particular training programmes will require and the benefits which they are expected to yield. Prioritising is important because training budgets are seldom large enough to meet every need. The findings must therefore be synthesised and expressed as recommendations for action. The recommendations should satisfy the following criteria. They should be:

- clearly in support of the organisation's operational plans and objectives
- consistent with the organisation's training policies, or where policy changes are needed, reasons given

- acceptable to senior management
- justified, with supporting evidence of actual training needs listed in priority terms
- feasible, in that the necessary resources are likely to be made available
- costed and, if appropriate, marked to indicate whether or not the proposed training is eligible for any funding from the local TEC or other grant
- practical and acceptable to those implementing and receiving the training
- specific, in naming who would be responsible for implementing the training and when it is required.

The recommendations and the evidence on which they are based are normally contained in a report for top management. In writing the report, the training officer bears in mind such points as: the initial and likely subsequent readers; the use of confidential information collected during the review; and how to express criticisms of managers who have apparently failed to train their staff, or perhaps of past training plans and/or methods, or even of learners who are resisting change.

Step 4: preparation for implementing the recommendations
When the review report is completed, there are still two key tasks to perform. First, to follow up her recommendations and help to get them accepted within the company and secondly, to see that they are implemented.

No experienced training officer assumes that all the recommendations will be adopted. Some managers will accept the assessor's specialist advice enthusiastically and use the training department's services fully. Others will disagree with particular findings or recommendations, but will be open to persuasion if the points can be substantiated with facts and figures. The apathetic manager, who superficially accepts the results of the assessment but takes no positive steps to implement them, is more difficult to win over.

The training officer should be prepared to spend a great deal of time discussing, persuading and marketing her services using the support of senior management, keen departmental managers, and the training committee. If she does not carry her colleagues with her, much of the value of a review will be lost. (For further details on corporate training needs identification, see Turrell (1980).)

After reading this chapter, you should by now be fully aware that:

1 The training effort must be directed to the most important organisation objectives. A survey of organisation needs or key areas is a logical step to ensure this. How it is carried out and to what extent, will depend upon a number of factors such as the culture, or the stage of development of the organisation. It is also the basis for the training plan and budget. Without any investigation into real needs, large sums of money might be invested with little positive result. If large capital sums were to be spent on the purchase of a machine, a detailed investigation into the need for it and its use and advantage to the company would be undertaken. The same discipline should be exercised in expenditure on training.

2 There are a number of approaches to identifying organisational needs, none of which is inherently 'good' for all situations; there is seldom likely to be one 'right' answer. Identifying 'own training needs' is an important part of some types of organisation activity, such as project groups. In these organisations the design and conduct of any review must take this into consideration.

3 The 'best' answer is likely to be that which appears to offer the 'best fit' in all the circumstances. To determine this may well involve the consideration of a number of different variables.

4 As well as being skilled in a range of techniques, a training officer needs diagnostic abilities of a very high order.

To return to the quotation at the beginning of this chapter, do you know of any organisation which completes a systematic analysis of training needs? Can you contrast it with one you know which does not? Why do you think this difference exists? And can you identify any effects of the two approaches?

FOR FURTHER REFLECTION AND DISCUSSION

1 Acting as a potential provider of training facilities, a local FE college has asked how your organisation's training needs are expected to change and/or develop over the next five years.

The request was sent to a senior executive, who is a member of the college governing body, and has been passed to the personnel department to construct an appropriate answer. How should the department set about establishing the facts and drafting the reply to be given to the college?

2 What are the essentials to a succession planning system? Who are the key contributors to the system, and how should their work be linked?

3 In a recent report on management training in the UK researchers concluded that there was no link between organisations' investment in management training activities and their commercial results. You have agreed to introduce a discussion on this topic at an IPM branch meeting, which you know will be attended by practising managers and students. Summarise your planned contribution to the meeting.

4 Who should be the various contributors to a periodic 'Training Audit' in an organisation employing over 1,000 people, and how might their work be integrated? What would you expect/require to be the types of output of such an audit?

SUGGESTED READING

BOYDELL T. H. *A guide to the identification of training needs.* British Association for Commercial and Industrial Education, London, 1983.

BRAMHAM J. *Practical manpower planning.* Institute of Personnel Management, London, 1988.

MOORBY E. *How to succeed in employee development*, Chapter 5. McGraw Hill, Maidenhead, 1991.

HARRISON R. *Training and Development.* IPM, London, 1988.

Chapter 8
TRAINING POLICY, PLANS AND RESOURCES

Training policy – policy development – annual training plan – training resources – from policy to training plan and budget.

INTRODUCTION

In Chapter 7, we suggested ways in which the organisation's training needs might be determined; we now consider the relationship between these requirements and the underlying training policy. We shall then examine how these two factors determine the content of a training plan and some of the typical resources that can be used to implement the plan, and we shall indicate some of the issues which can arise and the kinds of decisions which may have to be made in allocating the budget.

Most of the early training boards required a training policy as one of the conditions of awarding grants, but since their demise organisations are under no formal or statutory obligation to draw up such a statement, other than for training in health and safety (Health and Safety at Work Act 1974, Part 1, Section 2). A prerequisite of reaching the national standard for effective 'Investors in People' is a written plan setting out business goals and targets, as well as a consideration of how employees will contribute to achieving the plan, and how development needs will be assessed and met. (See Figure 1.2, page 25.) This might be considered to imply a policy, although that term is never actually mentioned and in any case there is no legal requirement to become an 'Investor in People'. Why then should organisations have a policy? And how formal should it be? We saw in Chapter 7 that in a survey (D of E, 1991), only about half of the participant organisations had formal written business and training plans and training budgets. About a further twenty per cent of establishments said they had such plans but on a less formal basis. As we discuss policy development and its uses, you might like to think of organisations you know, and try to gauge what their approach might be, and why.

TRAINING POLICY

The word 'policy' probably has its roots in the Greek word *polis*, meaning city – a term which in classical times conveyed notions of system, order and enforcement of laws. These ideas survive in our contemporary usage of the word 'police'. In a work context, a policy can be thought of as 'an expression of intention' which gives general guidance for the conduct of affairs. Thus an organisation's policy for training and development establishes the broad framework for its training plan. The plan, in turn, expresses the organisation's priority training interventions and the strategies to be followed during a given period of time (see Chapter 10 and Donnelly, 1991).

An organisation's philosophy towards the training and development of employees is reflected in its policy: this policy governs the priorities, standards and scope of its training activities. All organisations have a training and development policy: it may be explicit or implicit. Some policies are the outcome of a planned human resources management approach, others are reactive responses to requests and problems. Some are written, others not; some are regarded as being semi-confidential, others are promulgated to all staff. Some, where there is no organisational support for training, are negative; some apply only to certain job categories, others concern all employees; some are enforced, others honoured more in the breach than the observance.

Organisations develop training policies for four main reasons:

- to define the relationship between the organisation's objectives and its commitment to the training function
- to provide operational guidelines for management. For example, to state management's responsibilities for planning and implementing training; and in particular, to ensure that training resources are allocated to priority and statutory requirements (see Chapter 7)
- to provide information for employees. For example, to stress the performance standards expected; to indicate the organisation's commitment to training and development; and to inform employees of opportunities for training and development (including willingness to grant time off, and/or payment of fees for external courses)
- to enhance public relations. For example, to help attract high calibre recruits; to reassure clients and the public at large about the quality of the products (e.g. in pharmaceutical and food companies) or services (an airline's safety standards); or to project an image as a

caring and progressive employer by taking part in government sponsored 'social' training programmes such as Youth Training.

These four purposes overlap and are expressed in policy statements, in the organisation's plans for training, and in the rules and procedures which govern training access and implementation.

A corporate policy statement which aims to influence the outside world tends to be couched in broad terms, such as 'We offer training as part of our equal opportunities programme'. Corporate policy which regulates internal action may be published as a 'free standing' policy document (see page 216) or included in the organisation's training plan. Both typically include general statements of intent which set the corporate frame of reference for training and development activities, e.g. 'The Council will provide appropriate development opportunities for all its employees'; and specific statements which define the organisation's current priorities for training, for example, 'All managers and supervisors will attend a seminar on the company's industrial relations procedures'.

Corporate training policy at departmental level shapes the line manager's action plan by specifying what training will be provided for which staff, when it will take place, and who will be responsible for ensuring its implementation. It is at this level that policy can play the important role of helping to ensure equality of opportunity between employees working in different parts of the organisation. For example, published policy such as 'Junior office staff should be encouraged to attend appropriate day release Further Education courses', or 'All employees within two years of retirement are entitled to attend pre-retirement courses', will limit the discretion which a manager might otherwise apply unfairly.

Before 1964, it was unusual for training policies to be written, let alone published. This was because management had not generally been sufficiently interested in planned training, and because the expertise required to produce relevant policies was often lacking. Moreover, many top managements were cautious of 'publicly' committing themselves to policy which was untried and which they considered was better handled, at least initially, on a less formal basis.

Organisations have very varied approaches to training. Some have policies designed to gain the maximum benefit from training; in contrast, many others have no planned training and do not accept significant responsibility for training. The majority lie somewhere between these two extremes, with policies which permit training which is variable in quality, limited in scope, and to a greater or lesser extent lacking in direction. In these circumstances priorities are determined on an *ad hoc* or reactive, rather than a planned, basis.

POLICY DEVELOPMENT

An organisation's policy for training and development is influenced by a number of variables such as:

- size, traditions and prevailing culture
- products or services
- economic and social objectives
- obligations to provide professional updating (continuing) training, e.g. for nurses
- top management's views on the value of training
- availability of information about the organisation's training needs
- the labour market and the alternative means of acquiring skilled and qualified staff
- past and current training policies and practices
- training experience of its managers
- calibre of its specialist training staff
- resources that can be allocated to training
- expectations of employees and their representatives
- legislation e.g. health and safety, and government funded schemes e.g. Youth Training.

Training policy is more often determined by prevailing interest than principle, and as such tends to be impermanent and susceptible to change. This applies whether or not an organisation has adopted planned training. In the former situation, top management decide what contribution they want the training function to make in the achievement of the organisation's objectives. Their decision provides the framework within which training policy and plans are determined.

In organisations where planned training has not been adopted, policy for training results from the unsystematic growth of decisions, rules and procedures introduced to deal with particular problems. These decisions are typically made on a piecemeal basis and, with the passage of time, may be accepted as precedents and become 'policy'. *Ad hoc* policy development of this kind can give rise to inappropriate emphases and inconsistencies in application in different parts of the same organisation, particularly if changes in demand for skill and professional competences occur over short periods of time. A regular review of an organisation's training policy is essential to assess the relevance of existing priorities, rules and procedures in relation to current organisational objectives.

Other reasons can prompt an organisation to review its policy for training and development. These include: the availability of new methods of delivering training (see pages 221 and 222); and unexpected demand for training caused, for example, by restructuring to a flatter organisation (see Chapter 7 page 189); the need for retraining or retrenchment of training stemming from fluctuations in trading e.g. through recession; and changes in the work and role of particular groups of employees, e.g. maintenance engineering craftsmen (see Cross, 1985).

In the Scottish electronics industry (described by Cassels, 1985), although broadly the same number of people were employed, the relative proportions of different categories of staff altered dramatically through the effect of competition and new technology. There were increases of 94 per cent in the number of technologists and scientists in the industry, 26 per cent in the number of technicians, and 22 per cent in the number of managers. There were corresponding reductions in the numbers of craftsmen (nine per cent), administrative jobs (22 per cent), and of operators (18 per cent, but the greatest fall in absolute numbers). These changes affected company manpower profiles and, therefore, their human resource policies. In a rapidly changing environment, training policy can very quickly become out of date, and needs to be reviewed to ensure that it is appropriate to the provision of the required current and future skills and expertise.

It is clearly essential for an organisation to frame its policy to take account of potential problems and opportunities. Radical changes in organisational policy and objectives are more likely to secure wide support and to cause minimal anxiety when an 'open' consultative approach is used.

Tavernier (1971) stressed the need for:

'any policy regarding training [to] be in harmony with the company's personnel policies on recruitment, salaries, promotion and security of employment.'

This requirement is equally imperative today; for example, a policy of 'promotion from within', needs to be complemented by an appropriate training policy to prepare employees to climb the career ladder.

Top management are responsible for deciding training policy although the effectiveness of their decisions is likely to be increased if they have been based on consultation at all levels. It is suggested that when an organisation becomes an 'Investor in People', management should:

'develop and communicate to all employees a vision of where the organisation is going and the contribution employees will make to its success, involving employee representatives as appropriate.'

There are obvious benefits in involving employees in this way, notably that top management's decisions are likely to be more effective if they are consonant with the values and expectations of the employees in the organisation they direct.

Now put yourself in the shoes of the Training Director of an electricity board. During the reorganisation which followed privatisation the Training Department was designated a profit centre, selling its services and advice to management on request and in competition with external providers. When this change first took place, your staff were extremely concerned because they felt that the new system might not allow them to discharge their responsibilities in providing adequate training. A policy statement was issued which included a clarification that, in general, the onus for ensuring that employees were given access to sufficient training was upon line management, *not* the Training Department, but that to ensure uniformity, some training, such as certain aspects of health and safety training and induction, would remain the responsibility of the Training Department.

Without this statement much confusion might have arisen, and a policy should therefore clarify who is responsible, or who shares responsibility for different aspects of the training function and decision making activities, e.g. assessing needs, allocating resources, determining strategies, providing training, etc.

For the reasons we have mentioned above, training policies are unique, varying with the approach and requirements of different organisations. The following is an extract from a company's policy statement:

> 'The directors recognise the important contribution which training makes to the company's continuing efficiency and profitability. They further recognise that the prime responsibility for training rests with management. The Company Training Officer is accountable to the Managing Director and is responsible for submitting an annual assessment of organisational training needs, as well as advising and assisting all managers on training matters and providing the necessary training services. The annual training budget is approved by the Board and managed by the Company Training Officer.'

This company's training policy refers to all employees and aims to:

- provide induction training for all new staff and for those transferred to new departments
- provide day release facilities at the discretion of the appropriate departmental manager in consultation with the Company Training Officer
- ensure that appropriate training is available to enable individuals to reach and, through updating training, maintain satisfactory performance in their jobs
- provide the training required by those selected for promotion so that they are appropriately prepared for their new responsibilities
- provide information, instruction and training to ensure the health and safety of all employees.

There are a number of advantages to be gained from making the training policy widely known in the organisation. This approach clarifies the purpose of training and communicates top management's intentions; defines the organisation's responsibility for the development of the individual employee; helps those responsible for implementing training; clarifies the role and function of the training specialist; states in general terms the training opportunities available to employees and may indicate priorities. If the contents are progressive, publication enhances employer-employee relationships, but the success of a training policy is likely to be diminished if the 'public relations' element is overplayed or if the employees' expectations are not met. Employee resentment and, as a consequence, the possibility of more difficult problems, can result if an organisation fails to honour the development opportunities promised in published policy statements.

Writing a training policy is a task which requires considerable skill and attention to detail. The starting point is to clarify the reasons for introducing the policy and the objectives that it is designed to achieve. It is important that the staff categories to which the policy will apply are clearly stated. Account should be taken of any contingent precedents that may have been established, either in a formal way or by custom and practice. Discussion with representatives of those who will be affected is an essential part of the process of drafting a policy statement. It is important that the policy is written in an acceptable style, that the statement is positive (avoid using negatives) and that it contains no ambiguities.

ANNUAL TRAINING PLAN

An organisation's training plan should be a detailed and authoritative statement of the training which will be implemented over a given period. The plan results from a reconciliation of priority training needs, policy for training and development, and available resources, particularly budgets. (See also Chapters 5 and 7).

A range of requirements for training are identified prior to the preparation of the annual training budget and/or from a detailed investigation of the kind described in Chapter 7. These training needs should then be appraised against the criteria contained in the existing training policy statements: a process which may eliminate some requirements from the proposed plans. For example, a proposal from one department head for certain managers to attend a day release MBA course would not be included in the plan if there are to be no exemptions from a company's policy that staff over the age of 21 are not granted day release. In other cases, as we have seen above, it is the policy which has to be changed to meet the new conditions. Finally, training priorities have to be established by ranking, in order of importance, all the training requests received. As an organisation never has enough funds to meet all requests in full, it is important to remember that resources for training are likely to be in competition with provision for other purposes and that decisions about respective allocations may well be highly political. Obviously, those requests which appear most closely related to the organisation's strategic objectives are the most likely to be successful. For instance, the board of a company which has limited resources and is introducing an important new range of products in the coming year is more likely to allocate money to provide product training for its sales force than to what appears to be less urgent training in other fields, particularly if such training can be postponed without serious repercussions.

The training plan should therefore be drawn up with extreme care and political acumen. A typical plan would contain the following elements:

- details on a calendar basis (monthly, quarterly, half-yearly) of each department's training requirements by job classification and by number of employees involved e.g. accounts department, four clerical staff (BTEC qualifications) and two supervisory staff (NVQ junior management course); laboratory, one technician (attachment to raw material supplier); production department, an estimated 25 operatives (induction and initial training) and four managers (computer applications course)
- details on a monthly, quarterly, half-yearly, etc. basis of the projected training for categories of staff not permanently allocated to a department (e.g. five Youth Training trainees, three graduate trainee managers)
- specification, against each item of training, of the standard to be achieved, the person responsible for seeing that it is implemented, the training strategy to be used (e.g. self development, on-the-job coaching, internal or external course), how much the training will cost, its duration, when it will take place, and its target completion date
- a summary of the organisation's and each department's budget allocation for training: this may be divided into training which is continuing and to which the organisation is already committed, for example, craft trainees who are partway through their apprenticeships, and other training.

It should be noted that similar data can be collected and used to develop training plans of longer duration, e.g. two or three year rolling plans.

We know of one large organisation, with branches throughout the country, which produces such an annual document with fourteen sections, starting with a business review, followed by a section dealing with a projection of costs and of activities in each important aspect of the company's operation in the forthcoming year, thus linking all functions closely with corporate objectives. The following extract is the section which deals with training and development. It is a real case, altered only to conceal the identity of the company, and is, of course, backed up by a more detailed plan (too long to reproduce here), which provides a blueprint for the work of the training department.

The main thrust of our efforts during this year and next will be to achieve cost effective and more sharply focused training covering a wider group of people. Examples of current initiatives, actions and plans include:

1 Development of the Senior Management Team
A series of short lunchtime workshops has been arranged for all Directors and Department Heads. The programme of monthly sessions extending to the end of the year covers all aspects of the organisation under the headings Managing the Business, Managing Others and Managing Ourselves. Material from the Group Learning Resource Centre will be used as a basis for the sessions.

2 Hourly Paid Supervision
A series of training courses for first line supervisors has been launched. Subject areas include: an examination of their role; personal organisation and time management; effective delegation; use of branch diary; safety, etc. Use of existing materials, including company guidebooks and the Learning Resource Centre will be encouraged.

3 Development of Trainers
Greater emphasis is to be given to the use of senior/more experienced staff to provide guidance and training both on the job and during more formal courses.

4 Performance Review
Training sessions will be held to emphasise the importance of the review in the overall management and improvement of the business. The review is to be extended to include hourly paid supervision.

5 Trainees Under Agreement
Improved monitoring of training will be achieved next year and more of these trainees will be involved in the business review groups set up under the Total Quality Initiative.

6 External Training Professional Bodies

We continue to be involved in a wide variety of external committees and advisory groups covering professional bodies, local institutions of Further and Higher Education, Training and Enterprise Councils and BTEC Training Committees. The involvement allows us to influence the shape of future training within the industry and to draw on best practice from other industries/companies.

7 Personal Efficiency Programmes

Selected senior management (including Directors) are undergoing individual programmes of guidance on personal efficiency. This is leading to improvements in effectiveness.

At the beginning of this chapter, we pointed out that not all organisations have written training plans, but that some have plans on a less formal basis. This may be because of the factors illustrated by the Warwick University research described on pages 182–3, which make it impossible for some small to medium enterprises to make forward plans with any degree of certainty; could it also be that in times of rapidly developing technology and economic change, or recession, larger organisations no longer experience their former stability, and that their managements, too, are constrained from committing themselves to longer term planning and adopt an *ad hoc* approach? In this case, plans may well be discussed with managers and constantly reviewed to ensure that most urgent problems are addressed. Alternatively, the training may be phased – the precise pattern and content of each phase depending upon the outcome of those which preceded it. The optimum approach to planning may therefore have to be decided according to the context in which the organisation is operating. Whatever approach is used however, even short-term decisions should be recorded in writing with a proposed date for revision, and circulated to all concerned. Such documents can then act as a blueprint against which to monitor progress and evaluate what has been achieved.

TRAINING RESOURCES

We explain in Chapter 10 that when a training officer recommends or chooses a training strategy to meet an identified need she strives to achieve the 'best fit' consistent with the learning objectives, the organisation's policy, the learner's preferences and the resources available.

Training resources can be thought of as the input required to enable a training plan to be implemented. The range of resources that can be drawn upon by the training officer are considered later in this chapter and include people (e.g. the training officer herself), money (e.g. the training budget) and facilities (e.g. the self-learning packages, a 'walk-in' open access resource centre, a training room). However, it is often not so much the resources themselves that achieve results but the skill with which they are managed.

Central to the success of a training officer is her function as a manager of learning resources. Her credibility and influence are enhanced when she is accepted as the focal point in the organisation for advice and information about training activities (both internal and external); as the source of specialist knowledge and experience about learning in a work context; as the co-ordinator and monitor of the organisation's training policy, plans and budgets; as a competent trainer; and as a successful (line) manager of the training department, its staff, the training centre and learning aids. It is through contacts with top managers that the training officer benefits from the key resource of 'political' support for her activities.

During the last two decades, the work of many training officers has been dominated by organising and contributing to in-house courses and arranging attendance at external courses. The resources at their command are those required to carry out this restricted function, i.e. a limited training budget and a training room or area. In recent years, however, the benefits of structured on-the-job learning have gradually become more recognised. This recognition has extended to both the techniques and, through the greater involvement of line managers, the range of resources which an organisation can apply to planned training. Work-based projects, job rotation, and coaching, are examples of activities which can result in effective learning of a kind which, by itself, classroom-based training cannot achieve.

The recognition that successful training does not have to take place in a training centre has been powerfully reinforced by the application of the new technologies to training and development. These technologies are having three main effects.

First, computers, video tape-recorders, compact disc, interactive-video systems, and access to computerised data bases using modems and telephone lines (see Appendix 6) have greatly increased the choice and flexibility of learning systems available. Wherever there is a computer terminal there is a potential training resource.

Secondly, these applications of the new technologies are changing the perceptions of training. As a result, effective training is no longer so widely perceived to be primarily a classroom-based activity and few would now hold the simplistic view that, to be trained, employees had to attend an in-house course. However, in the right circumstances, the 'course strategy' (see Chapter 10) remains a very important method of achieving training objectives.

Thirdly, the new technologies are opening up opportunities for employees who in the past have been 'disenfranchised' from training and educational programmes because they worked shifts (i.e. could not attend 'normal' courses on a regular basis), or worked in dispersed units or in small organisations, or could not be released for training, or lived in an area without a local college. The new technologies have enabled the creation of sophisticated 'open learning' systems which make it possible for employees (and employers) to study at home, at work (even in the car on their way to and from work!) or wherever they wish; to embark on their studies when it is suitable for them (as opposed to the fixed enrolment date of an educational institution); to have access to a very wide range of courses, irrespective of where the learner happens to live, and to construct their own learning environment without having to cope with the 'going back to school' anxiety.

The trend to reduce what have come to be accepted as 'artificial' admission barriers to vocational educational courses (for example, traditional and notional minimum or maximum age regulations), and the parallel trend to recognise that in some circumstances adults' 'life experience' and high motivation to learn can more than offset their not having 'A' levels or other paper qualifications, have also opened up training and development opportunities for the 'unqualified' person. This characteristic of open learning is of particular importance in helping less well qualified technical personnel to acquire improved qualifications in the context of serious shortages of skills in the new technology industries, and in allowing personnel in all industries to update their skills and receive certification for units of NVQs. A number of large organisations now have their own open access training centres, where employees can use technology-assisted instruction at times to suit themselves, and many organisations have designed their own learning packages, which can be used by employees across a wide geographical area, either as distance learning, or as open access material supported by tutoring from local managers.

Clearly the role and expertise of the training officer in influencing and evaluating these approaches to planned training are very different from those required for traditional in-house training activities. For example, the explosive increase in the number and variety of open learning programmes becoming available presents a major challenge for the training officer to give advice as to which is the most appropriate programme for a particular employee.

As we saw in Chapter 5, all training resources ultimately cost money and the training officer is responsible for advising on the best use of the available resources to facilitate learning. To do this she requires an up-to-date knowledge of the resources on which she can draw and how they can best be employed. We now describe the three major categories of training resources: people, money and external facilities.

People as a training resource

Line managers

Many organisation training policies clarify that the training of their staff is ultimately a line management responsibility, and indeed, most learning takes place in the day-to-day work situation. Managers can act as coaches, mentors, appraisors and role models for their subordinates, as well as helping them to identify and use the many learning opportunities which occur in the course of normal work, and in the 'learning organisation' (see Chapters 1 and 12) increasing emphasis is being placed upon these aspects. In addition, successful off-the-job training relies heavily upon the trainees receiving suitable briefing by their managers prior to the training and being given support to transfer their learning to their work. Line managers' commitment to training is not only crucial to maximising the benefits of formal course training, it is also a powerful factor in creating and developing a climate which expects and supports training interventions as a normal part of organisational life. At an operational level, line managers, especially if they are good trainers, are an important source of lecturers for induction and other in-house programmes.

Training specialists

An experienced training officer is potentially one of the major contributors to her organisation's training operation. The extent to which her knowledge and skills are put to profitable use depends in practice upon many variables, in particular upon her credibility, technical competence and the degree of co-operation which she receives from fellow managers.

Trainers

The role of trainers is discussed in Chapter 6. They act as the essential link between the learner and the training programme and include managers (when coaching their own staff), company tutors overseeing trainee technologists, craft trainee supervisors and operator instructors.

Former trainees

Satisfied 'customers' are a training officer's best ambassadors in helping to create informed opinion about the training function. They can also be of great assistance in getting a new form of training accepted, such as outdoor training sponsored by an organisation (see Appendix 6). Again, because of their experience of a former programme and, in particular its subsequent value to them in their work, past trainees can often make helpful contributions as speakers or syndicate leaders.

Money resources

Training budget

Many training activities depend upon the availability of finance, and the preparation and monitoring of the budget is, therefore, a most important aspect of the training manager's job. Exactly how this is done will depend upon the following two key factors:

- the organisation structure which affects the way in which the training department relates to the rest of the organisation. For instance, as in our example on page 215, some training departments are designated as profit centres, supplying services to line managers on request and charging accordingly, and sometimes contracting their services and resources (premises, equipment) to external clients for a fee. Such departments are expected to pay their way, costing their services and overheads to determine the prices charged, and operating a profit and loss account. In other organisations, the training department is regarded as an overhead, and allocated a budget.
- the financial systems and controls which operate throughout the organisation. For instance, zero based budgeting assumes starting

with nothing and receiving an allocation justified by the estimated cost of carrying out the training plan, and possibly limited to agreed priorities. More usual is the annual budget allocation, the content and size of which depends on many factors. Of particular significance are the importance accorded to the training function, the level of its activity, and the training officer's tenacity and professionalism in 'fighting her corner' when budgets are being finalised! The size of the budget is likely to vary from year to year depending upon the profitability of the company or, in a public sector organisation, upon government policy. This is an added challenge for the training officer because training or retraining needs can be greatest when financial resources are at a premium. It is always necessary to plan well ahead and to assess the probable future requirements carefully so that whatever finance is available goes to the real, and acceptable, priorities. Regular monitoring of expenditure is essential, so that any discrepancies are noticed at an early stage, and corrective action taken before the situation becomes out of hand.

While budgets vary from one organisation to another, all require appropriate systems of forecasting the financial resources required for training and controlling the money which is allocated. Singer (1977) has specified certain main requirements of a budget and budgetary control in the training function. These are:

- adequate training plans
- the expenses incurred in achieving the training plan must have been identified and estimated (for a list of the main training costs, see Chapter 5, page 137)
- the responsibility for items of expenditure must have been allocated between training specialists and other managers
- account classifications must have been made so that expenditure can be allocated to specific cost areas
- cost information must be recorded accurately and a mechanism for feeding back the collated information must be present so that individuals can take corrective action when required.

Training officers should also be aware of the funding arrangements for national training schemes such as YT, and of grants which are available from their local TEC, as well as of the benefits they can gain from schemes such as Teaching Companies (see Chapter 11).

External training facilities

These can be grouped under six headings:

1 private sector courses and consultants
2 group training schemes
3 professional associations
4 public sector education and training services
5 programmes under the auspices of the TECs
6 courses run by trade unions.

Private sector courses and consultants

Numerous organisations offer a wide and, at times, bewildering variety of courses on almost every aspect of training. Although these providers suffered during the recession, the reduction in the number and size of training departments has resulted in some cases in an increased demand for external courses. Selecting the right course is a difficult but important task for a training officer if her company is to benefit from what can be a very considerable financial outlay. (See Chapter 10, pages 280 and 282, for criteria to use in selecting external courses).

Consultants are a valuable source of expertise and organisations considering employing them should apply similar criteria to those used in selecting courses. An external consultant can often achieve results which would not be possible by using internal staff. It is not only the wider expertise that a consultant is likely to bring, it is also the advantage of being unaffected by internal politics and value systems.

Group training schemes

These are formed by a group of employers, often in a similar industry, who join together to establish joint training facilities which individually they would be unable to afford. These schemes normally offer employers, particularly small employers, the facilities of a training officer, instructors, and an off-the-job training centre. Traditionally, group schemes were concentrated in the craft training area, particularly in first year off-the-job training and the decline in numbers of craft trainees has affected group training schemes, although some now cover the whole spectrum of training and may also include assistance with employee selection.

Professional associations

The growth of professionalism in many fields of employment in recent years has led to new professional bodies being formed. The training officer needs to be familiar with those professional associations relevant to her organisation. They can supply detailed information on training courses and programmes which lead to membership qualifications, and of post-qualification short courses to assist their members to keep up to date in specialist fields – courses an organisation could not normally afford to run internally.

Public sector education and training services

Universities and Institutions of Further and Higher Education offer vocational courses in a wide variety of subjects and skills. Many of these courses are geared to national examination syllabuses, but there is a trend for colleges to provide courses to meet specialised regional demands and the specific requirements of individual organisations. Some of these courses can, if required, lead to certificates which can be accumulated for NVQs (see Chapters 2, 5 and 9). The availability of courses 'tailor-made' to meet an organisation's specific training requirements is a well-established feature in management training, where it is closely associated with consultancy. Thus, in addition to their more traditional role as providers of standard courses, colleges and universities are increasingly regarded by industry and the public sector employees as 'resource centres' from which they can commission research and consultancy and obtain specialist guest lecturers.

Programmes under the auspices of TECs

As well as controlling the local funding for national schemes such as Youth Training and Employment Training, TECs offer a variety of different services to assist organisations to develop a training strategy linked to their needs and objectives, as well as measures designed to help overcome perceived local needs. Such provisions will obviously vary from time to time and from locality to locality, and training officers should therefore be thoroughly aware of the activities of their local TEC and ensure that they are kept completely up to date.

Trade Unions

Employers should be aware that trade unions run a wide diversity of training courses for shop stewards and union officials. Some of these courses are sponsored jointly by employers' associations and trade unions and are usually orientated towards a particular industry; most, however, are arranged by the TUC or by trade unions, sometimes in conjunction with colleges. Some trade unions have been quick to apply new technology for the benefit of their members, for example the Electrical, Electronic, Telecommunication and Plumbing Union pioneered the use of video discs and micro-computers for technical retraining at their Union College at Cudham (Chapple, 1984).

A training officer may wish to inform her directors of the possible consequences of their union representatives being better trained than their managers in the knowledge and skills of industrial relations!

FROM POLICY TO TRAINING PLAN AND BUDGET

A well known organisation in the electronics industry realised that because of increasing competition and rapid advances in technology, radical internal changes were required. The company had grown rapidly and there was no formal training policy; staff had been recruited for the expertise they already possessed, and had so far managed to update themselves and adapt their skills to new situations and challenges.

As the company developed, however, different departments grew at varying rates. Task teams had been very successful in masterminding various projects in the short term, but had lacked formal co-ordination with all departments concerned. In addition, there was now a mix of more recently recruited managers who had not undergone the learning process of 'growing up with the product'.

The Board decided that it needed to clarify the company's aims and make a clear statement of policies and strategies required to meet them. To overcome the problems being encountered, some structures and controls would be necessary, but because rapid technological development required constant change, the directors were determined not to introduce bureaucratic controls.

It was felt that the company could make better use of its own technological products to produce more efficient management information systems for use by all, and that it was necessary for employees to be aware of the new expectations of them, and to define the knowledge and skills they required.

Assistance was obtained from the local TEC in a pilot project to assess current skills against a profile of current and future skill requirements. It was found that managers needed an awareness of their own management style and that of others, and how to use their own strengths to achieve company objectives. They also needed to improve their problem solving abilities and there was an obvious requirement to develop techniques for effective teamwork.

As a result of this project, a short policy statement was drawn up. This related the training function directly to the achievement of organisation objectives, provided for a regular training budget and allocated specific responsibilities to managers and to a newly appointed Training Officer. The budget would include all normal training expenses, but not the cost of managers' time away from work undertaking learning/training initiatives, or acting as internal tutors.

The policy guidelines emphasised self development which was portrayed as a continuous process. The approach was to be directly related to business strategy and integrated in such a way that learning initiatives would be followed by action plans, review and related on-the-job coaching where required. In the short term the training budget was to be spent on in-house training, especially geared to the attainment of organisation objectives. Possibilities of sending staff on external courses and part-time qualification programmes would be considered in the longer term.

In consultation with representatives from all levels of management, the Training Officer drew up a detailed plan. This provided for short workshops featuring the core skill requirements highlighted by the analysis. Each workshop concluded with individual action plans with on-going 'clinics' at various levels to review and discuss progress.

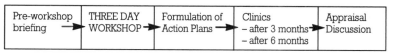

Figure 8.1
Training Plan

The discussions of responsibilities and accountabilities led to a new staff appraisal scheme and the individual action plans formulated at the workshops and discussed at the 'clinics' became an important feature of the appraisal interviews.

The programme was designed in several phases. Phase One consisted of five core workshops for senior managers as follows:

- Responsibilities and accountabilities in the 'new world'
- Interpersonal skills/Management styles
- Team management
- Presentation skills
- Time management.

Phases Two and Three concerned middle and junior managers and supervisors, the exact content to be determined as the result of discussions during Phase One, and after consultation with representatives of the groups concerned.

This training was costed and a budget sent to the directors for approval. A number of decisions had to be made, all of which had a direct relationship with the budget, as well as with the objectives of the training. Some of the issues were as follows:

- Should the workshops be held in-company, or would it be more beneficial if they were residential?
- Should they be conducted by internal or external staff?
- Should the pre-workshop briefings be held away from the participant's own department?

It was decided that it would be appropriate to make the team management workshop residential and that it should take place in a hotel, but that the others would be held in a specially designated conference room on the premises. External tutors were to be engaged for the team management and the time management workshops; the other workshops would be conducted by internal staff and the Training Officer.

The budget therefore included the following items:

- Appropriate proportion of the Training Officer's salary, national insurance and superannuation contributions
- Overheads on training room (proportion of heat, light, rent, depreciation on equipment)
- Tutor's fees (for Phase One, three days each to two external tutors)
- Residential fees (for Phase One this was a three-day workshop on team management only)

- Secretarial services
- Postage and
- Stationery and training aids.

Whilst the cost of Phase One could be calculated, it was only possible to use estimated figures for Phases Two and Three, as their precise content depended in part upon the results of Phase One.

Although this case has been simplified in the interests of conciseness and clarity, and takes no account of training needs of other categories of staff, it demonstrates the following points:

- *The training policy clarifies the* purpose *of training, defines* responsibilities *and provides* guidelines *for decision making*
- *It should be frequently* reviewed
- *The training plan translates the policy into strategies to meet specific situations*
- *The training budget is an estimate of the cost of the training plan*
- *As however, the budget is likely to be a fixed amount, it will affect the details of the plan*
- *As training needs unfold progressively (see also Chapter 7), training budgets should be constantly reviewed*
- *Although the training officer's accounts and budget estimations should be as professional as those of colleagues in other management functions, the full information required is unlikely to be available. Budget estimates therefore have to be based on 'best available' information. Making suitable adaptations is an important skill of a training officer*
- *Large organisations with a stable bureaucratic culture and planned training programmes for different categories of staff, e.g. craft trainees, technicians, middle and senior managers, are more likely to have detailed long-term training plans*
- *Rapidly developing organisations have the most difficulty in producing detailed training plans from which to derive budgets, and may be constrained to operate on an* ad hoc *basis. Plans should exist, but on a less formal basis. In any organisation, however, written policy statements and plans can be extremely useful documents in clarifying* objectives *and* responsibilities *and providing* guidelines *for decision making*

- *Whilst obtaining suitable finance is important and there is seldom sufficient funding to meet all needs, the most effective training programmes are not necessarily the most expensive. They are likely to be those which are 'owned' by management, directed towards strategic organisational objectives and integrated with other organisational systems, such as staff appraisal and mentoring.*

FOR FURTHER REFLECTION AND DISCUSSION

1 What do you see as the key requirements of a policy which aims to promote 'learning from everyday experience'? Explain the influence of these requirements on the following:

- Job descriptions.
- Job training manuals.
- Performance appraisal.
- Departmental meetings.

2 What are the main difficulties of translating corporate objectives into human resource objectives and plans, both generally and in any organisation with which you are familiar? How can these difficulties be tackled?

3 What in your opinion are the key areas to be addressed in an organisation's corporate learning strategy? What arrangements would you recommend within your organisation to ensure that departmental training plans reflect such a strategy?

4 What are the main influences on an organisation's policy or policies for employee development? Draft a proposed policy statement including each of the following issues, for an organisation that does not yet have a written employee development policy.

- Identification of training needs.
- Work experience opportunities for non-employees.
- Performance appraisal.
- Paid leave/release for educational purposes.
- Line management's training role.

SUGGESTED READING

HARRISON R. *Training and development*. IPM, London, 1988. (Chapter 6).

FARNHAM D. 'Corporate policy and personnel management'. *Personnel Management Handbook*, (ed. S. Harper), Gower, Aldershot, 1987.

MOORBY E. *How to succeed in employee development*. McGraw-Hill, London, 1991. (Particularly Chapter 6 and the Appendix to Chapter 6, for an illustrative case of an employee development plan.)

RICHARDS-CARPENTER C. *Relating manpower to an organisation's objectives*. Institute of Manpower Studies, Report No. 56, 1982.

SLOMAN M. 'Coming in from the cold: a new role for trainers'. *Personnel Management*, Jan. 1994, pages 24–27.

Chapter 9

ASSESSING TRAINING NEEDS – THE JOB AND THE INDIVIDUAL

Job Training Analysis – analytical techniques – carrying out an individual needs training analysis – assessing performance

INTRODUCTION

In Chapter 7, we demonstrated how an assessment of organisation needs can highlight problems revealing a variety of job-specific training needs for groups of people or for individuals. It is these with which we are now concerned. We shall consider two main questions:

- *how to identify the requirements of a particular job or task*
- *how to assess the existing competence and potential of the employee against these requirements.*

Fairbairns (1991) suggests that a third question is required, namely:

- *what skills/knowledge/personal attributes are likely to be encouraged, recognised, rewarded by the organisation?*

As you read this chapter, you might like to consider the implications of this third question, and, in particular, to relate it to the title of this book. We shall return to this issue later in the chapter. We shall now approach the first question by considering some of the different ways of analysing jobs for training purposes and some of the techniques which are commonly used, and then proceed to the second question of how an individual's performance may be assessed. However, the situation is not always quite so clear cut, as changes in organisations, such as the trend towards flatter structures, or matrices of project teams, may mean assessing the capability and potential of the team, rather than the individual. In fact, individual needs may vary according to the team mix; of equal importance as technical expertise may be the role each person plays as a team member and this may have to be assessed during the process of the teamwork itself. In addition, theories of experiential learning tell us that we need to reflect on what has happened and assess our own performance, determine how to improve and what help we need, and that this process is an essential part of the learning itself. In both these instances, the boundaries between our two main questions become less clear, but we will return to a consideration of these issues later in the chapter.

JOB TRAINING ANALYSIS

The use of job analysis is not confined to purposes associated with training and we therefore use the term 'job training analysis' to distinguish it from analyses carried out for recruitment, job evaluation, ergonomic or other reasons. Although the emphasis and the detailed information will vary, there is likely to be some overlap of the results of different types of analysis; for example, a training officer might find that an analysis for job evaluation purposes provided her with a useful starting point, and conversely, a job training analysis might be an aid in recruitment and selection.

In practice, jobs are varied and have many facets. Some consist of few tasks, others of many, some are relatively static and others subject to frequent changes, some require a high degree of discretion while others are mainly prescribed. Additional complications are caused by the range of social and physical environments in which they are carried out.

A wide variety of skills and knowledge may need to be analysed; for example, job skills may be manual, diagnostic, interpersonal, or decision making. The knowledge component may be technical, procedural, or concerned with company operations. Moreover, jobs vary widely in the range, variety and degree of skills and knowledge needed to perform them. With many different combinations of these components occurring in jobs, different analytical approaches and techniques are necessary. Until the advent of NVQs, to which we shall return later, it was customary to view a job as having requirements of knowledge and skill (and sometimes attitudes). This provided a framework in which to collect and organise information about a job, as well as a useful foundation from which to derive the appropriate content of a training programme, methods used to impart knowledge being different from those required to develop skills, which require opportunities to practise. From the analysis it is possible to determine 'behavioural objectives' specifying what the successful trainee is to be able to 'do' at the end of the programme, the standards required and the conditions under which the work will be carried out (see pages 269ff).

The ITBs introduced rigorous job training analyses, which fitted the higher proportion of routine manual jobs which existed at that time, and were also in accord with the philosophy of the day. Although these systems had drawbacks of being inward looking, time consuming to produce and neglectful of the needs of a team, or of problems of role conflict, they were in many cases a marked improvement on the previous 'common skills' or 'welfare' approach to training. Some of the techniques which evolved continue to be useful because, although automation and new technology has resulted in a trend away from routine manual, to more technical, jobs, some of the 'old type' skills are still required today. We therefore consider it relevant to give some examples. Currently, we have the rapid development of NVQs, which employ different terms and methodology. We shall briefly describe both approaches, terming the former 'traditional' job training analysis, and the latter 'approaches to competence'.

The process of 'traditional' job training analysis

As Boydell (1977) points out: 'Job analysis is a process of examining a job. Thus it is not a particular document, but rather gives rise to certain documents, the product of an analytical examination of the job'. A variety of documents can arise as a result of the analytical techniques; the main ones are as follows:

A job description

'A broad statement of the purpose, scope, responsibilities and tasks which constitute a particular job' (MSC, 1981). It contains the job title, the department in which the job holder works, to whom he is responsible and for whom he has responsibility, the purpose of the job, a list of the major tasks and, if appropriate, a brief description of any resources for which he is accountable. In a large organisation, it may be advisable to add the hours and precise place of work, as it can provide useful information in determining availability and suitable timing for any proposed training programme.

A job specification

'A detailed statement, derived from the job analysis of the knowledge and the physical and mental activities involved in the job, and of the environment within which the job is performed' (MSC, 1981). These activities are normally classified under the two headings of 'knowledge' and 'skill' and sometimes a third heading, 'attitudes' is added. In the case of a secretary's job, two of the tasks in the job description might be typing letters and answering the telephone. Associated physical and mental activities might be the interpersonal skills required in dealing with irate customers on the telephone, or knowledge of organisation style and format of letters.

A training specification

'A detailed statement of what a trainee needs to learn, based on a comparison between the job specification and the individual's present level of competence' (MSC, 1981). Methods of determining the latter may be by comparison with experienced workers' standard in the case of an operator, or in the case of a manager, by staff appraisal.

Task analyses

Give details of each of the tasks of the job, often in the form of Stages and Keypoints (see Figure 9.1). In the secretary's job an example might be the stages and important points to remember in using a piece of office equipment, such as a fax machine (see pages 241ff below).

Faults analyses

Give details of the faults which can occur in specific tasks.

Types of Analysis

The comprehensive analysis

In this approach, all facets of the job are examined with the aim of producing a detailed record of every task in the job, and the skills, knowledge and attitudes required for each. A less comprehensive and less expensive approach may often be adequate and the following criteria should be confirmed before a comprehensive analysis is carried out:

- the majority of work tasks which the trainee will have to do are unfamiliar to her, difficult to learn and the cost of error unacceptable

- time and other resources are available for a full analysis – the job is likely to remain basically unchanged and the resultant training programme used frequently by a number of trainees
- the job is closely prescribed and the 'correct' method of doing it must be learned.

A situation in which an exhaustive analysis might be worthwhile could be where new plant is to be installed in a factory, and because totally unfamiliar operating skills are required, the staff concerned need total retraining.

Having decided that a comprehensive analysis is necessary, the first step is to examine the job to gain an overall picture and write a job description. The next step is to examine in depth and produce a job specification. A useful sequence is to identify the main responsibilities of the job holder and record the constituent tasks for each of these, together with the skills and knowledge involved in carrying them out. For example, the responsibilities of a garage forecourt attendant may include accepting new stock and receiving payment for goods sold. Taking the first of these, a number of separate tasks can be identified, such as the handling of petrol deliveries, or receiving a consignment of new tyres. Each task is then analysed to find out what knowledge and skill is necessary. In the case of the petrol delivery, the attendant must know the relevant fire precautions and understand their significance, the sequences to be followed in dipping petrol tanks, the paperwork, procedures, etc.

Key task analysis

This is concerned with the identification and detailed investigation of the key or core tasks within the job. As far back as 1970, Wellens pointed out that job analysis as a means of determining training needs is at its most effective at the lower end of the organisation; the discretionary and ever-changing nature of supervisory and managerial jobs means that they cannot be predetermined or prescribed accurately. Indeed, often the most important task facing a manager is to determine what in fact he or she ought to be doing and this can involve a complicated balance of priorities. Although a breakdown into tasks and their requisite knowledge and skills can be of some use at supervisory and middle management levels, a total analysis would be costly, cumbersome and likely to obscure the critical areas of the job. At management level, therefore, job descriptions and specifications are usually expressed in more general terms, concentrating on objectives, targets and key areas. (However, definitions of responsibilities common to a number of supervisors and managers may be useful as a basis for standard in-house courses.)

Key task analysis is appropriate for any type of task where the following conditions apply:

- the job consists of a large number of different tasks, not all of which are critical for effective performance; it is assumed that the job holder does not normally require training in minor or non-key tasks, and
- the job is changing in emphasis or content, resulting in a continuing need to establish priority tasks, standards of performance and the skills and knowledge required.

Problem-centred analysis

This approach differs from those described previously in that no attempt is made to produce a description or specification of either the whole job or all of its key tasks. Analysis is limited to a difficulty considered to have a training solution, such as the chief chemist asking the training department to organise a report writing course for her technical staff because their reports were unclear and poorly structured. The analysis is concentrated on this particular aspect of the technical staff's work and excludes others unless they are directly relevant to the specific problem. A problem-centred approach is appropriate when:

- the need for training is urgent but resources are not available for a more extensive analysis
- the operational goal is essentially and uniquely linked to the resolution of one or more identified problems
- a fuller analysis is unnecessary, for example, where an employee's work is satisfactory except in a specific area.

Approaches to Competence

The concept of 'competence' has evolved over a number of years, originally in relation to management development, and it received a further impetus when researchers were trying to find ways in which participants on Youth Training schemes could be provided with learning experiences in one organisation which would stand them in good stead in another. The original solution was to identify a number of

'Occupational Training Families', 'Key Competences' and 'Transfer Learning Objectives' (Hayes, 1983). Later, the Management Charter Initiative (MCI, see page 28) adopted the competence approach and a national framework of management competences has been devised. Over the course of time, a number of different methodologies have been used to identify desirable competences, two of which are outlined below.

'Input' approaches
During the last twenty years there have been many studies of what it is that effective managers contribute to the job. Mintzberg (1975) identified eight basic groups of management skills, but the most comprehensive study involved 2,000 US managers and was carried out in 1979/80 by the American Management Association and documented by Boyatzis (1982). The researchers were trying to answer the question, 'What are the characteristics that distinguish superior performance by working managers?' They defined competency as 'an underlying characteristic of a manager causally related to superior performance in a management position.' This suggests that it is more than a set of skills; it is a mix of aptitudes, attitudes and personal attributes possessed by effective managers. In a useful discussion of the competency-competence debate, Woodruffe (1992) stresses that a competency is 'a dimension of overt manifest *behaviour* that allows the person to perform competently'. He explains that the reference to behaviour is important to the definition, stressing that a job analysis should isolate the behaviours which distinguish high performance.

The 'Outcomes' model (NVQs/SVQs)
Here we have a different methodology. Whilst 'input' models are concerned with what it is that effective employees bring to the job, 'outcomes' models focus on what high performers *achieve*.

The method of analysis used for NVQs/SVQs is dominated by two factors. They are *outcome-led*, and are based on *national standards* of competences ideally assessed in the workplace. Competence is defined as 'being able to perform ''whole'' work roles to the standards expected in employment in real working environments' (NCVQ, March 1991). The implication here is that 'whole work roles' involve more than just specific skills and tasks. As already mentioned in Chapter 2, identifying these competences is the remit of the Occupational and Industry Lead Bodies and the technique used is Functional Analysis (see pages 248ff). The approach assumes that the competence will be used at the workplace both to define training needs and to assess 'qualified' status, because standards are set in the form of performance criteria.

In this text we have used the term 'competence' in relation to the 'outcomes' approach and the term 'competency' with reference to the 'input' approach.

ANALYTICAL TECHNIQUES

Many different techniques have been devised to enable the variety of job skills to be analysed and recorded; among the best known are the following: stages and key points analysis, manual skills analysis, faults analysis, critical incident analysis, job-learning analysis and functional analysis.

Stages and Key Points Analysis

Imagine you are Nellie Brown, an Assistant Supervisor of an office in a branch of an international company. You have a very busy day ahead of you and a pile of queries to sort out. Your manager asks you to look after Mary, a YT trainee who started yesterday, and show her the work of the office, and in particular, how to use the fax machine. There are messages going out all the time, so there is plenty of opportunity; the only problem is that you have very little time this morning. You take her to the machine and let her watch you transmitting several messages. You ask Mary if she has any questions and are assured that she can manage, so you leave the last message for her to send to the United States, and just as she is starting you are called away to the telephone. When you come back you find Mary in tears because, although the letter has gone through the machine, and cost three minutes of telephone time, the concluding report indicates that transmission was not OK. One of the staff sitting nearby tells you that Mary had difficulty in putting the paper in straight at the beginning, causing the alarm bell to ring. Several people had come to help her, and eventually the fax went through. However, because there was now a queue at the machine, she had pulled the paper to hurry it as it came through, thereby interfering with the transmission. There were a number of key points that you should have made plain when you demonstrated to Mary, but because you were busy and your mind was on your own work, they did not come readily to your mind. The result was wasting money in useless telephone time, some disruption to others in the department, as well as the emotional upset to Mary and feelings of inadequacy on your part. When discussing this with friends over lunch, you discover that other departments have previously prepared analysis sheets which state very simply the main stages in routine tasks and the key points associated with them. Anyone demonstrating to new recruits can use these sheets to check that they have not omitted any important part of the instruction.

This technique can be applied to relatively simple tasks which are part of a more difficult job, but it is unsuitable for complex work, or tasks which require the frequent use of judgemental skills. A stages and key points analysis is normally undertaken by a trained instructor, supervisor or senior operator.

The analyst watches and questions an operator at work and using a stages and key points breakdown sheet (see Figure 9.1) records in the 'stage' column the different steps in the job. Most semi-skilled jobs are easily broken down into their constituent parts and a brief summary is made of what the operator does in carrying out each part. The analyst then examines the stages separately and for each one describes in the 'instruction' column, against the appropriate stage, how the operator performs each task. The description of the operator's skill and knowledge is expressed in a few words. At the same time, the analyst notes in the 'key points' column of the breakdown sheet any special points such as quality standards or safety requirements, which should be emphasised to a trainee learning the job. A 'stages and keypoints' breakdown sheet serves two purposes: it provides the *pro forma* which aids the analysis and, when completed, it is used as the instruction schedule. This is an efficient method of analysing relatively simple jobs. It is long established and has been used widely since its introduction from the USA as part of the TWI (Training Within Industry) Job Instruction programme during and after the Second World War.

Manual Skills Analysis

This is used to isolate the skills and knowledge employed by experienced

JOB TITLE: How to make a job breakdown		
Stage (what to do in stages to advance the job)	**Instructions (how to perform each stage)**	**Key points (items to be emphasised)**
1 Draw up table	Rule three columns. Allow space for column headings and job title	Use this sheet as example
2 Head the columns	On top line insert the title of job Insert: Column 1 (Stage) Column 2 (Instructions) Column 3 (Key Points)	Headings – summarise what worker needs to know to perform each job Watch for steps which are performed from habit
3 Follow through the job to be analysed	After each step, ask yourself – 'What did I just do?' Note places where the worker could go astray. Note items to be emphasised. Note hazards. Stress safety points	Write notes clearly and concisely Keep stages in order Ensure directions are complete – never assume they are
4 Fill in Columns 1, 2 and 3 as stage 3 above is performed	Make brief and to-the-point notes	Review and emphasise these 'Key Points' decisively
5 Number the stages	Follow the sequence a worker must follow when learning the job	
6 Follow the job through using directions in Columns 1 and 2	Follow the instructions exactly	
7 Check that all 'Key Points' are included	Record in Column 3 all points where the worker may be confused	

Figure 9.1
A 'stages' and 'key points' breakdown sheet

(Reproduced with acknowledgement to the former Ceramics, Glass and Mineral Products Industry Training Board.)

workers performing tasks requiring a high degree of manual dexterity. It can be used to analyse any task in which precision, manual dexterity, hand-eye coordination and perception are important features.

The hand, finger and other body movements of an experienced operative are observed and recorded in great detail as he carries out his work. This is a highly specialised technique and should be used selectively; those parts of the job which are relatively easy to learn are analysed in much less depth (a stages and key points approach may often be adequate) and an MSA is limited to those tasks (or parts of tasks) which involve unusual skills. These are the 'tricky' parts of a job, which, while presenting no difficulty to the experienced operative, have to be analysed in depth before they can be taught to trainees. In

Figure 9.2 we give an example of a typical pro-forma used in an MSA which illustrates the breakdown of the task of filleting raw fish in a food processing factory. It will be seen from this example that an experienced operative's hand movements are recorded in minute detail, together with the cues, (vision and other senses) which the operative uses in performing the task (see Chapter 3). Explanatory comments are added, where necessary, in the 'comments' column. Special training is needed to apply this type and level of analysis and, in particular, to identify the cues on which the operator depends in both normal and abnormal work conditions, and the senses by which he receives them.

DEPARTMENT : Fish-filleting		TASK: Fillet/trim small plaice			DATE:
Section or Element	Left hand	Right hand	Vision	Other Senses	Comments
Select fish	Reach to trough-grasp fish with T and 1 2 3 4 around belly, p/u and bring forward to board	P/u knife with T and 1 2 3 4 around handle. With sharp edge of blade to right of filleter	Glance ahead for knife position on board	Touch LH on fish	
			Glance ahead for fish position on trough		
		Knife hold:			
Position fish	Place fish on board so that the dorsal fins fall to the edge of the board and the head lies to the right hand side of the filleter.	Hold knife handle against first and third joints of the fingers. Place upper part of T (1st joint) against lower blunt edge of knife and the lower part of T against upper edge of handle. Do not grasp knife tightly. Do not curl tip of fingers into palm of hand.	Check position of fish	Touch LH on fish	Knife is held in the RH during the complete filleting cycle. If knife is held correctly it should be possible to move the knife to the left and right by 'opening' and 'closing' the knuckles (when T is removed from handle).

Key. LH = left hand, RH = right hand, p/u = pick up, T = thumb. 1 = first finger, 2 = second finger, 3 = third finger, 4 = fourth finger. Synchronous movements are recorded on the same line. Successive movements are recorded on succeeding lines.

Figure 9.2
Manual skills analysis

(Reproduced with acknowledgement to the former Food, Drink and Tobacco Industry Training Board.)

Faults Analysis

When analysing a job, information is collected about the faults which occur and especially those which are costly: 'the process of analysing the faults occurring in a procedure, product or service, specifying the symptoms, causes and remedies of each . . .' (Manpower Services Commission, 1981), is termed a faults analysis. The result of this analysis – a faults specification – provides a trainee with details of faults which he is likely to come across in his work, how he can recognise them, what causes them, what effects they have, who is responsible for them, what action the trainee should take when a particular fault occurs, and how a fault can be prevented from recurring. A faults specification is usually drawn up either in a tabular or 'logic tree' form and is useful both for instruction purposes and as a memory aid for an employee after completion of training.

Critical incident analysis

One way of defining the areas of a job with which the incumbent is having most problems is by examining incidents which he sees as the most difficult to handle. This information can be obtained by interview, although depending upon the status of the interviewer, employees may be reluctant to reveal their real problems for fear of making themselves appear inefficient. One of the classical criticisms of the critical incident technique is that people tend to select incidents which they think will put them in a good light, and therefore an atmosphere of complete trust and honesty is necessary if this difficulty is to be overcome.

An alternative way of obtaining the information is to ask the incumbent for a short written account at the end of each day of the one incident of the day which has been the most difficult to manage and to estimate how frequently he has to deal with a similar difficulty. The exercise is repeated for several days, or for several weeks on days chosen at random. The process is simplified if a special form is designed for the purpose. The forms can be returned anonymously and an overall picture can be gained, as a basis for general training programmes. The reported incidents can be camouflaged to make useful case studies. It is, however, very informative if the respondents are willing to identify themselves, so that individualised training can be devised, and in addition, particular problems can be localised, perhaps to one department, or to newly promoted supervisors. Assistance can then be given exactly where it is required.

As well as pinpointing trouble spots, this technique is useful in involving the employee. In a turbulent environment, change can be so rapid that management may be unaware of the problems and consequent stress which individuals are suffering and a simple technique such as this can often help to alleviate the situation. It is, of course, recognised that not all problems will have a training solution and that some will expose training needs for people other than the incumbent. Before embarking upon this type of exercise, therefore, it is necessary to be assured of management commitment at least to a *consideration* of possible ways of overcoming problems which cannot be solved by training. Having asked for employees' co-operation in writing daily reports, something must be *seen* to happen.

Job-learning Analysis

The types of analysis we have discussed so far have been concerned with the *content* of jobs and tasks; in contrast, job-learning analysis focuses on *processes*, and in particular upon the learning skills which are required. This technique is described in detail by Pearn and Kandola (1988), who give the definition of a learning skill as 'one that is used to increase other skills or knowledge . . . The learning skills represent broad categories of behaviour which need to be learnt.' They identify nine learning skills:

- physical skills
- complex procedures which have to be remembered or followed with the aid of written material
- checking/assessing/discriminating
- memorising facts/information
- ordering/prioritising/planning
- looking ahead
- diagnosing/analysing/solving
- interpreting or using written/pictorial/diagrammatic material
- adapting to new ideas/systems.

The analysis is carried out by interviewing the job incumbent, starting with a description of the main aim of the job, followed by the principal activities. Using nine question cards, each relating to a particular area of learning (see Figure 9.3), the interviewer probes each main activity in more depth, and the resulting analysis enables

CARD 1

Q1 PHYSICAL SKILLS

Are there physical skills involved in this activity which it tôok you a long time to get right or become proficient in?
What are they?

Probes

How much time did it take before you got it right?
What would the consequences be if you did not perform the physical skills correctly?

CARD 2

Q2 COMPLEX PROCEDURES

In this activity, do you have to carry out a procedure or a complex sequence of activities, either (a) relying solely on memory, and/or (b) using written materials, manuals, etc?

Probes

(a) What happens if you forget the sequence or procedure ?
    What are the consequences of forgetting the sequence or procedure?
(b) What written materials, manuals, etc do you use?
    How do you use them?
    When do you use them?
    How accessible are they?
    What are the consequences of not following the procedure correctly?

CARD 3

Q3 CHECKING/ASSESSING/DISCRIMINATING

In this activity, do you make adjustments/judgements based on information from your senses (sight, sound, smell, touch, taste)?
Give me some examples.

Probes

What senses, i.e. sight, sound, smell, touch, taste, do you use?
What adjustments/judgements do you make?
How do you make these adjustments/judgements?
What would the consequences be if you did not make the adjustments/judgements correctly?

Figure 9.3
Job Learning Analysis Question Cards

Source: Pearn M. and Kandola R. *Job Analysis: a practical guide for managers* (IPM, 1988)

trainers to design training approaches and material appropriate to the required type of learning. The aim is not only to ensure that the trainee can learn the content of the job, but that he has the skills to master work of a similar type. For instance, in a job where considerable memory work is involved, the trainee should learn the items he needs to know, but he should also be aware of ways of assisting the memory, such as visual association, mnemonics, etc.

The interviewer then probes each main activity in more depth and the resulting analysis enables trainers to design material and training approaches which are appropriate to the required type of learning. This method can be used in conjunction with other techniques. It is particularly suitable for jobs the content of which cannot be analysed by observation alone i.e. those involving planning ahead, diagnosing, analysing, etc. It also has the advantage of making the job holder aware of his own learning processes. It could usefully be employed by a project group, to determine their own training needs, redefining the nine 'learning skills', if necessary, to suit their own purpose. For further information about the method, see Pearn and Kandola (1988).

Functional Analysis

At the time of writing, this methodology is still being developed, giving rise to much debate. It is the method preferred by TEED in advising the Lead Bodies, and is accepted by NCVQ, as meeting their criteria. The statements of competence are derived by analysing employment functions; briefly, a statement of the key purpose of the overall area of competence is the first requirement. The next step is to ask the question, 'What needs to happen for this to be achieved?' This results in a breakdown into the primary functions which need to be carried out to fulfil the competence. The question is then repeated, generating a further breakdown of the primary functions into sub-functions, which are then divided further and so on (see Appendix 4).

In this way the function is broken down into units of competence and their constituent elements, the latter being accompanied by performance criteria. A unit of competence consists of 'a coherent group of elements of competence and associated performance criteria which form a discrete area of activity or sub-area of competence which has meaning and independent value in the area of employment to which the NVQ relates' (NCVQ, 1989). An example of elements of competence can be found in Chapter 6 (Figures 6.2 and 6.3 pages 150 and 151).

The elements and performance criteria should:

• be stated with sufficient precision to allow unambiguous interpretation by different users, e.g. awarding bodies, assessors, trainers and candidates

- not be so detailed that they only relate to a specific task or job, employer or organisation, location or equipment.

NCVQ (1989)

The NVQ statement of competence has a common format which contains:

- NVQ title
- units of competence
- elements of competence with their associated performance criteria.

Elements of competence are structured as below:

ACTIVE VERB	**OBJECT**	**CONDITIONS**
Implement and evaluate	changes to services, products and systems	related to all operations within the manager's line responsibility.

Performance criteria should each contain a critical outcome, which defines what has to be done for the relevant function to be successfully accomplished (see Chapter 6, Figure 6.3).

It is also customary to add Range Statements to the elements of competence. These specify the range of contexts, e.g. customers, products, settings, to which the element is expected to apply. By extending the range, it is possible to broaden the application of the competence to a national standard, rather than to the narrow requirements of one organisation. This, however, relies on the transfer of learning, about which too little is really known (see, for example, Duncan and Kelly, 1983), and further research is required.

When job training analysis is used purely for in-company purposes, the task of distinguishing the necessary knowledge and skills is facilitated because the circumstances under which the function is to be performed can usually be defined, and the necessary knowledge can be deduced without great difficulty. Broadening the competence nationally, to embrace any context, is an infinitely greater task. The first stage is to specify the range of application of each element (the Range Statement), but in one organisation or educational institution it is unlikely to be possible to practise or assess each element in all applications covered by the Range Statement. The question then arises as to how to facilitate learning which will transfer to these applications and how to test that it does.

Jessup (1991) argues that if the same *procedure* applied in all contexts, then transfer of learning could be assumed and cites the example of learning to drive one model of car, which transfers to other makes. Where this is not likely to be the case, if it were possible to provide experience and assessment in all likely situations, then there would still be no problem. As however, the range of work contexts throughout the country is vast, this is unlikely to be feasible. Jessup suggests two possibilities: first, to predict the likely main variations and ensure that learners know how to adapt accordingly; and second, to ensure that the learners understand the principles involved, thus enabling them to choose for themselves the correct responses to new situations. Resolving this problem is the challenge faced by NCVQ.

A further difficulty about national standards based on outcomes is that the different contexts in which functions are performed are so varied that in extreme cases it may be beyond the limit of any one person's competence to perform in them all. Imagine a barman in a public house in a run down inner city area, who is thoroughly competent in that situation, partaking in good natured daily banter with his customers, and effectively keeping order. If transferred to the bar of a luxury cruise liner he might never be suitable. The very skills which had contributed to his success in the first context might prove a hindrance in the second. The 'input' model of competence is needed here, despite any apparent national qualification.

Despite the critics of NVQs, there is no doubt that the identification of transferable competences would be a great step forward, particularly when in place in a national framework. This would be of use not just to employers, but for trainees, such as those on YT, who are not actually employees and who therefore need to learn skills which will stand them in good stead in entirely different types of employment. A national 'scheme' of competences which can be accessed by anyone, and provide certification for units which can be accumulated for qualifications is highly desirable. In addition, NVQ specifications are suitable for comparison with European awards and thus assist in mutual recognition of qualifications.

For a deeper discussion of NVQs see Jessup (1991 *op. cit.*), from which many of the ideas of this section have been taken.

CARRYING OUT AN INDIVIDUAL TRAINING NEEDS ANALYSIS

Steps in the analysis

Figure 9.4 shows the main steps in analysing a job for training purposes. The sequence illustrates a comprehensive analysis but the principles involved also apply to other forms of analysis.

Step 1
Gain co-operation of all concerned

Step 2
Carry out pre-analysis investigation

Step 3
Decide appropriate analytical approach

Step 4
Analyse the job

Step 5
Write the job description

Step 6
Write the job/training specification

Figure 9.4
The main steps in analysing a job for training purposes

Step 1: gain the co-operation of all concerned
Before carrying out any of the steps below it is necessary to inform everyone of the purpose and process of the investigation, or suspicions may be aroused when the analyst starts asking questions. Consulting and involving people at the outset also ensures a better chance of obtaining commitment to any training programme which might result, and constitutes the first step in a training intervention.

Step 2: carry out a pre-analysis investigation
It is first necessary to establish that a training analysis is needed because a problem which may appear to be due to lack of training may

have other causes, such as excessive workloads or poor organisation. When it is agreed that the problem is a training one, the next stage is to decide whether an analysis is really required. Questions, such as the following, clarify this point:

- What is the organisation losing in terms of production or services because the employee has not been formally trained?
- Is sufficient information available (e.g. from suppliers' manuals) to make an analysis unnecessary?
- How long does it take an average employee to learn the job without training? If a matter of hours then analysis may not be necessary.

Having established that an analysis is needed, a check is made to ensure that the job is unlikely to be changed significantly.

Step 3: decide the appropriate analytical approach
A stages and key points analysis may be appropriate for most of the tasks within a job, but possibly one or two tasks may need a faults analysis or even a manual skills analysis if a great deal of perception or intricate hand and eye movements are involved.

Step 4: analyse the job
The analyst needs to know the sources of information available, the appropriate methods of collecting it, and the depth of analysis required.
  Sources of information include the following:

- the job holder, who can often provide the bulk of the data required
- the job holder's superior, who will specify the purpose of the job and the necessary standards of performance; these points may be obvious for work where the content is largely prescribed, as in the case of most semi-skilled jobs, but it is often much less clear in other types of work, notably managerial jobs
- customers or clients. Information can be gained from records of customer complaints, or questionnaires, which are frequently issued by organisations such as hotels or garages, which provide a service
- organisation records such as job descriptions/specifications, organisation charts, policies, plans, procedures and sales and production records
- suppliers' manuals can be an essential source of information for

training purposes, particularly when new equipment is used for the first time.

Methods of Analysis

The analyst first identifies the job holder's responsibilities and tasks, and then finds out for each task what is done, why it is done and how it is done. This involves finding out what plans the job holder follows, what 'cues' he uses in initiating, controlling and completing a task or part of a task, and what skills and knowledge are required to respond effectively to the relevant cues at various stages in each task. The following methods are commonly used:

- *Observation by the analyst*

Very detailed and continuous observation is required when analysing the manual skill required by an operative in complex and short cycle repetitive work (see Chapter 3). Continuous observation is not normally warranted for jobs in which tasks are repeated at regular intervals, as sufficient information can normally be obtained by random sampling. Observation by itself, however, is inadequate, for instance observing a process operator reading a number of instruments on a control panel is of little help to the analyst.

- *Self observation*

This can be a useful method of collecting data on the purpose and content of a job but relies entirely on the job holder's willingness to keep a diary of his activities. The technique is used in the analysis of managerial and other work characterised by a high degree of discretion. Disadvantages are that the observer may be too close to the job to see it objectively and may, for his own purposes, under- or over-emphasize certain aspects at the expense of others. The job holder may be very busy and at the end of the day his recollections may not be strictly accurate. The required record should be kept as simple as possible, so that it can be kept up to date rather than becoming a chore to be completed later. One advantage of diary keeping is that it obliges the job holder to consider exactly how he spends his time – a very salutary experience to anyone who has never done so! It may be tempting to overestimate what one can do in a given period, and by drawing attention to this fact, keeping a diary may well arouse interest in the management of time.

● *Questionnaire*
This is a particularly useful technique if a significant number of analyses have to be made and can be used as a preliminary to an interview/discussion. It allows the job holder to think carefully beforehand and ensure that all relevant detail is included. Questionnaires and checklists can be designed for any job requiring analysis and can indicate the extent to which different tasks are performed within a job, and their level of difficulty. A further advantage is that they can be subjected to numerical analysis, by computer if necessary.

● *Fact-finding interview*
Discussions with the job holder and other relevant employees are an essential part of the job analysis. The analyst should be competent in the use of interview techniques, such as the framing of questions and careful listening, to gain the maximum benefits from this method.

● *Do-it-yourself*
One way of learning about a job is to try to do it. By putting himself in the position of a trainee, the analyst experiences at first hand the difficulties involved in learning the job. While this may be impracticable or unnecessary, there are certain situations in which it is a useful method of obtaining information. Tasks which are difficult to describe in words, such as those involving a high degree of manual dexterity, are amenable to this form of analysis.

Step 5: write the job description
It is possible that this is already in existence, but it is still useful at this point to check its accuracy. It might also contain extra details such as the incumbent's hours of work, and this might be helpful to know when arranging training programmes. It is also sensible to mark the date at the top of all job analysis documents.

Where the job holder has to liaise with a number of people in the organisation, it can often be illuminating to make an interactive diagram, see Figure 9.5. This depicts a 'role set'. Kahn *et al.* (1964) demonstrated that the conflicting expectations of the same person by various members of staff, can be a potent source of stress and difficulty. For instance, a production manager may have to maintain a delicate balance between the requirements of the production director, the sales manager, quality control, the progress chaser, his own subordinates, the shop steward and the production director. Developing strategies to cope with this situation is likely to be a key area of the job, and yet might easily lack emphasis in a traditional job description.

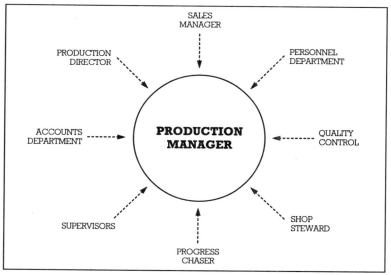

Figure 9.5
The role set of a production manager

Step 6: write the training specification
A job specification for training purposes gives much detail of the skills and knowledge (or the competences) required, and should reflect the environmental and 'job/role environment skills', as well as the tasks performed. The completed specification provides the yardstick against which a trainee's performance will be measured and any shortfall identified. It also provides the information necessary to devise an appropriate training programme (see Chapter 10). Before embarking on the training programme, the specification should be verified with appropriate managers and agreement obtained by all parties. It is particularly necessary to check the emphasis given to different items. One of the important benefits of a detailed specification is that it clarifies the job, as frequently the incumbent's conception of his precise duties and responsibilities is different from that of his superior.

ASSESSING PERFORMANCE

Self Assessment – Experiential Learning
As the rate of change accelerates rapidly, detailed job analyses become quickly outdated necessitating increasing emphasis on *self* analysis, *self* development and situations where employees take charge of their own learning. We are at the turning of the tide and this trend is likely to continue, so that situations where a training officer produces a job analysis and prescribes the necessary training are likely to become confined to lower level routine jobs. In Chapter 7, page 184, we raised the question 'How can we help people to develop themselves?', and one way in which we can do this is by helping them to learn from experience.

In Chapter 3 we explained the cyclical process of experiential learning (see Figure 3.2), and implicit in the reflection and conceptualisation stages of that cycle is the recognition of one's own shortcomings. Mumford (1989) has pointed out that managers tend to think in terms of managerial activities and problems first, whilst recognition of learning/training needs is a secondary stage in their thought processes. The requirement, therefore, is to accelerate this procedure and 'trigger' an acceptance of these needs and an awareness of remedial opportunities, many of which already exist in the working environment. There are numerous ways of encouraging this recognition; for instance, Mumford suggests a review based on the learning opportunities identified in Figure 3.3, which can encourage managers to realise how they can create learning events for themselves, often without the word 'need' being mentioned at all. (For a comprehensive treatment of this topic see Mumford, 1989, and Honey and Mumford, 1989).

Action learning 'sets' can provide a similar kind of 'trigger', particularly when the discussion centres round what is needed to overcome a particular problem. Regular entries in a personal log book help towards the gradual identification of needs and opportunities. This type of activity is at the far end of the continuum suggested in Chapter 7, and at the heart of the process of continuous development and the concept of learning organisations, where *reality* is the vehicle for learning. External help can be obtained through discussion with other people, but the process itself is internal and essentially self developmental because the assessment is an intrinsic part of the learning. It is a skill, the most vital of the 'competencies' which has to be acquired and gradually cultivated, as a prerequisite of 'learning to learn'. A recognition of one's own learning style is a helpful step forward and the Honey and Mumford Learning Styles Questionnaire (see Chapter 3) is a useful diagnostic instrument. Advice on how to practise and improve styles other than that originally preferred, helps the learner to become more versatile in completing all four stages of the experiential learning cycle.

Moving back along the continuum, various kinds of planned interventions can be used as stimulators for experiential learning, such as courses consisting of 'contrived' experiences (e.g. group task assignments, or in their extreme form, Outdoor Training). The debriefing which follows such activities can afford significant insights into strengths and weaknesses, and into the role each participant has played in the group.

Programmes can also be structured round questionnaires which identify preferred team roles, the two most notable being the Belbin Team Roles (see Chapter 12, and Woods, 1992), and the Margerison McCann Team Roles (see Margerison, 1992). Both of these feed information from a self perception questionnaire into a computer and produce individual print-outs relating to the way participants see their roles as team members. The new Belbin programme has an added dimension in that it incorporates information provided by colleagues or other course participants, thereby providing a more objective profile. The analysis into identifiable 'roles' enables a trainer to structure situations where participants can practise a variety of roles. These programmes and the learning needs they diagnose are particularly important in view of the increasing use of teamwork in organisations. They are also useful tools to help in the diagnosis of *group* training needs.

Other ways of helping people identify their own training needs are individual action plans. Sometimes it is useful to start these with a blank sheet, otherwise a little helpful structure can be provided in the form of questions such as:

- Where am I now?
- Where do I want to be?
- What is stopping me from getting there?
- What do I need to know?
- What do I need to do?
- Where can I get help?
- What targets am I going to achieve by . . . (dates)?
- How am I going to monitor and evaluate my performance?

When completing action plans, it is important that the targets are sufficiently specific to be recognised. For instance to plan to 'delegate more next year' is not a meaningful target as it can be very loosely interpreted. A more specific target would be 'By 13th March I will have reviewed all my work activities and found a suitable way of delegating twenty per cent of them'.

Assessing the new employee

A new employee, selected against a personnel specification, may already have, in broad terms, the necessary ability, achievement and experience and may therefore only require limited training. It is, however, advisable to check this, either by discussion with the person concerned, or, if appropriate, by administering a test. The new job may be very familiar in many respects but differ in one or two important aspects in which previous experience can hinder performance. Where safety controls are involved, it is imperative to be aware of the dangers of negative transfer (see Chapter 4). Possibly the only training which might be required would be to discuss the important areas of difference and provide practice in them.

A trainability test is 'a validated test designed to assess whether a job applicant has the potential to reach a satisfactory standard after training'. The applicant is required to perform an appropriate, carefully designed, short task after being given prior instruction . . .' (MSC, 1981). This type of test can be used for a variety of jobs ranging from fork lift truck driving, bricklaying, bottling, as well as social skills such as interviewing a client for a mortgage with a building society. It is also suitable for all ages of recruit and is regarded as more appropriate for older applicants than traditional selection tests.

Appraisal of Existing Employees

The two most common methods of assessing the performance of existing staff are performance appraisal and assessment centres. (For comprehensive coverage of a wide variety of assessment methods, including unconventional techniques, see Davey and Harris, 1982).

Performance Appraisal

A small chemical company in the UK received instructions from its parent in the USA to install a performance appraisal scheme as standardised by the parent company. The UK Personnel Manager protested that it would not suit the UK company, but his objections were overruled and the scheme was set in motion. The managers were called together and given some preliminary training in the operation of the scheme and in appraisal interviewing. Three years later, the scheme was deemed a dismal failure, because managers merely went through the motions of conducting the interviews, many of which took place in the bar of the local public house. The appraisal report forms contained noncommittal comments, which were no use for any purpose. The parent company still insisted that there should be an appraisal scheme operating in the UK, but reluctantly agreed that the standard scheme could be altered or modified to suit.

Knowing that introducing a new scheme would now be a tricky operation because of the attitudes which had already been created, the Personnel Manager enlisted the help of consultants. They set up task groups representing all grades of management, with a brief to discuss the difficulties of appraisal schemes, what the objectives of such a scheme might be, and how they might turn the request from headquarters to their own advantage by identifying the type of scheme which they felt would bring them some benefit. The suggestions from the task groups were modified at a conference where all managers were given the opportunity to voice their opinions. Only when it became apparent that there was general commitment was a new scheme drawn up on the proposed lines; groups of managers came together to clarify how they would operate the new system and, at their own request, to have further practice in conducting the interviews. After a difficult start because the first task groups still carried over negative views of appraisal from the former scheme, the new system ran smoothly.

Lack of commitment and unclear aims are the main reasons why appraisal schemes fail to realise the hopes of their instigators. It is expedient to use group discussions and participative approaches to draw up the scheme, thus making the design of the system and the assessment criteria the first stage of training. A further cause of failure is lack of ability and confidence to conduct the interview; accepting criticism is painful, particularly if it is given in a tactless manner. Managers are understandably reluctant to create resentment in subordinates with whom they are going to have to continue to work, and are often tempted to 'duck' important issues. Appraisor training, therefore, is an essential part of the process. In fact it is often said that appraisal can indicate more about the appraisor than the appraisee!

Some appraisal schemes emphasise joint assessment with the final report being owned and signed by both parties. In cases of disagreement a two part report may be submitted, or someone further up the hierarchy may be designated to discuss any points which either party wishes to raise. Performance appraisal needs to be complemented by regular review meetings; it is ineffective to initiate for the first time at an annual appraisal, discussion of an issue which arose several months previously.

Findings from the Price Waterhouse Cranfield Project on trends in Europe, indicate that performance appraisal is one of the major tools of management development in the UK as well as in Sweden, Switzerland and Holland, whilst on the other hand, it is less used in France, Spain and Germany, and rarely in Denmark. In all countries, including the UK, figures indicating the incidence of management training in appraisal are considerably lower than those relating to the regular use of the technique (Holden and Livian, 1992). A disturbing feature in view of the discussion above.

The purpose of appraisal may be to assess and improve current performance usually by defining training needs, or future potential, as well as salary review. It is not normally deemed advisable to attempt all three objectives at one time. Fear of losing monetary reward or promotion may inhibit an open discussion of training and development needs. It is indeed possible that one appraisor may not be appropriate for all three. For example, an immediate superior may be the most suitable person with whom to discuss current performance, but potential and promotion prospects may be the domain of someone further up the hierarchy. Some organisations make a practice of using more than one appraisor. For instance the 'grandfather' or superior's superior may be present at the interview, and we know of one organisation where a colleague of the appraisee is also present.

It is normally good practice to give advance notice of the interview and ask the appraisee to write a report on his/her own performance, and use this to start off the discussion. Some of the first appraisal schemes were designed on the basis of personal qualities such as enthusiasm, commitment, loyalty, etc., but current schemes are usually output based, reviewing performance against targets during the period under review, and formulating new targets for the forthcoming period. The interview should terminate with the identification of developmental steps, action plans and targets, with dates.

Objective setting and formal appraisal are at the centre of *performance management systems* (PMS), where individual goals and responsibilities are linked to the objectives of the work unit and key corporate objectives as a whole. A survey commissioned by the former Institute of Personnel Management found that organisations which operate PMS normally have a mission statement which is communicated to all employees, and express performance targets in terms of measurable outputs, accountabilities and training or learning targets. They use formal appraisal to communicate performance requirements and produce personal improvement plans and they also have a tendency to link performance requirements to pay, particularly for senior managers (Bevan and Thompson, 1991). Although the majority of companies in the survey had instigated PMS to improve organisational effectiveness, the researchers found no evidence to indicate that this link existed. Some PMS systems make use of computer programmes to subject data to statistical procedures and produce results which are as objective as possible. For a more detailed acount of such a scheme, see Moorby (1991). Despite the survey findings, the incidence of PMS is likely to increase and as the example in Chapter 7, page 181 demonstrates, it links very conveniently with NVQ competences.

Assessment/Development Centres

These have a history based in selection procedures and are still used for this purpose today. Many companies, however, have extended their usage to assessment for promotion and/or development centres to indicate strengths and weaknesses. Dulewicz (1989) claims that assessment centres were designed primarily as a predictor of potential *not* as a method for appraising current performance and that their record for doing this is far better than any other technique.

The first step in devising an assessment/development centre is to identify what strengths or characteristics are to be tested. As we have seen in considering the competences, two approaches are possible, the input approach, in which case personal attributes, such as leadership, might be tested, or the outcomes approach, in which discrete units of the job might be given as assessed tasks. In practice, most companies seem to employ input approaches, testing competencies, such as basic reasoning, strategic visioning, confidence, control, flexibility, interpersonal skills, etc., although with the advent of NVQs there may be a trend towards testing 'output' defined competences. There are a number of important questions to ask namely:

- What are the essential competences/(ies) the organisation/job requires?
- How can we monitor the competences/(ies) required in a changing environment?
- Can we devise tasks which really do assess these competences/(ies)?
- Does performance on the task actually transfer to the working situation?
- How can we evaluate the scheme as a whole?

Ways of arriving at answers to the first of these questions include: the use of the Repertory Grid technique (see Fransella and Bannister, 1977) to generate a list of the critical competences/(ies) exhibited by effective managers; surveys amongst staff; comparing results with those of similar organisations and interpreting any differences; considering the findings of other researchers; or adapting national standards such as those established within NVQs. Whatever methods are used it is necessary to monitor that the dimensions being assessed are still relevant to work aims and objectives, otherwise there is a danger that managers and assessors will subconsciously select in their own image and that this process of 'cloning' may hinder organisation development. Some organisations attempt to answer the last three questions by careful performance appraisal of staff who have previously been through the centre to compare their marks with actual performance. This is, of course, open to the criticism that since being assessed some development should have taken place. A more rigorous approach would be to rate managers in their current jobs, put them through the assessment centre and compare their scores with the ratings. Few organisations do this, because of the inconvenience it would cause. It may be thought ironic that standard selection tests are not marketed unless they have been thoroughly validated, and yet important career decisions may be made in many companies on the strength of procedures which have not been subjected to this rigour.

The training of assessors is obviously a crucial factor. Not only must they be capable of assessing the dimensions in question, but fairness also demands inter-assessor reliability; continuous training and updating is therefore required. Assessors may be senior managers who have themselves been through the centre and possibly assisted in its design. The full support of top management is vital in order to gain the commitment of managers at all levels, as the following quotation from L. Jackson (1989) shows:

> 'If anything, we underestimated the level of inertia and opposition which faced us . . . It was fortunate we had the full support of the directors . . . it was noticeable that the psychological barriers were more daunting than the administrative and technical ones.'

Now imagine that you are Jim Unlucky, and have just returned to work on Monday, having spent the end of last week going through your organisation's assessment centre. Attainment of certain standards is a prerequisite of being considered for promotion, and you have just been informed that unfortunately you did not make the grade, although after a suitable period you can apply for reassessment. You have been provided with a profile and asked to produce an action plan, to discuss with your superior and training officer, if required. You feel resentful about the whole business. You did not understand what one of the tests was getting at, and do not agree with the comments on your assessment sheet. You have just been to see your boss who said he did not understand them either. You wonder whether it is worth trying to make an action plan and apply for reassessment, or whether to start looking for other jobs because you do not seem to be getting very far in this one. You wonder whether your assessment centre scores will feature in an employer's reference.

A number of organisations (see, for example, L. Jackson, 1989), have found that merely feeding back the profile of strengths and weaknesses does not necessarily equip those assessed to take the required action. Short off-the-job follow up courses may be necessary to give a fuller understanding of the meaning of the profile, and to assist the manager to come to terms with it. Such a course is also a convenient occasion for drafting and discussing personal action plans, making learning contracts and enabling managers to begin to take charge of their own learning. This will not necessarily be related to weaknesses because, whilst 'training needs' are usually associated with limitations, one of the features of an assessment centre is that it also brings out strengths. Perhaps in the past we have dwelt too much on 'training gaps' and paid too little attention to helping people to learn how to build upon their strengths.

Griffiths and Goodge (1994) describe 'third generation' development centres where participants are actively involved in generating their own assessments.

For further accounts of assessment centres see Cockerill (1989), Dulewicz (1989) and Woodruffe (1990).

At the beginning of this chapter, we quoted Fairbairns (1991), in suggesting a third question which might be relevant in determining an individual's training needs:

'What skills/knowledge/personal attributes are likely to be encouraged, recognised or rewarded?'

This question brings us back to the title of this book, which is based on the philosophy that whatever approach is taken to training, or even if no formal training exists, an organisation is a learning environment with its own system of rewards and punishments of varying kinds. Unless there is going to be some organisational 'spin off' for attending to certain training needs, or unless there is some personal reason for wanting to learn, employees will not be motivated to do so. If training is required to run directly against the organisational flow, trainers must be prepared to overcome resistance. In assessing needs therefore, some attention must be paid to the organisational context. Fairbairns suggests isolating those needs which satisfy all three of the following criteria:

* *important in my job*
* *in need of training*
* *likely to be encouraged*

and describes how this methodology was used in two companies. Items which satisfied only one or two of the specified criteria were found to be barriers to training, or problems for the organisation as a whole, rather than individual training needs. Those which satisfied all three were described by managers as 'just what we need'. You might like to consider the relationship of that model with systems of performance related pay, or with methods of determining competences.

You should now realise that there has been a historical development of methodologies to determine training needs, influenced by the dominant job characteristics at different periods, as well as the philosophies propounded by national institutions such as training boards and the NCVQ. We are fortunate in having a heritage of approaches and tools from which to choose for specific occasions. It is likely, however, that the real challenge is yet to come; it is that of giving further impetus to the trend of encouraging individuals to assess their own and their team's needs. Start now, and look at Mumford's table, Figure 3.3, and identify occasions at work when you could take advantage of opportunities to practise some of the skills in the right hand column. Which skills do you think it would be most useful for you to develop further and why?

FOR FURTHER REFLECTION AND DISCUSSION

Consider how you would answer the following questions:

1 By what means should an organisation determine (a) when operational problems justify formal training solutions, and (b) how to make use of normal work activities as training opportunities?

2 What steps would you take in identifying the training needs of a group of college lecturers who have been in their posts for a number of years? What arrangements do you think colleges might make to ensure a regular updating of knowledge and skills?

3 How would you establish the training needs of a small group of experienced sales representatives, externally recruited following their being made redundant by a competitor?

SUGGESTED READING

BOYDELL T. H. *A guide to job analysis*. British Association for Commercial and Industrial Education, London, 1977.

FRANSELLA F. and BANNISTER D. *A manual for repertory grid technique.* London, Academic Press, 1977.

JESSUP G. *Outcomes: NVQs and the emerging model of education and training.* The Falmer Press, London, 1991 (particularly Chapters 5, 18 and 19).

MUMFORD A. *Management development: strategies for action.* IPM, London, 1989.

PATRICK J. *Training: Research and Practice.* Academic Press, 1992.

PEARN M. and KANDOLA R. *Job analysis: a practical guide for managers.* IPM, London, 1988.

Chapter 10
DETERMINING AND EVALUATING TRAINING INTERVENTIONS

Training interventions – determination of training objectives – determination of the appropriate training strategy – planning and implementation of the training – evaluation of the programme.

INTRODUCTION

Imagine you are the Training Director of XYZ Store, which has a large number of retail outlets situated throughout the UK. You have just attended a Board Meeting, at which disturbing figures were produced showing that in the past quarter retail shrinkage has increased dramatically. The situation is regarded as very serious, and was discussed as a matter of major concern and priority. Some of the comments made by your fellow directors were as follows:

'Our Branch managers need training – they don't seem to understand their responsibilities; they need to be made to see that shrinkage in their own branch is their pigeon. We should call them all in for a compulsory conference, and tell them it's not good enough.'

'That would be expensive. After the amount we have lost in shrinkage, we can't afford it. Perhaps the Regional Managers could hold their own conferences – make them realise their responsibilities as well.'

'I disagree; what we need is not more training, but better security equipment and alarms.'

'I agree. It will cost the earth to run a conference and anyway it isn't the managers who need training, it's the counter staff who let it all happen, and there is quite a high turnover there. We would be training for evermore.'

It was finally agreed, however, that you should produce a report to be discussed at a special meeting of the Board in two weeks' time.

This chapter will help to provide you with some criteria to use in deciding upon your recommendations. You will also see, however, that getting your recommended course of action approved by your colleagues, could be a political matter which you will have to take into consideration.

In Chapter 7, we gave an example of an incorrectly identified training need, and therefore before attempting to determine any training strategy, it is first prudent to verify that training really can contribute to the situation, as the third of the above comments questions. Once you have confirmed that this is the case, the main stages in devising a planned training intervention are illustrated in Figure 5.1:

- *identifying the training requirements; what do you want to achieve in terms of outcomes?*
- *setting training/learning objectives*
- *selecting the training strategy*
- *designing and planning the training*
- *implementing the programme*
- *evaluating the training.*

We considered the first of these stages in Chapter 9, with an investigation into methods of determining individual training needs. We now consider the formulation of specific objectives, the choice of strategy, and the planning, implementation and evaluation stages of training.

TRAINING INTERVENTIONS

We use the term 'training intervention' to include any event which is deliberately planned by those responsible for training to assist learning to take place. It includes a wide range of activities from formal courses to structured work experiences and we refer to these activities as strategies.

The logical first stage is to determine exactly what it is hoped to achieve by training intervention, i.e. formulate the objectives. It is then necessary to decide the best means of achieving these objectives, select a strategy, plan the training accordingly, implement and evaluate it.

Although it is convenient to consider these stages in logical progression, it should be realised that they are not entirely discrete; for instance, well defined objectives or competences should provide criteria which can be used as a basis for evaluation. It is sometimes necessary to employ training techniques, such as structured exercises, which will provide feedback of the learning which is taking place and which will thus form part of the evaluation. The final evaluation serves two purposes, it provides the trainer with feedback or knowledge of results, and draws attention to aspects of the objectives which have not yet been achieved. This involves a reconsideration of residual objectives and a return to the beginning of the cycle. In the interests of clarity, however, we shall deal with each of these activities in turn.

STAGE 1 – DETERMINATION OF TRAINING OBJECTIVES

A learning objective may be regarded as an intent, expressed in the form of a statement, describing a proposed behaviour change in the learner. The term 'criterion behaviour' is used to define what the learner is expected to do at the end of the training. It specifies the tasks, procedures and techniques that he should be able to carry out, the standards of performance required and the circumstances in which the work will be undertaken (see Mager, 1984). There are, therefore, three stages in compiling a behavioural objective. These are:

- Specify the behaviour the learner is required to demonstrate for the objective to be achieved
- Determine the important conditions in which the behaviour must be demonstrated. For example, the type or range of equipment to be used or the environmental constraints
- Determine the standard to which the trainee must perform. This can vary from a precise production specification, to criteria such as absence of customer complaints. It is frequently the most difficult aspect to define, but it is usually possible to find a way of describing what would be regarded as acceptable performance, even if in some instances it has to be 'to the satisfaction of the supervisor'.

An example of a behavioural objective is ' On completion of the training, the word processor operator should be capable of typing 'x' words per minute with no errors, using 'y' system, under normal office conditions'.

It is worth noting that some words in the English language, such as 'understand', 'know', 'appreciate', are open to many interpretations. For instance, if a person 'knows' how a refrigerator works, he might be able to design one, to assemble one, to repair one, or merely to describe its operation. Words such as these should not be used in compiling behavioural objectives. Preference should be given to more precise terms such as 'identify', 'differentiate', 'construct', or 'solve', which are more capable of describing specific behaviour.

It should also be noted that there is a difference between 'learner' objectives and 'trainer' objectives. Examples of the latter might be 'to give an appreciation of . . .', 'to provide an adequate foundation for . . .' These do not specify what the trainee is expected to do at the end of the training and should not be listed as behavioural objectives.

It is not always easy to structure an unambiguous behavioural objective in a training context, but the clearer the objective which results, the more likelihood there is of successful training. A trainee cannot be expected to know what he should be learning if the trainer's own objectives are uncertain! In some areas, such as management development, it is much more difficult to describe training objectives in strict behavioural terms, because the specific behaviour required may not be known at the time of training, or the possible behavioural outcomes may be too numerous to list. In such circumstances, one solution proposed by Gronlund (1978), is to state the general objective first, and then clarify it by listing a sample of the specific behaviour which would be acceptable as evidence of the attainment of the objective. For example:

> 'At the end of the training programme, the manager will be able to take greater responsibility for the development of his own staff. Indicative activities will include
>
> - carrying out satisfactory appraisal interviews
> - enabling his subordinates to recognise and accept their own training needs
> - conducting effective coaching and counselling sessions
> - delegating successfully to his subordinates.'

Objectives can also be formulated in this way without necessarily predicting the precise outcome. Many learning experiences raise open-ended questions, the answers to which have to be worked out when back on the job. It is unrealistic to set as a behavioural objective for a course on management styles 'participants will change styles immediately on returning to work', but it is possible to determine indicative activities, such as demonstrating an interest in developing new interpersonal skills, or initiating discussion on management styles with colleagues.

Training can often act as a catalyst for change, and it may be useful to make a distinction between training objectives and the ultimate outcome of an intervention. For example, a management conference might be called with the objective of arriving at some common agreement on the solution of a problem. A sub-objective might be that each manager would be able to identify the implications of the problem for his own department, and contribute to the solutions by putting forward practical suggestions. A second sub-objective might be attitudinal in that although possibly not in entire agreement with the ultimate solution, each manager would have recognised the many facets of the problem, and display some commitment to the final recommendations. In other words, the learning experience of discussion with colleagues holding varied viewpoints would give each manager a broader perspective and an understanding of the reasons for the decisions, rather than an opinion based on his own narrow experience.

A record of conference proceedings including the contribution of each manager, and a subsequent follow up of the implementation of the proposals, would be methods of ascertaining the fulfilment of the objectives. What could not be specified beforehand, however, would be the nature of the conclusions reached, i.e. the ultimate outcome. Top management may well have had some desired solution in mind and the conference may have approved it, but if, in the course of debate, sound reasons emerged for adopting a different approach, top management's credibility would be lost if these findings were to be totally disregarded and the pre-determined solution imposed from above. In these circumstances, such a conference may well have done more harm than good! Similarly, an intervention, such as a series of courses using Team Roles exercises, may have as its purpose an examination and evaluation of the work of a team, but the precise outcome of that programme cannot be predicted. Strict behavioural objectives and specifications of 'outcomes' are located at the analytical end of the continuum described in Chapters 7 and 8. As we move further along towards self development and experiential learning for the individual and the group, the outcome may be to trigger off change in a variety of ways which could not have been predicted beforehand.

It does not necessarily follow that the trainer alone should be formulating the objectives. The concept of continuous development implies that employees should be able to take increasing responsibility for their own learning, and therefore must be capable of drawing up their own objectives, although there may be some conflict between the desired objectives of the employee and those of her employer (see page 180). Assisting in the determination of training objectives can be an important motivator, and indeed part of the learning process itself for any trainee, but in particular for young people undertaking a general basic training, either as employees or under the auspices of a scheme funded by the local TEC. The same principle applies to students from schools, colleges or universities who are undertaking work experience placements.

Objectives and NVQs

In earlier chapters, we described how NVQs are based on the concept of competences, and both the learning required and its assessment are governed by statements of competence. The elements of competence bear some relationship with behavioural objectives in that they are defined by means of an active verb and also include a statement of the conditions. In addition, each element has performance criteria, setting out what must be achieved for successful performance. The performance criteria must always contain a critical outcome and an evaluative statement. The critical outcome stipulates what has to be done for the element to be successfully accomplished and the evaluative statement qualifies it in a quantitative or qualitative way. The performance criteria must relate to outcomes and not processes or procedures. They are concerned with *what* the learner can do, rather than *how* he has acquired the competence. Further detail about the required outcome is given in the Range Statement, which indicates the range of applications to which the element applies. The terminology of 'behavioural objectives' is not used, and Jessup (1991) suggests that a major difference between the two methodologies is that in the NVQ approach, the statement of outcomes is not limited by considerations of assessment. Some of the earlier attempts at defining behavioural objectives were focused on educational programmes with conventional assessment schemes.

STAGE 2 – DETERMINATION OF THE APPROPRIATE TRAINING STRATEGY

The link between job analysis and behavioural objectives should now have been clarified. At this stage it becomes obvious whether the necessary knowledge and skills, or in the case of NVQs the 'competences' have been investigated and described in sufficient detail. For instance, 'communication skills' is too broad a description to be of much assistance; it could give rise to a wide variety of objectives, for which appropriate training could range from report writing to learning how to chair a meeting. On the other hand, 'ability to give accurate and speedy information about train times to all telephone inquirers', gives a very clear indication of what is needed. Precise details are therefore essential to the design of a programme which requires specified outcomes.

At this point there may be a range of choices, and selection of the most suitable strategy can be critical. We have classified the possibilities under five main headings:

1 training on-the-job
2 planned organisation experience
3 in-house courses
4 planned experiences outside the organisation
5 external courses.

We shall shortly consider each of these in more detail. The four 'decision criteria' to use in determining the appropriate training strategy are:

- compatibility with objectives
- estimated likelihood of transfer of learning to the work situation
- available resources (including money, time and staff)
- trainee-related factors.

It is not possible to give specific rules which will hold good in every situation, not least because most cases are likely to result in a compromise between what is desirable and what is possible. The decision-making process is likely, therefore, to be one of 'best fit' and is exemplified in the following case:

A Training Officer was requested, as a matter of urgency, to arrange team-building training for a group of managers about to embark on a new project, the success of which depended crucially upon group effort. There was little time to undertake the training. Using the four criteria, the salient factors were:

* the objectives embraced knowledge of skills of group membership (for example of group interaction), as well as of attitude formation
* learning transfer to the work situation was essential; the organisation climate was influenced by a practical 'down to earth' management style, which was likely to be supportive of training based on real, rather than theoretical issues
* resources were very limited; time was short and there was little money left in the budget
* trainee-related factors; the managers had family commitments and would not have welcomed being asked to stay away from home, although they might ultimately have been persuaded to do so. They could not be spared from their departments for long periods.

The Training Officer considered the possible strategies. He rejected on-the-job training as being unlikely to achieve the objectives because each manager was isolated in his own department. Planned activity inside the company satisfied the criteria of good learning transfer, acceptability and credibility to the managers concerned. He deliberated how it could be arranged. He then considered external courses and re-read a brochure for an outdoor training course which he had previously thought looked useful. He knew this type of training was often effective in creating a team spirit and if all the managers were to go together there was a good chance the learning would transfer to the work situation. The timing was suitable, but the course lasted a full week. It would be difficult to arrange for all the managers to be absent from their departments so near the commencement of the project and the cost would use all that was left of the training budget. He recollected that one of the managers had a heart condition, which might cause difficulties. He considered other external courses and rejected them for similar reasons.

He then thought about the possibility of an internal course and decided that, because the objectives included attitudes and skill requirements, a course involving discussion sessions and group activities would be appropriate. There would be a better chance of learning transfer if it were possible to base sessions on real problems the managers would face in carrying out the project. From a resource perspective, the cost would be less than an outside course, and the timing could be arranged to suit the managers' availability. Although evening sessions might be included, they would not have to stay away from home which would save money; that could not be considered an advantage in achieving the objectives, but the training officer judged that in the circumstances it was the best compromise he could reach. A conference room and syndicate rooms were available.

The main difficulty was that time was short for him to prepare the programmes, but having considered his own commitments and those of his staff, he decided that it would be possible, especially as it might be beneficial to arrange certain problem-discussion sessions after the project had actually started. This would enable the course to be based partly on 'real' material which would help to ensure learning transfer similar to that provided by on-the-job training. He decided to consult senior management about the possibility of building some of the later sessions into the conduct of the project itself, and also to investigate what assistance he could obtain from his local college. In this way, he would be able to combine two strategies, an in-company course consolidated and made relevant by structured in-house activity. Training would thus be playing a direct and integrated role in implementing organisation plans.

This example is not intended to demonstrate that an in-house course is necessarily superior to outdoor training, which on another occasion might have been more effective; nor does it illustrate that courses are always the answer, but rather that each decision as to the most appropriate training strategy is contingent on the circumstances, and the resultant decision will reflect the 'best fit'.

We now turn to each of the five main forms of training strategies and the four 'decision criteria' in more detail and give examples of how they relate to each other.

The five main strategies

1 Training on the job

A discussion of the merits and demerits of off- and on-the-job training will be found in Chapter 4. This training can include the traditional 'sitting with Nellie' (watching an incumbent at work) or as in the case of a night watchman or sales representative, accompanying him on his rounds. In management development, it may take the form of coaching and advice from immediate superiors, or, in some instances, merely seeing the example of a good superior's work practices, and trying to perform according to her standards (i.e. modelling) may suffice. The whole process of agreeing key areas and targets, whether as part of a formal performance management scheme, or by individual agreement between boss and subordinate may also be viewed as invaluable on-the-job training in such aspects as time management, work organisation and planning.

Considered against the four 'decision criteria' the advantages of on-the-job training are that it is likely to be high in learning transfer and to appear inexpensive in terms of resources (but see examples of learning costs in Chapter 5). The learner may take longer to reach the desired objectives, because the environmental conditions may be unfavourable, but there can be some compensation in the fact that he may well be performing some part of the job during the training period. An important resource is the availability of a suitable on-the-job trainer. In Chapter 4, page 104, we suggest that training can be likened to a game of skittles, where in order to achieve one objective it may first be necessary to aim at another, and before commencing on-the-job training, it may be necessary to provide training, for example in coaching skills for a senior manager, or instructor training for an operator instructor in the case of manual tasks.

2 Planned organisation experience

This can be designed within existing organisational processes and wherever possible as an integral part of mainstream developments. It can include, planned experience in other departments or within the same department, or the assignment of special responsibilities, problem-solving discussion groups, quality circles, special projects, developing fresh aspects of activity such as a new sales promotion, or a system of records. These are likely to provide positive transfer of learning, provided there is organisational support. On the other hand, it is counterproductive to ask someone to undertake projects and special assignments when there is little hope of eventual implementation. Action learning (see pages 119ff and 183), involving 'learning by doing', provides a means whereby managers learn on the job, as well as acquiring awareness of their own developmental processes.

Opportunities for planned in-house activities are sometimes deliberately created, or may be planned to assist day-to-day running of departments. One organisation arranges for its graduate trainees to take over a production section for four weeks whilst the supervisor is on holiday. The graduate prepares for this by spending some time beforehand in the section, and actually takes over the week before the supervisor departs, continuing for a week after her return. This provides a challenging work experience for the graduate, while allowing the supervisor the privilege of taking her annual leave at a time other than the normal factory holiday.

Another form of training in this category, which is growing in popularity, is the use of mentors. It is suggested that mentoring originated in the concept of apprenticeship, and a mentor has been described as a 'role model . . . a guide, a tutor, a coach and a confidant' (Clutterbuck, 1991). The mentor is usually eight to fifteen years senior to the protégé, and may be the immediate boss, although this is not always satisfactory because the two roles can conflict. A more common arrangement, therefore, is that the mentor is a more senior individual above, and frequently to the side of, the protégé's own boss. Mentoring has the advantages of inducting newcomers efficiently to the organisation and of assisting them with organisation problems and personal development, thereby increasing motivation and job satisfaction. The mentor can also pass on the organisation 'culture'. A properly organised scheme of mentoring is an inexpensive and efficient method of employee development. (For an example of a framework for a training course on coaching see Moorby, 1991).

3 In-house courses

Many large organisations have a regular programme of in-house courses, for what might be regarded as 'maintenance' training. These can include updating courses in specific topics, or they may be general courses, such as those for junior, middle or senior managers, and attendance by those eligible for promotion is a routine practice. Other courses and conferences may be organised for specific needs, such as changes in legislation, company policy or industrial relations practice.

Some internal courses may be consultative in nature, for instance conferences to discuss future organisation development, or changes in structure or management style. Some organisations run their own part-time qualification courses, and the NVQ framework, assessed in the workplace, and offering certificates for the successful completion of units which can be accumulated to qualify for awards, lends itself admirably to this arrangement. For instance, 'retail skills' apprentices in a well known supermarket chain undergo in-company programmes for the NCVQ National Retail Certificates. As these must be assessed to national standard, they should be recognised by other employers, and can be used as a basis on which to build during later career development. Staff from local colleges are usually very happy to assist and help to plan in-house courses.

There is likely to be better learning transfer from internal, compared with external, courses, particularly if senior management are involved in some of the sessions. The training can be directed at real organisational problems which is likely to increase face validity and chances of effectiveness. Courses are useful when many employees require similar training at one time. A variation is open access in-house training. This can include the provision of computer-based training and the use of interactive video. For example a large motor vehicle manufacturer had the problem of training 600 engineers within a six week time-span, in a new specification system for vehicle components. With the help of a grant from one of the national schemes, the target was achieved on time, by the use of computer based methods, at half the cost of traditional training. This type of training has a number of advantages in that it can take place very near the trainee's place of work, and progress can be at his own pace and convenience. Training times can be reduced by the use of pre-tests, which enable the trainee to omit any items with which he is already familiar, while intermediate and final tests ensure that the material has really been mastered. This type of intensive course is now being used by many other large organisations. For instance, a large building society which was in the process of altering its operational systems, was able to train all the staff very effectively by means of computerised packages. Whilst the initial outlay was considerable, the overall cost per head was much lower than the estimated expenditure on 'traditional' hotel-based courses entailing travelling and residential expenses. Furthermore, the programme is always ready and available to train new members of staff.

4 Planned experiences outside the organisation

Secondments and visits to suppliers, or to the premises of important customers in order to obtain external views of the organisation's products and services can provide valuable insights. Visits are sometimes arranged to competitors or suppliers abroad, although these may be expensive. These experiences can, however, fulfil a number of objectives because, as well as imparting information, they often result in attitudinal change and can be used to provide a tangible reward for a recent job well done.

Whilst training objectives are derived from organisation needs, there can be circumstances when management is justified in encouraging employees to undertake self-developmental activities to progress their own careers, e.g. when promotion prospects are minimised and when current jobs afford little opportunity for challenge or development. Examples of such developmental activities include, undertaking a role within an appropriate professional body (resulting in contact and discussion with colleagues in other organisations), or experience in chairing or addressing meetings, or assisting in external projects for the local community or with local educational institutions (see Chapter 11).

Learning transfer will depend upon the particular experience, but some attitudinal change is likely to result which will enable the incumbent to view her job in a different light. Whilst there can be dangers in arranging learning activities of this kind, in that employees may gain useful experience which will enable them to move to other organisations, the importance of mental activity and stimulation is a central feature of the process of continuing development. There is therefore a case for making allowance for this factor when setting training objectives. It is necessary to balance the likely costs involved against the possibility of disillusioned employees who, having loyally carried out unchallenging tasks for the organisation for a number of years, discover that they are unable to adjust to change and find it difficult and threatening to learn new techniques and methods.

5 External courses

A plethora of leaflets and brochures advertising external courses is constantly arriving on the desk of every training officer, and to send someone on a course appears an easy, although frequently expensive option. External courses are broadly of two kinds: the short full-time variety, run by consultants, colleges and universities, and longer (usually part-time) courses often leading to a qualification. Educational institutions are usually very happy to co-operate and organise part-time programmes specially tailored to the needs of individual organisations, or by agreement, of a consortium of organisations. As there can be dangers in an organisation becoming too inbred it is useful for employees to find out what happens 'outside'; discussing the problems of others can often throw new light upon one's own situation. Where only one or two people require specialised knowledge, a course at the Open University or Open College, or one of the many distance learning programmes on offer is likely to be the best alternative.

Learning transfer is not likely to be high unless the organisation climate is supportive. For example, a study undertaken by the Marks Group (1985), on the effectiveness of management training, found that nearly a quarter of the participants had made no attempt to apply anything they had learned from their courses to their own organisations. The most commonly quoted reasons for this lack of transfer were 'company power structure', 'entrenched attitudes', and 'lack of resources'. The majority of respondents had, however, been satisfied with their courses. None of the participants in the Marks survey thought that attending the course would bring them any pay rise, nine per cent saw it as a prerequisite for promotion, seven per cent as a reward for past efforts and 42 per cent thought they had been offered the opportunity because of their status in the organisation. It is significant to note that there was no specific mention of the fulfilment of a training need.

If external courses are to be effective, they must be chosen with care. Having determined whether it is policy to cater for the particular need by an external course, and that the trainee would be prepared to attend, the main factors to be considered are the precise objectives. Do they match with those of the particular training need? Do the training methods and length of the course accord with its declared objectives? If the intention is to improve an employee's communication skills, what aspects of communication are covered and do they match the employer's requirements? Is there any opportunity for supervised practice and feedback? The acquisition of skill does not come through knowledge alone. Is there any indication of the level of the course? Who are the organisers? What experience have they had in the field? Is there any information to indicate their competence? What other organisations have supported the course? Is it possible to obtain feedback from them?

Is the cost related to the anticipated benefits? There is a temptation to judge the merit of a course by its price, but that can be misleading. A considerable proportion of the price of a residential course is the cost of accommodation. Does the venue appear to be suitable? This may seem unimportant but if, for instance, a senior manager is asked to attend a course held in surroundings which he considers uncongenial, he may approach the learning material with negative attitudes. Training officers should satisfy themselves on these points before committing their organisations to the expenditure and opportunity cost of sending members of staff on expensive courses. Briefing and debriefing sessions, preferably by the participant's superior, really are a prerequisite to gaining maximum advantage from an external course. Although they are very obvious and inexpensive steps to take, managers frequently fail in this respect, with the result that the participant may not have a clear idea of the objectives in sending him on the course and may fail to implement any new ideas on return, through lack of opportunity, or because he feels that no interest has been taken (see also page 315). To overcome this difficulty, some courses for supervisors and junior managers are preceded by short preliminary courses for participants' superiors.

Part-time courses, particularly those leading to a qualification, constitute a relatively long-term commitment and a considerable amount of personal study time. For instance, an MBA programme is likely to be extremely demanding, and might be difficult to manage at times of work crisis and overload. Requests to attend such courses often come from the employee, and are sometimes negotiated on a joint payment basis. From the company perspective it is very important that such a programme is integrated with the career development programme for the employee, and that at least one person from senior management takes an active interest in progress. Without this type of support, it is likely that if, on successful completion of the programme, the employee sees no immediate prospect of promotion or recognition, she will seek better opportunities elsewhere. There are now many types of MBA programmes; some have become specialised for particular categories of participant, such as staff from the Health Service, or from engineering, or for personnel staff, to mention but a few examples. Some are 'executive programmes' for relatively senior managers who must be sponsored by their organisations. Such programmes will normally have a Steering Committee composed of representatives of sponsoring organisations as well as staff from the university to advise on the programme and monitor its development. It is useful for the training officer from a sponsoring organisation to find out about this committee, because it is a vehicle through which she can exert influence on the conduct of the programme. Some MBAs are designed entirely for one organisation, or for a consortium. These and other part-time courses, such as those leading to professional qualifications, for instance those of the Institute of Personnel and Development, are normally regarded as a stage in career development rather than a remedy for an immediate training need.

The decision criteria

Objectives
Although we have argued that objectives should be formulated in as precise terms as possible, it does not necessarily follow that each can be fulfilled by matching it exactly with a particular strategy. Indeed, more that one strategy may be necessary to achieve a single objective. For instance, a junior manager may be unskilled in presenting a persuasive case at committee meetings: one way of bridging this 'gap' might be for him to attend an appropriate course which incorporates suitable skills demonstration and practice sessions; another method might be for a more senior member of management to give him appropriate coaching, followed by on-the-job experience including making presentations at specific meetings. In practice, probably a combination of all three would be useful.

Questions such as the following may assist in determining an appropriate strategy:

- Is the strategy consistent with the organisation's training policy and/or culture?
- Is the objective mainly concerned with long term career development, or a shorter term need? For instance seconding a manager to a long term part-time course is not likely to be suitable for overcoming his immediate problem of time management, and might even exacerbate it!
- Is the main requirement theoretical knowledge, or is the real need that of a thorough understanding of the organisation's policies and procedures? It has not been uncommon for managers to be sent on external courses covering, for example, principles and practices of marketing, when what is really required is a better understanding

of company marketing policies, procedures and objectives. It is acknowledged, however, that a familiarity with general principles helps to set company practices in perspective (and possibly bring about an improvement in them) and that what is often required is a mixture of both theory and company practice.

- Is the main need really knowledge or practical skill? A course on computing which does not give 'hands on' experience may help to change attitudes and arouse interest for further training, but is unlikely to help the participants with operational skills, or overcome possible anxieties about interacting with computers.
- Is part of the training requirement a general understanding and discussion of common problems? An important aspect of training can be an awareness and sensitivity to the total situation, and although this need might be partially met by dissemination of information, it will almost certainly require some kind of relevant experience, either a problem solving discussion, or possibly brief secondments to other departments. Training can sometimes assume the form of consultation: an example might be when a conference is called with a dual purpose of consultation about the introduction of total quality management, and possibly modifying the original plans as a result, as well as defining the knowledge and skill required to take part in the new style of management. It may be necessary to include general and theoretical material, but the organisational objective would not be met by sending staff individually on external courses.
- Does the objective involve introducing fresh ideas and new perspectives? Would it be best served by contact with people from other organisations, either by external course or visits or secondments?
- Is the objective associated with a need for reinforcement, reward or prestige? Managers have sometimes claimed that they have been offered the chance to attend a course as a reward. In the right circumstances this can be a valid training strategy. It is likely that the manager will approach the training with a favourable mental set and, if impressed, she may give more encouragement to her subordinates to attend courses.

Likelihood of learning transfer
In Chapters 3 and 4 we defined learning as a change in behaviour as a result of experience, and demonstrated that it was an inevitable feature of organisational life. The provision of planned training is therefore considered as an intervention into an informal, continuous and powerful

learning process, which affects the transfer of learning to the workplace in a way which should not be underestimated. It is not uncommon for staff returning from a course to be greeted with, 'You've had your holiday, now get on with your work'. A backlog of problems awaits, and often there is not even an inquiry as to whether anything useful was learned, let alone a follow-up session about the implementation of new ideas. Sometimes there might be direct opposition.

On page 264 we referred to barriers to training and it is certainly necessary to be aware of the many forms these barriers can assume including: inertia; autocratic opposition; bureaucratic procedures; work overload; interpersonal relationships; vested interests; fear of change and insecurity. Such barriers must be taken into consideration when devising a training strategy, as must the overall climate, dominant management culture and style, and sophistication and previous training experience of the organisation. For example, where there has been no previous planned training it might be unwise to start with a sophisticated form of interpersonal skills development for middle-aged supervisors, who have been employed there since leaving school. A short, practical course, where the job relevance is easy to determine would probably make a better beginning. They might then be encouraged to ask for further provision. In Chapter 3 we suggested that training might be regarded as the process of opening a door: when it is pushed ajar, it opens up vistas of other rooms with more doors. The view often generates a desire to penetrate further, but before this first door was opened, it was not possible to realise that there was anything beyond. A wise training officer will help to facilitate this process.

As a general rule, the more the training officer can take part herself in the mainstream organisation activity and can involve the sources of power in the actual training, the greater the likelihood of learning transfer. Examples might be:

- organising learning sessions as an integral part of mainstream events (see example on pages 273–5)
- emphasising the personal responsibility of managers in training their subordinates (see Chapter 6, page 147), and assisting them to do this;
- assisting managers to coach their subordinates
- ensuring that managers are directly involved in briefing and debriefing sessions for staff undergoing training
- if the occasion is appropriate, arranging for top management to attend a course first

- developing managers and supervisors as trainers in their own departments
- asking senior managers to lecture or lead sessions on in-house courses
- the use of mentors.

Some of these suggestions may involve training for superiors and achieving a particular objective may initially require an indirect approach.

Available resources
These include items such as:

- accommodation for running internal courses, or environmental constraints such as noise, space, for on-the-job training
- equipment, or availability of money to purchase the hardware and software required for the use of new technology; many organisations have a microcomputer on every desk providing a ready-made facility for the reception of in-house training programmes
- staff expertise in training techniques (e.g. coaching, writing programmes, delegating, acting as mentor)
- time span; how much time is available? Must the training be completed to particular deadlines?
- finance: the length of training time may be governed by policy decisions on appropriate expenditure of staff time. Opportunity cost as well as the money involved in wages and salaries is relevant. For instance, if all senior management attend a training course for a week, or if a store closes for staff training for half an hour per week, what business is likely to be lost because of the absence of relevant managers or what sales might be missed by shoppers taking their custom elsewhere?
- available external help: are there good facilities and staff in local colleges? Is suitable help available from other organisations such as suppliers, or professional bodies?
- availability of relevant external courses: some expertise is specific to organisations and is therefore unlikely to be found externally
- availability of external funding (e.g. in the shape of grants from the local TEC, or the European Social Fund).

For a further discussion on resources see Chapter 8.

Trainee related factors
These include the following:

- the experience and current expertise of the trainee; superfluous training in aspects well known can result in deteriorating performance through annoyance and boredom. Most computer-managed programmes incorporate pre-tests which enable learners to 'skip' aspects with which they are already familiar;
- learning style: the ultimate aim may well be to encourage employees to use a variety of different learning styles, but in the early stages of training, particularly if the content may be difficult for the learner, it is better to use a mode which appears to accord with his preferred or natural learning style. When attempting to convince trainees of the value of using different learning styles, it is advisable to start with content which is likely to be acceptable. For instance, many managers are interested in finding practical solutions to industrial relations problems. If training is required in this field, it might be useful to start with concrete examples and exercises which purport to find solutions, and subsequently progress to conceptual and theoretical aspects of the role of trade unions. On the other hand, a group of graduates with little or no experience of management, might well prefer the sequence reversed. It must also be noted that an overall objective should be to improve learning potential; an understanding of learning styles is one way of achieving this;
- age factor: (see also pages 97–9): older people should not be made to feel inadequate in front of younger people, particularly if they are feeling insecure because they are being retrained in entirely new skills. If, for instance, they have a knowledge deficiency in arithmetic, they may find it more acceptable to undertake a computer-assisted programme or a distance learning course, where they can work in private at their own speed and convenience;
- size of group: the number of trainees has an obvious influence on the technique to be used. It is not practicable to organise a discussion for one person! Closely associated with group size is the availability of trainees because, although the number may be considerable, if they are separated by geographical location, or shift working, the effect may be to reduce numbers available at any one time, and computer-assisted learning or distance learning packages may be suitable. These have the additional advantage of standardising instructions throughout a large organisation. For instance, British Airways uses

computer-based sales training, which is fully integrated with the training of booking clerks and includes such tasks as reservations, fare quotation and departure control;

- motivation: the likely attitude towards different styles of learning is relevant here, but other practical factors, such as the necessity to be away from home on a residential course should be taken into consideration.

STAGE 3 – PLANNING AND IMPLEMENTATION OF THE TRAINING

Where practicable, it is always advantageous to consult those concerned about the design of their programme; in all circumstances, careful briefing of trainees and their superiors is essential, if learning is not to be inhibited by conjectures as to why the training is taking place. Exactly what is involved in planning and implementing will depend upon the form of training which has been chosen. As the most comprehensive preparation is likely to be required in planning an in-house course, we have selected this training strategy for fuller discussion. The steps in the design of a structured in-house course are shown in Figure 10.1.

Step 1
Review the training objectives

Step 2
Determine appropriate learning activities

Step 3
Assess training times

Step 4
Construct the timetable

Step 5
Brief the trainers

Step 6
Organise the preparation of material and equipment

Figure 10.1
Stages in the design of a structured training programme

Designing and planning a structured internal training course

Step 1: review the training objectives

The objectives, and the knowledge, skill and attitudes required to achieve them, might be regarded as constituting the 'syllabus'. It is necessary to determine which objectives are the most important and therefore where the emphasis of the programme should lie, and then to arrange the material into a suitable sequence. This may be determined purely by logic but attempts should be made at the outset to create interest and utilise the participant's natural curiosity (see Chapter 4). It is important to arrange the material in steps of suitable size for the trainee to master, and (unless structured discovery learning is intended) to ensure that the programme proceeds methodically from the known to the unknown, and that where appropriate, each session serves as preparation and introduction for those which follow.

Although Figure 10.1 does not include any reference to monitoring and evaluating, the point must be made that these activities are intrinsically related to the objectives. At the stage of reviewing the objectives therefore, prudent trainers are already considering how they will monitor and evaluate. The more specific the objectives the easier will be these tasks.

Step 2: determine appropriate learning activities

Decide what sessions will be necessary and set sub-objectives for each, anticipating how the attainment of each objective might be evaluated. Determine the most appropriate training technique (or method), bearing in mind that a particularly important objective might require several sessions using a variety of training techniques. For example, during a course on organisational change, one of the objectives might be that the participants should be able to identify the barriers to change. This could be introduced by syndicate discussion sessions, where each participant describes some change he has experienced, and indicates areas of concern. Syndicates could then discuss the origin and alleviation of those worries and whether they could have been avoided. A case study might then follow allowing participants to apply and reinforce some of their findings and, after discussion of the case, the session might conclude with a short summary of the whole topic, accompanied by a 'handout' of the salient points. The trainer would receive some evaluation of the learning which had taken place by listening to the contributions to the case study, although there are dangers of evaluating group performance. It might also be possible to use a self-administered test before the final summary session.

The criteria to determine the most suitable training technique for each session are similar to the decision criteria for the strategy (see page 282ff).

The following example helps to explain the need for care in the structuring of precise behavioural objectives.

A group of craft trainees had to learn an electrical coding comprising nine colours and the job required instant association of a number (one to nine) with a particular colour. The objective would not be met if they learned the sequence of colours by rote, because each time they wanted to pair a colour and a number they would have to repeat the sequence, causing delay and allowing the possibility of error, which could have serious effects on safety. The training technique which was devised consisted of a visual presentation of well known objects associated with each colour, such as one brown penny, five green fingers. The use of vision and the association with previous knowledge quickly enabled the trainees to learn the information in the exact form in which it was required: a green wire immediately bringing to mind the number five.

The age of the trainees can also influence the suitability of a technique. Belbin and Belbin (1972) discovered that certain methods were more effective than others with older trainees. Discovery learning, or forms of 'deductive' learning (i.e. where the requirement is to reason out the answer) show the best results. Techniques which rely upon memory are not likely to be successful. Unlike older people, younger trainees enjoy a competitive approach, as in a quiz, and prefer frequent changes of topic. The former learn more effectively by concentrating on the same subject matter for longer periods; variety can be introduced by changing the training method. (For a more detailed investigation into methods of training older employees see Plett and Lester, 1991).

If course participants are at different levels of ability and have differing degrees of practical experience, flexible methods, such as computer-assisted learning, or sometimes discussion groups and case studies can be useful. Those with experience can be encouraged to assist but not dominate.

Step 3: assess training times
The time available for each session must be determined: participative methods may be the most effective in enabling learning transfer but they can be time-consuming, and it is therefore practicable to employ them for the most important aspects of the training. A further consideration is the time of day of each session; for instance, it may be considered wise to arrange a participative session straight after lunch, or after dinner in the evening of a residential course. Estimating the exact time required for each session is to some extent a matter of trial and error, and the requirements for the same programme can vary for different groups. An experienced trainer can usually gauge the timing reasonably accurately by consulting with those responsible for the various parts of the training, using the duration of similar programmes as a guide, and taking into account the age, experience and motivation of those to be trained.

Step 4: construct the timetable
The trainer should ensure that the timetable is flexible enough to be modified if required without affecting the whole programme, and determine the trainers for each session.

Step 5: brief the trainers
This is an important, and frequently neglected, step in the design process and misunderstandings can easily arise if the objectives for every section of the programme are not fully discussed and understood. The training technique to be used may well be discussed with the trainer but the final choice cannot be left to her entirely because of the need to obtain an overall balance. It is the course organiser who has to take this overall view. Otherwise, to quote the extreme case, it would be possible for each of several trainers to decide to show a film on the same day. Variety has to be planned, it cannot be left to chance. After briefing, the trainers then prepare the detailed material for their sessions. Information about the use of different training techniques will be found in Appendix 6.

Step 6: organise the preparation of material and equipment
Professionally prepared programmes, course manuals, log books and other references create a favourable impression. Unprepared or inadequate equipment suggests that the training is of secondary importance, and this can quickly affect the attitude of trainees.

STAGE 4 – EVALUATION OF THE PROGRAMME

Whilst it is generally accepted that there is a strong case for attempting to evaluate training, particularly in view of the very large sums of money which are spent on it, the attendant problems often appear insuperable. In fact, evaluation is one of the more difficult of the training officer's tasks, but it is not necessarily impossible.

The first difficulty is that it is necessary to know the exact knowledge and skill of each trainee before the start of the training. Without this information it would be impossible to assess what they have learned at the end. This would necessitate a pre-test, which is practicable in programmed or computer-assisted learning. It becomes more difficult when we consider an in-house course for managers. The first objective of every trainer in that situation is to establish rapport with the course members.

Presenting them with a pre-test, especially if they are unlikely to be able to complete it, is hardly in accord with this aim, nor is it likely to inspire them with confidence and a favourable mental set. Even if a pre-test were to be arranged, it could be argued that participants had learned from the pre-test not the training, and it would therefore really be necessary to set up a number of control groups. This is unlikely to be practicable, and therefore the training officer will realise from the outset that she can only do the best which circumstances permit.

A second difficulty is that an ongoing review tends to result in changes to the detail of the programme (and even to some of the objectives) before it can be evaluated.

The questions which need to be answered in evaluating a particular training programme are as follows:

1 Why is the evaluation required?
2 Who should do it?
3 What aspects should be evaluated and when should this be done?
4 What kinds of measurement will be used?
5 When will it be done?

1 Why is the evaluation required?

The answer to this question will affect the appropriate response to the other four, and five main reasons can be given: first, the evaluation enables the effectiveness of an investment in training to be appraised in general terms and provides data which can justify expenditure on training. One of the difficulties in obtaining money for a training budget is that the results are often regarded as intangible or an act of faith.

Secondly, it provides feedback to the trainer about her performance and methods and is therefore a part of her learning experience. Thirdly, it enables improvements to be made, either on the next occasion, or if the evaluation is ongoing, as the training proceeds. Fourthly, reviewing and evaluating his achievement to date is also an intrinsic part of the learner's progression round the experiential learning cycle, and therefore can be a part of the learning process itself. Finally, the evaluation indicates to what extent the objectives have been met and therefore whether any further training needs remain.

2 Who should carry out the evaluation?

This is a most important decision, as any suspicion of bias can invalidate the results, and also because receiving feedback can be a sensitive issue and may therefore need to be handled with extreme care. As, however, the process is itself a learning experience, it is obviously advantageous to involve those who could learn the most from it.

Tracey (1968) makes the point that:

> 'Evaluation must be co-operative. A one-man evaluation is little better than no evaluation, regardless of who does it, how competently he does the job, or how valid his findings may be. All who are a part of the process of appraisal, or who are affected by it, must participate in the process.'

Obviously the training officer, relevant managers and the learners need to co-operate in the process. However, each will bring a different perspective, and it may well be that the overall responsibility is best vested in a neutral party. This may be difficult, because even external consultants can have their own bias. Whoever takes overall responsibility, it is important that they are seen as impartial, having credible expertise and knowledge of the relevant processes, as well as possessing tact to deal with sensitive issues.

3 What aspects of training should be evaluated and when?

A number of different models have been suggested. The structure we describe below is after Whitelaw (1972) and Hamblin (1974), but for other alternatives see Warr, Bird and Rackham (1970) or Jones (1970). See Bramley and Newby (1984) for a useful framework of different concepts of evaluation, and a summary of appropriate techniques. Hamblin and Whitelaw suggest that training can usefully be evaluated at different levels each of which requires different techniques. An example of this type of model is given below.

Level 1: Reactions of trainees to the content and methods of training, to the trainer and to any other factors perceived as relevant. What did the trainee think about the training?

Level 2: Learning attained during the training period. Did the trainees learn what was intended?

Level 3: Job behaviour in the work environment at the end of the training period. Did the learning transfer to the job?

Level 4: Effect on the trainee's department. Has the training helped departmental performance?

Level 5: The ultimate level. Has the training affected the ultimate well being of the organisation, for example, in terms of profitability or survival?

It will readily be seen that these are sequential stages in the process: if it is found that behaviour on the job has not changed after training, unless evaluation has been carried out at Level 2, it will not be possible to ascertain whether the failure was due to lack of learning transfer or to the fact that the learning never took place at all. If the evaluation is to perform any of the functions we have outlined this type of detail is essential.

To facilitate evaluation, it is possible to set objectives at each of these levels. For instance, the objectives of a course providing an introduction to the organisation's networked computing facility, might be:

- that participants would recommend the course to their friends and wish to attend a further course themselves. This would involve a favourable 'reactions level' evaluation (Level 1)
- that participants should be competent in the use of a variety of software. This would involve objectives at Level 2

- that participants should request terminals on their desks and suggest how they could be used to make daily work practices more efficient (Level 3)
- that the introduction of desk terminals for the course participants should result in increased output in the department (Level 4)
- that this increased productivity in the department should contribute to the profitability of the organisation (Level 5).

It will be seen that the easiest levels to evaluate are 1 and 2 and that the process becomes increasingly difficult as Level 5 is approached. This is partly because of difficulties of measurement, but also because the problem of establishing cause and effect. Organisational changes are multi-causal, for example, it is usually impossible to determine how much of an increase in profitability is the result of a specific training intervention. There is also likely to be a time lag between the completion of the training and its effect on the organisation, and the relevant learning may have arisen from a later source. It can be said, however, that the more successful the evaluation at the earlier stages, the more likely is the training to affect overall departmental or organisational performance.

4 What kind of measurement will be used?

Different techniques and yardsticks are appropriate for each level of evaluation.

At Level 1, where an attempt is being made to assess the recipients' reactions to their training, techniques such as questionnaires, interviews, group discussion, individual interview or asking trainees to write a report can be employed. Care must be taken with the timing of these methods. For example, if participants have enjoyed a course, they may finish in a mood of euphoria which may not last after they return to work, and therefore a misleading impression might be conveyed if they are asked to complete a questionnaire at the end of the course (see Easterby-Smith and Tanton, 1985).

Similarly, trainees may not be in a position to know immediately whether what they have learned will be useful. It may be necessary to wait some considerable time before being able to obtain informed opinion. Furthermore, although ideally learning should be a helpful experience, it can at times be painful, and trainees may encounter difficulty or criticism and attempt to divert this to the training activities. If such trainees happen to be the most vociferous during an evaluation discussion, the trainer may obtain a completely false impression. Experienced trainers learn to interpret this type of feedback, and to use a series of techniques to obtain their information. For instance, they might use a short questionnaire and/or hold a general discussion, or interview the participants separately after an appropriate length of time has elapsed. Another method is to issue a questionnaire, ask the trainees to complete it, hold their own discussion session and present what they consider to be the most salient points to the trainer.

A number of other indicators can also be used to provide evaluation at this level, including requests from participants for further training, their recommendation to others to follow the same programme, or the return of past trainees for further help and advice. No single one of these can be taken out of context, but they can all assist to confirm or contradict an apparent trend.

At Level 2, the following techniques might be used:

Phased tests, as in craft training
These are beneficial in monitoring progress and providing feedback which can be used to modify the training as it proceeds. In addition, they provide intermediate targets and knowledge of results to trainees.

Final test
Workplace based tests of competence, such as those required for NVQs, are relevant here, and their incidence is likely to increase as more and more organisations become involved in these qualifications. Because jobs and the contexts in which they are performed are very varied, they can take a number of forms, such as the situation described on pages 121 and 122, where the learner sends a claim form, to Bus and Coach Training Ltd., and his performance is tested by a visiting assessor.

Final examination
This is still the most common type of evaluation in academic, and some professional, circles, although other types of continuous assessment have gradually been introduced. Final examinations have a number of disadvantages in that they are influenced by the trainee's ability to perform on a few chosen days and may therefore be affected by short-term memory, domestic circumstances or health. It is important that they are designed to incorporate a representative sample of the activities to be evaluated.

Projects

As well as being useful learning methods, these can provide valuable feedback on the ability to apply what has been learned to an organisational problem or issue.

Structured exercises and case studies

Performance on these can give the trainer indications as to how well people are learning. Structured exercises, such as interviews using closed-circuit television, are particularly helpful as it is possible to watch performance improving as the training progresses, and a record remains for comparison. Many of these activities, however, take place in groups and the trainer must beware of assuming that because a group has performed well, every member of that group has learned what was intended. One or two members can lead or inspire a group to the extent that it is difficult to realise that some people have contributed little.

Participation in discussion during training

This can be another indicator but requires skilled interpretation, as there can be a variety of reasons why trainees remain silent. They may feel overawed by prominent members of the group, or the entire group atmosphere may be alien to them. It is also possible that they have a different preferred learning style. An experienced trainer tries to interpret the meaning of such a situation and manage it.

Level 3 requires assessment of improved performance on the job. This is easiest in the area of operator training, where before and after measures can often be made. It becomes more difficult to evaluate performance further up the organisation hierarchy, where jobs are less prescribed and measurement imprecise. There is also likely to be a time-lag between training and the appearance of indicators of performance improvement. For instance, upon returning to work after attending a course on sales techniques, a salesman may immediately practise what he has learned and sow the seeds of extra future orders. These may not materialise for some time, after which other factors in the situation may have changed – there may have been some alterations to the product – and it is difficult, if not impossible, to attribute cause and effect. The Stroud experiment (see Whitelaw, 1972) was an attempt to note any change of behaviour on the job after the completion of training. This yielded some positive results, but must always be open to the criticism that if colleagues are asked to look for behavioural change, the implication has been made, and a mental set established, which would allow the perception (or imagined observation) of factors which otherwise might have passed unnoticed.

In general, it might be said that the more care that has been taken in the assessment of needs and the more precise the objective, the greater will be the possibility of effective evaluation. In the case of the salesman above, rather than an overall objective of increasing his sales it might be possible to be more precise by using sub-objectives such as increasing second sales, or reducing customer complaints directed at staff.

The 4th and 5th Levels are the most difficult to evaluate for the reasons given, and also because departmental and organisational results depend upon many people and it is difficult to apportion improvements to the efforts of specific individuals. Evaluation is therefore often related in a more general way to the health of the organisation. Evidence might be found in: overall profitability; lack of customer complaints; a favourable attitude to training; the standing of the training officer and the nature of requests made to her (is she, for example, included in discussions of matters which are central to the organisation?); a system of performance appraisal which works; the availability of suitable people to promote from within and a proactive labour force which will accept change.

The majority of training in the private and public sectors takes place in a busy working environment and a rigorous scientific approach to evaluation, involving pre- and post-training test, control and experimental groups, etc. although very desirable, is often not practicable. However, if adequate resources are not made available for evaluation purposes, the effectiveness will remain unchecked.

This dilemma can be resolved to some extent by adopting the following pragmatic approach:

- set clear training objectives, expressed as far as possible in behavioural terms, or in competences, specifying the performance evidence required and the range (see Chapter 6, Figure 6.3, and Chapter 9)
- include objectives for each level of evaluation
- evaluate systematically at as many levels as practicable to obtain the total picture.

Together, these three steps will go a long way towards helping an organisation maximise its benefit from investment in training. As Hesseling (1966) suggests:

> 'the main task of the trainer as evaluator is to test training effectiveness or to validate his professional claim that the selected training methods have brought about the desired result.'

To return to our case study at the beginning of the chapter: you should now have a good idea of the kinds of decisions which would have to be made and of the alternatives available. The Training Director's report was accepted and the recommendations successfully implemented as follows:

It was realised from the outset that the support of District and Regional Managers was vital, and a working party of representatives from these groups and from security staff, was appointed. A form of 'cascade' training was agreed upon and the store managers therefore had a key role to play. In reality, this was a very large project and it is not possible to give all the details here. In summary however, it was agreed that the first requirement was to raise managers' awareness of the problem. Secondly, managers needed to define their own key role in decreasing shrinkage, and identify the specific actions and procedures required to bring about an improvement. They then needed to raise awareness in their staff and encourage and give guidance on good practices. As the managers had little experience in training, they also required some assistance in this direction, and it was decided to produce a special training package for them, as well as material which could be used either as a guide for training their staff, or as self-instruction material for individual members of staff.

The actual package which was produced consisted of a video giving practical tips and portraying models of appropriate behaviour; posters made from stills of the video, as a constant reinforcement of the message; a booklet to assist managers to identify problems in the store and draw up appropriate preventative procedures; guidance for managers on introducing the staff package to store assistants; an individual booklet for staff, including a check list for regular use.

The training programme consisted of four team briefing sessions in each store. These took place over a four week period with store and departmental work and discussions during the intervals. The sessions were carried out by training department staff and store managers. The booklets and training materials were made by desk top publishing in-house, and could therefore be updated when required. The investment was therefore not for a 'one off' training event, but for material which could be used and modified for many years.

In this particular case the evaluation could be carried out on all of the levels above. A questionnaire at the end of the team briefings gave the reactions of the participants, and a question and answer sheet gave an indication of the learning which had taken place. The shrinkage statistics provided evidence for evaluation at departmental and store level, and the overall improvement in shrinkage costs was reflected in company profitability – Level 5.

This case is based upon, although does not exactly replicate, an assignment undertaken and written up in full detail by Bailey (1991).

FOR FURTHER REFLECTION AND DISCUSSION

1 Describe and critically review a course, conference or other learning event that you have attended, either as organiser or participant, during the past year.

2 'The main problem within Employee Development is the endless tendency for learners to revert to a state of dependency, leaving motivation to the teacher.' Discuss.

3 Choose either
   (a) An aspect of managerial behaviour you would like to eradicate,
   or
   (b) An aspect of managerial behaviour you would like to promote,
   and draft a suitable training programme to that end

– outlining and justifying the learning methods proposed. How would you evaluate the programme?

4 Before starting to evaluate a learning event, it is necessary to ask and answer a number of questions. What do you suggest these questions might be, and how would you set about determining appropriate answers?

5 'The trouble with textbooks and journal articles on the subject of "evaluating training" is that they always take a theoretical, scientific and logical approach which ignores mainstream operational aims.' Comment on this statement, and suggest practical evaluation measures within your organisation which can overcome this criticism.

6 What information would you seek for evaluation purposes from employees in your organisation who attend external courses? Construct an appropriate questionnaire, and explain how you would expect to use the information it provides.

7 You are preparing plans for your organisation to introduce a 'learning resource centre' – in which you intend to have the latest facilities available in technical and management subjects. Draft a suitable statement explaining the development to management, outlining the system for its use, and enlisting their support.

SUGGESTED READING

Appendix 6 of this book.

EASTERBY-SMITH M. and TANTON M. 'Turning course evaluation from an end to a means'. *Personnel Management*, April, 1985.

EASTERBY-SMITH M. and MACKNESS J. 'Completing the cycle of evaluation.' *Personnel Management*, May, 1992.

HARRISON R. *Training and development* (Chapters 12, 13, 14 and 15). Institute of Personnel Management, London, 1988.

JACKSON T. *Evaluation: Relating Training to Business Performance*. Kogan Page, London, 1989.

PLETT P. and LESTER B. *Training for older people*. International Labour Office, Geneva, 1991.

REID M. A. and KENNEY J. 'Selecting and evaluating training strategies'. *Personnel Management Handbook* (Harper S. ed.), Gower, Aldershot, 1987.

Chapter 11
TOWARDS 2000 – PREPARING TOMORROW'S WORKFORCE

Workforce entrants – making education more vocational – employers and educationalists working together – preparing and welcoming the newcomer.

INTRODUCTION

David Sainsbury, the Chairman of the well-known supermarket chain, gave an address to the TSB forum entitled 'Education for Wealth Creation'. (A similar philosophy is to be found in the May 1994 White Paper entitled 'Competitiveness: Helping Business to Win'.) How many reasons can you think of for choosing David Sainsbury's title? If answers do not spring immediately to your mind, you might refresh your memory by turning back to the beginning of Chapter 1.

Now imagine that you have been asked to give an address with that title to a forum of managers in your own locality. What issues would you raise and what do you see as the implications for your audience? Write down your answers, and later compare them with the content of the chapter you are about to read.

In previous editions of this book, a similar chapter has dealt almost exclusively with the role of education and training in helping young people overcome the problems in preparing for, and finding, employment to suit their abilities and aspirations. In recent years, however, changes in demography, new technology affecting work characteristics and patterns, and the need for continuous professional updating and upskilling, have resulted in more and more adults participating in vocational education, both before and during working life. Demographic trends are resulting in a substantial decrease in the number of school leavers in the job market, although the effect of this may be offset by variations in demand for labour, caused by economic trends. The main new category of employees available on the market will be women, many of whom wish to return to work after several years' absence. We therefore start this chapter by examining projections of the characteristics of new entrants to the labour force during the forthcoming decade.

A national pattern of vocational courses has been introduced with the aim of providing better preparation for work, and employers and educational institutions are liaising in many ways to help to bridge the gap between education and work. Three main themes emerge and are reflected in this chapter; the first relates to the revision and restructuring of educational provision to make it more vocational. However, altering content and structure of courses cannot alone achieve the required result; what is needed is increased understanding, leading to a degree of cultural change in educational institutions, and better preparation for newcomers by employing organisations. The second theme therefore relates to the collaborative measures between employers and educational institutions, which are resulting not only in providing students with experience of the working environment, but also in opportunities at staff level, to help to bring the two cultures of education and work closer together. We have included a brief survey of ways in which employing organisations and educational institutions can liaise. The final theme is that of inducting newcomers, including young people starting their careers under the Youth Training programme and Modern Apprenticeships. Induction is necessary not only to help young people in their transition to work, but for all employees as they move through their training and career development.

WORKFORCE ENTRANTS

Young People

Young people represent an investment in the future. In these days of rapidly changing technology they can bring energy and ideas into an organisation and rejuvenate an ageing workforce. They represent an invaluable resource which the nation cannot afford to underutilise.

The number of young people in the labour force will continue to decline until the turn of the century, but will then gradually increase until 2006. The proportion who are from ethnic minorities is increasing and the evidence suggests that the labour market does not currently make the best use of their skills and potential, and that they have higher unemployment rates than their white counterparts (Employment Department Group 1994). It is therefore vital that *all* young people are provided with a strong base of general competences upon which they can draw as they prepare to take their place in the workforce and as their careers progress.

Youth unemployment was a characteristic of the 1980s and early 1990s, and unless young people have been equipped with marketable skills, they are likely to be early victims of any recession. The pattern of the 1980s was that of a sharply rising *duration* of unemployment of young people and wide regional variations. This is a problem for all the major EU countries; as far back as 1976, the question of transition from education to working life was investigated by the Commission of the European Communities which reported that:

> 'finding employment is only the first step, making sure of congenial and suitable employment, adjusting to it, finding satisfaction in it and learning how to progress in a career are quite as important parts of the process of transition . . . The period of economic recession and the dramatic unemployment situation affecting young people have served to highlight in starker terms, the problems for each generation of young people making effective transition from education to working life, and being sufficiently adaptable to meet changing circumstances later in life.'

Some of the problems highlighted by the Commission's report are:

- the need for work experience, which is particularly important to help young people compete with adults in times of unemployment
- the special help required for certain groups, such as girls (intensive guidance is needed for girls, and their parents and teachers, to combat the effects of stereotyped attitudes regarding suitable careers for women)
- migrants who may have linguistic or social and cultural difficulties
- those who are ill prepared for work because of lack of qualifications or low motivation
- the need to strengthen relationships between education and employment
- the necessity of obtaining information on the attitudes of young people leaving school.

Although this report was compiled some sixteen years ago, we quote it because it is still relevant today and explains the philosophy behind our current national provisions.

If we reflect on some of the considerations in Chapter 4 (see particularly pages 97–8), the following picture emerges. In general, learning takes place more easily in youth and, as people grow older, those with lower cognitive ability show greater deterioration than those whose potential is above average. Age is not the sole determinant of the retention of mental ability; previous learning experiences (including 'learning to learn'), may transfer and assist the acquisition of new knowledge and skills. Thus, unless some appropriate form of training is provided at the time when they are most able to take advantage of it, a considerable proportion of young people, particularly those at the lower end of the intelligence scale, may never have the chance of reaching their full potential. Not only is there a great danger of underutilisation of potential strengths and of insufficient skills for the nation's needs, but also of the creation of underprivileged sectors of the population, low both in motivation to seek employment and in ability to learn new skills. Furthermore, older workers are another important group in the workplace and learning experience in later life can have an important influence upon their ability to acquire new skills. The necessity for action is economic, social and moral.

Fortunately, the proportion of young people participating in education beyond the statutory school-leaving age has been increasing and

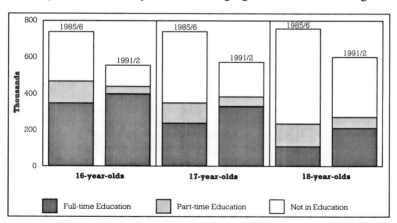

Figure 11.1
Fewer young people but more staying on

Source: *Labour Market and Skill Trends 1994/5*. Crown Copyright; reproduced with the permission of the Department of Employment.

continuing education is becoming the norm. In 1987/8 less than 47 per cent of 16-year-olds in Britain continued in full-time education. By 1991/2 the figure was 64 per cent and provisional figures suggest a further rise to 69 per cent for 1992/3. Over half of 17-year-olds now stay on in education, the estimated figure for 1992/3 being 52 per cent compared with only 32 per cent in 1987/8, whilst a third of 18-year-olds in England now study full-time (Department of Employment Group 1994). See Figure 11.1.

An increasing proportion of the population of working age now holds qualifications, the total having risen by over 1 million from 60 per cent in 1984 to 73 per cent in spring 1993 (Department of Employment Group 1994). The proportion of young people seeking qualifications has increased in respect of both academic and vocational courses. In 1992/3 over 35 per cent of 16-year-olds in England studied A or AS (Advanced or Advanced Supplementary) levels, and the national availability of Advanced GNVQs from September 1993 has attracted large numbers. Rising participation in full-time education is leading to higher attainment. In 1991, 22 per cent of 18-year-olds in England had gained two or more A level passes compared with 17 per cent in 1987/8. There is a growing demand for further and higher education and an increase in the number of places. The overall effect will be that the 'demographic time bomb' will cause only a small fall in the number of new graduates available for work in the mid-1990s, but there will be a dramatic drop in the numbers of 16-year-olds seeking work.

The advent of an increasingly well qualified population is encouraging in view of the fact that in this respect, the UK has appeared to lag behind her competitors. For instance, in 1986, participation rates in full-time education for 16-19 year olds in the UK were lower, at 33 per cent, than those for most other countries, although at 31 per cent the UK had the second highest rate for part-time education (DES, 1990). A series of enquiries produced by the National Institute of Economic and Social Research in the 1980s indicated that in the lower half of the ability range, British children seemed to lag two years behind their counterparts in Germany, whilst at the age of fifteen, pupils' attainments in core subjects in Japan were higher than here. The significance of this shortcoming is brought home by a consideration of the projected requirements of the future labour force.

New specialisms are arising from advancing technology, and there is increasing demand for professional and managerial qualifications. For example, information technology is likely to be required by workers at all levels, and more operationally purposeful application of IT is likely to be needed by businesses if they are to remain competitive. Not only does this reduce the number of routine jobs, but it causes changes in organisation structures, which often require new communication and managerial skills. There is likely also to be an increase in the number of IT professionals. Markets are becoming global and there is a growing demand for international marketing and linguistic skills, as well as the ability to cope with different cultures. The EU and the opening-up of Eastern Europe are likely to present new opportunities. Between 1991 and 2000 almost 1.7 million extra jobs are expected in Managerial, Professional and Associate Professional and Technical Operations (Institute for Employment Research 1993). See Figure 11.2.

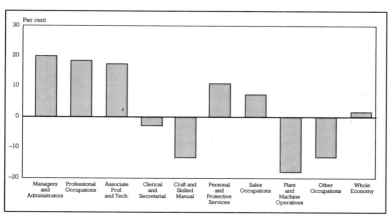

Figure 11.2
Occupational employment projections: percentage change 1991–2000

Source: *Institute for Employment Research, 1993.* Crown Copyright; reproduced with the permission of the Department of Employment. (In Labour Market Quarterly Report Nov. 1993.)

These trends are matched by a projected increase in demand for qualifications as shown in Figure 11.3.

The European Union
As part of the work programme arising out of the Social Charter the Commission is to bring forward proposals to update the general

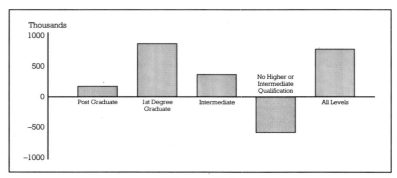

Figure 11.3
Projected change in employment by qualification
1990–2000

Source: *Labour Market and Skill Trends 1992/93*. Crown Copyright; reproduced with the permission of the Department of Employment.

principles of EU policy on vocational training. One of the aims is to set up a 'European space' for training and education, in which training agencies will operate in European, rather than national markets, allowing individuals new opportunity for training and mobility. The trend is towards dynamic interaction between education and training, and a merging of their boundaries. Vocational training should be designed with an 'eye to the labour market' and the 'status' of technical and vocational education is an issue. Uncertainty and turbulence are seen as continuing features, requiring a flexible workforce, the traditional division of labour being eroded by giving more responsibility down the line to operator level, thus strengthening quality control.

A 'European market of qualifications' is beginning to emerge, with the prediction that accessing qualifications with a European standing will become essential in many professional occupations. Interchangeability of qualifications with those of other member states will be of increasing importance, and training will assume a European dimension with international networks for trainers. The EU will have to develop its capacity to cover mutual recognition of qualifications to ensure free movement. A further concern of European social policy is the training and qualification of women, particularly in view of the demographical trends illustrated above, which are not merely a characteristic of the UK. Those countries which find the best solutions to encouraging women and girls to enter high-quality jobs will find themselves at a considerable advantage in combating skills shortages. For an overview of the education and training systems of other countries within the European Community, see Incomes Data Services (1992).

Women entrants to the employment market

Women are playing an increasing part in employment in Britain. In spring 1984 there were 9.6 million women in employment, and this number had increased to 12.2 million by 1992 (Employment Department Group 1993). This trend is likely to continue and large numbers of women returners are expected to join the labour force during the next decade, thus counteracting the 'demographic time bomb'. Figure 11.4 indicates a projected 13,564 women in the labour force in 2006 (Employment Department Group 1993). This increase is attributed to age groups over 35. In line with the general trend of an ageing workforce, the projection shows a significant decline in the numbers of women in employment who are aged between 16 and 24.

Women have traditionally been employed in a narrow range of industries and there is much unrealised potential; they are significantly under-represented in managerial positions in many professional occupations and in a wide range of jobs at technician level.

Many of these women are returning after a career break to bring up a family. Some may have had little or no working experience and may be apprehensive about entering a totally different environment; careful induction is needed. Some want part-time work; flexible learning

	1992 (Thousands)			2006 (Thousands)			Percentage Change 1992–2006		
Age	Men	Women	Total	Men	Women	Total	Men	Women	Total
16–19	1,016	919	1,935	1,088	995	2,083	7.0	8.3	7.6
20–24	1,833	1,503	3,335	1,445	1,328	2,773	–21.2	–11.6	–16.9
25–34	4,163	3,043	7,207	3,424	2,823	6,247	–17.8	–7.2	–13.3
35–44	3,562	2,921	6,482	4,254	3,782	8,035	19.4	29.5	24.0
45–54	3,054	2,507	5,561	3,385	2,937	6,321	10.8	17.2	13.7
55–59(f)/64(m)	1,818	787	2,605	2,178	1,099	3,277	19.8	39.6	25.8
Over 60(f)/65(m)	312	528	840	303	601	904	–2.9	13.8	7.6
All ages	**15,757**	**12,208**	**27,966**	**16,076**	**13,564**	**29,640**	**2.0**	**11.1**	**6.0**

Figure 11.4
Labour force projections (Great Britain)

Source: *Labour Market Quarterly Report*, May 1993. Crown Copyright: Reproduced with the permission of the Department of Employment.

provision will increasingly be required, so that it can be combined with domestic responsibilities. Courses at the Open University or Open College will be helpful in this respect, as will self-learning materials, technology assisted learning, distance learning and open access programmes of all kinds. If, during their previous education the new entrants have 'learned to learn' their task will be much easier. For this, and many other reasons a 'learning to learn culture' is rapidly becoming an essential requirement of modern life.

Flexible arrangements will also be required to cope with career breaks. Some organisations already have internal schemes to enable women to return for short periods to update themselves and maintain their skills during a career break. Corresponding educational facilities will be needed including part-time work experience. Courses which can be undertaken *during* the career break would be welcomed by the women concerned and would assist the quickest possible return to work.

Many women will have received vocational education earlier in their lives and many will have work experience. Whilst they may need refresher and updating courses in certain aspects, they will not necessarily require to undertake a whole programme from beginning to end. Courses which have rigid entry requirements, and offer no facility for accrediting previous experience or learning, are likely to be unsuitable, prolonging the necessary education and training time, as well as running great risks of boring the participants. The national framework provided by NCVQ (see Chapters 2 and 5), together with the flexibility of the CATS and APL schemes (see pages 319–20), which afford facilities for the accreditation of appropriate prior learning or prior experience, should go a long way towards helping vocational education to meet the needs of these women.

Older Workers

During the eighties, older members of the workforce were being encouraged to retire early (sometimes to reduce costs, sometimes to make way for the promotion of younger workers). Whilst 'downsizing', involving massive early retirement, is still going on in many sectors, the accent in the nineties appears to be on encouraging older people to continue working or to take up 'post first retirement' jobs. There is a need for others to create jobs for these early pensioners, a striking example being a large self service, DIY chain store which opened one branch staffed entirely by people over 50, and has found the experiment extremely successful. The new workers were found to be better at product knowledge and customer care than their younger counterparts in other stores, and there was less incidence of absenteeism and labour turnover (Hogarth and Barth, 1991).

Some of these 'older returners' may reappear in the educational system (possibly to take NVQs as an addition to existing qualifications). They are also likely to require flexible programmes. (A discussion on special training methods for older people is given in Chapter 4). (See also Plett and Lester, 1991).

All these factors point to two urgent needs:

1 to make education more vocational, more flexible and more accessible
2 to ensure that newcomers are properly welcomed and inducted into the organisation.

MAKING EDUCATION MORE VOCATIONAL

Let us now return to David Sainsbury's address. After pointing out that if we want to set performance standards for our educational system, we must be clear about the knowledge and skills which need to be developed, he identified three main general needs relating to the skills we need as a country if British industry is to regain its technical edge:

- *A well-educated mass labour force, not just a small well-educated elite. (David Sainsbury suggests that the high productivity of Japanese factories is due to the ability to push responsibility down to operators on the factory floor, and involve them in such matters as statistical process control, preventive maintenance and machine set-up time.)*
- *More people with managerial and financial responsibilities in industry who understand the technological potential of their industry*
- *More people who are generalists rather than pure specialists.*

The last two of these requirements emphasise the need for top management to have both technological understanding and modern management skills.

These requirements should be borne in mind when considering the following outline of developments during the last decade. We begin with a brief outline of developments in schools and in particular of the National Curriculum.

The field of vocational education and training is vast and rapidly developing, and here we can do no more than outline the main trends and emergent issues. For further study you are recommended to read specialised texts such as Raggat and Unwin (1991) or Jessup (1991) as well as constantly updating by means of newspapers or journal reports.

The National Curriculum

Under the Education Reform Act of 1988, the 'National Curriculum' for state schools in England and Wales is prescribed by the Secretary of State for Education and Science, who consults the Schools Curriculum and Assessment Authority (SCAA). The SCAA constantly reviews all aspects of the curriculum and consults regularly with a wide range of employers. This is the first time the government has imposed a standard curriculum. The aim is to give pupils adequate preparation for adult life (including, of course, *working* life) in Europe and the wider world, by providing a broad and balanced framework of study for all throughout the whole period of compulsory education. (The system in Scotland is somewhat different; the Scottish Consultative Council on the Curriculum (SCCC) is the principal advisory body of the Secretary of State for Scotland on all matters relating to the curriculum for 3–18-year-olds in Scottish schools. It is responsible for keeping the Scottish school curriculum under review, and, in agreement with the Secretary of State, for issuing guidance on the curriculum to education authorities and schools. The curriculum of an individual pupil derives from a national framework based on consensus and a set of nationally-defined courses, from which education authorities and schools make provision suited to local circumstances; curricula suited to the needs of individual pupils are negotiated.)

In England and Wales, the Curriculum is made up of Core Subjects (science, mathematics and English) and Other Foundation Subjects (such as technology, a modern foreign language and physical education). With the addition of religious education and sex education, this work takes about 60 per cent of teaching time, leaving 40 per cent for option choices. For each subject there are:

- *Attainment targets*, which define what pupils are expected to know at each stage
- *Programmes of study*, which detail what pupils should be taught in order to reach the targets
- *Assessments*, on a 10-level scale based on the attainment targets. As well as evaluating progress, it is intended that the assessments will be diagnostic in that they will pinpoint where pupils need help.

In addition, five focal themes are seen as essential:

1 Economic and industrial understanding
2 Careers education and guidance (including a period of work experience)
3 Health education
4 Education for citizenship
5 Environmental education.

A Record of Achievement is maintained for each pupil, whose property it is. It gives a record of the assessments and also contains an account of experience and attainments, written by the pupil in question. The record of achievement will be available for inspection by potential employers and should provide full information about a young person's attainment and all-round performance. The concept of a record of achievement emphasises the fact that the learner is the *client* of the learning. See also pages 316 and 317.

The 'General Diploma'

A new 'general diploma' will be introduced from 1995 in England and Wales, to be awarded to 16-year-olds gaining GCSEs at grades A–C in English, Mathematics, Science and two other subjects or vocational equivalents. The vocational components are likely to consist of 'part one' GNVQs (see page 124), selected from a wide range of choices such as manufacturing, leisure or tourism. The first of these courses will be piloted in 1995. The 'part one' GNVQs can then provide the basis for intermediate or advanced level GNVQs, the latter having the status of A levels.

16-17-year-olds at school

Those who stay on at school take A level or AS courses which were introduced in 1987 to broaden the studies of sixth-formers, and a range of vocational courses under the auspices of the Technical and Vocational Education Initiative set up in 1983, originally as a five-year experiment, with the aim of opening 'to young people within education, across the whole range of ability, a technical and vocational route to recognised national qualifications' (HMSO, 1984). TVEI has played a major role in encouraging schools to respond to the changing needs of the world of work and in giving the curriculum a greater focus on the needs of working life. Schools and colleges have been encouraged to work in consortia to develop a wider range of educational opportunities than could be provided by one institution and new teaching and learning styles directed towards active learning have been developed. When the General NVQ (see page 124) is fully implemented, it is likely to embrace these developments and TVEI will have fulfilled its purpose. (For further information on TVEI, see Appendix 3.)

A new system is to start in Scotland in 1997 involving a unified curriculum and assessment system for academic and vocational courses offered by the Scottish Examination Board (SEB) and SCOTVEC, the awarding body for Scottish vocational qualifications. The GSVQ, the equivalent of the General National Vocational Qualifications (GNVQs) in England and Wales, will be part of this unified structure. The main objective is to end the academic/vocational divide and dispel any lingering association of 'vocational' with 'low-level' education.

National Developments in Further and Higher Education

A few years ago, it would have been possible to structure a discussion of education under neat headings, such as 'Initial Full-Time Education', and 'Further and Higher Education'. The flexibility of today's system no longer makes this strictly possible. For instance the work of the National Council for Vocational Qualifications (see Chapters 2 and 5), ranges from schools to universities. General NVQs (see page 27) were introduced in schools in 1992, with the intention of widening options for young people; NVQs can be taken by students in colleges of Further Education or in adult education institutes: most vocational courses can now be pursued on a part-time basis whilst working, or by studying full-time. Boundaries are becoming blurred and some of the features of Further and Higher Education we shall describe below are also applicable to the National Curriculum.

The term 'Further and Higher Education' can be used in a general sense to cover all post-school education. Accessibility to learning facilities is an essential ingredient of continuing development and the flexible system (full-time, part-time, distance learning) allows people to acquire whatever level of qualifications their abilities, time and motivation permit.

Many students take advantage of part-time or distance learning facilities which enable them to complement their employment with relevant study. The employer's support is of the utmost importance; this can include the granting of day release and the facilities to undertake a work based project, but of equal importance (often not realised by employers) is the *interest* shown by management. Imagine undertaking a year's work-related course, either by day release or in your own time in the evenings, and your own manager giving the impression of having no interest! Attempting to integrate the learning with the work environment or with general career planning is also critical and will usually cost very little; it will not only make the educational programme more effective, but will help to retain the employee afterwards. It is disheartening and commercially naive, if students successfully complete a course observing that they must now look for a new job, because their company has no interest in what they have just learned. As well as discussing progress with students, employers can contact tutors, or in many cases can attend 'open days' or 'sponsors' evenings where they can also meet other participants on the programme. They can often offer useful visits of students to their premises to discuss aspects of particular interest.

The end of the eighties and beginning of the nineties has been a period of rapid change in education, and although the ultimate aim is to achieve a coherent system, the emergent new developments and qualifications may well cause initial confusion to employers. A number of common themes can be observed which include:

- the necessity for an education system which imparts the knowledge and skills required by adult life and a competitive workforce
- change in orientation from academic to workplace-led programmes and qualifications
- parity of esteem for academic and vocational qualifications
- greater opportunity for employers to influence and become involved in national education and training schemes

- the positioning of many diverse qualifications within a co-ordinated national framework with defined levels
- accreditation of prior learning
- transfer of credits from one programme to another
- assessment based on targets and outcomes
- records of achievement
- work experience for all.

National Council for Vocational Qualifications (NCVQ; SCOTVEC in Scotland)

NVQs embrace a wide spectrum of education. The attainment of NVQs at Level 2 (minimum), is now the main target of YT and funding is becoming contingent upon these qualifications. Adult training is increasingly being linked with NVQs, through national targets, profes- sional qualifications and in-company schemes. (In the second chapter of this book, we warned against too rigid a view of the distinction between education and training.)

All NCVQ awards are based on so-called 'national standards' expressed as statements of competence in performing a wide range of work-related activities. These have been described and illustrated in Chapters 2, 5, 6 and 9.

Criticism of the content and structure of new vocational qualifica- tions will be addressed in a review of all National Vocational Qualifications to be completed by April 1996.

The National Record of Achievement (NRA) was launched in 1991 to provide each individual with a lifelong record of achievement in education, training and employment. Central concepts are a commit- ment to lifelong learning and self management of learning, including the transition from one stage to another e.g. school, college, work. The development of the NRA is managed by NCVQ and SCOTVEC. Contents include:

- *A Personal Record* which can include such items as a summary of school records, qualifications obtained, and CV
- *An Action Plan* based on targets for the current programme, includ- ing details of the units of competence to be undertaken in NVQ pro- grammes
- *An Assessment Record* detailing units, elements and performance criteria, together with the completed assessment

- *Unit Credits* including certificates already gained in the current and previous programmes
- *Qualifications* including qualification certificates already gained.

The provision of a permanent record such as this should encourage continuing development, as additions can be made throughout life.

Questions have been raised as to the narrowness and occupational specificity of the NCVQ approach, particularly in view of the fact that the participation rates of 16–18 year olds in full-time education have been low and many may therefore lack the necessary broad foundation. This concern was endorsed by the CBI:

> 'As employers increasingly require the skills for adaptability and innovation in employment, education and training needs to be broadly based, concerned not just with technical understanding of the job but competence in the broader work context. Broader occupational competence should be concerned with adaptability, management of roles, responsibility for standards, creativity and flexibility to changing demands. Task competence is not enough to meet this need although some employers concentrating on their short-term needs may believe that it is.'

CBI (1989)

For a more comprehensive examination of NVQs see Raggatt and Unwin (1991) and Jessup (1991), both of which are a mine of information.

The number of bodies whose awards are accredited by NCVQ is large and rapidly increasing. Three of the main bodies are described below:

The City and Guilds of London Institute (CGLI)
The CGLI is a large curricular and examining body. Although financially and educationally independent, it maintains a close relationship with the DES and in 1973 when the Business Education Council and the Technical Education Councils were being established (now BTEC, see below), it was asked to provide administrative backing. To avoid duplication, it withdrew some of its own technician courses but continues with pre-vocational courses, higher post experience qualifications and a small range of professional examinations. Like other examining bodies its courses are gradually being brought within the NCVQ framework (see above).

RSA Examinations Board

In 1987, the RSA Examinations Board was given autonomy by the Royal Society for the Encouragement of Arts, Manufactures and Commerce (RSA), and the two now exist as separate organisations. The RSA Examinations Board, based in Coventry, offers more than 200 qualifications in:

- business administration
- information technology
- secretarial and clerical work
- retail, warehousing and wholesaling
- languages
- teaching and training
- pre-vocational and enterprise skills.

There are more than 900,000 candidate entries every year, at around 9,000 centres worldwide, from pre-vocational up to postgraduate levels. Many RSA qualifications are either NVQs or have been developed in line with the framework established by NCVQ.

The Business and Technology Education Council (BTEC)

Awards from these bodies are important qualifications for young people. All the courses are modular in design and are of three levels: General, National and Higher National. General or first level awards are suitable for trainees starting work at sixteen and include core areas of study as well as option modules. Examples of core areas for the business studies area are: communications, human relations, organisational structures and environment, office services and clerical skills. National awards are for students who have attained credit standard in BTEC first level awards, or the required number of GCE 'O' level passes. Higher National awards have an entry qualification of BTEC National award, or a required number of GCE 'A' and 'O' level qualifications or the equivalent. Many of the subjects studied are similar to those in the lower level courses but are taken to a higher standard.

The Council has always been particularly mindful of the necessity to integrate employment needs and education. For example, business studies courses are designed to provide rungs on the ladder for those who are aiming at professional qualifications and foster knowledge and skills for those planning careers in business or public administration.

Study for the awards can be full-time, part-time or on a sandwich basis, and successful students can obtain some exemptions from the examinations of appropriate professional bodies, for example, personnel, purchasing and accountancy. BTEC courses are being assimilated at appropriate levels into the NCVQ framework.

The 1992 Higher Education Act has provided that colleges of further education (which already have employer-led governing bodies) have new funding arrangements, taking them out of local authority control. By linking output targets with NVQs, these funding arrangements will in all probability influence institutions to integrate with the NVQ system.

Credit Accumulated Transfer Scheme (CATS)

A national scheme was evolved, whereby to ease progression from one programme to another, specific courses (i.e. qualifications or parts of qualifications), may be given a credit rating towards exemption from similar content on other programmes. These credits may be transferable from one institution to another. It is for individual institutions to decide precisely how many credits are given for any specific qualification, but the candidate may be required to 'confirm' this notional points score by undertaking a 'portfolio exercise' as determined by the institution to which application is being made. CATS is already being extended to NVQ programmes (see Jessup *op. cit.*, Chapter 9). This will make the national framework even more flexible.

Accreditation of Prior Learning

There is now greater readiness on the part of further and higher educational institutions to take account of prior learning, thus avoiding situations where students are obliged to cover the same ground twice. There are two forms of recognition:

- Accreditation of Prior Learning based on evidence of successful completion of a relevant formal programme (APL)
- Accreditation of Prior Experiential Learning based on evidence of learning through work experience (APEL). This evidence will normally consist of a portfolio of relevant documents and may also include such written assignments relating to work experience as the educational institution concerned deems relevant.

Both APL and APEL enable students to gain exempting credits (entry with advanced standing), on many degree courses. Some professional bodies are co-operating to link APEL with second degrees and professional qualifications. Accreditation of prior learning can also apply where appropriate, to entrants on NVQ programmes (see Jessup, 1991, Chapter 8). These schemes, as well as the provisions under CATS, are in harmony with the concepts of continuous development and continuing professional development, and make further and higher education more accessible and attractive to adults.

Assessment
Many traditional forms of assessment might be described as 'norm referencing', because the results would be expected to conform more or less according to a normal curve of distribution (where the majority cluster around the average, with small numbers obtaining either very high or very low marks). Although these systems afford the facility of comparing trainees with each other, or with a given standard, they provide a general grading rather than a clear picture of what the trainee can actually do. The extreme case might be where one student obtains a first-class honours degree and another student obtains a third-class degree; an employer might judge the first student to be a better resource than the second. It is, however, still not apparent what either student can actually do; the second student might have other attributes such as self-presentation skills, which might make him a better choice for an appointment in sales management than the student with first-class honours.

'Criterion-referenced' assessment, on the other hand, involves assessing performance on a number of specified dimensions. These may be competencies (such as leadership, tolerance of stress, negotiation) or outcomes (such as ability to use a micrometer or to operate a duplicating machine). The assessment may consist of awarding a grade for each dimension, which can then be recorded on a 'profile'. Ideally trainees should be involved in monitoring their own progress and in drawing up their own profiles, which should be completed with more than one tutor or work place supervisor, in more than one context (e.g. shop floor, classroom). In this way, the 'profile' serves both as a record and a learning tool. The ability to evaluate one's own strengths and weaknesses might be regarded as one of the essentials of self development. A useful dimension of the assessment profile is 'the ability to learn new competences', which is of interest to any prospective employer.

Valid assessment requires explicit trainee/pupil objectives. In the case of the National Curriculum, these are expressed as targets in the form of standard assessment tasks for each level, and assessment takes the form of assigning one of ten grades. In the NVQ context, what is to be assessed is stated in terms of elements of competence, performance criteria and range statements, which give details of the conditions under which the competence is to be measured. Those conditions are designed to equate as closely as possible with those in the working environment under which the activity normally takes place (see Chapter 5). Whilst this is a laudable concept, its implementation is not without problems. The implication is that assessment will be locally delivered, but as the context of the working environment can vary greatly from one organisation to another, the achievement of national standards at the workplace might be disputed and there is no guarantee that all supervisors/managers will be impartial, and external verification is likely to be expensive. NCVQ will insist that assessors are 'competent', and Lead Bodies and Assessment Bodies will require those who are to undertake the assessment to be properly trained to do so; nationwide this is an enormous and continuous undertaking (in the case of secretarial and clerical work alone, the number of supervisors is vast); possibly education and training agencies may be accredited to assess, but at whose expense?

These difficulties, however, are not necessarily insurmountable, and in some ways are reminiscent of arguments put forward in the late 1960s when colleges first started to set and assess their own papers on behalf of external examining bodies. Imagine yourself in the place of a prospective employer and consider whether you would prefer to accept school leavers whose education and training had endowed them with useful basic practical competences rather than young people with none of the skills required in the working environment. Think back to your own school days and early education and reflect whether you felt most motivated when learning something apparently for learning's sake, or alternatively for some purpose which you could see would be practically useful.

Whilst these developments are encouraging in terms of their commercial and economic value, there remains a strange paradox: as workers are gradually gaining more leisure time, there is still a good argument for maintaining that the prime function of education remains to produce good citizens who, as well as being employable, can use their spare time wisely, and – if need be – can stand back and indulge in healthy criticism of organisations and institutions. Mistakes may have been made in the past, and some spheres of education may have tended to isolate pupils from industry instead of encouraging them to take part in wealth creation, and the fact that school-leavers need skills to compete with adults in the labour market may not have been accorded sufficient attention. The danger however, remains the familiar one of throwing out the baby with the bath water, in that tomorrow's citizens will require more than the sum of a collection of workplace competences.

EMPLOYERS AND EDUCATIONALISTS WORKING TOGETHER

The recent revisions to the structure and content of courses aim to make education a better preparation for working life, but full benefit will not be obtained without a change of ethos. Whilst it is neither practical nor desirable for the cultures of education and the working environment to be exactly the same, one way of assisting to bridge the gap between school and work is to bring these cultures closer together. This is beginning to happen in a variety of ways including the provision of work experience to pupils and students. The White Paper (HMSO 1994) states that in the year before GCSE all pupils are to receive a week of work experience and all pupils aged 16 to 18 in further education are to receive a further week. This is considered such an important goal that the government is to provide £23 million between 1994/5 and 1997/8 to achieve it. Of equal importance, however, is the exposure of teaching staffs to work norms outside education, so that they can better comprehend the needs of employers, understand their objectives and appreciate how managers think. These perceptions are essential for effective debriefing of young pupils and students returning from organisational visits or placements, for advising on future arrangements, and for the integration of what has been learned into the teaching/learning programme.

The situation is not totally one-sided. A better understanding of the educational system, the teaching/learning methods used and the objectives of tutors is helpful to employers in recruitment policies as well as in formulating realistic expectations of new entrants and providing appropriate initial training and induction programmes. At another level there is potential benefit to both parties from collaborating in research to solve organisational or industry wide problems, particularly at the 'leading edge'. Much progress has been made in these respects during the last decade, and there are many national schemes and examples of informal collaboration. For a detailed account of one international company's experience in liaising with educational institutions see Marsden and Priestland (1989).

Before proceeding to outline some of these measures, we return to the second of our questions at the beginning of this chapter, concerning the implications of these changes for employers in your own locality. Consider the following examples, which we have chosen from many;

A large chemical company endows a Chair in chemistry at the local university. Joint research takes place.

The engineers from a large petroleum company work with local teachers as part of an organised programme of development of a relevant science course for primary and secondary schools.

Staff from a company help their local college of Further Education with mock interviews.

For many years, and particularly during the last decade, employers have stressed the need for a change in the UK education system. With the current emphasis on a market-led approach, they have more influence in this field than at any time in history, as well as opportunities and invitations to assist in bridging the gap between education and work. They can exert their influence through membership of TECs (LECs in Scotland), Lead Bodies, as governors of educational institutions, and as external examiners, whilst at the same time giving practical assistance to the learning process in a great variety of imaginative ways. The accruing benefits can be mutual.

Work-Related Experience

This can take a variety of forms such as visits to organisations by individuals or groups, assignments, projects and research; a number of examples are discussed in more detail below. The benefit gained is likely to be in proportion to the preparation accorded beforehand by *both* parties. For instance, it is unlikely that a group of schoolchildren, who have received no prior briefing, will have a profitable experience from a 'standard' organisation visit, where no effort is made to consider their particular needs. How much better it would be to lead up to such a visit by integrating it with other aspects of the curriculum, thus providing lead-in sessions beforehand, and working with the host organisation in defining what is required.

Work Shadowing

Jack's class at school was split into very small groups, each of which spent three days shadowing a student taking a vocational course at a College of Further Education. Jack was pleased that his group was allocated to a student of hairdressing, as this was one of the ideas he had in mind for his own career. They attended some of the student's sessions at college and he also talked to them about the practical work he was undertaking. Each member of the group was then given an opportunity to spend a day in a salon, shadowing a hairdresser. The class then met to discuss their experiences, and each group produced a paper on what they had learned.

This is a useful way of giving an insight into a particular role or job. It can be used as an aid to vocational guidance, or for greater understanding of the working environment, as when teachers shadow a manager in industry or commerce. It can also be used to enrich more formal studies, as when an organisation arranges with a college to 'adopt' a full-time personnel management student, who visits at various times of the year and shadows a personnel manager. A discussion of the matters which arise during the course of the personnel manager's day, makes an important contribution to the student's learning.

Compacts

During her last year at school, Brenda spent one afternoon a week at a leading London hotel, where she learned many things, including how to use the telephone, how to set a dining room table, how to make beds professionally and how to deal with awkward customers. She had never really seen the need to be able to write grammatical English, but she now began to realise that the ability to write business letters and to express herself clearly on the telephone was important. She liked the idea of working in an hotel and was told that if she attained certain targets at school, including a good record of attendance, the hotel would give her application first consideration. The previous year, Brenda's teacher had spent two weeks gaining work experience in the hotel, and so was well equipped for the debriefing session when Brenda returned to school.

The Compact concept originated in the USA and was aimed specifically at inner city public high schools, an example being the Boston Compact in Massachusetts. Local schools and industries collaborate to define goals and targets young people should attain. The employers then make a commitment to offer a job with training, or training which will lead to a job, to pupils attaining the defined standards. Martineau (1989) gives the following examples of goals set by employers to improve school/industry collaboration in the London Compact:

- provide places for work experience
- take teachers on secondment
- release staff to work in schools
- guarantee jobs for pupils who achieve Compact goals.

For their part, the young people will:

- reach agreed targets for attendance and punctuality
- secure qualifications in English and maths
- show commitment and satisfactorily complete two weeks of work experience.

The Compact Initiative is now extended nationally.

Enterprise in Higher Education (EHE)

A group of students on a hospitality management degree programme carried out research for the trustees of a hostel which had fallen into disuse and was owned by the Church. The students identified how they would make the most effective use of the accommodation and produced a report for the Church which included all relevant information regarding costs, suppliers, contacts from companies and budgets (Smyth and McKenna, 1991).

EHE is an Employment Department initiative launched in December, 1987, with the aim of increasing the competence of graduates to cope with a variety of work skills, such as the ability to work with others, communications, and the ability to apply powers of reasoning and habits of learning. These competences are to be gained, at least in part, through project based assignments undertaken in a real economic setting, and jointly assessed by employers and the relevant educational institution. It is expected that staff development and curriculum development will take place and that partnerships with employers will be extended and strengthened. All Higher Education institutions, individually or in consortia, were eligible to make bids and, if successful, were awarded up to one million pounds for the five years of the contract. Employers are also involved in contributing in cash or in kind. By the end of the five years the educational institution is expected to have adopted measures to make the programmes self sustaining.

Three main models are being used: cascading, where a small number of staff take part in intensive development and pass on their skills to their colleagues; integrated curriculum development; and organic growth, where the lead in demonstrating the value of EHE is taken by resourceful departments and understanding gradually spreads throughout the institution. An external evaluation during 1991 by the National Foundation for Educational Research (NFER) of the second year of the initiative showed that the vast majority of students found projects containing a 'real-life' dimension an effective learning method. Some 65,000 students are so far involved. For further information see Holden and Gold (1991).

Teaching Companies

A large engineering company, recognising the necessity to devise an innovative skills audit for the shop floor, entered into a Teaching Company agreement with a local university. A senior member of staff acted as supervisor and the two students, who registered an M. Phil degree at the university, were employed by the organisation to carry out the work.

An employing organisation and an educational institution join together on a particular project (at the instigation of the former). The educational institution provides a tutor/supervisor, and Associates, who may be registered for a research degree; the Associates are paid by the organisation which can claim a proportion of the salary in grant. There are often several Associates during the life of a programme and their tenure overlaps to allow for a smooth turnover. A Teaching Company arrangement should result in the solution of a problem for the organisation and a valuable learning experience for the Associate and the tutor.

Work Experience

Work experience is distinguished from work related experience in that the student or pupil actually carries out the job as closely as possible to the conditions in which an employee would work, although the emphasis is obviously on educational aspects. If carefully planned, supervised and debriefed, there is no doubt about its value. One of the provisions of the National Curriculum is work experience for all fifteen and sixteen year old pupils. This is already a requirement of many of the other programmes such as those under TVEI or sandwich degree courses. Of practical importance is the question of whether this experience can be spread over the teaching year, or is to be concentrated in the summer term only, as training officers are in danger of receiving requests from many sources simultaneously and there is a strong argument for some form of local co-ordination, in terms of numbers to be placed. Careful co-ordination is also required between the tutor and work supervisor, in setting realistic objectives and timescales for placements, as well as evaluation and discussion with the students. A number of large organisations have already found the necessity of appointing a work experience tutor or co-ordinator.

Work experience is a commendable inclusion in the educational curriculum, but it is not an easy option, particularly in times of recession. To be successful it demands careful planning, time and resources from the host organisation. Unless students have a very clear idea of what they are trying to gain, there is a great danger that within the short time available they will obtain a superficial impression or that they will not take the opportunity seriously. An ITV programme followed the fortunes of twelve schoolchildren who experienced their work preferences over four-week work experience attachments, ranging from hospital to laboratory work, and from shipbuilding to the army. The filmed records showed much learner fascination, but all twelve ultimately decided on new preferences.

The attitude and commitment of teaching staff is of prime importance; liaising with organisations over student placements and joint assessment of progress is extremely time-consuming and therefore proper time allowance must be allocated. Careful preparation by the host organisation is also necessary to enable the student to gain full benefit from the placement. The Institute of Personnel Management (1984) urged its members to manage work experience placements professionally by taking the following steps:

- finding out about the programme of which the work experience will form a part
- setting learning objectives for work experience in collaboration with the young person's tutor
- reviewing the work experience against the learning objectives at the end of the placement
- bringing young people together for common work experience sessions e.g. induction
- producing written material to avoid duplicating instructions
- updating the work programme continuously in the light of experience.

Work experience is increasingly in demand for teachers and tutors, which can result in additional strain upon employers. The timing can cause particular difficulties if there are only certain times of the year when some teachers can be spared from their duties, or a substitute can be found. There have been a number of imaginative developments, such as offering places on company management development programmes to head teachers, and the Compacts schemes usually include placements for teachers, who then become very familiar with the environment into which their pupils are going. These are all obviously commendable initiatives, but the question must be raised as to how much industry and public sector employers can provide, particularly in times of recession.

PREPARING AND WELCOMING THE NEWCOMER

Careers Guidance

The White Paper (HMSO 1994) specifies that for the first time young people will have an 'entitlement' to careers guidance and that advice should be given at ages 13, 15 and 17 for those still in full-time education. The Careers Service is charged with this responsibility and is to receive an extra £87 million for this purpose. Help with course choices is also to be included within the scope of its advice.

Youth Training

The current Youth Training programme (YT) was introduced in 1990, having developed from the Youth Opportunities Programme (YOP) and the Youth Training Scheme (YTS). It is a two year programme aimed at two main groups of young people who are guaranteed an offer of a place:

- sixteen and seventeen year olds not in full-time education or employment
- young people aged eighteen or over who are not in full-time education or employment and who have not previously been able to partake in YT or YTS because of disability, ill health, pregnancy, custodial sentence or care order.

A wide range of organisations is involved in YT. Some, as Managing Agents in their own right are responsible for planning and delivering an individual's overall programme. Others supply one or more elements of training under contract to the Managing Agent. For instance, Colleges of Further Education may provide an off-the-job programme, or a Managing Agent such as the Construction Industry Training Board, may organise training on employers' premises. The scheme is very flexible and there is no standard model; the TECs/LECs are responsible for the YT programme and each monitors the standard of quality in its own locality.

The current scheme retains many features of its predecessors and offers the opportunity of a two year period of training or planned work experience, combined with work-related education. The new focus, however, is upon NVQs (and SVQs), the aim being that as many trainees as possible should obtain an NVQ at Level 2 of the national framework. More emphasis is also placed on craft and technician level skills. Although a main aim of the preceding YOP and YTS schemes was to assist the young unemployed, it is hoped that increasingly those who are in their first years of working life will be registered under the YT scheme. Those not employed by the organisation have the status of trainee and have a special training contract or traineeship agreement.

Special attention must be given to health and safety. In Chapter 3, page 71, we emphasised that trainees, particularly those in strange surroundings, are more prone to accidents than experienced workers. In the early days of the scheme insufficient care was taken in this respect and several serious accidents occurred. It is therefore mandatory that the induction (see pages 332ff below), which must precede each element of the programme, contains sufficient safety training and develops a realistic appreciation of hazards.

There must be a planned programme of practical experience as well as occupationally based education, and a number of specified core areas must be incorporated. These are: number and its applications, communications, problem solving and planning, manual dexterity, and introduction to computer literacy and information technology. Guidance and counselling must be available.

In September 1993 there were approximately 276,400 young people on YT (including Youth Credits – see below). Of those who left YT from April 1992 to March 1993, 48 per cent went into a job, and 64 per cent had achieved positive outcomes (jobs, full-time education or training) and 31 per cent gained a full qualification (Employment Department, Feb. 1994).

Youth Credits (formerly Training Credits)
In 1991, eleven TECs operated pilot schemes whereby credits were issued to school-leavers. In some regions they were issued to all school-leavers, whilst in others they were targeted on priority skills or industrial sectors. The young people present the credits to an employer who can offer them suitable training, or if they are unable to find employment, they can be presented to a specialist provider of training. The credits can only be used for training which conforms with the minimum requirements for YT and therefore must be aimed at qualifications at least to NVQ Level 2 or its equivalent. Equal Opportunities and Health and Safety requirements must be observed. Most of the pilot schemes include initial in-depth career interviews leading to the development of individual Action Plans, to enable the young people to make the best use of their credits. By 1995/6 every 16- or 17-year-old school- or college-leaver will have the offer of a Youth Credit (Employment Department Feb. 1994).

Modern Apprenticeships
Modern apprenticeships should not be confused with the old-style time served schemes associated primarily with manufacturing and construction. The new system was announced by David Hunt in 1993 when he launched widespread consultation with industry to establish model

schemes of training up to NVQ Level 3 or above. TECs throughout the country are working with ITOs and employers in many sectors of industry and commerce to develop successful Apprenticeships in their areas. Hunt announced that 'The Modern Apprenticeship initiative is one of partnerships. The lead players are employers working with TECs, ITOs and others . . . it is not a tinkering with the existing system, but rather a fundamental reform of a critical part of the country's training arrangements'. It offers industry and commerce the chance to develop even further the progress they have made from YT programmes to those leading to NVQ Level 3. Individual sector models will be based on a common framework of core criteria to ensure quality and consistency. These criteria are outlined as follows:

Training – contents and outcomes
Training must lead to an NVQ at Level 3 or above and provide for breadth and flexibility according to sector and employer needs, drawing on units from related GNVQ or NVQs. Sectors should also consider multi-skill schemes. The core content is to emphasise standards of literacy and numeracy as well as technical skills. Problem solving, the ability to get on with people, assuming responsibility and selling ideas will also be prominent. There will be no time-serving, training outcomes must be achieved in the shortest and most realistic time-scales and progress will be measured by target milestones.

Trainees – rights and expectations
The programme will provide equal opportunities for girls as well as boys. The normal age-range will be 16 to 17, but an 'accelerated modern apprenticeship' extending the scheme to students leaving full-time education at age 18 and over was announced in the May 1994 White Paper. There will be a written 'pledge' between the employer and the young person underwritten by the appropriate TEC. Ideally, employment status should be given at the start of the training.

Funding and administration
ITOs working with TECs will be responsible for designing models on a modular basis. TECs will be responsible for delivery. National funding will be available for pump priming, but the sectors and individual employers will be expected to contribute. The scheme will involve small to medium as well as large companies. As at March 1994, 14 sectors are developing the first Prototype Apprenticeships, ranging

from Engineering Construction to Childcare and Travel Services. The first prototype schemes are planned to start in September 1994, with a general start of refined modules in September 1995.

Induction

Whilst all the above measures help to decrease the gap between education and work, thereby easing the transition from one to the other, the way in which new entrants are received into an organisation is a critical factor in forming their attitudes and ensuring that they reach the desired standard of performance as quickly as possible. The process of induction begins with the initial contact between the new employee and the organisation, as this is when first impressions are formed which can be long lasting; induction can therefore be considered as including the whole of the recruitment process. The main aims of induction are to welcome new employees into the organisation and department, to ensure that they understand core information about the job and its environment, and to help them into their new jobs. Thus it is the one type of training necessary for all trainees, whether young or old, unqualified or qualified, whether they are newcomers or have changed their work within the same organisation. Labour turnover is frequently highest among those who have recently joined an organisation. The term 'induction crisis' is used to describe the critical period when new starters are most likely to leave. A well planned induction programme can help to decrease labour turnover by ensuring that new starters settle quickly in their jobs and reach an efficient standard of performance as soon as possible.

Legislation, for example in the field of health and safety, has caused employers to review the content and effectiveness of their induction arrangements and these reviews have led to two major conclusions. First, an awareness that the traditional 'standardised' induction course which all employees attend often disregards the particular needs of special groups, such as school leavers, YT trainees, immigrants, the disabled, or adults being trained for new jobs. While such staff will share some common induction needs, their programmes must also reflect the differences and, as a result, should vary both in content and duration from one category to another. Secondly, employers recognise that the wider induction objectives cannot be achieved in an initial short course of training. The following quotation from the MSC (1975) study on the vocational preparation of young people is still highly relevant:

INDUCTION CHECKLIST

SUBJECT	DATE	TRAINEE'S SIGNATURE	CORE SKILLS	DATE	TRAINEE'S SIGNATURE
1. Mission Statement			1. Customer Care		
2. Store Tour			2. Refund & Replace		
3. Store Structure			3. Price Indication		
4. Staff Dress			4. Chill Chain		
5. Personal Hygiene			5. Food Handling		
6. Contract of Employment					
7. Hours of Work					
8. Sickness & Absence					
9. Staff Shopping					
10. Trade Unions					
11. Wages/Payslip					
12. Days off and Holidays					
13. Security – Personal Belongings					
14. Staff Searches					
15. Prevention of Customer/Staff Theft					
16. Health and Safety at Work Act					
17. Dealing with Accidents					
18. Prevention of Fire					
19. Pensions					

All subjects listed above have been explained to me.   Signed ——————— (Trainee)

A satisfactory level of understanding has been achieved in all subjects listed above.   Signed ——————— (Trainer)

I confirm that I have received and read my copy of the Staff Handbook and accept   Signed ——————— (Trainee)
its provisions and agree to abide by the rules and procedures laid down.

Figure 11.5
Extract from Basic Skills Training Card

COMPETENCE ACHIEVED			
LISTED BELOW ARE YOUR KEY AREAS OF RESPONSIBILITY	SIGNATURE OF DEPARTMENT	SIGNATURE OF TRAINEE	DATE
1. CUSTOMER CARE			
1. Establish contact with the customers			
2. Receive and direct visitors			
3. Establish and meet the needs of the customers			
4. Serve customers			
5. Deal with customer complaints			
2. HYGIENE			
1. Carry out hygiene routines			
2. Demonstrate Company Policy on personal hygiene			
3. Demonstrate Chill Chain procedures			
3. HEALTH AND SAFETY			
1. Use equipment provided within the limits of authority			
2. Carry out relevant procedures in the event of an accident			
3. Carry out safe lifting and carrying procedures			
4. Implement the control of substances hazardous to health (COSHH) regulations			
4. PRICE INDICATION			
1. Handle customer pricing queries as per Company Policy			
2. Demonstrate the use of point of sale material			

Figure 11.6
Extract from Basic Skills Training Card

Reproduced by kind permission of Safeway

'What is needed . . . is a personnel policy specifically for young entrants which recognises the special problems they face in the transition to the new environment of adult working life, at a time when they are also experiencing the personal problems of growing up. Such a policy would reflect awareness of the teaching methods in use in schools, the common attitudes of young people towards work and the community; their ideals and expectations; the difficulties faced by young people in . . . adapting to working life, in working with older people, and in understanding and accepting the discipline of the workplace. Particular attention would also be given to trying to see that those close to the entrants, particularly their supervisors and workmates were able to guide them in their development, both as individuals and as capable members of the working community, and that the young people themselves know where they can go to get advice, whenever they need it.'

From this it follows that induction cannot be carried out by the training officer or central personnel unit alone, but must be an overall managerial responsibility. Many induction needs are concerned with the immediate working environment; a most important part must be played by the supervisor and those working in the vicinity. For these reasons, induction must be regarded as an integral part of the organisation's training plan and its importance should be stressed in the training given to all employees and especially to managers and supervisors.

Induction should not be regarded as a requirement for new employees only. Recruits need a short induction period for each phase of their programme, particularly if they are progressing through different departments, and established employees may need similar treatment when moving to new duties or departments. Induction should include a discussion of the objectives and expectations of the learner and organisation or department, as well as any necessary knowledge about the new environment. Students or pupils on work experience programmes also require induction although their programmes may be different in emphasis and depth of detail from those designed for permanent employees.

The following list indicates the points which may need to be covered during the induction period:

- *Conditions of employment:* the contract of employment, payment procedures, holiday arrangements, relevant legislation, absence and sickness procedures, meal and tea breaks, disciplinary procedures

- *Welfare:* pension and sickness schemes, welfare and social activities, medical services
- *The organisation:* foundation and growth, products, standards, market, future of the organisation
- *Introduction to workplace:* meeting the supervisor and fellow employees, geography of department (e.g. canteen, toilets), the job, who's who, any impending workplace changes
- *Safety:* hazard areas, fire alarm procedure, fire points and exits, no smoking areas, first aid and accident procedures, safety rules (e.g. safety clothing), security arrangements, safety committees, safety representatives
- *Training and education arrangements:* person(s) responsible for training, content of training programmes, further education, including release arrangements and awards made
- *Organisation facilities:* clubs, discount schemes
- *Pay and rewards system:* how to read a pay slip, performance related schemes, overtime and incentive payments, share option and pension schemes, income tax and other deductions
- *Non-financial benefits:* rest rooms, canteens, clothing, products
- *Discipline and Grievance Procedures:* rules and regulations; how to register a grievance
- *Trade unions and staff associations:* the role of trade unions, joint consultation.

The content and approach to induction training should be planned around the needs of the new employee. In some cases a few hours' induction is adequate but in others it may last for several weeks. It is preferable to split the content of longer programmes into several sections, providing the learner with the information as she needs it. As an extreme instance, a school leaver is unlikely to be interested in details of the pension scheme the minute she has arrived on the premises. Her first concern is more likely to be, 'Will I be able to do the job?' and 'What will my supervisor and co-workers be like?' In Chapter 4, we discussed the value of curiosity; the appropriate timing of the sessions can be a decisive factor in effectiveness. One way of appealing to the curiosity motive is to set the newcomer a list of questions or a series of tasks which involve going around the organisation 'finding out'.

The UK company, Safeway, which has comprehensive competence based training programmes, issues each new employee with a Basic

Skills Training Card. This includes an induction checklist (see Figure 11.5), and a record of key areas of responsibility and competences achieved (a short extract is given in Figure 11.6).

Each of the key areas is the subject of a section in a specially prepared training manual. There is a separate section of the Skills Training Card for health and safety training, particularly in relation to dangerous substances and machinery. The Card also has spaces to record details of three Reviews; after four weeks, eight weeks and twelve weeks.

For a fuller discussion of Induction see Fowler (1990) and ACAS (1982).

Graduates have special requirements which are likely to fall into four main categories:

- Organisation knowledge encompassing most of the items mentioned above
- The political system and in particular the types of management behaviour that tend to be respected and rewarded. Sensitivity to organisation culture
- Management skills, such as delegation, time management
- Technical and/or professional knowledge and skills. Although they should provide an excellent basis for further learning, even highly specialised degrees are unlikely to encompass the precise needs of an organisation, or to be 'at the leading edge' of the company's particular interest.

Care should be taken that the graduate does not receive conflicting messages. If the recruitment brochure has given the impression of immediate responsibility and rapid career progression, it can be demoralising to spend a lengthy period merely observing what happens in different departments. It is likely that attitudes to the job are developed at an early stage and become internalised, and it can be extremely beneficial to set reasonably demanding projects, which will not only help to solve organisation problems, but will require the graduate to find out useful information about the company.

Mentors and coaches can be an invaluable resource for new graduates, particularly in acquiring sensitivity to organisation culture and practices. (Further discussion of graduate trainees will be found on page 44.)

We now return to the address on 'Education for Wealth Creation' we asked you to imagine you were to give. We hope that by now you have identified more issues than you are going to be able to explore in one hour and that you appreciate the ambitions and contradictions of the current scene; for example, closely defined competences for NVQs alongside an emphasis on the self-generating nature of student centred learning; the need for people with ever deeper technological knowledge and skills, who must still have generalist competences. The challenge is enormous and complex, but we cannot afford to fail. You should now be able to distinguish the main current trends in vocational training; if you are not already familiar with the situation, a useful exercise would be to investigate what is happening in your own local schools and colleges and see how many examples you can find of liaison between educational institutions and employers. If you are employed, what does your company do in this respect, and how effective is it?

FOR FURTHER REFLECTION AND DISCUSSION

1 'Records of Achievement' are an attempt by the educational world to provide employers with comprehensive information on school-leavers. What would you like to see included in such records? How might this information influence initial training decisions?

2 Draft a short report to your top management team, explaining the Youth Training (YT) or Modern Apprenticeships programme, incorporating firm recommendations concerning your organisation's future involvement or otherwise.

3 Draft a letter to the journal 'Personnel Management', in which you offer personal comments on current moves at national level to ensure that vocational qualifications reflect competence at the workplace.

4 FE college bodies now contain over 50 per cent 'employment interest' governors. What do you see as the main responsibilities which these governors must carry? What would you look for when identifying suitable people to undertake this role?

5 You have been asked by your organisation to prepare plans for a conference which will bring together a mixed group of internal managers and external teachers, the theme being 'Making Work Experience Work'. Summarise your draft plans and compose a briefing statement which explains the conference aims and method.

6 Describe your organisation's induction training arrangements. How would you set about improving these arrangements?

SUGGESTED READING

FOWLER A. *Getting off to a good start: successful employee induction.* London, Institute of Personnel Management, 1990.

JESSUP G. *Outcomes, NVQs and the emerging model of education and training.* London, The Falmer Press, 1991.

PLETT P. C. and LESTER B. *Training for older people.* Geneva, ILO, 1991.

RAGGATT P. and UNWIN L. 'Quality Assurance and NVQs'. *Change and Intervention.* Raggatt P. and Unwin L. (Eds.), London, The Falmer Press, 1991.

HOLDEN R. and GOLD J. (Eds.), 'Enterprise in higher education: Lighting the blue touchpaper'. *Education + Training*, Vol 33, No. 2. 1991.

INSTITUTE OF PERSONNEL MANAGEMENT. *Switch on to records of achievement.* London, IPM, 1992.

Chapter 12
CONTINUOUS DEVELOPMENT – THE ULTIMATE INTERVENTION

Defining CD – the evolution of CD – key CD concepts – later history – the ultimate intervention.

INTRODUCTION

In the first section of this book, you were encouraged to accept that Continuous Development (CD) offers a unique approach to managing employee development. Our own view is that whilst CD is unique, interventions based on CD do not necessarily APPEAR different from other training interventions: its uniqueness is not a reflection of unique learning theories or training techniques, not a batch of different training methods or procedures or priorities, but essentially an attitude that promotes learning at all times.

The chapter may appear different in style from its predecessors. Instead of a logically structured framework, we offer an anecdotal review of CD's own development – which itself is something of a CD case study in its own right. This is partly because, apart from the example of a three-times-revised IPM (IPD) Code (later Statement) on CD, and a single book published by the same Institute, written material on the subject does not exist. But the main reason is that, although CD thinking has been influenced by developments in fields of psychology, sociology and business studies during the past 30 years, the CD movement has been developed essentially by practitioners, offering reflections on their own operational experiences and ambitions rather than the results of controlled research or sustained theoretical discipline. Perhaps the main reason why research findings and discipline have been scarce is that those resources are less a 'requirement' of CD than operational purpose and creative thinking – a fact which is illustrated by the lack of a single, unanimously agreed definition of CD. And as operational purpose and

*creative thinking vary dramatically between situations, 'standard'
conclusions are rare.*

*Nevertheless, CD advocates have at times deduced principles from
their empirical observation of their own real life experience of CD.
They have, in other words, demonstrated both a monitoring and a
learning process, and an ability to communicate the essentials of those
processes. We have tried to ensure that those essentials, and the probable reasons for their emergence, are included in what follows.*

*Before we embark on the main text, you might like to consider three
questions:*

---

1 **How can development be continuous?**

2 **If CD does not offer new theory, new techniques,
new methods, new procedures, nor new priorities, how can it offer a unique approach?**

3 **What do you think are the main differences
between learning in formal courses, and learning
from day-to-day experience?**

DEFINING CONTINUOUS DEVELOPMENT

Early in the book *Continuous Development: The Path to Improved
Performance* (ed. Sue Wood, IPM, 1988), we read:

> 'Individuals can and should create their own definitions [of CD]
> . . . each individual will arrive at a personal understanding of
> the term through his or her own experiences which, of course,
> will be determined by unique changing circumstances.'

The book then offers two examples of work situations. In the first, a
brand manager in a marketing oriented company sees CD as linked to
making the factory more versatile whilst making assistant brand managers more creative; in the second, a librarian sees CD illustrated by
the introduction of a new computerised index facility which library
staff and clients must learn to use. A year later, each has a different
concern, but is still an advocate of CD. The point is made that the only
consistent element in their definitions (which are not formalised in

words) is the concern for some sort of improvement, with some sort of learning to that end.

The important word here is 'concern'. CD is not a specific type of development activity, nor a specific system or set of procedures, nor a finite body of knowledge, nor a collection of skills or techniques. It is an attitude, or set of beliefs, which condition thinking. It is this which allows the term *continuous*: the beliefs remain constant regardless of whether development is actually occurring or otherwise.

It is perhaps worth noting that this CD concept is actually broader than that in the evolving 'Continuing Professional Development' (CPD) movement, although both have much in common. CPD's preference for the word 'continuing' reflects an acceptance that development activities are formalised alternatives to other activities, and that they represent periodic learning periods; organisations such as the Royal Institute of Chartered Surveyors, the Institute of Chartered Accountants, and the Law Society have built CPD into their membership systems, but have limited their CPD definition to include only clear-cut professional education courses, with minimum time requirements to be satisfied. CD, on the other hand, proposes and stimulates *all* kinds of learning in *any* situation, the trigger being the *attitude*; the concern for learning to effect some sort of improvement is seen as the all-important focus. This in turn, as we shall see later, leads CD enthusiasts to stress *self* development as potentially superior to traditional diet-driven teaching programmes prepared by others.

But CD enthusiasts also see the learning environment as important, in that it may help or hinder the concern for learning. They see learners as responsible for developing their learning environments as well as themselves, and indeed for promoting *group* learning, which again can sustain the necessary CD attitude.

We can perhaps now offer no less than three tentative definitions of Continuous Development:

- for the organisation – 'The management of learning on an ongoing basis through the promotion of learning as an integral part of work itself'
- for the individual – 'Self-directed, lifelong learning, with a strong element of self direction and self management'
- in general – 'The promotion and management of learning in response to a continuous attitude in favour of improvement'.

The first two of these definitions appear in the IPD Statement on CD; the third is our own. Other alternatives exist; CD encourages the learner to create definitions relevant to his own aims, providing only that they incorporate support for learning.

THE EVOLUTION OF CD

In the early 1980s, the National Committee for Training and Development (NCTD) of the Institute of Personnel Management (IPM) – and more particularly its Employee Development Working Party (EDWP) – spent several successive meetings agonising over a number of papers and reports published by other national bodies. The common element in these documents was an attempt to suggest what was wrong with the UK training scene, and how it might be changed to improve the nation's economic prospects. Recommendations also had a common element: they all suggested variations of collective, national, prescribed, but essentially static, systems. The NCTD and EDWP comprised practitioners from organisations at the forefront of training developments; and they unanimously criticised the 'conformist' and standardised approach. Their experience had taught them that training was at its most effective when it was unique to a particular workplace need, that national programmes increased learner dependency at the expense of learner motivation, and that the prime goal was to bring about the integration of learning with work.

Typical comments at these NCTD/EDWP meetings were as follows:

- '. . . they want everybody to think alike . . . it isn't like that . . . the differences are greater than the similarities . . .'
- '. . . why should we have to conform to a system which is built for those who DON'T train, when we have already gone past that level of development . . .'
- '. . . why should we have to work together? The logic of competition is that we do different things . . . we are right now trying to be better at training than our competitors . . .'
- '. . . they talk about technical skills . . . it isn't about skills . . . it's about attitudes . . .'
- '. . . training is at its best when it is specific to the actual workplace, producing improved performance from ANY level of achievement – I mean from the level you've actually got . . . Today's performance

is the springboard for tomorrow's target, regardless of how good it is
nationally . . .'
- '. . . the real need is for everybody to want to learn . . . and for
  everybody to know more about learning itself'.
- '. . . they're still thinking in terms of closed systems . . .'

The speakers were reflecting their own learning during the past decade.
Some of them had been active as members of ITB committees; their
experiences here had made them cynical of 'nationalised' approaches,
which seemed inevitably entwined with bureaucratic methods, often
diverting funds from training activities *per se*, or promoting 'lowest
common denominator' training practices. But much more important
were three other influences:

1 The belief that turbulent workplace conditions were producing new-
  style learning needs which were inextricably linked with the detail
  of work itself, and which could only be satisfied within the work
  framework
2 Recent theory relating to learning, plus a new wave of sociological
  thinking, which explained some of the operational problems and
  changes that were emerging, and offered new training material and
  new training designs. This thinking typically saw modern organisations as inevitably needing to become dynamic learning systems
3 Experience of recent advances in training method, notably relating
  to management training and the training of groups. The essence of
  these advances was a move away from teaching towards learning
  methods.

We will explore each of these three influences independently in greater
detail. The IPM committees did not themselves review the three
influences independently, nor did they at any time suggest a ranking
order. Our own order of treatment attempts merely to recapture the relative importance of each as determined by its contribution to the debate
and its later influence on the ensuing IPM campaign (about which more
later).

The Turbulent Workplace
NCTD/EDWP members were, for the most part, personnel and training
practitioners. During the seventies they had increasingly been wrestling

with problems of improved performance – the improved performance of established staff rather than newcomers (in some 'back home' situations recruitment had been dramatically curtailed as profitability had dropped). Operational attempts to improve performance were for example aimed at:

- reducing manpower
- making existing manpower more versatile (i.e. able to cover more jobs)
- increasing productivity (often via negotiated deals)
- reducing overtime
- reducing lost time
- removing one or more levels in the organisational hierarchy
- formal work improvement programmes involving new job standards.

These attempts were often linked with technological developments, notably involving the application of computers and (in the late seventies) the emergence of new methods of communication. These developments were to be seen on the organisation charts: new planning units were appearing, for example, working alongside marketing, sales and distribution staff; new technical development units alongside production departments; and electronic specialists alongside electricians. Lead times (the periods between plans being first created and 'goods in the warehouse') were often dramatically reduced as computers allowed the handling of complex 'late' data. Promotional schemes often made long work runs on standard products a thing of the past, and introduced complexities into all kinds of operations, from storage and distribution to accounting.

The extent to which organisations saw their own trainers as having a key role in such changes varied, of course. Outside consultants were sometimes used; for example, a move from shorthand typing to word processing might involve the purchase of training as part of a software package, and consultants offering work improvement packages usually included similar initial training facilities, notably for first level management. But a very large proportion of the changes were not 'packaged' at all, yet workers at all levels were required to expand roles and acquire new technical or procedural knowledge. Furthermore, their traditional 'teachers' – the foremen, supervisors and junior managers – often were unable to fill the teacher role: they themselves were needing to learn.

In one large company, which marketed and made fast-moving consumer goods for the grocery trade, central computerised planning allowed new sophistications to product promotion: money-off packs, banded packs, free gift packs, competition packs, 'two-for-the-price-of-one packs' and the like proliferated. The company marketed more than a dozen products, each in a variety of sizes; promotions often ran alongside each other, but did not always cover all pack sizes, and might be targeted for selected regions instead of the country as a whole. Quantities of promoted pack were always limited: hence it was normal for standard, non-promoted, pack sales to be linked. Production runs were all determined by planners, production supervisors no longer taking decisions on machine loadings and overtime. Sales representatives were given 'allocations' of special pack, plus overall targets; area managers issued briefs at cycle meetings, but had no inside knowledge justifying allocations or targets.

Inevitably, this enormously complex operation, which proved a major competitive success (and was continued for many years despite the enormous strains it placed on people), produced daily problems. Warehousing was a nightmare, because of the multitude of different packs and the varied requirements for delivery vehicle loadings; daily changes stemmed from such matters as returns of damaged stock, or the switching of goods to take advantage of a sudden opportunity (e.g. the opening of a new supermarket). Warehousemen often had to take spot decisions on how to rearrange stocks following a midnight call to 'change the plan'. Sales representatives could no longer sell 'as much as possible'; and in order to keep as nearly as possible to their targets, they needed to find out first what the supermarket stockroom (usually out of bounds to outsiders) held. Their contacts invariably wanted more promoted pack than was available. Like the warehousemen, therefore, they had to take new on-the-spot decisions, and hope they were not building ground for complaints (especially complaints of non-delivery and an out-of-stock position) when they next called.

In another company, manufacturing animal feedstuffs, new production machinery arrived from Italy with all instruction manuals in Italian, which no-one in production spoke. It took two weeks for one of the buyers to produce a translation; during that time, commissioning had begun under the direction of a

Technical Development Officer, who introduced a number of adjustments which he considered necessary or worthwhile. During the early days, technical problems led to an unacceptable level of machine performance; the Italian suppliers were called in, and made further adjustments to compensate both for the commissioning work and for several agreed design defects. The manuals were now useless. Factory operatives played a large part in the establishment of a new set of operating instructions, dominating the discussions, and consistently focusing discussion on the improvement of performance beyond what had been achieved before the new machinery arrived.

Operational problems which changed the nature of workplace competence were not confined to the impact of new technology. Flexible work plans made workers more mobile: for example, fitters who had earlier maintained a small group of machines in one department might be required to operate throughout several departments. The assumption that 'qualified' employees had generic skills that could be applied anywhere was often found wanting; it emerged that those skills had often been sharpened to cope with the idiosyncrasies of the machines in the first department, and that the 'new' machines' idiosyncrasies needed similar but different refinements. Under these circumstances, fitters often complained about machines, which led to internal disputes which supervisors felt unable to resolve easily. Such disputes were often accepted as 'inevitable', 'reasonable', even 'necessary', in order to resolve problems; management no longer took the view that there was only one tenable view (their own), in the face of frequently superior detailed contributions from their subordinates.

NCTD/EDWP members had lived through much operational turbulence of this kind, and had themselves been engaged in many workplace discussions. Often their involvement came via appraisal data for individuals who were reported as needing 'to know more about x', or 'to develop team leadership skills', or any of an increasingly wide catalogue of subjects. Discussion on external course facilities often foundered on the issue of workplace relevance: the real need was invariably not one of general appreciation but of specific development. Increasingly, trainers found themselves suggesting and setting up special workplace discussion sessions (in one instance, in the 'promotion-ridden' company exemplified above, following participation by sales representatives in a 'Stockturn' business game which the trainer had himself devised); in these discussion sessions, they often used internal specialists (e.g. planners), and sometimes even participants' colleagues, as discussion leaders.

In another company, a Statistician from Head Office visited the Marketing Department every Tuesday afternoon, discussing with a group of brand managers possible applications of statistical theory to their own marketing aims. Typically, managers one week would outline one or more operational needs: for example, to understand better the strength of a brand, or the contribution made to a brand's strength by its theme advertising. During the time between this and the next meeting, the statistician would explore possible statistical methods which might serve this end. Ideas which caught on influenced the type of market research data commissioned, and the ways in which brand plans were presented. This company developed such concepts and practices as 'dynamic difference' and 'key purchase analysis'; these and other innovations influenced strongly, for several years, the ways in which brand managers planned the fortunes of their brands.

Examples such as these were at the centre of NCTD/EDWP discussions, which majored on the theme that new national offerings were never going to meet the real operational needs, which could only be met properly by workplace learning itself. Essentially they were feeling their way towards the concepts of 'the learning organisation', 'learning to learn', and 'self development', which we introduced in Chapter 3; see especially the 'CD spiral' (Figure 3.4 on page 80). Much of their discussions also centred on obstacles: the frequent refusal to acknowledge the need for learning time, and the impotence of top management. It was strongly suggested that top management had no idea how to stimulate a learning culture, and that they simply assumed (wrongly) that line management would somehow arrange for relevant learning to take place. The ideas that learning itself might be efficiently managed (or not), that organisational changes were making it less than certain that management could offer a traditional teaching resource, and that traditional teaching resources might not be appropriate seemed to NCTD/EDWP members to need much wider distribution.

Three important 'basic principles' were fairly quickly agreed at these discussions, and were amalgamated into a fourth:

1 learning was now an endless and vital part of work for employees at all levels
2 adult motivation to learn must be raised
3 given commitment, learners were usually the best people to direct their own learning
4 substantial operational success flowed from developments which allowed the integration of learning with work, and its continued management by committed learners themselves.

Related Theories

The IPM committees at no time considered that such principles could be met simply by publicising (or 'teaching') up to date theory on learning and/or organisation. They did nevertheless think that part of the nation's problem was its 'anti-development' culture, which failed to acknowledge recent research contributions.

In the field of *learning*, Kolb's learning cycle (see page 74) was seen as highly relevant to the debate. Its essence is 'learning from experience', the nature of which is described as a continuous cycle or process. There were some problems: for example, Kolb's 'abstract conceptualisation' stage was felt to be more correctly a description of what might be termed 'academic learning', workplace learners being considered as moving straight from reflection to decisions, which were viewed by NCTD/EDWP members as neither abstract nor conceptual in nature. Honey and Mumford's adaptation of the Kolb cycle (see Honey and Mumford, 1986 and 1989) was much favoured for its use of 'learning styles' (activists, reflectors, theorists, pragmatists), which were seen as more relevant to the world of work and significant aids for trainers who wanted to develop interest in learning, and particularly in self development.

Belbin's work on *management teams* (see Belbin, 1981) was also much respected: his classification of eight roles (Developer, Shaper, Company Worker, 'Plant' (creating new ideas), Resource Investigator, Monitor, Team Worker, and Finisher) was seen as relevant to team development. Belbin's roles were believed to be incomplete (missing for example the 'learner' role), but it was recognised that Belbin had been describing what he found, and not necessarily suggesting all that was needed – and the inclusion of roles such as maintenance ('team worker') and process review ('monitor') was respected. Perhaps his strongest appeal accrued from his definition of management as a set of roles, and not necessarily as attaching to any particular title or titles. Belbin's research was of course into the characteristics of 'winning teams', and not just 'effective managers'; hence the formula could apply to teams in general, regardless of their degree of formal management structure. But despite its attraction, and despite accepting that an acquaintance with Belbin's roles could help any team to define its own, NCTD/EDWP members were reluctant to champion these research findings as their own mainstream vehicle. Publicising 'standard answers' was felt to distract learners from their own all-important learning process. The precise mixture and meaning of roles in a given team needed to be learned (and to continue to be learned) from within the team, and the real need was for the team to establish its own role classification, with definitions which included references in workplace jargon to specific tasks and responsibilities.

Towards the end of the seventies there had been considerable journal reference to 'self organised learning', 'self development', and 'self directed learning'. *Skills involved in learning* were often tabulated – for example, the ability to listen, to accept help, to plan one's learning. Amongst these skills was the 'ability to understand obstacles to learning', which undermine the opportunity to identify the need to learn (see Mumford, 1980). Exercises to stimulate self development had been published (see especially Pedler, Burgoyne, and Boydell, 1978). NCTD/EDWP found these exercises stimulating, and they wholeheartedly supported the ideas that self development should be promoted, and that developing the skills of experiential learning was a major need. To that end, they felt people, and managers in particular, should be exposed to theoretical differences between traditional and experiential learning processes (see Figure 12.1):

We will leave the issue of how people might be exposed to these theoretical ideas until we deal with 'training methods' below. It is arguable that Figure 12.1 does less than justice to traditional learning processes, ignoring for example the stimuli to learning that specially-designed tests and exams have offered, and simply ignoring the many ways in which reflection and understanding have been promoted. In experiential learning, the learner may not be aware of what has been learned, and may instinctively avoid the conceptualisation stage (see the Kolb cycle, page 74) unless there is provision for a formal summary of learning outcomes (e.g. by keeping a log), or less formal discussion activity. NCTD/EDWP members' bias, if it existed, stemmed from their prime interest in work

	Traditional Learning	**Experiential Learning**
Learning is for . . .	Individuals	Individuals + Groups
Learning provides . . .	Knowledge	Knowledge + Understanding
Plans are based on . . .	Content	Content + Process
Participants . . .	Listen; memorise; prepare for exams	Participate; discuss; reflect; decide
Trainers . . .	Teach; lecture; present; evaluate; challenge via questions; carry responsibility	Facilitate; participate; stimulate share responsibility

Figure 12.1
Traditional versus Experiential Learning Processes

outcomes – and although they tried to generate debate wherever possible on learning theory, they rarely argued that 'traditional' and 'experiential' approaches were mutually exclusive.

But the most valued theoretical contribution was from the Tavistock Institute of Human Relations (see Rice, 1965; Emery, 1981; Trist, 1981), whose consultants had over the past two decades explained the evolving nature of what they called '*socio-technical organisations*' and '*open systems*'.

To the Tavistock researchers, work organisations are 'socio-technical systems' – that is, they should be understood as *combining* the characteristics of technical systems (in which work is designed and carried out, resulting in economic performance) and social systems (in which people achieve some common goals or purpose, resulting in job satisfaction). The simplest of several models of the socio-technical system is seen in Figure 12.2 which lists its key elements.

Managing the system requires that the *relationships* between the elements are understood and influenced in the service of the system's goals. NCTD/EDWP saw this as a critical issue at the dynamic workplace; the relationships were constantly changing, and on-the-job learning was endlessly needed to understand the changes and manage them. The socio-technical model appeared to describe, albeit in an unrealistically 'static' form, the basic requirements of workplace learning.

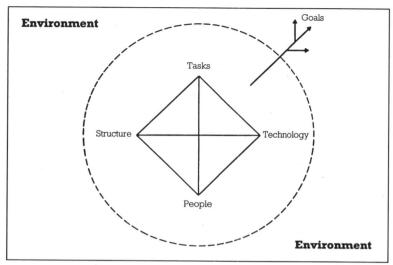

Figure 12.2
The Socio-Technical System

Source: H. Barrington, *Learning about Management.*

Tavistock researchers also distinguished between 'closed' and 'open' systems, and argued that the modern dynamic world was making systems increasingly 'more open'. 'Closed' systems are managed as if they are independent of their surroundings – the basic assumption is that any problems can be analysed and dealt with solely on the basis of internal structure – and hence that the organisation simply does not need to respond to changes in external technology or law or public opinion. In such systems, management is typically aimed at producing an 'ideal' set of procedures, and then at imposing these procedures for ever; needless to say, command structures predominate. 'Open' systems, on the other hand, accept that change has to happen in response to external developments that cannot be ignored; procedures change through time, leadership is much more shared, and team working evolves. (See Figure 12.3.)

It will come as no surprise that NCTD/EDWP members believed – or perhaps we should say, came to believe – that open systems were now the norm in UK society, and a critical problem lay in the fact that management were still trying to manage as if closed systems were extant and necessary.

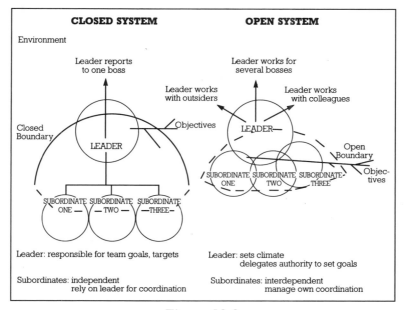

Figure 12.3
'Closed' versus 'Open' Systems

Adapted from a Bridger Study-Group Handout.

Several principles emerged from the dialogue on theory:

- that modern systems are predominantly 'open systems'
- that continuous workplace learning is needed (especially by managers) if they are to understand and be able to manage socio-technical relationships
- that self development should be urged as 'part of working life'
- that learning about learning itself is a key need for self development.

Training Methods
Much time was spent discussing recent and current training methods, in the hope that something might be championed and offered as 'the answer to the nation's needs' – that is, 'the' way to satisfy the principles so far established. No such conclusion proved possible; but the

debate yielded interesting light on what was being attempted, and allowed several more principles to be established.

In-depth explanation of each method is not possible here; for substantial coverage see M. L. and P. J. Berger's 1978 collection entitled *Group Training Techniques* and other texts mentioned against specific sections. Some methods were identified as less useful than others:

Organisation Development
OD (a collective term for a number of methods – see Beckhard, 1969 and Bennis, 1969) was seen as effecting organisational change but not closely enough linked to workplace learning.

Managerial Grid Training
MGT (see Blake and Mouton, 1978) was believed to be at odds with the participative workplace setting.

Action Centred Leadership
ACL (see Adair, 1978) enjoyed a theoretical base which was believed to be relevant to the turbulent workplace, but did little to promote the 'learning organisation'.

T-Groups
T-Groups (see Smith, 1969, and Cooper and Mangham, 1971) were respected for their ability to develop sensitivity to group processes, but criticised heavily for their adoption of *taskless* group settings.

Coverdale Training
Coverdale Training (see Taylor, 1979) was praised for its emphasis on improvement, and its acceptance that the real work team was the effective learning unit. Members felt the need was to get something approaching Coverdale into many organisations as part of the ongoing work reality.

Two methods easily outshone the others in apparent relevance:

Action Learning (AL)
In AL (pioneered by Revans – see Revans, 1983), tailor-made programmes of several months' duration were created 'for the development of managers . . . based on real life problems'. Volunteers (called 'fellows') were enrolled in groups, and assigned to work on specific

challenges set by participating firms. The design of programmes was detailed: for example, a challenge must involve more than a short-term emergency, and fellows were required to work on equal terms with staff in participating firms whom they might normally consider 'unqualified' or 'lower level'. Each group (called a 'set') had a set adviser attached to it; the adviser offered help in understanding the challenge in academic terms (e.g. psychology, economics), and in providing a sounding board against which process ideas might be tested. In the early eighties, AL was applied *inside* a number of large firms (e.g. IBM UK), and with the aid of Manpower Services Commission and the City University, in some 90 new entrepreneurial developments; supporting academic work was here expanded to include business studies, including such subjects as formal organisation theory, salesmanship and cash flow forecasting.

NCTD/EDWP members saw AL as wholly appropriate to the needs of managers in the changing work scene, and its promotion inside firms as potentially a major answer to the nation's problems. They hoped in-house AL would grow. Their main concern was that to date AL seemed to favour the one-off project approach. It was also expensive, fees charged being high; and the investment in managers' (i.e. 'fellows') time seemed too much for UK business to accept on a wide scale.

Study Groups

The London Tavistock Institute, and (independently) several of its own consultants, ran variants of T-groups under the heading 'study group' or 'learning group'. One important version of these was offered by Bridger, whose groups had one important difference – they observed their behaviour against the backdrop of an agreed task. Staff members, who were known as 'process consultants', intervened as in T-groups to help members appreciate their own group dynamics, but interventions were usually geared to illuminating how the group was progressing in relation to its work goals. Managing both task and process was openly seen as a requirement for an effective team. Bridger-type study groups were reported to be highly successful in the Philips organisation, and in Lever Brothers, where groups could study their own reality whilst collectively addressing a real work need. In both these organisations, these methods had become a fundamental part of management trainee training. A fictional account of a Bridger-type study group, in which a group of management trainees explore management concepts and simultaneously study their own organisation-building process, can be seen in Barrington (1984).

As with AL and Coverdale training, NCTD/EDWP members could not see industry generally investing the necessary management time to promote widespread study groups. But they liked the concepts inherent in 'task versus process' management and 'process review', and the emphasis on group cohesion; they saw these as wholly relevant to the real life work situation and the needs of the learning organisation.

Other methods (e.g. one based on role negotiation and confrontation skills) were discussed, and rejected as too far removed from the basic need.

As already suggested, 'the' answer to the nation's needs did not seem to exist. But reviewing what was on offer yielded several more 'principles':

- for team development in a modern setting, training methods must be based on learning rather than teaching processes
- learning to manage change requires both individual motivation and a group setting, with the latter supporting the former
- discussion is an essential vehicle to allow the transformation of new perceptions into confident ideas
- process review skills are as important as problem solving techniques.

The 'ABCD' Campaign

The IPM committees now had a list of principles, and a wish to transform them into some sort of persuasive activity. They quickly established their ideal as a 'continuous development' (CD) culture. But the list of principles was not an easy one to communicate; indeed, traditional communication methods (off-the-job courses and conferences, general articles, text books) seemed inappropriate to the message. It was also felt that to attempt too much at one stroke might undermine the message; CD needed its own evolutionary development, adjusting its own reality continuously in the light of its own experience.

More importantly, the situation was itself one which mirrored the workplace reality. The world was changing around IPM, whose committees were being drawn into it. Internally, IPM members were becoming less dependent, more challenging, more diverse in their views. Membership regulations were being adjusted with increasing frequency; the IPM professional education syllabus was being reviewed and amended on virtually an annual basis. The personnel profession was itself illustrating the national problem: personnel managers were no longer able to see themselves as parts of a military-style culture, but as politicians needing to consult and facilitate, instead of simply imposing decisions. (For an insight into the politics of training management in a changing world, see Moorby, 1991.) In short, CD principles seemed relevant and appropriate to the evolution of CD itself.

A five-year campaign was decided upon, with a mnemonic title 'ABCD' – standing for 'A Boost for Continuous Development' – which was intended to suggest the opposite of revolutionary or doctrinaire ideals. The NCTD became the trainer-facilitator, or 'set adviser'. Three 'sets' were initially targeted: IPM members, including students; the media; and other national organisations. The underlying aim was to generate and increase understanding of CD principles, and to that end to start a nationwide learning process about operational learning itself. The essential first objective was to generate discussion; to that end, a Code was published, IPM branches were encouraged to insert CD meetings into their calendars, journal articles were prepared, and IPM's national committees were asked to put the theme on their agendas (the national Education Committee quickly lifted the gauntlet, and CD was also introduced into the professional studies syllabus at its next rewrite).

The Code was the most important catalyst produced. Even in its third (1990) form (now called a 'Statement' – reproduced in this book as Appendix 7), it can be seen that much of the CD message has been omitted. This reflects the 'slowly, slowly' strategy. The emphases in the Code are first on self development, and second on creating the organisational culture in which it can flourish. Later, the integration of learning with work was to be added. The architects of the Code were highly conscious that CD seemed best able to flourish in operating organisations which had already developed a 'training infrastructure' – training policy statements, learning objectives written into forward plans, appraisal aiming at improved performance – and they reasoned that the introduction of an appropriate system was as much part of the promotion of CD as the development of employee attitudes.

The media showed little interest (the national press did not carry a single article on CD throughout the eighties, and apart from IPM's own journals – the IPM Digest carried a regular, periodic ABCD report – editors preferred to wait until support was voiced on a widespread scale). Existing IPM members, both individually and in branches, were interested but cautious; they asked many questions, most of which could be interpreted as implying that they thought ABCD must have some unspoken ulterior political purpose. This reproduced the problem: the political purpose was not unspoken, nor ulterior, but open to all who could learn. A great deal of success was however forthcoming from other national organisations, who seemed to appreciate the CD message and wanted to talk about it. Discussions were held with a wide variety of bodies, from the Institute of Manpower Studies to the Engineering Council, from the Industrial Society to the Confederation of British Industry. All these bodies showed interest and voiced support for the principles which were being preached; before the end of the decade, several (e.g. the Engineering Council, who were by 1990 to develop a national CD system for all engineers) had produced their own supporting reports. A great deal of interest also came from the colleges, where IPM lecturers were quick to help students to understand the links between learning theory, organisational developments and the Code.

KEY CD CONCEPTS

The dialogue during the mid-eighties significantly sharpened and extended overall understanding of what CD was all about. Most importantly, it focused attention on what came to be regarded as the two critical elements in CD thinking: self development, and the integration of learning with work.

These two elements took on added meaning and sophistication. What CD meant for the individual self developer was increasingly well defined; Figure 12.4 provides an example of such definition.

But it also became increasingly clear that the concept of self development is as relevant to the team as to the individual: indeed, while working as an effective group, team members both help individuals to develop themselves and generate collective learning. Similarly, it emerged that people who are brought by discussion to appreciate the existence of 'barriers' to their learning are more motivated to want to break those barriers than people assessed as having 'weaknesses'; and that motivation can be stimulated by such devices as 'prompt lists' (lists of questions to which a job holder should have answers), 'learning contracts' (learners' statements of real-life problems, together with planned learning activities and predictions of achievement); and 'learning logs' (learners' diaries of conclusions, and the process of arriving at them)

Ann Gray is a recently-qualified Personnel Officer in an NHS hospital. She has been asked to recommend ways whereby staff costs can be reduced without affecting hospital services to patients and the local community.

1 Ann reviews her learning needs in the light of the task, and decides:
   - she must sharpen her awareness of what the patients and public expect
   - she needs to know more about NHS finance and accounting norms
   - her task has a political dimension which must be managed

2 She assesses learning opportunities, and decides:
   - fellow professionals in the hospital and the local authority are her best sources of information
   - she must operate without a budget for her learning

3 She considers her own learning styles/preferences, and decides:
   - she must actively seek opportunities for learning
   - she must gain entry to selected 'planning' meetings
   - she must develop a 'team member' image
   - she must find and make use of any relevant documents
   - she must interpret information for herself

4 She creates a 'learning agenda', and decides:
   - she must list potential barriers to her learning, and create positive ways of overcoming them
   - she will list the 'planning' meetings to which she can reasonably expect access, and 'sell' the need for her attendance
   - she will prepare briefing notes for each meeting she attends, explaining her mission, outlining benefits to the listeners, and listing the information she needs

5 She adds priorities to her 'learning agenda', and decides:
   - she must develop presentation skills by practising at home
   - she must learn who are the key members of the meetings she will attend, and what they themselves support
   - she must create a 'prompt list' (questions to which she needs answers)

6 She investigates resources to facilitate learning, and finds:
   - two of her Personnel colleagues are happy to provide information
   - once her attendance at a meeting is agreed, past minutes of the meeting are easily available
   - local councillors are available for discussion
   - the local paper has recently carried several relevant letters

7 She anticipates possible difficult eventual outcomes, and decides:
   - her recommendations must not be open to charges of insufficient evidence or bias or incompleteness

8 She reads, attends meetings, discusses, reflects, interprets, concludes, writes. She checks her conclusions with her contacts, sharpening her awareness of their responses and strengthening or modifying her opinions in the light of what emerges. By the time she presents her final report, she confidently believes her recommendations represent the most professional contribution that ANYONE can make.

Figure 12.4
An example of self-development within a work role

Adapted from internal IPM material prepared by Sue Wood.

(see Gold, 1990). Perhaps most importantly, it slowly became appreciated that treating workplace learning as relating simply to a person is not quite appropriate: the significance of the turbulent workplace is to make the learning need one which can reasonably be seen as stemming not from the person alone, but from the 'person in the job'.

The *integration of learning with work* was given new meaning by examples such as this. Although at the level of the organisation it means (as the IPM CD statement implies) the introduction and maintenance of systems and procedures which naturally promote learning (e.g. the identification of learning needs), at the level of the work team it means organising time to allow for the learning process (and especially the discussion activity), and at the level of the individual it means more conscious appreciation of how learning can happen – which includes appreciation of the learning skills needed. In the mid-eighties, researchers working with Kolb at Case Western University in the USA published their own new definitions of such skills, linked to the well-known four-stage Kolb learning cycle (see Figure 3.2 on page 74). It is shown in Figure 12.5.

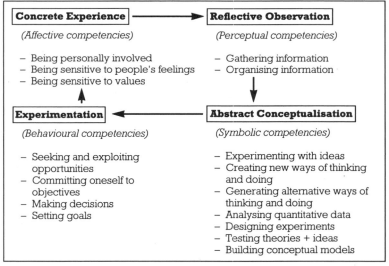

Figure 12.5
Experiential Learning Skills

Constructed from material in Kolb *et al.*, 'Strategic Management Development: Using Experiential Learning Theory to Assess and Develop Managerial Competences', in *Journal of Management Development*, Vol. 5, No. 3, 1986.

They called these learning skills 'specialised adaptive competencies', and viewed them as generic; but they also suggested that each needed to be further sub-divided into lower level skills in any specific organisational setting to identify actual learning needs which might apply. And they further acknowledged something they called 'integrative competence', which was needed to add dimensions such as the level of complexity and uncertainty. As they saw it, the 'unmet need' for education in 'integrative competence' would continue to grow; 'integrative learning' demanded learning conditions that are different, and at times in opposition to, other approaches:

> 'integrative learning is more concerned with process, with learning how to learn rather than simple skill acquisition . . . It is more concerned with executive problem solving about which competence to apply in which circumstance . . . As such, it is more internalised and specifically tailored . . . There are no simple answers, or, more specifically, only *one* correct answer in each unique . . . circumstance'.

> Kolb *et al.* (1986)

These ideas put into rather more complex terminology what the NCTD/EDWP members had increasingly been thinking. Their CD ideal involved raising individual performance by raising the ability to understand one's immediate work situation as an endless learning situation – both in terms of learning needs and the learning process. The ideal also involved managing work in such a way as to share that learning process, allowing time for discussion on it and acknowledging that adult learners learn best when they are acknowledged as experts and equals. Managers in such circumstances are still managers, and probably have superior understanding of group processes; but they remain part of the learning organisation themselves, and their main role in an open system is to help the learning to happen, with their main vehicle the 'process review' dialogue, in which they learn along with other team members. Decisions on how to promote this cannot be divorced from the work situation, nor can they be permanent. Hence the justification for the continuous improved performance attitude.

You might like to look again now at the three definitions of CD which we tentatively offered early in this chapter (page 342), with a view to creating your own personal definition. Should there be reference in it to 'learning to learn'? To the provision of learning time? To 'process skills'? To 'integrative learning'? Or mangers as learners? Or is it enough to define CD simply as 'development on an endless basis'?

LATER HISTORY

But the environment of the eighties was not naturally kind to CD and its supporters. Indeed, environmental change offered a number of significant challenges to progress along the CD route.

1 The economy thrived, and took with it most new management thoughts about workplace learning. Many previously over-manned organisations had been slimmed down during the recession of the seventies; participative movements declined as trades unions weakened and employers rekindled confidence in their ability to manage in the old authoritarian and 'closed system' ways (paradoxically, the prevailing open market views of government were often interpreted by top management as a guarantee of freedom from outside interference). A new view of double-tiered organisations, comprising 'core' workers who were the 'permanent staff' and others who were less permanent, gained ground; simplistic commentators implied that this reduced, or at least simplified, the employer's training responsibilities. The ITBs were now finished, and the new training spokesunit, the Manpower Services Commission, put its eggs into its new anti-unemployment basket, Youth Training. And the formula seemed to work: the economy grew, and profits and cash returned, without any need to worry about internal learning systems. Recruitment and initial training became once again the main focus for trainers. Teaching resumed its key role; self directed learning, by individuals or groups, changed its direction towards 'distance' learning, with its prepackaged teaching methods.

2 The MSC's preoccupation with new centralised developments like YTS made it difficult for them to champion an unstructured, evolutionary, 'learning' approach. The MSC did provide funds for a report on CD as a management tool (the material was eventually published by IPM in the book 'Continuous Development'); but they had separately funded the much more ambitious study into management development which led to the Handy report and the appearance of the Management Charter Initiative (see Chapter 1). Handy's recommendations suggested a

relaunch of management development in the UK, but made no clear reference to CD; the charter group's charter and code of practice included CD elements, but equally saw training as 'getting the best out of people'. MCI at no time concentrated any energy on how to transform these elements into working criteria. MCI appeared as simply devoted to yet another prescriptive management model.

3 The UK business world became very interested in a new import from Japan – 'Total Quality Management' (TQM). For a thorough outline of TQM, see Collard (1989). TQM philosophy is not unlike that of CD: it is attitudinal, and aspires to endless improved performance. Indeed, its early pioneers all saw that improvements are dependent upon employees (usually managers) being motivated towards learning, and one of its crucial principles is that 'in discussing quality we are dealing with a people situation'. TQM of course wholeheartedly supports the idea of learning within work. The main differences between TQM and CD lie in the absence of any commitment to promote 'learning about learning' in TQM, and its much greater support for direction and control. In TQM, quality circles are a key instrument; but they are always led by an immediate supervisor, they must meet according to a set calendar pattern, and so on. Management quality circles are not held; ideas from quality circles must be agreed by management before implementation. In other words, TQM attempts to sustain the hierarchical organisation that the Tavistock researchers believed was naturally a 'closed system' phenomenon. It is probably true that in doing this, TQM proved more in harmony with the wishes of most management in the UK during the boom years of the eighties.

4 The National Council for Vocational Qualifications was born, and with it the idea that all workplace competence could be transformed into national standards. We have already noted in earlier chapters government's sustained attempt to bring education and training together; that attempt has included the hierarchical arrangement of qualifications, but has to date ignored both learning methods and the further learning of the 'qualified' worker (NVQs do not normally incorporate a commitment to go on learning, nor competence in self directed learning – although it is argued by Jessup (1991) that the national framework of NVQs provides new opportunities for any with the ambition to go on learning). Employers (and many trainers) have nevertheless seen NVQs as offering a simple answer to their

training problems: little workplace planning is needed, the content of training being dictated by the national standards and the responsibility for the learning once again being given in the vast majority of cases to a college lecturer. It is ironic that learning needs and work needs can thus remain separated in an initiative which is said to bring them together.

5 Politicians from all parties took the lead in promoting their own debate on education and training, and omitted all reference in it to the importance of workplace learning. Training moved to somewhere near centre stage in the run up to the 1992 election, with the unsuccessful Labour and Liberal Democratic parties including new training measures in their manifestos; but politicians' views were limited to government's own activity, and hence to formal national programmes and their funding (the Labour party promised a return to employer levies; the Liberal Democrats promised compulsory two-days-a-week vocational studies for all who had left full-time education up to age eighteen). The political arguments rarely extended to ways whereby industry might be helped to help itself: one ex-politician's comment that 'economics is essentially about people' was a rare exception to the more normal comments on trainee or student numbers and the need for training levies. Somewhat surprisingly, the Conservative election manifesto did not even make great economic claims for its training interventions.

THE ULTIMATE INTERVENTION

And yet, CD philosophy remains relevant. It is the 'ultimate' intervention, in that it allows and encourages all other training interventions: as an attitude of mind, an approach, a philosophy, which attempts to promote endless learning, and designs environments to that end, CD cannot properly be viewed as an alternative to any other intervention, national or otherwise. We must remember that the IPM committees found themselves unable to move at one jump to their ideal of integrating learning with work; they acknowledged that for many the necessary building blocks were not yet in position. Similarly, CD advocates have been quick to acknowledge the importance of formalised programmes to ease unemployment problems. Perhaps the nation must, like the organisations who moved ahead of the ITBs in the sixties, move through a period when attention is focused on standardised programmes and systematic approaches, with their formal procedures and analytical practices, in order to appreciate the additional need for more organic models to improve workplace learning.

The similarity with the sixties is not a close one. Organisational development in the sixties meant 'top downward' manipulation; it now increasingly means the evolution of 'flatter', participative organisations *from interventions in the middle*, and indeed it means the evolution of *'learning organisations'*. The 'Learning Pays' and 'Learning Organisation' movements which we mentioned in Chapter 1 clearly support CD ideals, albeit with different emphases: they represent further attempts to satisfy on an ongoing basis the important requirements we explained towards the end of Chapter 4. The growing support for these attempts can be gauged from reading a 1992 report (Jones and Hendry) commissioned by the Human Resource Development Partnership, entitled 'The Learning Organisation'; the recommendations at the end of that report point the way to further research during the nineties. Professional bodies are also rapidly coming to expect continuing professional development from their members, who constitute an increasingly large proportion of the nation's managers. The 'Continuing Professional Development' (CPD) movement is gaining ground: the IPD's decision to require evidence of continuous development for the upgrading of members, and eventually for the retention of membership, is a clear demonstration of their belief in CD. The existence of mandatory CPD schemes in a number of professional bodies is a clear indication of the growing belief in CD. The IPD and other professional bodies can be expected to explore new ways to relate CD concepts to membership requirements and to find ways of assessing CD achievements.

Higher education is increasingly committed to adding 'preparation for work' to its academic syllabuses, and is beginning to advertise learning skills as a necessary part of that preparation. The Open University has developed as one of its EHE initiatives a 'portfolio approach to personal and career development' which is basically a self-study and self-development course in 'learning about learning'. The next generation of personnel managers can be expected to have at least a theoretical understanding of CD concepts. Moreover, the fruits are now appearing of a number of development projects mounted in the higher education sphere by the Employment Department during the eighties. Many of these projects were related to promoting 'enterprise' within universities and polytechnics; but one group of ten went under the collective title 'Learning Through Work', and had as their focus the integration, assessment and accreditation of work-based learning *within academic programmes*. The work (summarised in reports dated 1990 and 1992 from the Higher Education branch of the Employment Department – see Bibliography) has made inroads into defining skills development opportunities within undergraduate courses, and the contribution of work experience to such courses. Separately, a number of pilot arrangements between universities and professional bodies have pioneered post-graduate courses leading to both academic awards and professional qualifications. It is not simply that these initiatives erode the distinctions between education and work; they also give work-based learning a new level of respectability.

The 'Investors in People' initiative will stimulate at least the basic structure on which organisations can then build their unique systems.

Self development can also be expected to grow quickly as new technology makes self directed learning more feasible. Computer-based training (CBT) methods already offer home study packages to those with their own personal computers (a steadily increasing percentage of the population). Compact disc technology widens this opportunity, allowing massive amounts of data to be stored on a single cheap disc; linkage with the video recorder allows a mixture of still and moving, and sound and vision, material. The application of artificial intelligence (AI) is making programmes much more adaptive, more able to reproduce the sophistications of the real world, more able to respond to the learner's questions without having to predict them in advance, more able to simulate the workplace learning situation in so far as standard 'rules' are concerned. Separately, satellite broadcasts promise educational options, with tutorial resources available by telephone (see Appendix 6 for more – albeit brief – information on technology-assisted training methods and techniques). The ability to marry these methods with a turbulent workplace is still some way off, but there will be researchers addressing this need as well as sophisticating their own products.

Perhaps most importantly of all, we can expect work organisations to continue to make their operations more open and flexible; hopefully, the deep recession of 1991/92 will eventually be seen as a collective calamity, brought about as much by industry's inefficiencies as by any governmental mistakes, and necessitating a stronger spotlight on the learning processes that can attack those inefficiencies. The Total Quality Management movement will surely also grow, and may be expected to refine its views on the contribution that employee development can make.

Whatever the future, learning must surely grow in importance in the eyes of the UK community. That being so, greater interest in CD seems more rather than less likely, at least in the long term. If the nation reaches the point when the majority of its workforce believes in continuous development, the ultimate move will have been made, generating its own ongoing, infinite number of interventions into the nation's continuous learning process.

FOR FURTHER REFLECTION AND DISCUSSION

1 How do YOU see the future for CD?

2 Do you agree that CD offers a unique approach to employee development?

3 Assuming for at least one moment that you support CD as an ideal, what would you recommend as the best way(s) to promote it?

SUGGESTED READING

There is only one text on CD itself. Edited by IPM's Training Manager Sue Wood (now IPD's Policy Adviser), it is entitled *Continuous Development: The Path to Improved Performance*. Our own Appendix 7 (the IPD CD Statement) out-dates the IPM CD Code printed in that book.

GARRATT B. *'The Learning Organisation'*. Fontana, London, 1989. Covers team learning and the integration of learning with work; its title (and that of the 'learning company') is increasingly becoming used to describe organisations that seek to manage change on a continuous basis – embracing elements such as worker participation, power/control, and management systems as well as employee development *per se*.

The 1992 report which we mentioned in the text (with the same title, *'The Learning Organisation'*), commissioned by the Human Resource Development Partnership and compiled by Warwick University's A. M. JONES and C. HENDRY, provides a comprehensive review of 'literature and practice', and includes twelve case studies summarised from journal articles – although surprisingly it does not mention CD. Among the report's many references, that of *Self-Development in Organisations* (edited by M. PEDLER *et al*. McGraw Hill, Maidenhead, 1990) is worthy of emphasis.

FOR FURTHER REFLECTION AND DISCUSSION

What would you like to see as the 'next training intervention' in your own organisation, and why?

Which parts of this book have made the biggest impact on you?

How can you build whatever you have learned into your
   (a) roles?
   (b) life?

APPENDIX 1

A positive policy for training and development

This policy was devised by the former IPM's National Committee for Training and Development in 1983. It was revised in 1990. It is written in terms of principles and not in terms of current initiatives.

Purpose of the paper
1 The purpose of this policy paper is to assist members, IPM Officers and members of staff as they respond to, or seek to influence, national training developments. From this base, the IPM will continue to put forward its considered views on the necessary shape and style of the training infrastructure at national and local level. And will, of course, continue to contribute to and comment on major national initiatives.

Introduction – the challenge for training
2 The prosperity of the nation depends upon the creation of wealth: that is the 'value added' in the production of goods and services. Of equal importance, the quality of life of our people depends upon national prosperity which enables the efficient provision of those public services which are essential for the well-being and protection of the population. All types of employing organisations are thus interdependent. The nation relies upon UK businesses competing successfully in markets at home and abroad, and such success can only come through continuous improvements in efficiency and productivity (the key to which is training).

3 Faced with the accelerating pace of technological and social change – and its profound impact upon employment patterns and work organisation – and with increasing and increasingly more pervasive competition

from abroad, our employing organisations must possess workforces which are not only well organised, motivated and skilful, *but which are also capable of adapting to changing demands.* Within the workforce, each individual should be encouraged and equipped to contribute to the fullest of his or her abilities, otherwise potential will be squandered (and personal ambition remain unfulfilled). Thus there is national, commercial and personal profit in each individual making his or her maximum contribution in a changing world; this contribution will depend to a large extent on the education, training and development the individual receives.

4 The costs of learning should be shared by its beneficiaries – the individual, employing organisations and the State – in appropriate proportions depending upon the status of the learner (young person or adult, employed or unemployed).

5 The need for training before and throughout working life is made apparent when viewed against the background of changes which have already occurred. The nature of work has changed and continues to change: white-collar jobs now outnumber blue-collar, reflecting in part the decline of job opportunities in the manufacturing sector, the growth in service industries and the introduction of modern technology. Less skilled work is fast diminishing, leaving unqualified school leavers and unskilled and semi-skilled workers particularly vulnerable to unemployment.

There is an increasing demand for technical skills of a type or in a combination not anticipated a decade ago. Thus continuous change should be expected and individuals should be prepared to face it. For economic AND social reasons, training should be available to all. Clearly the acquisition of skills and knowledge through training and development is becoming more important as a prerequisite for entry into the productive workforce, and skills once acquired are likely to need updating or modifying to match changing requirements.

A period of initial training no longer provides a sufficient skills base (if it ever did): continuous development is necessary. Training must match the changing needs of industry, commerce and the public sector, and so our traditional education and training systems must adapt and change. Educators themselves need to continue to adapt and learn and to anticipate the needs of a changing clientele.

Education and vocational preparation

6 Preparation for adult and working life begins at school. Every young person should receive an education which prepares him or her to participate in and contribute to society. It must therefore include the basic skills necessary to cope with modern life and to become a responsible citizen; it must also impart an understanding of modern society (including the wealth creating role of industry and commerce and the social support role of the public services). Education must focus on the individual however, and provide young people with the means to begin to develop their own individual interests and talents to the fullest of their capacity.

7 Each school pupil should have early and continuous help in identifying his or her potential, in clarifying his or her aspirations and interests, and in setting targets for achievement. It is important that the school leaver should have learned to set goals for learning and to recognise and use a variety of learning resources to achieve these goals. Until, in the area of basic skills and personal development the school system FULLY meets the needs of young people, it will be necessary to incorporate much of this in post-school programmes.

8 Before starting full-time employment, every school leaver should have an opportunity of an integrated programme of training, work experience and related further education (apprenticeship is one form of this).

All full-time further or higher education courses, including Polytechnic and University courses, should incorporate or be followed by an appropriate work introduction programme.

9 All training programmes for young people must lead to a nationally recognised qualification (or part qualification) based on the young person's experiences and achievements, and including achievements on educational courses. It is important that parents, employers and young people themselves understand, accept and value new forms of certification and see them as relevant to progress in the real world. Such programmes should be realistically based on one or more of a set of grouped occupations – each group requiring broadly similar basic skills and knowledge – and should aim to give each young person many opportunities to experience achievements in a variety of contexts and provide first-hand experience of the world of work.

10 Further and higher education must also respond to the changing needs of society. There is mutual benefit in much closer liaison between the education sector on the one hand and industry, commerce and the public services on the other. The academic institutions can provide resources and research results of direct use to organisations in changing and developing both products and methods. There is value and inspiration for the teaching institutions in using (and perhaps resolving) real problems from the world of work as part of the learning process.

Initial training

11 Job-specific training programmes which build on vocational preparation programmes need to be developed by industrial, commercial and public organisations in anticipation of demand. The importance of initial training is not diminished by better vocational preparation, although its scope and nature may need to change. An imaginative long term view is required in programme design, one which recognises the likelihood of continuing change in many job-specific skills. Initial training must be fairly broadly based, and it must be carefully constructed to emphasise *the context* in which specific job skills will be employed.

12 Initial training is the foundation upon which further learning will be built. Trainees need to be made aware of the importance of continuing to learn after initial training, particularly in response to developments in technology and work organisation. Thus, initial training programmes should reflect the fact that learning must be a continuous process. It is important, therefore, that in initial training programmes – the primary aim of which is the acquisition of 'product' skills – attention should also be paid to 'process' skills, that is, learning skills, in order that the trainee is equipped to acquire new product skills quickly and easily later on as circumstances demand.

13 Initial training will continue to be provided mostly by individual employers. Within realistic constraints however, young people should be given maximum freedom to choose opportunities which best match their interests, aptitudes and aspirations. In order to begin to achieve this it is essential to develop sound information systems and careers guidance, with easy access to both.

Continuing training

14 Because of the continuous demand for new or more advanced skills, adults must be encouraged to continue to develop their skills and knowledge throughout their lives, whether in employment or not. It is recognised that self-motivation may be more of a problem for some unemployed people seeking to re-enter employment. Counselling, to assist in the choice of path for further development, will be essential. Employers must meet the need to update or change the skills and knowledge of employees as a result of technological innovation and new working practices. A less obvious but equally important priority is to ensure that employees learn to cope with participative methods of management where these emerge or are demanded, and to develop the new forms of organisational structure which will result. (Training methods appropriate for continuous development are themselves subject to change. Reference is made to learning methods later.)

15 It is for the State to make provision for the training of those who are unemployed and to stimulate the provision of training, advisory and support services for those who are or wish to become self-employed. Imaginative provision of this sort will be needed to create opportunities for people to develop organisations which contribute to society and reward those who labour in them. Innovations in employment patterns and types of employment are necessary if a high rate of unemployment is to be avoided. Radical means of sharing work are needed in order to organise the work to suit available workers' needs. Such innovations themselves require an educational, training and development effort, particularly in the spheres of attitudes to employment and continuous development.

The role of management

16 Managers must take a long term view of their organisation's corporate strategy. They need to understand the organisation in the context of its complex relationships with:

- its employees
- other organisations
- the public
- the State

– all of which are dynamic – and in the context of the organisation's reactions to changes in:

- products and markets
- the attitudes and demands of employees
- public taste and expectations.

Survival in such a complicated and ever-changing environment demands not only a high level of managerial skill and team work but also the development and maintenance of a workforce competent to perform, adapt and change as the situation demands in the search for greater productivity and/or effectiveness.

17 Cost effective employee development is crucial. The IPM does not consider that the considerable sums spent on education and training are spent sufficiently productively. To be effective, learning for work activity must be rooted in work activity. There will of course be circumstances when learning takes place, quite properly, away from the workplace but – as stated earlier – most learning takes place through the performance of the job itself.

In helping employees to continue to learn from their own experiences at work, that is, in instilling a learning culture, chief executives particularly, and all levels of supporting management, have key responsibilities: the rewards for the organisation can be very significant. For example, creating an environment in which self-directed development is encouraged and rewarded, which allows employees to question what they do and how they do it and to experiment with new ways of working, can lead to increased job satisfaction, greater individual commitment, closer identification with corporate objectives, and hence, to more effective job performance and increased efficiency.

18 Systems of continuous employee development and the allocation of resources in this area can only be brought about at the initiative of, and with the whole-hearted consent of, the chief executive and senior management. In gaining acceptance of the need for employee development programmes, managers must be convinced of their value and benefit to the organisation.

Programmes will demand full management commitment and ingenuity in design; managers must become aware of learning methods including self and group development. Personnel professionals have an important role to play in persuading, advising and supporting their management colleagues in taking appropriate initiatives and in assessing, maintaining and building upon the systems they create.

Delivery mechanisms

19 Increasingly, in considering employment issues, the importance of the local labour market and the local community is being recognised. This makes it imperative that more responsibility for programmes of initial training and retraining is put into the hands of the local community, with 'Area Boards' representing local employers, local employees, local authorities – including education authorities and other education and training establishments – plus other concerned groups, playing an active part. Such training bodies, to be credible and effective, need to be given executive authority to take action within a clear, flexible framework: a framework which is perhaps devised by the Area Board but which has the approval of all local interest groups. To enable local bodies to take responsibility for their community's training needs (to include unemployed people, disabled and disadvantaged people as well as training within employment) a broad allocation of funds from central government will be required and must be maintained. The funds should be used to establish training programmes, support trainees where necessary and to cover administrative costs and the fees of professional staff. In addition, Area Boards need to be able to charge fees for the services each provides locally (so raising additional funds).

20 There is a need for a nationally agreed framework for vocational training standards: standards must be linked to measures of performance and proficiency rather than to age, length of training or the possession of general qualifications.

Learning methods

21 Education and training systems must be so designed as to be capable of responding to totally new and rapidly changing needs. The training programmes should be sufficiently flexible to suit the learner, that is, should accommodate learners of varying ability and at varying educational levels. The trainee should not be required to fit into rigid education and training patterns. In view of the speed of change and its unpredictable nature, there is a need to encourage individuals to accept greater responsibility for their own learning. Individuals need to be

given assistance to establish their own unique set of learning objectives and in the preparation of a training strategy to meet these needs. Thus, teachers and trainers should be developed to serve as managers of the learning environment, as 'enablers', and to act as a resource rather than merely giving instruction.

22 The importance of learning from the experience of work itself, of coaching by the 'boss' and of learning from peers and subordinates cannot be over-stressed. It follows that the development of the skills of 'learning how to learn' and of coaching must be encouraged. To be successful, it is essential that a supportive learning environment is engendered at all levels of the organisation, and most important that all such systems have the full support and involvement of the chief executive.

23 The methods of learning used must be appropriate to the learners concerned and to the subject matter. There will still be a place for instruction in the 'classroom', but such a technique should be used thoughtfully, that is, used only when it is judged to be the most effective method of imparting appropriate skills and knowledge. Not only will the management of training need to alter, but the use of participative, project based and discovery methods – which focus on the learner – must be developed. Open learning systems – flexible in timing, place and pace of learning, age and stage of client, status of learners – by overcoming obstacles to learning, vastly extend the range of ways in which learners can be helped to learn AND CAN HELP THEM-SELVES. In addition, it is vital that those who train the trainers themselves use the methods they advocate for others' use.

Finally
24 Training policy cannot be viewed in isolation: it must be part of the strategic plan for every organisation, and part of the policy for change in society itself. The aim of training should be to contribute to the continuing well-being of society in all its constituent parts. The training infrastructure must be so designed as to be capable of responding appropriately, and with speed, to ever changing demands.

APPENDIX 2

List of abbreviations

ACAS	Advisory Conciliation and Arbitration Service
AI	Artificial Intelligence
APEL	Accreditation of Prior Experiential Learning
APL	Accreditation of Prior Learning
BGT	Business Growth through Training
BIM	British Institute of Management
BTEC	Business and Technology Education Council (formerly Business and Technical Education Council)
CATS	Credit Accumulation and Transfer Scheme
CBI	Confederation of British Industry
CBT	Computer Based Training
CD	Continuous Development
CGLI	City and Guilds of London Institute
CRE	Commission for Racial Equality
CSE	Certificate of Secondary Education
DFE	Department For Education
DV-I	Digital Video-Interactive
EHE	Enterprise in Higher Education
ET	Employment Training (now Training for Work TFN)
EU	European Union (superseded the European Community 1993)
FA	Functional Analysis
FE	Further Education
GCSE	General Certificate of Secondary Education
GNVQ	General National Vocational Qualification
IIP	Investors in People

ILB	Industry Lead Body
IMS	Institute of Manpower Studies
IPD	Institute of Personnel and Development
IPM	Institute of Personnel Management*
ITB	Industrial Training Board
ITD	Institute of Training and Development*
ITO	Industry Training Organisation
LEC	Local Enterprise Company
LEN	Local Employer Network
MBA	Master of Business Administration
MCI	Management Charter Initiative
MSA	Manual Skills Analysis
MSC	Manpower Services Commission (no longer in existence)
NACETT	National Advisory Council for Education and Training Targets
NCITO	National Council of Industry Training Organisations
NCVQ	National Council for Vocational Qualifications
NLP	Neuro-Linguistic Programming
NRA	National Record of Achievement
NROVA	National Record of Vocational Achievement (now replaced by NRA)
NTA	National Training Awards
NTTF	National Training Task Force
NVQ	National Vocational Qualification
OC	Open College
OU	Open University
PMS	Performance Management System
PSLB	Personnel Standards Lead Body
RSA	Royal Society for the Encouragement of Arts, Manufacturers and Commerce
SCAA	Schools Curriculum and Assessment Authority
SCOTVEC	Scottish Vocational Education Council
SVQ	Scottish Vocational Qualification
TA	Training Agency (no longer in existence)
TDLB	Training and Development Lead Body
TEC	Training and Enterprise Council
TFW	Training For Work
TUC	Trades Union Congress

* Merged in 1994 to become the Institute of Personnel and Development IPD.

TVEI   Technical and Vocational Education Initiative
TWI   Training Within Industry
YOP   Youth Opportunities Programme (now YT)
YT   Youth Training
YTS   Youth Training Scheme (now YT)

APPENDIX 3

A 'quick guide' to national and European training schemes, programmes, initiatives

Accreditation of Prior Learning (APL)
A national methodology providing for specific learning experiences (e.g. in-house courses) to be (a) assessed as satisfying some or all of the national standards for a given vocational qualification, and (b) formally accredited, in order that portfolios of evidence can be built up that will justify the award of appropriate qualifications.

Arion
EU exchange scheme for those concerned with education and training policy.

Business and Technology Education Council (BTEC)
Established in 1983, BTEC promotes 'work related studies' and awards 'work related qualifications'. The main occupational areas are Business and Finance, Engineering, Science, Hotel and Catering, and Computing. There are four levels of award – First, National, Higher National, and Continued Education; at each level BTEC offers both a Certificate and a Diploma, the latter involving longer and more concentrated study. Many BTEC awards are now also approved as National Vocational Qualifications (NVQs) q.v.

Business Growth Through Training (BGT)
An 'enterprise' initiative aimed at small businesses, and administered by Training and Enterprise Councils (TECs) q.v.

CEDEFOP
EU training research agency. Moving from Berlin to Thessaloniki in 1994.

City and Guilds of London Institute (CGLI)
An independent examining body which for over 100 years has set nationally recognised standards for operatives, craftspersons and technicians through its wide range of certificates. Individual subject exams are usually classified into three performance levels. Many CGLI awards are now also approved as 'National Vocational Qualifications' (NVQs), q.v.

Comett
EU training programme for cross-border cooperation between education and industry on new technology.

Compacts
Partnerships between specific employing organisations and specific educational institutions, offering to students training opportunities, to educationists updating in changing techniques and processes, and to employers a flow of potential recruits. A key service is the provision of Work Experience q.v. for students and staff alike.

Continuing Professional Development (CPD)
An uncoordinated series of initiatives designed to promote the ongoing development of professional people. Most initiatives emphasise formalised learning.

Continuous Development (CD)
An approach to learning, pioneered by the former Institute of Personnel Management (now IPD), which emphasises self development and the integration of learning with work.

Erasmus
EU exchange programme involving students in higher education.

Eurotecnet
EU training programme for cross-border cooperation on hi-tech programmes.

Force
EU programme to promote occupational vocational training.

General Certificate of Secondary Education (GCSE)

UK's single system of examining at 16+, introduced in 1986/8, and designed to cater for all abilities. Emphasis is on using knowledge and skills, not just memory. The exam is taken on a 'subject by subject' basis: grades are awarded against performance in each, grades A to G being considered 'Pass' grades, with work below grade G remaining unclassified.

General National Vocational Qualifications (GNVQs)

Qualifications approved by NCVQ q.v., available to full-time students in schools and FE colleges. GNVQs are 'broader-based' than NVQs q.v., and are grouped under 14 occupational headings at Levels 3 and 4.

Industry Training Boards (ITBs)

(No longer extant.) Statutory bodies established by the 1964 Industrial Training Act covering most, but not all, industries, and empowered to raise levies from employers within scope (NB small organisations were usually outside scope). Grant and levy exemption schemes were designed to promote training. Some 30 ITBs dwindled to six when the statutory basis was removed in the early eighties; the remainder disappeared in 1990/1.

Industry Training Organisations (ITOs)

Voluntary (i.e. non-statutory) successors to ITBs q.v. – representing most industries (over 100 ITOs exist), and advising/influencing their respective industries towards 'best training practice'. In recent years, ITOs' main national role has been to operate as Lead Bodies q.v. in defining standards of competence for use with National Vocational Qualifications (NVQs) q.v.

Investors In People (IIP)

An initiative aimed at increasing employers' commitment to training 'activities and attitudes' throughout the UK. Whilst managed and promoted by an independent organisation 'Investors in People UK Ltd', Training and Enterprise Councils (TECs) q.v. have been given the role of assessing employing organisations against a 'standard' (see Figure 1.2 for details). National Training Targets q.v. include one whereby at least half of the 'medium and larger' employing organisations are brought to qualify as IIPs by 1996.

Iris
EU initiative concerned with vocational training and retraining for women.

Lead Body
An industry- or occupation-wide body set up to identify and maintain 'standards of competence' covering jobs in their area of interest. The National Council for Vocational Qualifications (NCVQ) q.v. is required to reassure itself that any qualification submitted to it for approval as a National Vocational Qualification (NVQ) q.v. conforms to the standards laid down by the appropriate Lead Body/Bodies.

Learning Pays
A Royal Society of Arts initiative, aimed at stimulating interest in post-compulsory education and training in the UK. The initiative involves the gathering of information, its dissemination, and the generation of debate on issues of lifelong learning. It also aims to forge stronger links between schools, colleges, industry and commerce.

Leonardo
EU action programme from 1995 concerned with vocational training.

Lingua
EU foreign language training programme.

Local Enterprise Companies (LECs)
See 'Training and Enterprise Councils' below.

Management Charter Initiative (MCI)
A UK initiative in which employers combine to promote higher standards of management practice, by sharing resources, exchanging information, devising new management qualifications, and observing a Code of Practice. MCI have issued lists of management competences which they recommend as the bases for future management qualifications.

Manpower Services Commission (MSC)
(No longer extant.) A semi-independent agency, established and funded by government, which managed government's unemployment and training activities during the 1970s and 1980s. The MSC introduced the Youth Training Scheme (YTS) q.v., led Industrial Training

Board (ITB) q.v. activity, liaised with Industry Training Organisations (ITOs) q.v., and mounted a wide variety of training initiatives.

Modern Apprenticeships

Initiative launched 1994 with target of 150,000 'apprenticed' young people following new-style programmes (to be devised by 1995 by Industry Training Organisations (ITOs) q.v.). A key element in each programme will be training and education to NVQ/SVQ q.v. Level 3. Training and Enterprise Councils (TECs) q.v. will coordinate arrangements involving employer commitment to 'start-to-finish' training, and similar pledges from the trainees. 'Accelerated' programmes planned for 18–19-year-olds.

National Council for Vocational Qualifications (NCVQ)
and
Scottish Vocational Education Council (SCOTVEC)

Established in 1986, NCVQ exists to develop and maintain national standards of occupational competence, and to oversee a national framework of National Vocational Qualifications (NVQs), q.v. Standards are not themselves defined by NCVQ, but by Industry and Occupation 'Lead Bodies', q.v. NCVQ does not seek to influence the routes or methods by which people study for NVQs. (In Scotland, the system is managed by the Scottish Vocational Education Council (SCOTVEC), with a framework of Scottish Vocational Qualifications (SVQs).)

National Curriculum

Prescribed parts of UK's secondary education curriculum – introduced via the 1989 Education Reform Act and implemented via a timetable over the following six years.

National Record of Achievement (NRA)

A sequential portfolio system of collecting and collating qualifications and reports on vocational studies and training. Supervised nationally by the National Council for Vocational Qualifications (NCVQ) q.v., the system replaced an earlier system termed National Record of Vocational Achievement (NROVA).

National Training Awards

A national awards scheme, managed by the Training, Enterprise, and Education Division (TEED) of the Department of Employment (DE), giving public recognition to organisations and training providers who claim to have demonstrated 'excellence in the training field'. Award winners are selected from an annual batch of entrants.

National Training Targets
Targets originally devised and launched in 1990 by the Confederation of British Industry as 'World Class Targets' for the UK; adopted and renamed by government as 'national' targets in 1991. Specific goals relate to NVQ/SVQ attainments during the 1990s by young people and employees generally, and the attainment of 'Investors In People' (IIP) q.v. status by employers. See page 29 for details.

National Vocational Qualification (NVQ)
A term used to describe any qualification which has been approved by the National Council for Vocational Qualifications (NCVQ) q.v.; 560 NVQs exist (July 1994) covering 150 occupations. Qualifications are initially awarded by independent organisations (e.g. CGLI, BTEC, q.v.), but the 'NVQ' kite-mark appears alongside that of the awarding body. NVQs are arranged in a hierarchy of five levels, from 1 (the most basic) to 5 (management and professional level). 'General' NVQs (GNVQs) are available for those young people still in full-time education.

Open College (OC)
A 'distance learning' organisation, established 1987 on lines similar to those of the Open University (OU) q.v. – but primarily addressing vocational skills training needs.

Open University (OU)
A 'distance learning' organisation, offering degree-level and other courses on a national basis through flexible learning methods. Apart from receiving learning material by mail, students study by watching prepared TV programmes, completing planned assignments and attending residential workshops.

Petra
EU action programme for the vocational training of young people.

Records of Achievement (ROAs)
Records issued (from mid 1991) to those leaving full-time secondary schooling, reporting academic and other successes already achieved.

ROAs do not cover the wide range of data that earlier pilot 'Profile' documents covered. See also National Record of Achievement (NRA), which has taken the approach into the post-school education and training field.

Sandwich Training
Arrangements whereby degree and diploma students from UK universities and polytechnics spend periods of time working in industry or commerce (e.g. in a laboratory or a marketing department) – essentially as part of their course. Sandwich students usually receive special rates of pay, and are given 'real' jobs of work.

Scottish Vocational Education Council (SCOTVEC)
See 'National Council of Vocational Qualifications'.
and
Scottish Vocational Qualification (SVQ)
The Scottish equivalent of National Vocational Qualifications q.v.

Socrates
EU programme which extends Erasmus q.v. and Lingua q.v. to all levels of education. Encourages distance learning and mobility.

Technical and Vocational Education Initiative (TVEI)
An educational initiative (NB not a course, but usually involving a course, and a recognised qualification) aimed at providing vocational education for 14 to 18 year olds in UK schools. Curricula vary, but include subjects such as Business Studies, Information Technology, and Community Studies; provision is made for a wide range of abilities. Employer involvement is a 'must', Work Experience (q.v.) a norm.

Tempus
EU scheme which supports the development of higher education in Central and Eastern Europe.

Training Agency (TA)
(No longer extant.) Government's successor to the Manpower Services Commission (MSC) q.v., which introduced a new Youth Training (YT) q.v. programme, and produced the ground rules for the network of Training and Enterprise Councils (TECs) q.v.

Training, Enterprise and Education Division (TEED) of the Department of Employment (DE)
Government's successor to its Training Agency (TA) q.v. TEED manages the funding of Training and Enterprise Councils (TECs) q.v., and of those national schemes which are implemented through the TECs. TEC full-time staff are DE-employed.

Training and Enterprise Councils (TECs)
and (Scotland)
Local Enterprise Companies (LECs)
Employer-led bodies, established 1989/90 (coincident with the ending of Government's Training Agency (TA) q.v.); their main tasks are to manage in the locality national training schemes such as Youth Training (YT) q.v. and Training For Work (TFW) q.v., and to promote skills development in line with predicted local need – for which they dispense government funds. Training Credits schemes (see Youth Credits q.v.) and Career Development Loans (to help adults pay for their own training) are also managed by these bodies. An Investors in People (IIP) q.v. initiative allows them to give public recognition to any employing organisation which meets certain training standards.

Training For Work (TFW)
A national training scheme for long term unemployed adults, administered through training providers by Training and Enterprise Councils (TECs) q.v., using government funds. Programmes vary, dependent upon TECs' priority skill aims. (Formerly Employment Training ET.)

Work Experience
and
Work Shadowing
Arrangements made between employers and educational institutions whereby students spend periods of time within industry and commerce, experiencing the world of work. Schemes vary, sometimes involving projects and group work; some schemes are integral with courses such as TVEI or Business Studies GCSE q.v. Wages are not normally paid.

Youth Credits
(Also known as Training Credits and Training Vouchers.) Schemes involving 'vouchers' which can be exchanged for 'approved' training e.g. a Youth Training (YT) q.v. traineeship. Details of schemes, and

the value of vouchers, vary between Training and Enterprise Councils (TECs) q.v., who are the administrators.

Youth Training (YT)

A national training scheme for young people leaving full-time education between the ages of 16 and 18. Limited government funding is provided via Training and Enterprise Councils (TECs) q.v. Trainees may be engaged as 'employed' (i.e. on normal employment contracts) or as 'non-employed' (i.e. on special training contracts). Training programmes combine planned, supervised work experience and attendance at further education classes; apart from 'special needs' (e.g. disabled) trainees, all aspire to attaining NVQ q.v. Level 2 awards. Minimum weekly allowances are paid, plus travel allowances in certain cases. Programmes range from engineering to hairdressing, from catering to motor vehicle repair.

Terms relating to the EU have been taken selectively from the 'Glossary of EU Terms', *European Update*, Institute of Personnel Management, London, Aug–Sept 1994, pages 21–5.

APPENDIX 4

The Training and Development Lead Body's National Standards for Training and Development

Area A: Identify training and development needs

A1 IDENTIFY ORGANISATIONAL REQUIREMENTS FOR TRAINING AND DEVELOPMENT

- **A11** AGREE AND OBTAIN SUPPORT FOR THE CONTRIBUTION OF TRAINING AND DEVELOPMENT TO ORGANISATIONAL STRATEGY
  - **A111** Agree the contribution of training and development to organisational strategy
  - **A112** Promote and support decision makers' commitment to the agreed contribution of training and development

- **A12** IDENTIFY ORGANISATIONAL TRAINING AND DEVELOPMENT NEEDS
  - **A121** Identify the human resource implications of organisational strategy
  - **A122** Identify the priority human resource needs arising from organisational strategy
  - **A123** Specify training and development needs to support current organisational strategy
  - **A124** Identify training and development needs to support long term organisational strategy
  - **A125** Specify and agree priority training and development needs

- **A13** AGREE PRIORITIES FOR DEVELOPING THE TRAINING AND DEVELOPMENT FUNCTION
  - **A131** Evaluate the current capacity of people to meet priority training and development needs
  - **A132** Evaluate the capacity of physical resources and systems to meet agreed training and development needs
  - **A133** Identify priorities for developing current capacity in order to meet training and development needs

A2 IDENTIFY THE LEARNING NEEDS OF INDIVIDUALS AND GROUPS

- **A21** IDENTIFY THE CURRENT COMPETENCE OF INDIVIDUALS
  - **A211** Provide information and resources to enable individuals to identify their current competence
  - **A212** Provide information and resources to enable others to identify the current competence of individuals and groups
  - **A213** Define the current competence of individuals and groups

- **A22** AGREE INDIVIDUALS' AND GROUPS' PRIORITIES FOR LEARNING
  - **A221** Agree learning objectives which meet current performance requirements
  - **A222** Agree learning objectives which meet changes in performance requirements and work roles
  - **A223** Agree the learning objectives which meet the long term aspirations of individuals
  - **A224** Negotiate and agree priorities between learning objectives
  - **A225** Promote and encourage commitment to enable individuals and groups to achieve agreed priorities

B1 DESIGN ORGANISATIONAL TRAINING AND DEVELOPMENT STRATEGIES AND PLANS

B11 DEVELOP TRAINING AND DEVELOPMENT STRATEGIES
- B111 Identify potential strategies for meeting organisational requirements
- B112 Evaluate and select strategies which meet organisational requirements
- B113 Agree a strategic plan which meets organisational requirements

B12 IDENTIFY RESOURCES REQUIRED TO IMPLEMENT A STRATEGIC PLAN
- B121 Identify human resources required to implement a strategic plan
- B122 Identify physical resources required to implement a strategic plan
- B123 Identify systems required to implement a strategic plan

B13 SPECIFY AN OPERATIONAL PLAN WHICH MEETS ORGANISATIONAL TRAINING AND DEVELOPMENT REQUIREMENTS
- B131 Identify options for implementing a strategic plan
- B132 Evaluate and select options against strategic requirements
- B133 Agree an operational plan

B14 NEGOTIATE AND AGREE THE ALLOCATION OF RESOURCES
- B141 Prepare a training and development budget
- B142 Negotiate and agree a training and development budget
- B143 Agree a plan for allocating resources

B2 DESIGN STRATEGIES TO ASSIST INDIVIDUALS AND GROUPS TO ACHIEVE THEIR OBJECTIVES

B21 IDENTIFY AND AGREE TRAINING AND DEVELOPMENT STRATEGIES THAT MEET LEARNING NEEDS
- B211 Agree a specification of requirements
- B212 Identify individuals' previous learning experiences and needs
- B213 Identify and select options for meeting training and development requirements
- B214 Agree learning strategies to meet training and development requirements

B22 DESIGN LEARNING PROGRAMMES WHICH MEET LEARNING NEEDS
- B221 Select and specify training and development processes
- B222 Define and agree learning programme components
- B223 Specify processes and methods for evaluating progress towards objectives

B23 SPECIFY THE RESOURCES NEEDED TO DELIVER PROGRAMMES
- B231 Specify strategies for evaluating learning programmes
- B232 Specify the human resources required to deliver programmes
- B232 Define the physical resources and systems required to deliver programmes

B24 TEST, ADAPT AND AGREE LEARNING PROGRAMME DESIGNS
- B241 Identify and select strategies for testing learning programme designs
- B242 Test and assess learning programme designs
- B243 Adapt and agree learning programme designs

B25 AGREE LEARNING PLANS TO DELIVER INDIVIDUALS' AND GROUPS' OBJECTIVES
- B251 Provide information and advice for individuals to select and implement personal learning strategies
- B252 Develop and agree learning plans which meet individual and groups' objectives
- B253 Negotiate & agree the roles & resources required to support the achievement of personal learning objectives
- B254 Identify and select processes for monitoring and reviewing achievement of planned outcomes

B3 DESIGN AND PRODUCE LEARNER SUPPORT MATERIALS

B31 SPECIFY LEARNER SUPPORT MATERIALS
- B311 Identify and agree learner requirements
- B312 Identify and select options to meet learner requirements
- B313 Specify the materials required to support learners

B32 DESIGN LEARNER SUPPORT MATERIAL
- B321 Agree the media and systems required to deliver learner support materials
- B322 Agree the design requirements and formats for learner materials
- B323 Originate learner materials to support the achievement of objectives
- B324 Originate materials to support learners' management of their personal learning programmes
- B325 Originate material to support the assessment of progress towards objectives

B33 TEST AND ADAPT LEARNER SUPPORT MATERIAL
- B331 Select and plan methods to test materials
- B332 Test the effectiveness of learner materials
- B333 Modify learner materials to meet the requirements of specifications
- B334 Identify and implement adaptations of materials to meet changes in the support requirements of learners

Area C: Provide learning opportunities, resources and support

C1 OBTAIN AND ALLOCATE RESOURCES TO DELIVER TRAINING AND DEVELOPMENT PLANS

- **C11** OBTAIN RESOURCES TO DELIVER TRAINING AND DEVELOPMENT PLANS
  - C111 Obtain people to fill the roles identified within plans
  - C112 Obtain resources and services specified within plans
- **C12** ALLOCATE RESOURCES TO MEET THE REQUIREMENTS OF TRAINING AND DEVELOPMENT PLANS
  - C121 Allocate people to agreed roles to meet the requirements of operational plans
  - C122 Allocate physical resources and services to meet the requirements of operational plans

C2 PROVIDE LEARNING OPPORTUNITIES AND SUPPORT TO ENABLE INDIVIDUALS AND GROUPS TO ACHIEVE OBJECTIVES

- **C21** PREPARE AND PRESENT DEMONSTRATIONS AND INFORMATION AND PROVIDE ADVICE TO SUPPORT LEARNING
  - C211 Select and adapt learning materials and facilities to support oral and visual training methods
  - C212 Present information to learners
  - C213 Demonstrate skills, methods and procedures
- **C22** PREPARE AND PROVIDE OPPORTUNITIES FOR INDIVIDUALS AND GROUPS TO LEARN BY COLLABORATION
  - C221 Select, prepare and adapt exercises and simulations to support collaborative learning
  - C222 Provide opportunities for groups to exchange and interpret information and ideas
  - C223 Co-ordinate collaborative simulations and exercises which support learning objectives
  - C224 Provide feedback which enables groups to learn from their experience
- **C23** PREPARE AND PROVIDE OPPORTUNITIES FOR INDIVIDUALS AND GROUPS TO MANAGE THEIR OWN LEARNING
  - C231 Select, prepare and adapt resource materials to support self managed learning
  - C232 Identify and prepare locations and environments for self managed learning
  - C233 Provide information and advice to support individuals in managing their own learning
- **C24** SUPPORT THE ACHIEVEMENT OF INDIVIDUALS' LEARNING OBJECTIVES
  - C241 Provide information/advice to enable learners to identify & take opportunities to achieve their learning objectives
  - C242 Agree and provide learning opportunities to support the achievement of individual learnin objectives
  - C243 Provide materials to support the achievement of individual learning objectives
  - C244 Provide information and advice to support individuals review and modification of learning objectives
  - C245 Collate information about learner progress in order to provide guidance to learners
- **C25** PREPARE AND PROVIDE INFORMATION TECHNOLOGY DEPENDENT LEARNING RESOURCES TO SUPPORT INDIVIDUAL AND GROUP LEARNING
  - C251 Select and specify information technology dependent learning material
  - C252 Commission and set up information technology based learning equipment
  - C253 Advise users on the function and operation of ITDL equipment
- **C26** CO-ORDINATE THE PREPARATION AND DELIVERY OF LEARNING OPPORTUNITIES
  - C261 Agree learning support roles with contributors
  - C262 Coordinate the roles of contributors
  - C263 Monitor and assess the effectiveness of contributors
- **C27** ASSIST AND SUPPORT THE APPLICATION OF LEARNING
  - C271 Assist individuals to apply learning
  - C272 Provide advice to support the application of learning
  - C273 Monitor and assess the effectiveness of the learning process
- **C28** ORIGINATE TRAINING SUPPORT MATERIALS
  - C281 Originate training and development materials
  - C282 Originate training exercises, learning experiences and assignments
  - C283 Originate visual display and support materials

Area D: Evaluate the effectiveness of training and development

D1 EVALUATE THE EFFECTIVENESS OF TRAINING AND DEVELOPMENT

D11 PLAN AND SET UP SYSTEMS FOR EVALUATING THE TRAINING AND DEVELOPMENT FUNCTION
- D111 Agree criteria for evaluating the training and development function
- D112 Select processes for evaluation
- D113 Obtain and allocate resources for evaluation

D12 EVALUATE THE TRAINING AND DEVELOPMENT FUNCTION
- D121 Gather evidence to evaluate the training and development function
- D122 Analyse and interpret evaluation evidence

D13 MODIFY SYSTEMS AND PRACTICES TO IMPROVE TRAINING AND DEVELOPMENT
- D131 Identify modifications in systems and practices
- D132 Plan improvements in training and development practice
- D133 Implement plans for improving training and development practice

D2 EVALUATE INDIVIDUAL AND GROUP ACHIEVEMENTS AGAINST OBJECTIVES

D21 PLAN AND SET UP SYSTEMS TO EVALUATE THE ACHIEVEMENT OF OBJECTIVES
- D211 Agree criteria for evaluating the achievement of objectives
- D212 Select processes for evaluation
- D213 Obtain and allocate resources for evaluation

D22 EVALUATE THE ACHIEVEMENT OF OUTCOMES AGAINST LEARNING OBJECTIVES
- D221 Evaluate individual and group performance against objectives
- D222 Evaluate learning programmes against the achievement of objectives

D23 MODIFY AND ADAPT LEARNING PLANS
- D231 Modify and adapt learning programmes
- D232 Modify and adapt individual learning plans
- D233 Provide feedback to individuals on their achievements
- D234 Provide feedback about individual and group achievements

D3 ASSESS ACHIEVEMENT FOR PUBLIC CERTIFICATION

D31 DESIGN ASSESSMENT SYSTEMS
- D311 Design methods for the collection of performance evidence
- D312 Design methods for the collection of knowledge evidence

D32 ASSESS CANDIDATE PERFORMANCE
- D321 Identify opportunities for the collection of evidence of competent performance
- D322 Collect and judge performance evidence against criteria
- D323 Collect and judge knowledge evidence to support the inference of competent performance
- D324 Make assessment decision and provide feedback

D33 ASSESS CANDIDATE USING DIVERSE EVIDENCE
- D331 Determine sources of evidence to be used
- D332 Collect and evaluate evidence
- D333 Make assessment decision and provide feedback

D34 CO-ORDINATE THE ASSESSMENT PROCESS
- D341 Provide advice and support to assessors
- D342 Maintain and submit assessment documentation
- D343 Undertake internal verification

D35 VERIFY THE ASSESSMENT PROCESS
- D351 Provide information, advisory and support services for centres
- D352 Verify assessment practice and centre procedures
- D353 Maintain records of visit and provide feedback to awarding body

D36 IDENTIFY PREVIOUSLY ACQUIRED COMPETENCE
- D361 Help candidate to identify areas of current competence
- D362 Agree an assessment plan with candidate
- D363 Help candidate to prepare and present evidence for assessment

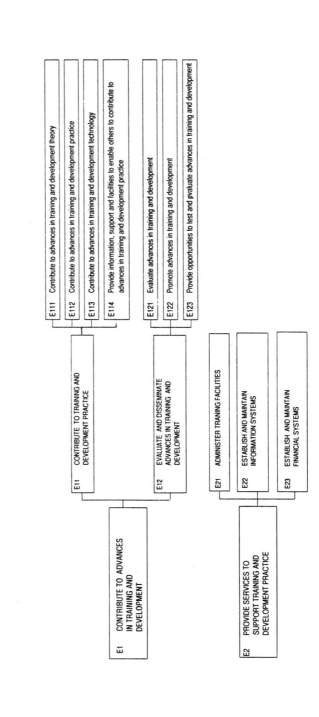

Area E: Support training and development advances and practice

E1 — CONTRIBUTE TO ADVANCES IN TRAINING AND DEVELOPMENT

E11 — CONTRIBUTE TO TRAINING AND DEVELOPMENT PRACTICE
- E111 — Contribute to advances in training and development theory
- E112 — Contribute to advances in training and development practice
- E113 — Contribute to advances in training and development technology
- E114 — Provide information, support and facilities to enable others to contribute to advances in training and development practice

E12 — EVALUATE AND DISSEMINATE ADVANCES IN TRAINING AND DEVELOPMENT
- E121 — Evaluate advances in training and development
- E122 — Promote advances in training and development
- E123 — Provide opportunities to test and evaluate advances in training and development

E2 — PROVIDE SERVICES TO SUPPORT TRAINING AND DEVELOPMENT PRACTICE
- E21 — ADMINISTER TRAINING FACILITIES
- E22 — ESTABLISH AND MAINTAIN INFORMATION SYSTEMS
- E23 — ESTABLISH AND MAINTAIN FINANCIAL SYSTEMS

APPENDIX 5

The former Institute of Training and Development's Code of Professional Practice

Introduction
The Institute's mission is:

- to lead in the development of a learning world;
- to serve the professional interests of members (individuals and organisations);
- to uphold the highest ideals in Human Resource Development.

The term Human Resource Development embraces that process whereby people develop their full potential in life and work.

Objective
The Code lays down standards of practice for all members of the Institute to follow in their professional relations with their employers, clients, fellow practitioners, trainees, students, and the general public. Whilst the Code is prescribed primarily for members of the Institute, it is hoped that all engaged in training and human resource development will adopt these precepts.

The Code of Professional Practice
The Code of Professional Practice relates to five aspects of members' behaviour, namely:

- Behaviour and Personal development.

395

- Equal opportunities.
- Relations with individuals for whose training, development or guidance members are responsible.
- Relations with the employing or client organisation and its employees or trainees.
- Relations with other organisations.

Behaviour and Personal Development
Members shall:

Work to the highest standards complying not only with the law (including the law on copyright) but also with published codes of practice and generally accepted best practice as it affects training and development.

Conduct their work based activities with a high standard of courtesy and integrity and respect the dignity and privacy of individuals.

Accept responsibility for their own work and the effective use of the resources entrusted to them; demonstrate by personal example and ordered approach the self-discipline and conduct expected of the professional. Accept assignments within their own competence or when required seek appropriate expertise from properly qualified individuals.

Strive to enhance the good standing of the Institute and its members and of the HRD profession at large.

Maintain a personal programme of Continuous Professional Development (CPD) and keep abreast of changes and developments relevant to the profession.

Equal Opportunities
Members shall:

Be aware of relevant legislation, statutory codes and recommendations.

Promote equality of opportunity for individuals, avoiding prejudice and refraining from discrimination on the grounds of ethnic origin, gender, class, marital status, age, beliefs, disability, sexual orientation or perceived contribution to society.

Accept personal responsibility for assisting under represented groups to develop in the profession.

Relations with Individuals for Whose Training, Development or Guidance Members are Responsible
Members shall:

Establish and maintain relationships with individuals to ensure that effective learning and development takes place.

Establish realistic plans to meet stated learning objectives and defined standards of competence.

Ensure the safety and well-being of those personnel within their responsibility or sphere of influence by adhering to both legislation and relevant advisory codes at all times.

Relations with Employing or Client Organisation Employees
Members shall:

Respect the confidentiality of information gained in the course of work and refrain from using such confidential information for personal benefit or in a way that may be damaging to any employing or client organisation.

Inform the client or employing organisation immediately of any personal interest which may conflict with the employer's interests.

Act honestly and loyally in carrying out the lawful policy and directions of the employing or client organisation and refrain from damaging its image or reputation.

Relations with Other Organisations
Members shall:

Make clear in any public statement whether they are acting in a personal capacity or representing the Institute or any other organisation.

Be ready to share the results of research, new knowledge and skills; to acknowledge the work of others and to give professional assistance in public affairs insofar as commercial confidentiality allows.

Comply with and be subject to the Articles of Association of the Institute and the regulations from time to time in force.

Co-operate with investigations conducted by the *ad hoc* sub-committee of the Professional Standards Committee of the Institute, arising from complaints against members who may have infringed the Code.

Discipline
Any breaches of both the spirit and standards set out in this Code of Practice may form the basis of action under Articles 19 and 30 of the Institute's Memorandum and Articles of Association.

Reproduced with permission of the Institute of Training and Development.

APPENDIX 6

A 'quick guide' to training methods and techniques

Adapted and expanded from Paper No. 5 of the former Ceramics, Glass and Mineral Products Training Board. Entries have been arranged in an order which moves from traditional and relatively simple methods and techniques, through those which are more complex and require more planning, to those which make use of sophisticated technology.

METHOD: WHAT IT IS	WHAT IT CAN ACHIEVE	POINTS TO WATCH
LECTURE Structured, planned talk. Usually accompanied by visual aids, e.g. slides, OHP foils, flipchart.	Suitable for large audiences where participation is not wanted. Content and timing can be planned in detail.	Lively style needed. Communication of material may be limited if no provision for feedback to lecturer.
FILMS/VIDEOTAPES 'Visual lectures' – but often presented in dramatised form.	As 'Lectures' – but addition of moving images and drama can significantly aid motivation. Useful as precursor to discussion; can be 'stopped' at key points for discussion.	Tailor-made products are expensive. Care needed to ensure material (not just title) is relevant.
CASE STUDY Examination of events or situation – often real life – usually aimed at learning by analysing the detailed material or defining, and posing solutions for, problems.	Opportunities exist for both exchange of views on 'what matters' and problem solving. Especially useful for analysis of financial/statistical data. Can incorporate exercises.	Simple cases may give wrong impression of reality. Difficult to reproduce the 'political climate'.

METHOD: WHAT IT IS	WHAT IT CAN ACHIEVE	POINTS TO WATCH
PROMPT LIST List of 'questions to which a person should have answers'.	Useful basis for self-study or discussion in cases where opinions are important but no clear 'correct' answer exists.	Can highlight inter-personal differences in terms of values – and hence stimulate conflict.
DISCUSSION Free exchange of information, opinions, etc. a 'controlled' discussion may follow a planned path, the leader controlling the agenda; an 'open' discussion may mirror members' priorities.	Especially suitable for development or adjustment of attitudes and opinions. Promotes group cohesion. Also offers feedback to trainer on learning achievement.	May be time consuming – especially if discussion wanders or 'process problems' emerge. Attitudes may harden rather than adjust. Individual participation may be affected by group composition.
INSTRUCTION Formula-based 'teaching' session: 1 Tell – how to do 2 Show – how to do 3 Do (supervised practice) 4 Review process and results.	For introducing skills, usually in line with a planned breakdown of small sequential practice stages. Confidence is built by mastery and link-up of stages. Typically must follow input of knowledge, the skills to be learned being those of application.	Skill may be best addressed as a whole rather than in parts –but lengthy stages 1 and 2 yield memory problems. Design/balance of session important.

METHOD: WHAT IT IS	WHAT IT CAN ACHIEVE	POINTS TO WATCH
LANGUAGE LABORATORY Individual booths equipped with audio programmes and linked to a central tutor.	Allows learner-paced language tuition and practice, without 'speaking in public'. Machine management seems to promote motivation.	Good for early stages but cannot replace eventual need to practise in public.
DISCOVERY LEARNING 'Learning without a teacher' – but usually in a controlled (i.e. pre-designed) set-up, and under supervision.	Offers challenge, and builds confidence as learner masters new skills. Best suited to tasks involving dismantling, checking, adjusting, rebuilding. Helps understanding of principles.	Considerable design work needed. Safety paramount – may need special adjustments, and so be unrealistic.
EXERCISE Carrying out of a particular task along prescribed lines. Often a test of knowledge earlier communicated.	Highly active form of learning; satisfies need for practice to apply knowledge or develop skill. Often linked with test to judge extent of learning.	Exercise must be realistic, objectives attainable.

METHOD: WHAT IT IS	WHAT IT CAN ACHIEVE	POINTS TO WATCH
PROJECT 'Large-scale exercise', but leaving most of the process within learner discretion. Frequently involves collecting and reporting data, then offering conclusions and recommendations for improvement.	Like exercises, offers practice and simultaneously 'tests'. Stimulates analysis + creativity; also reporting skill.	Like exercises, needs realism and attainability. If 'real life', must have support of those responsible for reality. Ideally will be 'actioned'.
ROLE-PLAY Enactment of role(s) in protected training environment.	Mainly used to practise face-to-face skills (e.g. selling) combined with review critiques from trainers and/or other learners.	Unless disciplined, can cause embarrassment. Realism of set-up important.
ROLE-REVERSAL Enactment of reversed roles by two or more learners in simulated situation.	Mainly used to help those who operate in face-to-face situations to appreciate their contacts' needs and feelings.	As with role-play, needs discipline and realism.

METHOD: WHAT IT IS	WHAT IT CAN ACHIEVE	POINTS TO WATCH
SIMULATIONS/BUSINESS GAMES Dynamic exercises or case studies – usually involving 'coming to terms with' a situation, then managing it via a set of imposed decisions. Computerised models offer complex data, and often decisions which interact.	Offers practice in management – observation, analysis, judgement, decision making, etc. Interactive element generates enthusiasm, notably when teams are in simulated competition. Can be linked with team development.	Model can be challenged as unrealistic.
STUDY GROUPS Task-briefed groups which also practise process review, aided by a process consultant, who does NOT operate outside this role.	Offers appreciation of need for both task and process management; also group learning processes.	Some learners dislike lack of structure. May generate stress.
OUTDOOR TRAINING Dynamic open-air exercises, usually carried out in teams.	Offers practice in management, in challenging or problematic circumstances; also leadership and teamwork opportunities, as well as self-analysis.	Physical challenge can be tough. Some learners may not accept relevance of unusual environment.

METHOD: WHAT IT IS	WHAT IT CAN ACHIEVE	POINTS TO WATCH
VIDEO-CONFERENCING AND TELE-CONFERENCING Two-way audio and two-way visual link-up (see Hogan 1993).	Participative training sessions: trainers in different locations. Can interact with each other and with a tutor.	Special training needed for tutor. Careful preplanning essential.
ELECTRONIC BRAINSTORMING Participants sit in a laboratory at individual PCs connected through a local area network. One computer acts as a file server (see El-Sherif and Tang 1994).	By using special packages e.g. Meeting Ware, each participant can contribute anonymously by computer to a brainstorming session. The results are analysed by computer.	Careful preparation needed. Experienced team guide required.

METHOD: WHAT IT IS	WHAT IT CAN ACHIEVE	POINTS TO WATCH
SELF-MANAGED LEARNING: READING Learner-paced coverage of printed material, with or without basic learning plan	Knowledge retention can be good if learner motivation is high. Learning packages are often augmented by audio- and/or video-tapes.	Motivation often declines if reading is difficult/'dull'. Tutorial help can be important.
RADIO + TV BROADCASTS	Large potential audiences permit costly programmes. Often linked with national (e.g. Open University) courses and qualifications. Satellite TV is likely to offer new and wider subjects. Can be linked with tutorial assistance by phone.	Viewing times often unsocial.

METHOD: WHAT IT IS	WHAT IT CAN ACHIEVE	POINTS TO WATCH
SELF-MANAGED LEARNING: TECHNOLOGY-ASSISTED Learner-managed coverage of programmed material, usually involving keyboard and screen.	Many varied uses. Computer-based training (CBT) can offer workplace simulations and link with videotape to provide still or moving pictures. Compact Discs offer huge information storage, with visual additions. Moves to introduce artificial intelligence (AI) yield prospect of using machine as a tutor and managing one's own learning process.	Hardware may be expensive. Present state of technology makes logic-based programmes most reliable.
Computer-based Training (CBT) (Learner uses keyboard in line with screen instructions, calling forth information and responding to questions)	Screen material can be complex and include animation. Good for presenting statistics. With addition of 'artificial intelligence' (CBT – AI) learner responds to computer question, computer interprets response and adjusts own programme.	Compatible hardware and software needed; perhaps also tutorial help.

METHOD: WHAT IT IS	WHAT IT CAN ACHIEVE	POINTS TO WATCH
Compact Disc Training (CDT) (Hardware linking CD to TV screen plus keyboard allows operation similar to CBT)	CD 'Read Only Memory' (CD-ROM) offers high capacity data store on each disc, which becomes a reference source equal to many books (and even more computer packages). Retrieval can be in text and picture and sound form.	Special hardware needed. Limited to retrieval of stored data.
	CD 'Read Only Memory – Extended Architecture' (CD-ROM-XA) allows learner to 'play with' material, practising analysis and/or synthesis. Particularly suitable for work involving assembling, dismantling, diagnosis; the disc effectively 'packages expertise' in these things.	Learner needs some basic awareness of data in order to manipulate it.

METHOD: WHAT IT IS	WHAT IT CAN ACHIEVE	POINTS TO WATCH
	CD 'Interactive' (CD-I) is similar to CBT-AI (see page 407) in allowing learner much greater control of the learning process, the programme adjusting to learner questions and responses.	May not reproduce realistic workplace language; hence tutor may also be needed.
	'Digital Video' Interactive (DV-I) offers CD-I together with the facility to videotape the learner's own actions, and replay the results. Ideal where the learner must perfect a PHYSICAL movement (e.g. golf swing, or sign language), and needs to see the result.	Hardware and software are likely to be costly.

NB: CBT, CDT and video can be combined in 'multi-media programmes', which can offer both (a) information, and (b) practice in using the information to specific ends e.g. problem-solving. These programmes are naturally expensive to produce, and require expensive hardware.

APPENDIX 7

An IPD Statement 'Continuous Development – People and Work'

1 Introduction and Aims
Continuous development (CD) is not a body of theory, nor a collection of techniques; it is an approach to the management of learning.
Continuous development means:

- learning from real experiences at work;
- learning throughout working life, not confined to useful but occasional injections of 'training'.

For the individual, CD means lifelong learning with a strong element of self direction and self management. For the organisation, CD means the management of learning on a continuing basis through the promotion of learning as an integral part of work itself.

An organisation's success depends upon its people. If the organisation is to become more successful, employee learning must be stimulated and managed – not specifically and separately, but constantly – in relation to all work activities. The essential basis for this management is not a set of prescribed techniques but an attitude of mind; it is this attitude which justifies the CD label and generates the desired growth.

This Statement, *Continuous Development: People and Work* is designed to help all managers, especially personnel professionals, to broaden their views about learning and training, to help them to anchor their learning activity firmly in the organisation's day to day activities, and – most important of all – to promote the development of the CD attitude. The IPD considers that such a Statement is necessary because, in the UK, training has too rarely been thought of as a continuous process. Rather, it has been treated as a series of short-term expedients, and usually in reaction to change, not in anticipation of it.

These issues are further explored in the Statement under seven key headings, as follows:

The essential conditions for a CD culture
Policy
Responsibilities and roles
The identification of learning opportunities and needs
The integration of learning with work
The provision of learning resources
Benefits and results

2 The Essential Conditions for a CD Culture

If learning activity is to be fully beneficial to both the organisation and its employees, the following conditions must be met:

- the organisation must have some form of strategic operational plan – and the implications of this plan should be spelt out in terms of the knowledge, skills and concerns of all employees
- managers must be ready, willing and able to define, give priority to, and meet learning needs as they appear. Not all such needs can be anticipated. In the early stages of developing the CD culture, encouragement must be given to employees to suggest learning needs from the problems and challenges, and the successes and failures encountered in their day to day activities
- learning and work must be integrated. This means BOTH (a) dovetailing plans for learning with other operational plans, AND (b) devising and maintaining systems and processes which stimulate learning activity. But it also means, wherever possible, arranging work activities which themselves incorporate a learning element
- the inpetus for CD must come from the Chief Executive and members of the top management team. They must regularly and formally review the way in which the competence of both management and the workforce are being developed. In the early stages, one senior executive should be charged with overall responsibility for overseeing the practical aspects of the introduction of the CD culture
- investment in CD must be regarded by the top management team as being as important as investment in research, new product

development or capital equipment. This investment – in terms of both time and money – is not a luxury which can only be afforded in the 'good times'. Indeed, the more severe the problems an organisation faces, the greater the need for learning on the part of its employees and the more pressing the need for investment in learning.

Successful CD demands:
- rapid and effective communication of priority operational needs
- the availability of appropriate learning opportunities, facilities and resources as a normal part of working life
- processes which naturally integrate learning with work
- recognition by each employee that he or she shares ownership of any collective learning plans to meet the priority operational needs
- recognition by each employee that he or she has a responsibility to communicate and otherwise share new information, again with the purpose of meeting priority operational needs
- recognition by each employee that he or she is able to and allowed to create a personal development plan
- a clear understanding, by everyone in the organisation, of their responsibilities for learning.

3 Policy

Most organisations find STATEMENTS of policy useful. Any statement of general policy relating to the management of people should indicate:

- a firm corporate commitment to continuous development;
- that self development is a responsibility of every individual within the organisation;
- the need for employees, clients and customers to understand as much as possible about how individuals and groups of people learn, and why it is important;
- the organisation's commitment to acknowledge improved performance, to use enhanced skills operationally, and to provide appropriate rewards;
- 'who carries responsibility for what' in the identification of learning aims and the promotion of learning activity;
- ways in which operational aims and objectives are communicated to all employees;
- agreed procedures and methods for performance appraisal and assessment;

- avenues, procedures and processes for career development and pro-gression;
- facilities provided for learning during work time, including paid or unpaid leave for this purpose;
- the organisation's policy on employee involvement, especially that relating to involvement in reviewing education and training facilities and resources.

If the statement of general policy is not to be a sterile document of mere good intent:

- top management must be committed to it and should periodically request feedback on its implementation;
- senior executives and middle and junior level managers must be given the opportunity to suggest amendments in line with what they regard as 'current operational reality';
- the document must regularly be discussed with representatives of the workforce;
- the organisation must satisfy itself that it is making best use of research and development findings in the human resource develop-ment field (and perhaps get involved with such research activity).

4 Responsibilities and Roles

All members of the organisation should be encouraged to view the operational life of the organisation as a continuous learning process, and one in which they all carry responsibilities.

Senior executives have the responsibility to ensure that policy state-ments and practices promote continuous development and that forward plans incorporate future management needs, particularly to improve performance – taking into account the impact of key changes in legal requirements, technology, work patterns and (not least) ideas. They must encourage managers to plan learning activities to facilitate the process of change.

Managers, as part of their responsibilities for getting the best out of their staff, must give regular attention to subordinates' continuous develop-ment: discussing needs, creating plans, coaching, mentoring, counselling and introducing changes which make learning easier and/or more effec-tive. Managers must engender their own 'learning about learning'.

Personnel professionals have very many responsibilities in the CD field. They should provide an information service on resources, and continuously monitor the extent and quality of learning activity in the organisation. If they feel that the learning activity is inadequate to support the operational needs of the business, they should take the initiative in generating strategic and/or tactical discussions, recommending appropriate action as necessary. They should ensure that review discussions happen at least once a year within the senior executive group and within any consultative groups. Internal personnel department review discussions should take place frequently: personnel professionals must constantly seek to improve their own performance and the service they provide to their organisations.

All learners (including the three groups above) must appreciate that they are responsible for clarifying their own learning goals within the framework established by forward plans, standard procedures and discussions with management. They should raise their problems with management; review their own performance impartially; suggest what they themselves should learn, and how; seek new information without waiting for it to be delivered; alert others whenever important new information is received; ask for explanations whenever a communication is not understood; aim, generally, to use new learning whenever possible. The ultimate goal is for everyone to contribute to the identification of learning opportunities, and for learners to manage most of their learning for themselves.

The chief responsibility for ALL learners is to seek constant improvements in performance: no matter the base of 'learning sophistication' from which learners set out, improvement is always possible.

5 *The Identification of Learning Opportunities and Needs*
It is worth repeating that everyone needs to contribute to the identification of learning opportunities using the information available to them.

Operational plans: every proposal for a new operational element or instrument, that is, a new product, a new item of plant, a new procedure, a new organisation structure, a new department, a new member of staff, a new accounting convention – a new *anything*, should be accompanied by an estimate of:

- which employees need to learn something;
- what needs to be learned;
- how the learning is to happen.

If these things cannot be defined with confidence, the proposal should include a plan which allows this to be completed later. Some needs are indirectly related: for example, new technical systems may demand not merely instruction in the system itself, but also new levels and types of maintenance. Removing existing resources (machines, materials and perhaps people) may also demand a learning plan.

Job descriptions and specifications: documents outlining management responsibilities should normally include references to:

- the roles as appraiser, counsellor, tutor;
- the responsibility to develop an understanding of learning processes;
- the manager's responsibility to include learning elements in operational plans.

All job descriptions and specifications (regardless of level) should also emphasise the job holder's responsibility for self development on a continuing basis.

Appraisal: appraisal should normally include joint appraiser/appraisee discussions on the extent to which self development is taking place, and again on the implementation of management-inspired learning plans. Ideally, informal appraisal discussions will happen all the time; a standard question would be 'how long is it since we/you/I learned something new at work?'.

Special reviews and audits: parts of the learning system should be specially reviewed from time to time. Inter-departmental working parties, joint consultative committees, trainee groups, and, not least, particular individuals, can be charged with collecting and analysing data, and reporting to senior executives or to personnel management. These reviews are particularly useful in those parts of the learning system where knowledge or awareness needs to be periodically updated or revived: 'health and safety' is a good example.

Prompt lists: it is helpful to create lists of questions in a style and in a sequence which will prompt job-holders to think about aspects of the performance of the job which can be improved through new learning or increased awareness. The lists should include questions to which no demonstrably 'correct' answer is known but which prompt educated opinion; and also, questions to which the answer will change over time. These lists can be used as the basis of learning needs identification, and/or for one to one and team review discussions which lead to explicit definition of training needs.

6 The Integration of Learning with Work

Learning must be integrated with work: unfocused learning is akin to recreation. When organising work, 'learning time' should be built in – and not just in the early stages of any development. Formal learning events should always be planned as part of operational work plans, their timing being fixed to minimise impact on other work requirements, but their priority being given EQUAL weight. A number of organisational devices should be promoted to ensure that employees are naturally involved in the learning process; to that end:

- joint appraiser/appraisee discussions should aim at joint definition of objectives and the means to achieve them;
- quality circles, briefing groups, and any other special organisational groupings, should explicitly contain 'improved performance' and 'management of change' aims, and should devote time to discussing the learning aspects of any proposals for future activity;
- when new plant or equipment is planned and introduced, suppliers should be encouraged to provide more than just written manuals: active dialogue between suppliers and those who are to operate and maintain the new equipment (including contract staff where appropriate) is needed;
- project or work teams should encourage a 'multi-skills' approach to their future operations, playing down divisions between jobs and making the most of the flexibility that goes with increased versatility;
- where joint consultative arrangements exist, policies relating to training should regularly be discussed with employee representatives at all levels;
- reference should be made to training policies, and to any current learning priorities, in progress reports, house magazines and other communication channels. Through such channels, every opportunity should be taken to reinforce self development goals.

7 The Provision of Learning Resources
Self development, team learning, and continuous operational development, all require resource material and facilities. The organisation should have clear policies and practices on the following:

- training/learning budgets;
- authorities to approve training/learning plans and expenditure;
- facilities and support for study during and outside standard working hours, including paid and unpaid leave;
- open and distance learning;
- financial assistance with courses, travel, books, tapes, and other facilities;
- awards and/or scholarships;
- access to internal and external advisers, counsellors and facilitators;
- coaching and tutorial resources;
- management's responsibility to create an environment in which continuous development can prosper and succeed.

All employees should be made aware of these policies and the range of facilities and opportunities for learning which are available. Increasingly, individuals are coming to expect their employers to have policies which enable them to develop their competence and will choose employing organisations which take learning seriously. Some learning will lead to national vocational qualifications, or part qualifications. Some learning will be required by an individual's professional body (to which the individual will have a natural loyalty). This learning is subsumed by the concept of continuous development and is, indeed, a spur to learning generally.

8 Benefits and Results
Strategic plans, or research and development expenditure, are not expected to yield precisely quantifiable benefits. They are a means to an end. So, too, should expenditure on education, training and development be regarded as a necessary and calculated investment, yielding consequent 'pay-offs' in terms of enhanced business performance. The following benefits can be expected:

- strategic plans are more likely to be achieved;
- ideas will be generated and in a form which relates to operational needs;

- everyone in the organisation will recognise the need for learning effort on their part if the organisation is to succeed in its endeavours and thereby make their jobs more secure;
- by enabling employees to make the most of their talents, the organisation will be in a position to deploy individuals most effectively; to fill skills gaps from internal resources; to create and retain a motivated workforce;
- and, in general, the organisation can expect fewer mistakes, fewer accidents, less waste, higher productivity, higher morale, lower staff turnover, better employee relations, better customer service, and hence, *greater returns to the organisation.*

The major benefits are, first, improved operational performance, and second, the simultaneous development of people and work.

The CD culture has many and varied characteristics, and each individual organisation which promotes CD will develop its own unique version. There are nevertheless certain key characteristics which are likely to emerge:

- all understand and share ownership of operational goals;
- immediate objectives exist and are understood by all;
- new developments are promoted; change is constructive, welcomed and enjoyed, not forced and resisted;
- managers are frequently to be heard discussing learning with their subordinates and colleagues;
- time is found by all the team to work on individual members' problems;
- reference documents (manuals, specification sheets, dictionaries and the like) are available to all without difficulty, and are used;
- colleagues use each other as a resource;
- members of teams do not just swap information; they tackle problems and create opportunities;
- team members share responsibility for success or failure; they are not dependent upon one or more leaders;
- individuals learn while they work, and enjoy both.

BIBLIOGRAPHY

NB. Bracketed figures at the end of each entry denote chapter numbers of this book, to which they apply.

ADAIR J. *Training for Leadership.* Gower, Farnborough, 1978 (12)

ADVISORY, CONCILIATION AND ARBITRATION SERVICE. *Induction of new employees.* Advisory Booklet No. 7, ACAS, London, 1982. (11)

ANNETT J. in *Psychology at work.* Warr P. (ed.), Penguin Education, Harmondsworth, 1974. (4)

ARGYRIS C. and SCHON D. *Organisational Learning: A Theory of Action Perspective.* Addison Wesley, New York, 1978. (5) (12)

ARMSTRONG P. and DAWSON C. *People in Organisations.* Elm Publications, Cambridge, 1983. (1)

ATKINSON R. L., ATKINSON R. C. *et al. Introduction to psychology.* (10th edition), Harcourt Brace Jovanovich, New York, 1985. (3) (4)

BAILEY D. 'Training to reduce retail shrinkage'. *Training and Management Development Methods*, Vol 5, 1991. (10)

BANDLER J. and GRINDER J. *The Structure of Magic: Parts 1 and 2.* Science and Behaviour Books, California, 1968 (3)

BARON B. in *Managing Human Resources.* eds. Cowling A. G. and Mailer C. J. B. Arnold, London, 1981. (2)

BARRINGTON H. *Learning about Management.* McGraw-Hill, London, 1984. (12)

BASS B. M. and VAUGHAN J. A. *Training in industry – the management of learning.* Tavistock Publications, London, 1966. (3) (4)

BECKHARD R. *Organisation Development: Strategy and Methods*. Addison-Wesley, Reading, Mass., 1969. (12)

BELBIN E. and BELBIN R. M. *Problems in adult retraining*. Heinemann, London, 1972. (10)

BELBIN R. M. *Employment of older workers. No. 2, Training Methods*. OECD, Paris, 1969. (4)

BELBIN R. M. *Management Teams: Why they Succeed or Fail*. Heinemann, London, 1981. (12)

BENNIS W. G. *Organisation Development: Its Nature, Origins and Prospects*. Addison-Wesley, Reading, Mass., 1969. (12)

BENNISON M. and CARSON J. *The manpower planning handbook*. McGraw Hill, Maidenhead, 1984. (7)

BERGER M. L. and P. J. (eds.) *Group Training Techniques*. Gower Press, Farnborough, 1978. (12)

BEVAN S. and THOMPSON M. 'Performance management at the crossroads'. *Personnel Management*, Nov. 1991. (9)

BLAKE R. R. & MOUTON J. S. *The New Managerial Grid*. Gulf Publishing, Houston, 1978. (12)

BOYATZIS R. *The competent manager*. John Wiley, Chichester, 1982. (9)

BOYDELL T. H. *A guide to job analysis*. British Association for Commercial and Industrial Education, London, 1977. (9)

BOYDELL T. H. *A guide to the identification of training needs*. British Association for Commercial and Industrial Education, London, 1983. (7)

BOYDELL T. H. and PEDLER M. (eds.) *Management Self Development*. Gower, Aldershot, 1981. (12)

BRAMHAM J. *Practical manpower planning*. Institute of Personnel Management, London, 1988. (7)

BRAMLEY P. and NEWBY A. 'The evaluation of training: clarifying the concept'. *Journal of European Industrial Training*, Vol. 8, No. 6, 1984. (10)

BRIDGER H. *Towards a Psychodynamic View of Man*. (The 1980 Malcolm Millar Lecture) Aberdeen University Press, Aberdeen, 1980. (12)

BROMLEY D. B. *The psychology of human ageing.* Pelican, Harmondsworth, 1975. (4)

BROMLEY D. B. *Behavioural gerontology. Central issues in the psychology of ageing.* Wiley, Chichester, 1990. (3) (4)

BURNS T. and STALKER G. M. *The Management of Innovation.* Tavistock, London, 1961. (1) (12)

BUS AND COACH TRAINING LIMITED. *Vehicle Engineering Competence Assessment Scheme.* Bus & Coach Training Ltd, Rickmansworth, 1990. (5)

CASSELLS J. 'Education and training must be geared to match the demand for more skills in British industry today'. *The Times*, 18th June, 1985. (8)

CHAPPLE F. 'A report on the Electrical, Electronic, Telecommunication and Plumbing Union's retraining programme'. *The Times*, 13th March, 1984.

CHILD J. *Organisation: A Guide to Problems and Practice.* Harper and Row, London, 1982. (6)

CLUTTERBUCK D. *Everyone needs a mentor.* Institute of Personnel Management, London, 1991. (10)

COCKERILL T. 'The kind of competence for rapid change'. *Personnel Management*, Sept. 1989. (9)

COLLARD R. *Total Quality: Success Through People.* Institute of Personnel Management,. London, 1989. (6) (12)

CONFEDERATION OF BRITISH INDUSTRY. *Towards a skills revolution – a youth charter.* CBI, London, 1989. (11)

CONFEDERATION OF BRITISH INDUSTRY. *World Class Targets.* CBI, London, 1991. (1)

COOPER C. L. and MANGHAM I. L. (Eds.) *T-Groups: A Survey of Research.* Wiley, New York, 1971. (12)

COULSON-THOMAS C. and COE T. *The Flat Organization.* BIM Foundation, Management House, Cottingham Road, Corby, Northants NN17 1TT, 1991. Also cited in *Skills and Enterprise Briefing.* Issue 3/ 92 Feb. 1992, Skills and Enterprise Network, PO Box 12, West PDO, Leen Gate, Lenton, Nottingham NG7 2GB. (7)

COURSES AND OCCUPATIONAL INFORMATION CENTRE. *Knowledge and Competence.* (Published by COIC in conjunction with the Employment Department Group) HMSO, London, 1990. (5)

CROSS M. *Towards the flexible craftsman*, The Technical Change Centre, London, 1985. (8)

CUMING M. *A manager's guide to quantitative methods*. Elm Publications, Kings Repton, Cambridge, 1984. (7)

DAVEY D. MACKENZIE and HARRIS R. *Judging people: a guide to orthodox and unorthodox methods of assessment*. McGraw Hill, Maidenhead, 1982. (9)

DEPARTMENT OF EDUCATION AND SCIENCE. *Statistical bulletin*. January 1990. (11)

DEPARTMENT OF EMPLOYMENT. *see also* EMPLOYMENT DEPARTMENT

DEPARTMENT OF EMPLOYMENT. *Training for Employment*. (Cm 316). London, HMSO, 1988. (1)

DEPARTMENT OF EMPLOYMENT. *Higher Education Developments: The Skills Link*. Department of Employment, Sheffield, 1990. (1)

DEPARTMENT OF EMPLOYMENT. *1990s: The Skills Decade*. Department of Employment, Sheffield, 1990. (1)

DEPARTMENT OF EMPLOYMENT. (Qualifications & Standards Branch). *Setting Standards for Training: National Standards for Training and Development*. Employment Department, Sheffield, 1991. (6)

DEPARTMENT OF EMPLOYMENT. (Qualifications and Standards Branch). *The Development of Assessable Standards for National Certification*. Employment Department, Sheffield, 1991. (6)

DEPARTMENT OF EMPLOYMENT, *Skill needs in Britain 1991*. IFF Research, October 1991. Reviewed in *Labour Market Quarterly Report*, Nov. 1991, Employment Department, Room W801, Moorfoot, Sheffield. (7) (8) (9)

DOBSON C. B. HARDY M. *et al*. *Understanding Psychology*. Weidenfeld and Nicolson, London, 1990. (3) (4).

DONNELLY E. L. 'The need to market training'. *Gower Handbook of Training and Development*. (Prior J. ed.). Gower, Aldershot, 1991. (8)

DONNELLY E. L. *Training as a Specialist Function – an Historical Perspective*. Working Paper No. 9, Faculty of Business Studies & Management, Middlesex Polytechnic. Middlesex Polytechnic, London, 1984. (6)

DULEWICZ V. 'Assessment Centres as the route to competence'. *Personnel Management*, Nov. 1989. (9)

DUNCAN K.D. and KELLY C. J. *Task analysis, learning and the nature of transfer.* Manpower Services Commission, Sheffield, 1983. (3) (4) (9)

EASTERBY-SMITH M. and TANTON M. 'Turning course evaluation from an end to a means'. *Personnel Management,* April 1985. (10)

EASTERBY-SMITH M. and MACKNESS J. 'Completing the cycle of evaluation'. *Personnel Management,* May 1992. (10)

EL-SHERIF H. H. and TANG V. 'Team focus electronic brain storming'. *Training and Management Development Methods,* Vol. 8, 1994.

EMERY F. E. (Ed.) *Systems Thinking.* Penguin, London, 1981. (2) (12)

EMPLOYMENT DEPARTMENT. *see also* DEPARTMENT OF EMPLOYMENT

EMPLOYMENT DEPARTMENT, *Labour Market Quarterly Report.* Employment Department, Moorfoot, Sheffield, Nov. 1993. (11)

EMPLOYMENT DEPARTMENT, *Skills and Enterprise Network.* Feb. 1992, Room W801 Moorfoot, Sheffield. (11)

EMPLOYMENT DEPARTMENT. *Prosperity Through Skills: the National Development Agenda.* Employment Department, Sheffield 1993. (1)

EMPLOYMENT DEPARTMENT. *Knowledge and Understanding: Its Place in Relation to NVQs and SVQs.* Number 9 in 'Competence and Assessment' Briefing Series. Employment Department, Sheffield, Dec. 1993. (6)

EMPLOYMENT DEPARTMENT. *Labour Market Quarterly Report.* Employment Department, Moorfoot, Sheffield, May 1993. (11)

EMPLOYMENT DEPARTMENT. *Labour Market Quarterly Report.* Employment Department, Moorfoot, Sheffield, Feb. 1994. (11)

EMPLOYMENT DEPARTMENT GROUP. *Competence and Assessment Compendium Nos. 1 and 2.* Employment Department, Sheffield, 1990 and 1992. (5) (9)

EMPLOYMENT DEPARTMENT GROUP. *1990s: The skills decade.* Employment Department Group, Moorfoot, Sheffield, 1990. (11)

EMPLOYMENT DEPARTMENT GROUP. *Learning Technology in the 90's* (2 Videotapes) Employment Department, Sheffield, 1992. (12)

EMPLOYMENT DEPARTMENT GROUP. *Labour Market and Skills Trends 1992/3.* Employment Department, Sheffield, 1992. (11)

424   *Training Interventions*

EMPLOYMENT DEPARTMENT GROUP. *Labour Market and Skill Trends 1994/5*. A Skills and Enterprise Network Publication. PO Box 12, WestPDO, Lean Gate, Lenton, Nottingham NG7 2GB. (1)

EMPLOYMENT DEPARTMENT GROUP (Higher Education Branch). *Higher Education Developments: The Skills Link.* Employment Department, Sheffield, 1990. (12)

EMPLOYMENT DEPARTMENT GROUP (Higher Education Branch). *Higher Education Developments: Learning Through Work.* Employment Department, Sheffield, 1992. (12)

ENGINEERING INDUSTRY TRAINING BOARD. *The EITB: 1964–1991. The Lessons To Be Learned.* EITB, Watford, 1991. (1)

ESTES W. K. *Learning theory and mental development.* Academic Press, New York, 1970. (3)

ETZIONI A. *A Comparative Analysis of Complex Organisations.* Free Press, Glencoe, Illinois, 1961. (6)

EUROPEAN ECONOMIC COMMISSION. *Preliminary Guidelines for a Community Social Policy Programme.* Brussels, Sec (71) 6000 Final, 17 March 1971. (1)

EUROPEAN COMMISSION. *Commission Memorandum on Vocational Training in the European Community in the 1990s.* European Social Policy Document, February 1992. EEC, Brussels, 1992. (1) (11)

EUROPEAN COMMISSION. *Growth, Competitiveness, Employment: the challenges and ways forward into the 21st century.* White Paper. European Commission, Brussels, 1993. (1)

FAIRBAIRNS J. 'Plugging the gap in training needs analysis'. *Personnel Management*, Feb. 1991. (9)

FARNHAM D. 'Corporate policy and personnel management'. *Personnel management handbook* (S. Harper ed.), Gower, Aldershot, 1987. (8)

FAYOL H. *General and Industrial Administration.* Durod, Paris, 1915. (5)

FESTINGER L. *A theory of cognitive dissonance.* Row Peterson, Evanston, Illinois, 1957. (4)

FLEISHMAN E. A. and HEMPEL W. E. 'The relationship between abilities and improvement with practice in a visual discrimination task'. *Journal of Experimental Psychology*, 49, 1955. (4)

FOWLER A. *Getting off to a good start: successful employee induction.* Institute of Personnel Management, London, 1990. (11)

FRANSELLA F. and BANNISTER D. *A manual for repertory grid technique.* Academic Press, London, 1977. (9)

FURTHER EDUCATION STAFF COLLEGE. *A Guide to Work-Based Learning Terms.* Training Agency. HMSO, London, 1989. (Intro)

FURTHER EDUCATION UNIT. *How do I learn?* 1981. (3)

GARBUTT D. *Training Costs with reference to the Industrial Training Act.* Gee and Company Limited, 1969. (5)

GARDNER H. 'The theory of multiple intelligences'. *Annals of Dyslexia*, Vol. 37, 1987, pages 19–35. (3)

GARRATT B. *The Learning Organisation.* Fontana, London, 1989. (12)

GLASER R. *Training Research and Education.* Wiley and Sons, New York, 1965. (2)

GOLD J. 'Learning to learn through learning contracts', in *Training and Management Development Methods*, Vol. 4, No. 4. MCB University Press, Bradford, 1990. (12)

GOLDSTEIN I. L. 'Training in work organisations', in *Annual Review of Psychology* 31, 229–72, 1980. (5)

GREGORY R. L. (ed.), *The Oxford companion to the mind.* Oxford University Press, Oxford, 1987, pages 740–747. (3)

GREINER L. E. 'Evolution and revolution as organizations grow'. *Harvard Business Review*, July–Aug. 1972. (4)

GRIFFITHS P. and GOODGE P. 'Development Centres: the third generation'. *Personnel Management*, June 1994, pages 40–43. (9)

GRONLUND N. E. *Stating behavioural objectives for classroom instruction.* Macmillan, London, 1978. (10)

HAMBLIN A. C. *Evaluation and control of training.* McGraw Hill, Maidenhead, 1974. (10)

HAMMOND Valerie and WILLE, Edgar. 'The Learning Organization', in *The Gower Book of Training and Development* (Prior J. ed.). Gower, Aldershot (12)

HANDY C. *Understanding Organisations.* Penguin, London, 1985. (6) (7)

HANDY C. *The Making of Managers.* National Economic Development Office, London, 1987. (1)

HANDY C. *The Age of Unreason*. Hutchinson, London, 1989. (2) (12)

HARRISON R. *Training and Development*. Institute of Personnel Management, London, 1988. (2) (6) (8) (10)

HAYES C., FONDA N., POPE N., STUART R., and TOWNSEND K. *Training for skill ownership*. Institute of Manpower Studies, Brighton, 1983. (4) (9)

HAYES C. *et al*. 'International competition and the role of competence', *Personnel Management*, September 1984. (3)

HESSELING P. *Strategies of evaluation research*. Van Gorcum, 1966. (10)

HEWSTONE *et al*. (eds.) *Introduction to social psychology*. Blackwell, 1990. (4)

HMSO. *Industrial Training Act, 1964*. HMSO, London, 1964. (1)

HMSO. *White Paper: Training for Jobs*. HMSO (Cm 9135), London, 1984. (1) (11)

HMSO. *White Paper: Education and Training for Young People*. HMSO, London, 1985. (1)

HMSO. *White Paper: Working Together: Education and Training*. HMSO (Cm 9832), London, 1986. (1) (6) (11)

HMSO. *White Paper: Employment for the 1990s*. HMSO, London, 1988. (1)

HMSO. *White Paper: Education and Training for the 21st Century*. HMSO (Cm 1536), London, 1991. (1) (11)

HMSO. *White Paper: Competitiveness: Helping Business to Win*. HMSO (Cm2563), London, May 1994. (11)

HOGAN C. 'How to get more out of videoconference meetings: a socio-technical approach: experience of CURTIN University of Technology'. *Training and Management Development Methods*, Vol. 7, pages 5.01–5.32, 1993.

HOGARTH G. and BARTH M. *Why employing the over 50s makes good business sense*. Publications Department, Institute of Employment Research, University of Warwick, 1991. (11)

HOLDEN L. and LIVIAN Y. 'Does strategic training policy exist?: some evidence from ten European countries'. *Personnel Review*, Volume 21, Issue 1, 1992, pages 12 -23. (7) (9)

HOLDEN R. and GOLD J. (eds.), 'Enterprise in higher education: Lighting the Blue Touchpaper'. *Education + Training*, Vol. 33, No. 2, 1991. (11)

HONEY P. and MUMFORD A. *Using your learning styles.* Second edition, Peter Honey, Ardingly House, 10 Linden Avenue, Maidenhead, 1986. (3) (12)

HONEY P. and MUMFORD A. *The manual of learning opportunities.* Peter Honey, Ardingly House, 10 Linden Avenue, Maidenhead, 1989. (12)

HONEY P. and MUMFORD A. *Manual of learning styles.* Third edition, Honey, Maidenhead, 1992. (3) (12)

INCOMES DATA SERVICES. *European Management Guide, Training and Development.* Institute of Personnel Management, London, 1992. (1) (11)

INDUSTRIAL SOCIETY. *Training Initiative.* Industrial Society, London, November 1987. (12)

INDUSTRIAL SOCIETY. *Training Trends: the Industrial Society Training Survey.* Industrial Society, London, 1992. (1)

INSTITUTE OF MANPOWER STUDIES. *Employer Response to the Decline in School Leavers in the 1990s,* by Hilary Metcalf (IMS Report No. 152) IMS, Brighton, 1988. (1)

INSTITUTE OF PERSONNEL MANAGEMENT. *TVEI recommendations on improved school/work liaison.* IPM, London, 1984. (11)

INSTITUTE OF PERSONNEL MANAGEMENT. *The IPM Code: Continuous Development: People and Work.* IPM, London, 1984 and 1986. (12)

INSTITUTE OF PERSONNEL MANAGEMENT. *Professional Education Scheme.* IPM, London, 1991. (6)

INSTITUTE OF PERSONNEL MANAGEMENT. *Towards a National Training and Development Strategy,* and *An Action Plan for the UK.* IPM, London, 1992. (1) (12)

INSTITUTE OF TRAINING AND DEVELOPMENT. *Human Resource Development: Diploma in Training Management – Syllabus, Regulations and Approved Centres.* ITD, Marlow, 1992. (6)

JACKSON L. 'Turning airport managers into high fliers'. *Personnel Management,* October, 1989. (9)

JACKSON T. *Evaluation: Relating training to business performance.* Kogan Page, 1989. (10)

JAMES R. 'The use of learning curves'. *Journal of European Industrial Training,* Vol. 8, No. 7, 1984. (4)

JENNINGS S. and UNDY R. 'Auditing managers' IR training needs'. *Personnel Management*, February, 1984. (7)

JESSUP G. *Outcomes: NVQs and the Emerging Model of Education and Training*. Falmer Press, 1991. (5) (9) (10) (11) (12)

JOHNSON P. R. and INDVIK J. 'Using brain hemisphericity to enhance career management'. *The International Journal of Career Management*, Vol. 3, No. 3, 1991, pages 3-10. (3)

JOHNSON R. 'Neuro-Linguistic programming'. *Handbook of Training and Development* (Prior J. ed.), Gower, Aldershot, 1991.

JONES A. M. and HENDRY C. *The Learning Organisation: A Review of Literature and Practice*. The HRD Partnership, London, 1992. (12)

JONES J. A. G. *The evaluation and cost effectiveness of training*. Industrial Training Service, London, 1970. (10)

KAHN R. L., WOLFE D. M. *et al. Organizational stress studies in role conflict and ambiguity*. Wiley, London, 1964. (9)

KAMP D. 'Neuro-Linguistic Programming'. *Training and Development*, Oct. 1991, pages 36 and 38. (3)

KAY. H. 'Accidents: some facts and theories'. *Psychology at work*, Warr P. (ed.), Penguin Education, Harmondsworth, Middx, 1983. (3)

KENNEY J. P. J., DONNELLY E. L. and REID M. A. *Manpower training and development*. Institute of Personnel Management, London, 1979. (3)

KENNEY J. P. J. and REID M. A. *Training Interventions*. 2nd Edition (Revised) Institute of Personnel Management, London, 1989. (Various)

KING D. *Training Within the Organisation*. Tavistock, London, 1964. (3) (6)

KOHLER W. *The mentality of apes*. International Library of Psychology, Routledge, 1973. (3)

KOLB D. *Experiential Learning: Experience as the Source of Learning and Development*. Prentice Hall, Englewood Cliffs, New Jersey, 1984. (12)

KOLB D. A., RUBIN I. N. and McINTYRE J. M. *Organizational psychology; a book of readings*. Prentice Hall, Englewood Cliffs, NJ, 1974. (3)

KOLB D., LUBLIN S., SPOTH J., and BAKER R. 'Strategic Management Development: Using Experiential Learning Theory to Assess and Develop Managerial Competencies'. *Journal of Management Development*, Vol. 5, No. 3, 1986. (12)

MAGER R. F. *Preparing instructional objectives.* Fearon, California, 1984. (10)

MANAGEMENT CHARTER GROUP. *The Management Charter Initiative.* MCI, London, 1987. (1)

MANCHESTER UNIVERSITY. *All Our Futures.* Centre for Education and Employment Research, University of Manchester, Manchester, 1993. (5)

MANPOWER SERVICES COMMISSION. *Vocational preparation for young people.* MSC, Sheffield, 1975. (11)

MANPOWER SERVICES COMMISSION. *Training of Trainers.* Two reports from the Training of Trainers Committee. HMSO, London, 1978 and 1980. (6)

MANPOWER SERVICES COMMISSION. *A New Training Initiative.* Manpower Services Commission, Sheffield, 1981. (1)

MANPOWER SERVICES COMMISSION. *Glossary of Training Terms.* Manpower Services Commission. HMSO, London, 1981. (Intro) (6) (9)

MANPOWER SERVICES COMMISSION. *Development of Assessable Standards for National Certification: Guidance Notes 1 to 7.* Manpower Services Commission, Sheffield, 1988. (2)

MARGERISON C. 'Margerison and McCann discuss the Team Management Wheel'. *Industrial and Commercial Training* Vol. 24, No. 1, 1992. (9)

MARKS GROUP. 'Alfred Marks Group quarterly survey'. *Personnel Management,* August, 1985. (4) (10)

MARSDEN C. and PRIESTLAND A. *Working with education: a framework of business objectives and activities.* A working document produced for 'BP in Education European Conference 1989'. BP Educational Services, PO Box 30, Blacknest Road, Blacknest, Alton, Hampshire GU34 4PX, 1989. Also reprinted in *Training and Education,* Vol. 32, No. 2, 1990. (11)

MARTINEAU R. 'First term report on the London compact'. *Personnel Management,* April, 1989. (11)

McGREGOR D. *The human side of enterprise.* McGraw Hill, Maidenhead, 1960. (4)

MINTZBERG H. 'The manager's job: folklore and fact'. *Harvard Business Review,* July, 1975. (9)

MOORBY E. *How to succeed in employee development.* McGraw Hill, Maidenhead, 1991 (7) (8) (9) (10)

MUMFORD A. *Making Experience Pay.* McGraw-Hill, Maidenhead, 1980. (4) (5) (12)

430   *Training Interventions*

MUMFORD A. *Management Development.* Institute of Personnel Management, London, 1989. (3) (9) (12)

NATIONAL ADVISORY COUNCIL FOR EDUCATION AND TRAINING TARGETS. *Report on Progress.* Employment Department, Cambertown, 1994. (1)

NATIONAL COUNCIL FOR VOCATIONAL QUALIFICATIONS. *National Vocational Qualifications: Criteria and Procedures.* NCVQ, London, 1989. (1) (5) (9)

NATIONAL COUNCIL FOR VOCATIONAL QUALIFICATIONS. *General National Vocational Qualifications.* NCVQ, London, 1991. (1)

NATIONAL ECONOMIC DEVELOPMENT OFFICE (in conjunction with the MANPOWER SERVICES COMMISSION). *People: The Key to Success.* (An 'Action Pack', comprising videotape and literature – prepared for NEDO/MSC by consultants Peat Marwick McLintock) NEDO, London, 1987. (1)

NATIONAL ECONOMIC DEVELOPMENT OFFICE. *Young People and the Labour Market: A Challenge for the 1990s.* NEDO, London, 1988. (1)

NATIONAL INSTITUTE OF ECONOMIC AND SOCIAL RESEARCH. Report in *Sunday Times,* 31 May 1988 (11)

NEALE F. *The handbook of performance management.* Institute of Personnel Management, London, 1991. (7)

NFER. *Second year national evaluation report on EHE.* Employment Department, W437, Moorfoot, Sheffield, 1991. (11)

NORD W. R. 'Beyond the teaching machine: the neglected area of operant conditioning in the theory and practice of management'. *Organizational behaviour and human performance,* Vol. 4, 1969. (3) (4)

OPEN UNIVERSITY. *Enterprise in Higher Education – Annual Report 1993.* Open University, Milton Keynes, Jan. 1994. (12)

OTTO C. P. and GLASER R. O. *The Management of Training.* Addison Wesley, London, 1970. (4)

PATRICK J. *Training: Research and Practice.* Academic Press, 1992. (3) (4) (9)

PEARN M. and KANDOLA R. *Job Analysis: A Practical Guide for Managers.* IPM, London, 1988. (5) (9)

PEDLER M., BURGOYNE J. and BOYDELL T. *A Manager's Guide to Self Development.* McGraw-Hill, Maidenhead, 1978. (12)

PEDLER M., BURGOYNE J. and BOYDELL T. *The Learning Company Project.* Training Agency, Sheffield, 1988. (1) (12)

PEDLER M., BURGOYNE J. and BOYDELL T. *The Learning Organisation.* McGraw-Hill, Maidenhead, 1992. (12)

PEDLER M., BURGOYNE J., BOYDELL T. and WELSHMAN A. (Eds.) *Self-Development in Organisations.* McGraw-Hill, Maidenhead, 1990. (12)

PEPPER A. D. *Managing the Training and Development Function.* Gower, Aldershot, 1984. (5) (7)

PERSONNEL STANDARDS LEAD BODY. *A Perspective on Personnel.* PSLB, London, 1994. (6)

PERSONNEL STANDARDS LEAD BODY. *Functional and Occupational Survey Results.* PSLB, London, 1994. (6)

PERSONNEL STANDARDS LEAD BODY. *Personnel Standards.* PSLB, London, 1994. (6)

PETERS, T. *Liberation Management.* Pan Books, London, 1993. (1) (6) (12)

PETTIGREW A. M., JONES G. R. and REASON P. W. *Organisational and Behavioural Aspects of the Role of the Training Officer in the UK Chemical Industry.* Chemical & Allied Products Industry Training Board, Staines, 1981. (6)

PETTIGREW A. M., SPARROW P. and HENDRY C. 'The forces that trigger training'. *Personnel Management*, December 1988. (1) (5)

PLETT P. and LESTER B.T. *Training for Older People.* ILO, Vincent House, Vincent Square, London SW1P 2NB, 1991. (4) (10) (11)

PRASHAR U. 'Evening up the odds for black workers'. *Personnel Management*, June, 1983. (7)

RAGGATT P. and UNWIN L. 'Quality Assurance and NVQs'. *Change and Intervention* (Raggatt P. and Unwin L. eds.), Falmer Press, London, 1991. (11)

REID M. A. and KENNEY J. 'Selecting and evaluating training strategies'. *Personnel Management Handbook* (Harper S. ed.), Gower, Aldershot, 1987.

REVANS R. *Action Learning.* Blond & Briggs, London, 1980. (12)

REVANS R. *The ABC of Action Learning.* Chartwell-Bratt, London, 1983. (5) (12)

RICE K. *Learning for Leadership.* Tavistock, London, 1965. (12)

RICE A. K. *The Enterprise and its Environment.* Tavistock, London, 1963. (2)

RICHARDS-CARPENTER C. *Relating manpower to an organization's objectives.* Institute of Manpower Studies, Report No. 56, 1982. (8)

RICHARDSON J. and BENNETT B. 'Applying learning techniques to on-the-job development: Part 2'. *Journal of European Industrial Training*, Vol. 8, No. 3, 1984. (3)

RODGER A., MORGAN T. and GUEST D. *A Study of the Work of Industrial Training Officers.* Air Transport and Travel Industry Training Board, Staines, 1971. (6)

ROSE C. *Accelerated Learning.* Accelerated Learning Systems Ltd., 50 Aylesbury Road, Aston Clinton, Aylesbury, 1991. (3)

ROYAL SOCIETY OF ARTS. *Learning Pays: The Role of Post-Compulsory Education and Training.* RSA, London, 1991. (1)

SAINSBURY D. 'Education for Wealth Creation' (address given to TSB forum). *Education and Training*, Vol. 33, No. 1, 1991, pages 27–31. (11)

SCHEIN E. H. *Organisational Psychology.* Prentice Hall, New Jersey, 1970. (2) (6)

SELIGMAN M. E. P. *Helplessness.* Freeman, San Francisco, 1975. (3)

SEYMOUR W. D. *Industrial Training for Manual Operatives.* Pitman, London, 1954. (6)

SEYMOUR W. D. *Skills analysis training.* Pitman, 1968, London. (3)

SHRIVASTAVA P. A typology of organisational learning systems, *Journal of Management Studies*, Vol. 20, No. 1, 7–28, Basil Blackwell, Oxford, Jan. 1983. (5)

SINGER E. *Training in industry and commerce.* Institute of Personnel Management, London, 1977. (8)

SINGER E. *Effective Management Coaching.* Institute of Personnel Management, London, 1979. (6)

SKINNER B. F. *Science and human behaviour.* Free Press U S, New York, 1965. (3)

SKINNER B. F. *Walden Two.* Collier Macmillan, London, 1976. (3)

SLOMAN M. 'Coming in from the cold: a new role for trainers'. *Personnel Management*, Jan. 1994, pages 24–27. (11)

SMITH P. B. *Improving Skills in Working with People: the T-Group.* Department of Employment and Productivity Training Information Paper No. 4, HMSO, London, 1969. (12)

SMITHERS, Professor Alan. *All Our Futures.* Centre for Education and Employment, University of Manchester, 1993. (5)

SMYTH S. R. and McKENNA M. A. 'Developing industry-based projects in hospitality management'. *Education and Training*, Vol. 33, No. 3, 1991, pages 9–16. (11)

STAMMERS R. and PATRICK J. *Psychology of Training.* Methuen, London, 1975. (3)

STRINGFELLOW C. D. 'Education and Training', in *Industrial Training International*, Vol. 3, No. 2, 1968. (2)

TALBOT J. P. and ELLIS C. D. *Analysis and Costing of Company Training.* Gower, Aldershot, 1969. (5) (8)

TANNEHILL R. E. *Motivation and Management Development.* Butterworths, London, 1970. (2)

TAVERNIER G. *Industrial training systems and records.* Gower Press, Aldershot, 1971. (8)

TAYLOR B. and LIPPITT G. (Eds.) *Management Development and Training Handbook (2nd Edition).* McGraw-Hill, Maidenhead, 1983. (Various)

TAYLOR M. *Coverdale on Management.* Heinemann, London, 1979. (12)

TAYLOR N. *Selecting and Training the Training Officer.* Institute of Personnel Management, London, 1966. (6)

THOMAS L. F. 'Perceptual organization in industrial inspectors'. *Ergonomics*, Vol. 5, 1962. Quoted in *Experimental psychology in industry.* Holding D. H. (ed.), Penguin, Harmondsworth, 1969. (3)

TORRINGTON D. *et al. Employee resourcing.* Institute of Personnel Management, London, 1991.

TRACEY W. R. *Evaluating training and development systems.* American Management Association, 1968. (10)

TRAINING AGENCY. *Standards for Action.* (Videotape + booklet) Training Agency, Sheffield, 1990. (1)

TRAINING AGENCY. *Training Workers: Priorities for Action 1990/1*. Training Agency, Sheffield, 1991. (1)

TRAINING SERVICES AGENCY. *An Approach to the Training of Staff with Training Officer Roles*. TSA, Sheffield, 1977. (2)

TRIST E. *The Evolution of Socio-Technical Systems*. Ontario Ministry of Labour/Ontario Quality of Working Life Centre, Ontario, 1981. (12)

TRIST E. *et al. Organistional Choice*. Tavistock, London, 1963. (2)

TURRELL M. *Training analysis: a guide to recognizing training needs*. Macdonald and Evans, Plymouth, 1980. (7)

VERNON P. E. *Intelligence and attainment tests*. London University Press, London, 1960. (4)

VOGT O. 'Study of the ageing of nerve cells'. *Journal of Gerentology*, No. 6, 1951. (4)

WARR P. B., BIRD M. and RACKHAM N. *Evaluation of management training*. Gower Press, Aldershot, 1970. (10)

WARWICK UNIVERSITY, Centre for Corporate Strategy and Change. *Study for Department of Employment*, 1991. Reported in *Skills and Enterprise Briefing*, February 1992, Employment Department, Moorfoot, Sheffield. (7)

WELFORD A. T. 'On changes in performance with age'. *Lancet*, Part 1, 1962. (4)

WELLENS J. *The Exploitation of Human Resources*. In *The Times* 16th August 1968. (2)

WELLENS J. 'An approach to management training'. *Industrial and Commercial Training*, Vol. 8, No. 7, July 1970. (5)

WHITELAW M. *The evaluation of management training – a review*. Institute of Personnel Management, London, 1972. (10)

WILLIAMS A., DOBSON P. and WALTERS M. *Changing Culture*. Institute of Personnel Management, London, 1989. (6)

WOOD S. (Ed.) *Continuous Development: The Path to Improved Performance*. Institute of Personnel Management, London, 1988. (1) (12)

WOODRUFFE C. *Assessment Centres: Identifying and Developing Competence*. Institute of Personnel Management, London, 1990. (9)

WOODRUFFE C. 'What is meant by a competency?' *Designing and achieving competency*. Sparrow P. and Boam R. McGraw Hill, Maidenhead, 1992. (9)

WOODS M. and THOMAS E. 'The Belbin Interface 111 – an expert system to assist personnel and trainers in personal and team development'. *Training and Management Development Methods*, Vol. 6, Section 2.01, 1992. (9)

WRIGHT D. S. and TAYLOR A. *Introducing psychology – an experimental approach*. Penguin Education, Harmondsworth, 1970. (3)

Index